The Theory and Practice of
Corporate Communication

This book is dedicated to my mother, Daisy Belasen,
for her love and supportive communication.

The Theory and Practice of
Corporate Communication

A Competing Values Perspective

Alan T. Belasen

State University of New York — Empire State College

SAGE Publications
Los Angeles • London • New Delhi • Singapore

For information:

Sage Publications, Inc.
2455 Teller Road
Thousand Oaks, California 91320
E-mail: order@sagepub.com

Sage Publications Ltd.
1 Oliver's Yard
55 City Road
London EC1Y 1SP
United Kingdom

Sage Publications India Pvt. Ltd.
B 1/I 1 Mohan Cooperative Industrial Area
Mathura Road, New Delhi 110 044
India

Sage Publications Asia-Pacific Pte. Ltd.
33 Pekin Street #02-01
Far East Square
Singapore 048763

Printed in the United States of America

Library of Congress Cataloging-in-Publication Data

Belasen, Alan T., 1951-
The theory and practice of corporate communication: a competing values perspective/Alan T. Belasen.
    p. cm.
Includes bibliographical references and index.
ISBN 978-1-4129-5035-0 (pbk.)
    1. Communication in management. 2. Communication in organizations. 3. Corporate culture.
4. Communication in management—Case studies. 5. Communication in organizations—Case studies.
6. Corporate culture—Case studies. I. Title.

HD30.3.B447 2008
658.4'5—dc22   2007014604

This book is printed on acid-free paper.

07   08   09   10   11   10 9 8 7 6 5 4 3 2 1

Acquisitions Editor:	Todd R. Armstrong
Editorial Assistants:	Katie Grim and Sarah K. Quesenberry
Production Editor:	Catherine M. Chilton
Copy Editor:	Sarah J. Duffy
Typesetter:	C&M Digitals (P) Ltd.
Proofreader:	Caryne Brown
Indexer:	Sheila Bodell
Graphic Designer:	Janet Foulger
Marketing Manager:	Amberlyn Erzinger

Brief Contents

Introduction   xiii

Foreword: The Science of Corporate Communication   xxi

PART A. WHY A NEW BOOK ON CORPORATE COMMUNICATION?   **1**

1. Corporate Communication as a Field of Study and a Community of Practice   3

PART B. STRATEGIC CORPORATE COMMUNICATION: AN INTEGRATED VIEW   **9**

2. Competing Values Framework for Corporate Communication   11
3. External Image, Internal Identity   27
4. Identity, Reputation, and the Functions of Corporate Communication   41

PART C. FUNCTIONS OF CORPORATE COMMUNICATION   **55**

5. Media Relations   57
6. Investor Relations   73
7. Government Relations   85
8. Employee Relations   101

PART D. EXTERNAL AND INTERNAL COMMUNICATION   **121**

9. Marketing Communication and Corporate Advertising   123
10. Financial Communication and Corporate Social Responsibility   135
11. Organizational and Management Communication   151

PART E. ANALYSIS AND CONTROL   **177**

12. Stakeholder Analysis   179
13. Communication Audits Within Organizations   199

PART F. CRISIS COMMUNICATION AND PATTERNS OF CORPORATE RESPONSE   **215**

14. Crisis Communication and Message Strategies   217
15. Conclusion   235

Contents

Introduction   xiii

Foreword: The Science of Corporate Communication   xxi
     Elliot Luber

PART A. WHY A NEW BOOK ON CORPORATE COMMUNICATION?   1

Chapter 1. **Corporate Communication as a Field of
Study and a Community of Practice**   3
    The Missing Link of Corporate Communication as a Field of Study   3
    Corporate Communication as a Community of Practice   4
    Attempts to Integrate the Field of Corporate Communication   5
    The Challenge to Identify the Construct Space of
       Corporate Communication   6
    Overhauling the Field   7
    The Need for a Theoretically Based Organizing Framework   8
    Summary   8
    Review Questions   8

PART B. STRATEGIC CORPORATE COMMUNICATION:
AN INTEGRATED VIEW   9

Chapter 2. **Competing Values Framework for Corporate Communication**   11
    Communication Perspectives   12
    Functionalism   15
    Interpretivism   15
    Critical Approaches   16
    Self-Efficacy   16
    Communication as Organizing   17
    • Apollo 13   18
    High-Reliability Organizations   19
    Communication Systems and Goals   22
    Balancing Competing Tensions   22
    Summary   24
    Review Questions   24
    Case Study: Satellite Systems   25

Chapter 3. External Image, Internal Identity   **27**
        Integrated Corporate Communication   29
        Sustaining and Managing Identity Programs   29
        Primary Functions of Corporate Communication   32
        Media Relations   33
        Employee Relations   33
        Government Relations   34
        Investor Relations   35
        The Communication Process   35
        Summary   37
        Review Questions   38
        Case Study: Starbucks Coffee Company   *38*

Chapter 4. Identity, Reputation, and the Functions of Corporate Communication: A Strategic View   **41**
        • GE: Managing Image and Corporate Identity   45
        • Target: Managing Corporate Reputation   47
        • McDonald's: Promoting the New Image   49
        Effective Communication Strategies   51
        External Communication   52
        Summary   53
        Review Questions   53
        Case Study: The Power of Symbols: Creating Corporate Identity at Agilent Technologies   *54*

PART C. FUNCTIONS OF CORPORATE COMMUNICATION   **55**

Chapter 5. Media Relations   **57**
        Reputation and Media Relations   58
        Enhancing Public Image Through Issue Management   60
        Branding the Image and Identity   60
        Public Relations and Media Relations   61
        • Johnson & Johnson   62
        Public Relations and Investor Relations   63
        The Corporate Spokesperson   63
        Summary   64
        Review Questions   65
        Case Study: Adolph Coors Company   *65*

Chapter 6. Investor Relations   **73**
        Stakeholders   74
        Working With Financial Analysts   75
        Managing Stockholder Confidence   76
        Financial Reporting   77
        Investor Relations and Corporate Reputation   79

Corporate Social Responsibility   80
Financial Performance and Corporate Reputation   80
Investor Relations Success Story   81
Financial Ethics   83
Summary   83
Review Questions   83
Case Study: The Press and the Stockholders   84

Chapter 7. Government Relations   **85**
Externally Derived, Internally Enforced   85
Policy Fields   87
Importance of Government Relations   90
• Altria   91
• American Red Cross   92
Regulations and Boundary Spanning   93
Interdependence   95
Shaping Favorite Policies Through Issue Management   96
Supplier Relations   97
Summary   97
Review Questions   98
Case Study: The Anti-trust Case Against Microsoft   98

Chapter 8. Employee Relations   **101**
Aligning Identity With External Image   102
Strategic Conversation   103
Asking the Right Questions Rather Than Giving Solutions   104
Motivating Employees   104
Integrating and Assimilating Employees: The Role of Culture   105
Mapping Culture in the Training Organization   107
Avoiding the Trap of Knowing-Doing   109
Positive Communication Relationships   110
Message Orientations   111
Mapping Message Orientations   111
A Diamond Model of Interactions   115
Managing for Organizational Integrity:
    The Social Contract With Employees   116
• FedEx   117
Summary   118
Review Questions   118
Case Study: Hanover Software   119

PART D. EXTERNAL AND INTERNAL COMMUNICATION   **121**

Chapter 9. Marketing Communication and Corporate Advertising   **123**
Integrated Marketing Communication   123
• Southwest Airlines   124
Sustainability   125

Issue Management and Corporate Advertising   125
PR and Corporate Advertising   126
Nonprofit Organizations   127
Managing Organizational Constituencies   128
Marketing Communication in Nonprofit Organizations   128
Marketing to Employees in Nonprofit Organizations   129
E-Channels for Nonprofit Organizations   129
Marketing Communication and Ethical Advertising   130
Summary   132
Review Questions   132
Case Study: Wal-Mart and Its Communications Strategy   133

Chapter 10. Financial Communication and Corporate Social Responsibility   135
• Enron: The Corporate Tactics   136
• Arthur Andersen: Turning the Blind Eye   137
• Tyco: Stealing the Vanity   138
• WorldCom: The Giant Falls   139
• Union Carbide   140
Financial Communication: The Sarbanes-Oxley Act of 2002   141
Implementation Challenges   143
Enforcement   144
Summary   145
Review Questions   146
Case Study: Illinois Power and 60 Minutes: Communicating
    About the Communications   146

Chapter 11. Organizational and Management Communication   151
Rule Theory: Rationalistic Approach to Communication   152
The Humanistic Approach   153
Rationalistic and Humanistic Communication Roles:
    A Competing Values Perspective   153
Facilitating Vertical Communication   156
Information Communication Technology   157
The Role of Informal Networks in Management Communication   160
Aligning Communication With Structures   161
Horizontal Management   162
Aligning Communication Processes in Loosely Coupled Structures   164
Managerial Ethics and Social Responsibility   165
The CEO and the Board of Directors   167
Structural Regulations   168
Policies and Standards   168
Reforms   169
The Ethical CEO   169
Communication Between the CEO and Board Members   170
Building an Effective Board of Directors   170
Summary   171

Review Questions   172
Case Study: The Paradoxical Twins—Acme and Omega Electronics   172

PART E. ANALYSIS AND CONTROL   177

Chapter 12. Stakeholder Analysis   179
Communicating With Stakeholders: A CVFCC Approach   180
Firm-Stakeholder Relationships   181
• StarKist   183
Principles of Stakeholder Management   185
Communicating Messages to Stakeholders   186
Steps in Stakeholder Analysis   188
Sources of Power   191
Assessing Stakeholders' Perceptions Using the CVFCC   192
Summary   193
Review Questions   195
Case Study: Granite City: Doing More With Less   195

Chapter 13. Communication Audits Within Organizations   199
Functionalism   199
Interpretivism   200
Uncertainty Reduction   201
The Process of a Communication Audit   202
Benefits   202
Identifying Communication Activities Across Managerial Levels   203
The Importance of Contextual Factors   204
Assessment of Managerial Communication Roles and Skills   205
Diagnosing Organizational Culture   206
Cultural Types   208
Cultural Audit in a Health Care Organization   209
Summary   210
Review Questions   211
Case Study: Planning the Project   212

PART F. CRISIS COMMUNICATION AND PATTERNS OF CORPORATE RESPONSE   215

Chapter 14. Crisis Communication and Message Strategies   217
Fire at Deloitte Office Tower in Madrid:
    Deloitte Spain Maintains Activity   218
• Southwest Airlines   218
Communication Failures   219
• Failure at Dow Corning   220
• Failure at the University of Maryland   221
• Success for NASA   223

- Success for Texas Eastern Transmission Corporation   224
- Verizon: Effective Corporate Communication   224
Protecting the Image   225
Organizing the Exchange of Information   227
Restoring the Image   228
Stages of Crisis   229
The Importance of Culture in Managing Crises   231
Summary   232
Review Questions   232
Case Study: Tylenol Tampering Scare   232

Chapter 15. Conclusion   **235**
Corporate Communication: The Maestro   235
Strategic Corporate Communication   236
The Theory and Practice of Corporate Communication   238
Integrative Case Study: The Acquisition of Abbott Hospital   239
Case Study: Mt. Mercy Acquires Abbott   243
Case Study: The End of the First Six Months   245
Integrative Case Study: BelBeck Production   246

References   **249**

Index   **259**

About the Author   **271**

Introduction

Corporate communication as an academic field and as a community of practice must be broad enough to allow for the integration of ideas and the development of agreement among theoreticians, researchers, and practitioners. It also needs to be specific enough to allow for differentiation of distinct contributions to the field. The organizing framework should reflect the paradoxical nature of corporate communication in which unity and variety, consistency and creativity are practically recognized and academically accepted. This book, *The Theory and Practice of Corporate Communication: A Competing Values Perspective,* responds to these requirements.

This book offers an integrative approach to corporate communication. It covers theoretical aspects and uses practical examples and case studies to illustrate a broader, strategic view of the field of corporate communication. The book draws on an adaptation of the Competing Values Framework to provide a fuller and more coherent view of corporate communication in which a dynamic interplay of complementary and often competing message orientations takes place.

The Competing Values Framework (CVF) depicts organizations as inherently contradictory systems. Managers are expected to perform well and use various communication roles and behaviors in different contexts of organizational performance. For example, in the innovator and broker roles, managers rely on creativity, persuasion, and communication skills to stimulate innovation and development. The monitor and coordinator roles are more relevant for system maintenance and coordination of activities, and they require project management and supervision skills. Thus,

the CVF highlights the importance of aligning managerial values and communication roles with contextual variables. As a teaching/learning medium, the CVF enables learners to see the big picture (system view) and at the same time recognize the interconnectivity and synergistic effects among the different parts and functions of corporate communication. A CEO's vision may include growth through market development, but without aligning resources, capabilities, roles, and communication systems with that vision, the company may miss its target goals.

The benefit of the CVF lies in its diagnostic and predictive power. That is, professors and students can use the model to examine communication systems and goals, identify current and desired targets, conduct gap analysis, and highlight areas for organizational improvement. Similarly, the CVF can be used as a communication audit tool to chart organizational core values and culture and examine the alignment of existing communication roles and skills with the profile of the organization. Doing so allows students to develop a better understanding of communication strengths and weaknesses (at managerial as well as organizational levels) and to suggest ways to improve communication processes and practices.

The Competing Values Framework for Corporate Communication (CVFCC) is an adaptation of the original CVF model. It provides an integrated and broad perspective for addressing the diversity of corporate communication as a field of study and a community of practice. As an organizing schema it helps capture the richness, complexity, and interdependence of communication theories (e.g., rationalistic humanistic), functions (e.g., media relations, employee relations, investor relations, government relations), culture (e.g., development, hierarchy), managerial roles (e.g., broker, director, mentor, innovator), and organizational stakeholders (e.g., employees, investors, customers, regulators, reporters). As a practical approach it highlights the fact that corporate communication executives and professionals operate under the burden of contradictory and often inconsistent expectations coming from diverse constituencies. Responding to these expectations is vital for building a strong identity and sustaining a credible organizational image.

The CVFCC brings the whole (corporate communication) and parts (marketing communication, financial communication, organizational communication, management communication) into a more sophisticated theoretical treatment of corporate communication that goes beyond merely discussing best practices. As echoed later in the book, existing textbooks on corporate communication do not integrate diverse practices (e.g., public relations, media relations, investor relations, employee relations) into a coherent theoretical framework. Professors can use the CVFCC to articulate a systematic framework with which to group and differentiate different functions and common practices according to common principles and criteria.

The CVFCC allows students to combine theory (deductive thinking) with practical examples and case studies (inductive learning). The model helps students of corporate communication develop the language needed to understand the field's different functions while also enriching their learning by broadening their understanding of how the different pieces fit into the whole. It is like a giant puzzle that shows not only the bigger picture but also how well the pieces fit together.

The CVFCC is based on more than 15 years of consulting work, academic teaching, curriculum development, conference papers, and publications in the areas of communication, management development, cultural transformation, and

organizational leadership as also evident in my previous book, *Leading the Learning Organization: Communication and Competencies for Managing Change* (State University of New York Press, 2000). The current book presents a balance among the four perspectives on corporate communication: marketing communication with its emphasis on media relations, financial communication with its emphasis on investor relations, organizational communication with its emphasis on government and supplier relations, and management communication with its emphasis on employee relations.

The primary audiences for this book are departments of communication (undergraduate courses in organizational communication), graduate programs in corporate communication, MBA programs, and schools of management emphasizing broad communication skills for managing internal and external organizational stakeholders. The book is also attractive to company executives and communication consultants and directors who are responsible for external affairs and public relations.

The field of corporate communication is recognized throughout the world, particularly in Europe and North America. Many variants of corporate communication are taught in most departments of communication (like mine at the University at Albany). Some schools, like Emerson College, have unique programs in organizational and corporate communication. The structure and approach used in this book allow for flexible adaptation of the entire book or parts of it to supplement existing organizational communication curricula or to enrich topics taught in corporate communication courses. This book can be used in undergraduate core courses on topics such as research and theories in organizational communication, communication theory for leading change, management and communication, and functions of corporate communication. The book is also geared toward graduate specialized courses in corporate communication on topics such as media management strategies, stakeholder analysis, strategic planning and corporate environments, crisis communication, communication audits and consulting, corporate communication dynamics, and integrated corporate communication. The examples and case studies used throughout the book draw on diverse organizations from a wide range of industries and sectors in different countries.

Although most of the existing books on corporate communication advance the need for a broader, integrated view of the field, each approaches the field from a different perspective, usually by focusing on a particular function. Cornelissen (2004), for example, places heavy emphasis on marketing communication, whereas Goodman (1994) focuses on public relations and media management strategies. Oliver (1997) describes the "fragmentation of the discipline" and the "subsequent credibility gap" (pp. 11–12) as the main reasons for the shift that she advocates toward a systems perspective that combines both internal and external communications with functional and strategic approaches to corporate communication. *The Theory and Practice of Corporate Communication: A Competing Values Perspective* is aimed at doing just that—closing the gap and enhancing the credibility of the field of corporate communication.

The theoretical framework introduced in this book, the CVFCC, advances the notion of communication systems that are both independent and interdependent. The framework is particularly useful in helping communication researchers, professors, and practitioners form a better understanding of the scope and range of communication activities that affect organizations both internally and externally. Moreover, the book promotes the development of communication responses that consider the objectives and consequences of employing different messages when addressing different audiences.

Contents

The contents of this book are arranged logically and conform to accepted categories used in the field. From "Corporate Communication as a Field of Study" to "Crisis Communication and Patterns of Corporate Response," the book starts out broadly describing the CVFCC and becomes more specific as the corporate communication functions are discussed. The CVFCC is integrated throughout most of the book, providing the necessary road map for navigating the diverse range of activities and organizational functions that fall under the heading of "corporate communication." Chapters 2–15 each end with a case study to help teachers and learners of corporate communication make sense of the connections between actual situations (What happened?) and theory (How do we make sense of what happened?). The CVFCC as an integrative approach that helps bring meaning and coherence to the functions of corporate communication comes full circle in the concluding section of the book. Corporate communication is treated as a serious subject amenable to intellectual study and analysis.

Chapter 1 lays the foundation for the justification of the book and the need for a more integrated approach to corporate communication. Although most corporate communication researchers and executives could benefit from using an integrated and more systematic framework, unfortunately the academic field of corporate communication is scattered, divergent, and lacks coherence.

Chapter 2 provides the rationale for using the CVFCC. Drawing on Quinn (1988) and Belasen (2000), the CVFCC was developed primarily to address concerns about the wide dispersion of the field and the need for greater focus in attending to important stakeholders. Even though the existing conventions of corporate communication (i.e., media relations, public relations, customer relations, government relations) have broadened our thinking about the scope of corporate communication tasks and responsibilities both internally and externally, there is still a need to explore the context of corporate communication as a unified, highly interdependent function.

Chapter 3 sets the stage for linking the primary functions of corporate communication both internally (identity) and externally (image). Viewing internal and external communication as connected functions shifts the focus to answering questions about how an organization can communicate consistently to its many audiences in a way that represents a coherent sense of self. That sense of self is needed to maintain credibility and reputation inside and outside the organization through strong organizational identity and positive external image.

Chapter 4 reconstructs the need for a more holistic approach to corporate communication by highlighting strategic issues and concepts. Strategic issues include orienting communication toward an organization's priorities as well as the external environment. Internal and external priorities include responsibility to investors, media relations, a strong organizational culture, and relationships with government and regulatory agencies—the areas covered by the CVFCC. Organizations must attend to the needs of their stakeholders through strategic corporate communication in order to build image and identity and maximize credibility. Chapter 4 brings closure to the issues of identity and image through the prism of the CVFCC. Communication should co-create an image that conveys the company's vision or mission and that reflects the organization's interests. The questions of *who, how, when, where,* and *why* typically provide a starting point for developing communication strategy.

Chapter 5 connects reputation with image. Diverse communication roles and activities are important in obtaining corporate communication goals across the four areas. The practice of media relations requires communicators to be creative, inspiring, and adaptive in establishing a professional and productive relationship with the press. Maintaining such a relationship is an ongoing effort that must be nurtured carefully because it can provide an organization with the ability and voice to paint a certain picture of events.

Chapter 6 shifts the emphasis to financial markets and stockholder communications. The area of investor relations requires the communicator to be a taskmaster and possess the competency of promotional communication efforts, which if handled correctly and honestly can help improve the company's financial position. The role of the communication taskmaster involves establishing organizational dialogue to facilitate understanding of financial expectations and the long-term corporate outlook. This promotional ability fits together the information provided to investors and analyzers in order to reflect a complete, unified message of the organization's financial outcomes and vision for the future.

Chapter 7 focuses on business-government relationships and regulatory environments that require compliance and greater control and accountability. The area of government relations has become increasingly important in the midst of the increased influence of government on domestic issues and the ever-changing role of companies in international business operations. With the onset of such fluid combinations of business groups and constituents, it is paramount that a corporate communicator follow suit with a corresponding flexible, rapid communication repertoire that can develop a communication system around the supply chain of the organization. A communicator must be able to tap into the skills that enable such systems to be coordinated, which include negotiation, facilitation, consensus building, and developing familiarity with the inside workings of the industry, regulatory concerns, and technical standards and procedures.

Chapter 8 completes the circle of corporate communication functions, as depicted by the CVFCC, by covering important employee relations issues. The area of employee relations demands that a communicator be a motivator and possess the competency of relational communication efforts that go beyond writing and editing the company newsletter. Employee relations staff specialists use strategic conversations across organizational lines to help bring an outside-in perspective and inform employees about marketing and strategic initiatives that might affect their quality of work life. This area becomes critical in the face of the equivocal future of many employees' jobs and the state of the economy since the early 1990s; the demands on employees have increased significantly, and the need to address, value, and retain employees has become increasingly important.

Chapter 9 (and the following two chapters) opens up the discussion of the primary areas of corporate communication by covering important theoretical models and practical applications in each approach (i.e., marketing, finance, organization, and management). Marketing communication has significantly increased in value as global markets have become more interdependent, with companies using creative distribution channels to reach their customer bases. Rapid change and having to respond to multiple stakeholders also has led many companies to scale up their media relations activities, intensify public relations efforts, and use extensive corporate advertising and direct marketing to manage their brand image. Although public relations and marketing communication are viewed as distinct corporate functions, they also share many important similarities and complementary relationships, primarily cultivating favorable perceptions toward the corporate image among key audiences and stakeholders.

Chapter 10 covers financial communication, the primary objective of which is to promote the value, credibility, and reputation of the organization in order to achieve a favorable market image about its financial strength. Institutional investors and analysts receive a company's communications regularly, which helps them evaluate the company's earning potential and its intentions to materialize its potential and attain short- and long-term goals. This means producing and distributing financial reports and analyses regularly through annual meetings and quarterly distribution of mandatory reports, answering shareholders' questions and concerns, addressing long-term strategic issues with major institutional investors, and sending information to securities analysts and other Wall Street parties. This chapter also discusses financial management issues and reforms enacted

following the recent executive frauds and corporate scandals.

Chapter 11 deals with management communication. One of the main points that the literature makes is the need to encourage internal corporate identity through various management communication initiatives. When management communication aligns with the organization's vision and when organizational leaders assume the role of communication champions, building trust and gaining members' commitment, organizational members develop shared reality and accountability toward the attainment of corporate communication goals. Unlike vertical authority lines, horizontal structures eliminate the need to devote resources to formal systems of coordination. The internal machine of a flatter organization uses fewer resources that rely heavily on communication lines and networks as effective substitutes for hierarchy. The chapter also covers ethics, governance, and social corporate responsibility issues. Managerial accountability systems are necessary and important to improve trust within and around the organization as well as create better communication relationships between board members and top executives.

Chapter 12 is an important milestone of this book. It draws on the CVFCC to help determine the most important stakeholders, as well as their values and bases of power, and how corporate communication executives and professionals strategically address the concerns of influential stakeholders. This chapter covers important methodologies, case studies, and analyses to illustrate the concept of the stakeholder and its importance to the field of corporate communication both in theory and in practice.

Chapter 13 focuses on how corporate communication professionals can use the CVFCC to initiate self-improvement processes in their organization. Communication audits draw on models of assessment and intervention to improve corporate communication in all areas of the CVFCC. Most of this chapter covers important facets of communication audits that I conducted through previous consulting and research. Personal and corporate self-evaluation can help managers diagnose their roles and skills, identify strengths and weaknesses, and develop action plans for improvement. At the personal level, the results of communication audits often promote an increase in productivity and improved interpersonal communication, decision-making, and problem-solving practices. Many experts agree that internal communication audits help managers increase confidence in their communication abilities and skills and gain greater proficiency in dealing with employees, customers, and executives. Managers who used the CVFCC audit tools reportedly developed better understanding across managerial and functional lines and worked together as a management team. At the corporate level, managers are able to develop a shared understanding of the core leadership competencies required to support organizational capabilities and business-growth strategies.

Chapter 14 shifts the emphasis from managing daily corporate communication tasks and routines to handling crises and communicating uncertainty. A crisis usually causes an interruption in what is going on and poses certain risks to an organization, potentially affecting reputation, image, brand equity, credibility, publicity, financial viability, legitimacy, and community standing. Because an organizational crisis is a situation that can potentially escalate in intensity, fall under close government or media scrutiny, jeopardize the current positive public image of an organization, or interfere with normal business operations, an organization could be at serious risk for survival. The chapter describes models of dealing with crisis and failure and discusses success stories from different industries.

The book concludes with a recap of corporate communication as a strategic function.

Acknowledgments

Writing a new book is a challenging task. It requires high tech for locating relevant knowledge and a soft touch for putting that knowledge to the test. It demands not only intense discipline to structure the thread of ideas convincingly and coherently but also the energy necessary for keeping up with current trends and constantly updating the material. Authors also need the courage to share a work in progress with others and the grace to accept criticism and revise content areas accordingly. Writing a new book is especially challenging when the requirement to meet the publisher's tight deadlines competes directly with academic, professional, social, and personal responsibilities (whether teaching, fine-tuning a conference paper, attending to a family, or conducting a consulting project). This is exactly why the book benefits from any kind of support, whether in release time, research funds, data collection, case applications, feedback on work in progress or earlier drafts, family and collegial support, and a host of little things such as library research, scanning material, typing manuscripts, following up with publishers and authors, and so on.

A number of individuals reviewed earlier drafts of the manuscript and helped improve the quality of this book and shape its overall direction: Merry Buchanan (Department of Mass Communication, University of Central Oklahoma), Leonard M. Edmonds (Hugh Downs School of Human Communication, Arizona State University), Nancy Miller Frank (Master of Business Administration Program, State University of New York–Empire State College), Joseph W. McDonnell (College of Business, Stony Brook University), J. Gregory Payne (Department of Organizational and Political Communication, Emerson College), Gary P. Radford (Department of English, Communication, and Philosophy, Fairleigh Dickinson University), and Stuart J. Sigman (Department of Academic Affairs, Naropa University). Gary Radford's systematic review and insightful comments were particularly helpful in fine-tuning a number of sections in this book. Thanks, Gary!

I would like to recognize the important insights of Rosalyn Rufer, who helped with sequencing the parts and chapters of this book, as well as the intellectual stimulation of Nancy Frank, both of whom are my MBA colleagues at Empire State College. Nancy Frank, my CBF research partner, also helped fine-tune my thinking about the applicability of the CVFCC to stakeholder analysis and organizational culture. From the Department of Communication at the University at Albany, Teri Harrison and Anita Pomerantz provided me with many opportunities to teach corporate communication, conduct site visits, and bring guest speakers to my classroom. Rocco Padula's comments and insights on the initial draft were helpful in improving later drafts.

I would also like to recognize the contributions of my students from the Department of Communication: Yi-Fen Chen, Kori-Ann Taylor, Karla Jaime, Lisa W. Grigg, Gustavo Berganza, Travis Minnaugh, Yolanta Karwowski, Shifay Cheung, Christine Decatur, Marissa A. Poletti, Mary Lille, Christine A. Moore, Jun Zhang, Alicia Mosteller, Christine Decatur, Chun Lee Li, Heather D. Sanger, Marissa A. Poletti, Christina Havlin, Lisa Sorrentino, Xiaoxia Liu, Ann

Custodero, Julie Tracy, Jing Dong, Chris Kulle, Tanja Ohlson, Steve Palenscar, Christine Ji, Eileen Sullivan, Mark DeSanctis, Wen Ji, Beth Novak, Liani Rosa Swingle, Wei Qingxia, Darcy Scheyer, Alexandra (Xiaoying) Li, Erica Ropitzky, Karen Habel, Stephen Palencsar, and Tracy Nicholson. And from Union Graduate College, I would like to thank Adrienne Ringer, Lisa Troyano, Dipankar Basnet, Nick Campitello, Kathy Ebert, Jordon Heffler, Lisa Troyano, and Kristen Pero. Special thanks to Ellen Raphael for her stamina and commitment working on the early draft of this book.

I would like to acknowledge the academic development funds provided by Empire State College to cover my research-related costs and my trips to several conferences. Special thanks to Doreen DeCrescenzo for her diligence and meticulousness in following up on my correspondence with various publishers. Special thanks go to Suzanne Hayes, manager of Library and Instructional Services at Empire State College, for the invaluable access to multiple databases that supported the research for this book.

This book could not have been possible without the high commitment and continuous support of Katie Grim, Sarah Quesenberry, and Deya Saoud, led by Todd Armstrong, senior acquisitions editor at Sage, whose early endorsement of the idea for this book helped bring it to fruition. Catherine Chilton, my production editor, was instrumental in providing the structure and logistical plan for book production. Many thanks go to Sarah Duffy, my copy editor, whose dedication, diligence, high standards, and insightful queries and suggestions helped improve the clarity and quality of this book. Sarah's inquisitive skills, positive attitude, passion, and supportive communication made the task of bringing this book project to closure both mind stretching and fun!

Special thanks to John and Brenda Greenberg for the motivation, constant encouragement, and admirable support that gave me the strength to complete this important book project.

And for cheering me on while I worked on this book, I will always admire my wife, Susan, and our five children, my five As: Ari, Amy, Anat, Amanda, and Abby.

Foreword

The Science of Corporate Communication

Elliot Luber
Internal and Executive Communication, IBM Corporation

Gods and General Managers

The great physicist Albert Einstein was said to have died peacefully in his sleep on April 18, 1955, the result of a ruptured aorta, but he could have easily died of a broken heart. Historians paint the waning Einstein as an unhappy though accepting man.[1] His quarter-century obsession to prove a unified field theory covering all of physics went unfulfilled. He first proposed this in 1929, when he was 50. As a somewhat religious man, Einstein believed a universal theory would tie together all of physics and evidence what is now called *Intelligent Design*. One framework evidences belief in a single creator. Said Einstein, "Try and penetrate with our limited means the secrets of nature and you will find that, behind all the discernible concatenations, there remains something subtle, intangible and inexplicable. Veneration for this force beyond anything that we can comprehend is my religion."[2]

Alas, Einstein lived to see neither the establishment of a unified field theory nor today's heated debate over intelligent design. For the purpose of this book, I take no stand on that issue and won't try to predict what Einstein's inclination might be today. A scientist first, however, Einstein was said to have congratulated attorney Clarence Darrow in their one chance meeting for having successfully defended John T. Scopes's teaching of evolution in Tennessee in 1925,[3] though Einstein would later proclaim he was no atheist. Those on both sides of the argument today should feel free to read this book and thus be empowered to take advantage of the communication framework it outlines in asserting their beliefs. You will understand why about five paragraphs down when I discuss maximizing market share, but we're discussing more lofty subjects for the time being.

Although modern physicists have not made the leap to intelligent design, they have recently made substantial progress toward the development of a unified field theory of physics called String Theory (see Table F.1). Among other things, String Theory holds that the universe can be explained through the understanding of how four primal forces influence the vibration of matter, much like the plucking of a guitar string.[4] These four forces are strong molecular force, weak molecular force, electromagnetic force, and gravitational force. Luckily, communications majors are rarely graded on the basis of their ability to grasp "rocket science," but those are the theory's basic underpinnings. It was Einstein who reportedly said, "If you can't

Table F.1   The Four Forces of Nature: String
                  Theory

Weak molecular force	Electromagnetic force
Gravitational force	Strong molecular force

explain something simply, you don't understand it well enough." He could have easily been speaking about communications, a discipline that has long escaped a simple explanatory academic framework—until now.

For many years the business world has also hunted for a unified theory that would explain the management process. It seems we all have our own gods, and for years business academics and journals searched high and low for one of their own—beginning naturally enough with the CEO, who in corporate mythology sits closest to God in the corner office. For a long time academics shadowed, interviewed, and published accounts of successful business leaders to glean the secrets of their success, only to learn that valuable knowledge quickly turns to hubris with the discovery of personal fortune and fulfillment. But such tales of swashbuckling business heroes do well in the bookstore and largely outsell more serious books sold on campus. Thus a discussion of business became a big business, but more serious students were deprived of the level of discussion they required. Here Adam Smith might agree with Karl Marx: Business case history is economic.

L'Essence de l'Éléphant

In one interesting twist of fate, we see business imitating the physical universe and perhaps its "supreme manager" as well. In recent decades management thought leadership has followed four distinct strings of its own. These can be categorized as many flavors of (a) innovation, (b) rational goal setting, (c) process improvement,

and (d) human resources. For example, Michael Porter wrote about geographical disadvantage being the mother of innovation, Lou Gerstner wrote about getting elephants to dance—an analogy to planned execution at larger companies, Michael Hammer and James Champy wrote about reengineering the corporation, and Peter Senge penned a manifesto on personal mastery, the optimization of human resources. These have been delightful fodder for deep academic discussion and have led to considerable advancements in the practical world of management—things like Six Sigma certification. No one ever suspected they would all relate to one another directly or, for that matter, to the "black art" of communications.

The academic world eventually came to understand that these four distinct strings of management academics resembled the fable of the three blind men and the elephant. Each man (modern tellers may substitute woman) could feel only the part of the elephant in their proximity— the trunk, tail, or belly—yet none possessed the full pachydermal perspective—*l'essence de l'éléphant*. Then suddenly, in 1983, Quinn and Rohrbaugh discovered that the four strings of academic discussion were really quadrants along two axes, one running from internal to external and the other from flexibility to control.[5] That is, innovation represented external flexibility, and human resources represented internal flexibility. Rational goals were the external manifestation of control, and process improvement was the internal focus on control (see Figure F.1).

Is not innovation the opposite of strict conformity? Companies are trying to compete by innovating while saving money by enforcing conformity. It cannot be done without some sleight of hand we call *management*. Are not improving corporate climate and meeting sales quotas paradoxical achievements? The harder one pushes, the more employees resent it. So here was a framework that not only unified the four strings of management theory but also provided insight into their interactions in a way that was repeatable and, more important

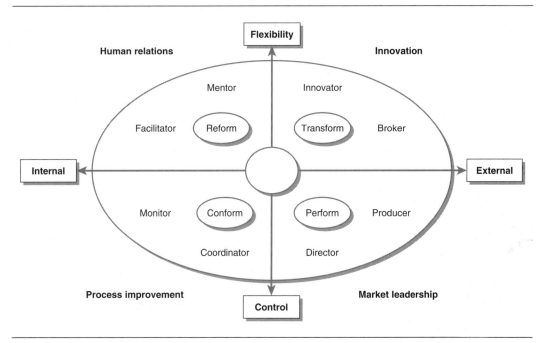

Figure F.1   Competing Values Framework: Organizational Environments and Managerial Roles

SOURCE: Adapted from Quinn, R. E., *Beyond Rational Management.* Copyright © 1988, San Francisco: Jossey-Bass. Reprinted with permission of John Wiley & Sons, Inc.

to number-hungry executives, measurable. Graphically depicting the implications of String Theory has proven a bit tougher—even for physics majors.

Professors at business schools had for years taught that the hardest part of being a manager was managing paradoxical situations by developing softer impact *either and* instead of *either or* decisions that slyly break the rules. For example, large market shares can be maintained by striking difficult partnerships with numerous competing vendors in an ecosystem rather than dividing the potential market by getting close to only one segment. So someone selling communications textbooks would want to address both sides of the intelligent design debate rather than limit his or her market potential to only one faction on the issue. Some managers, like Alan Greenspan, made great careers from engineering soft landings—in his case, softening the landing

of a downward economy by manipulating investor confidence.

Now, armed with the CVF, managers could balance aggressive moves in one direction by at least touching on the opposing discipline to ward off anticipated backlash. It was Einstein who likened life to riding a bicycle because one had to keep moving in order to maintain a balance.[6] The CVF, in fact, explains business cycles in this manner. It depicts the stages of a project life cycle by simply renaming its quadrants: transform, perform, conform, and reform, instead of innovation, rational goals, process improvement, and human resources. Information technology consultants may be more familiar with this diagram using the terms *build, run, scale,* and *innovate,* and marketing professionals may recognize this as the *Marketagon,* a map of the product life cycle phases in which you innovate, launch a product, market it aggressively, then focus on improvements for the next-generation product.

Thus managers should heed Einstein's remarks about balance, for therein lies a key to success. In any event the CVF helps practitioners and academics alike better understand and manage paradox tightening or loosening various controls at their disposal both internally and externally. In Greenspan's case, the tool was doublespeak to soften the market blow of direct pronouncement by calming and perhaps befuddling investors while often delivering bad news.

But it is useful to discuss other ways that the original business model obviously impacts communications before considering Belasen's extensions to follow. As a young news reporter, I was taught to look for inconsistencies in an executive's story because they would prove the Achilles heel to attack with questions. "Let them slide off the hot seat once, and you'll never corner them again," I was told. Today, I suddenly recognize this executive inconsistency as the mark of a great manager rather than a half-truth, thanks to the CVF. Indeed, Alan Belasen began his management lessons on the CVF by quoting F. Scott Fitzgerald, who wrote that "the test of a first-rate intelligence is the ability to hold two opposed ideas in mind at the same time and still retain the ability to function."[7] So functioning despite paradox is the sign of a great mind, which may help explain Einstein's belief in god amid his relentless pursuit of a scientific explanation for the universe.

Using the CVF for management, human resources professionals could suddenly develop a comprehensive list of eight key managerial competencies, as well as metrics to quantify an individual's strengths and weaknesses in each area to create a manager map, both for candidate comparison and for in-service development. In the first shadows of the CVFCC, Belasen (2000) wrote that, as a means to best communicate, executives could frame their wishes ranging from direct orders to vague suggestions to match the organization's prevailing CVF culture.[8] For example, a large, control-oriented organization would traditionally issue orders, but could instead stress

innovation and trust as a means to loosen up the culture and break itself out of a mold.

So by assigning a communication tone of voice to each of the quadrants, and rotating the CVF one quadrant counterclockwise, Belasen was able to create a chart to readily predict the most appropriate tone for addressing the overriding culture of an organization. Practitioners could select an alternate voice for strategic purposes. Moving counterclockwise from process improvement to rational goals to innovation to human resources, you would either *tell, sell, suggest,* or *ask* audiences for their suggestions. This process of rotating the CVF cycle on its side adds new meaning to the idea of "spinning" a story, and realigning the two axes adds new mechanical meaning to the term *designated spokesperson*. It's all about spokes, and cycling to maintain balance.

The wrong tone for a given culture can be upsetting, as Greenspan knows. Academics themselves generally get nervous when people start discussing things in absolute terms such as *universal* despite working at a *university*. You see the CVF in play when they choose softer terms such as *unified* to balance strong claims with the burden of later having to prove them because far-reaching descriptions approaching hyperbole tend to open professors' work to peer criticism and the one counterexample that immediately kills all talk of universality. For the CVF to be somewhat universal, it must apply to various aspects of business. That was the basic idea behind Belasen's assignment to his MBA class in 2002, in which I was enrolled.

I had gone back to graduate school to better understand what business leaders were trying to achieve. I felt this would help me communicate better to audiences about how my company's solutions would benefit line-of-business executives. The online program at Empire State College first caught my eye because of time constraints, but I was surprised to see that one of the core professors, Alan Belasen, also taught graduate corporate communications classes at the sister State University of New York institution, the University at Albany. I figured this could only help make my studies more relevant to my career. That turned out to be an understatement.

When I took Belasen's Leading in Complex Organizations class, he gave out what seemed like a pretty straightforward assignment. We students had to apply the CVF to whatever it was we did for a living. I had an undergraduate degree in liberal arts/journalism rather than communications, so I was completely ignorant of the communications function's long inability to be academically characterized at the macro level. People were always subdividing the definition of the word *public* in public relations, but no one had successfully seen the big picture, or at least written about it convincingly. To complete the assignment I simply wrote about my job at the time as an IBM publicist promoting enterprise-computing solutions to the aerospace and chemical industries.

I categorized my job as a brokering role because I made deals with influencers such as reporters. I wrote about balancing that job in the innovation quadrant with the monitoring and coordinating roles in the opposing process improvement quadrant. I learned the lesson that it is not enough to develop contacts in the media. You have to align spokespeople and customer references to develop a comprehensive, successful story—and great press is worthless unless you find it first and then merchandise your success to the entire team. But there was a greater lesson to be learned, and it was, I readily admit, beyond my comprehension at the time.

Continuing to ignorantly outline CVF roles for communications jobs, it was my subsequent alignment of the corporate communications function with the CEO in the director role of the rational goals quadrant that sparked Belasen's interest. I placed corporate communications in this role for communicating earnings, the attainment of corporate goals, rather than the process improvement quadrant for the monitoring role, where you would find accounting. The implications, I soon learned from Belasen, were staggering. I had no idea I had just upset the

apple cart. I didn't even know there was an apple cart. It may have led to Belasen's "aha" moment, but I'll let him tell his own story.

Just in Time. . . .

The creation of a unified theory that enables integration of communications could not have come at a better time for communicators or students of communications. Certainly mass communications media are presently undergoing revolutionary change in terms of both the technology and the socialization of that technology. These communications tools are called *Web 2.0* because the Internet is evolving from a publisher-to-reader model (I refrain from using the hated term *paradigm*) to a more democratic publisher-to-publisher model in which equal access theoretically allows for a true marketplace of ideas, where the best authors and ideas are elevated by their hit rates and not—necessarily at least—from pedigree or affiliation.

Where once people surfed the Web to view content, today nearly everyone with access can not only comment but also become a publisher, a blogger, a podcaster, a videocaster, a Skype Internet telephony user, an instant messaging *pinger*. Blogging has had the most societal impact, but I feel videoblogging will quickly surpass it as individuals learn to package news stories or satire. People can break news faster than the established media, and the marketplace will correct the content in similarly rapid fashion. They can create and or participate in a Web-based poll that delivers results faster than can professionals at Reuters/Zogby or Quinnipiac. It is no secret that Matt Drudge gets more readers than *The New York Times*; he just hasn't earned the same level of credibility.

From a traditional corporate communication perspective, communicators need to understand the technologies and be able to use them not only to further corporate initiatives but to respond to and counter challenges and falsehoods. The thought of someone parodying your brand on YouTube is frightening to many, but particularly to those who are removed from the practice of today's egalitarian new media. There will be a serious cultural divide among those in the communications industry, similar to a corporate cultural divide that is developing between younger employees who are accustomed to social networking tools and traditional employees who are not. Knowing how to e-mail is no longer enough, particularly for corporate media practitioners. Those who fear the tools are relinquishing any influence they might have had.

A Brave New, Flat World

As Thomas Friedman points out in *The World Is Flat*, only those with the ability to horizontally integrate disparate people and processes will be successful by using communications media to think and act like a larger player.[9] By breaking down the pyramid of communications control through an environment of trust—much the way desktop publishing first challenged established media—smart entrepreneurs will be able to integrate a culture of open communications in which organic innovation and good ideas bubble up by inertia and important news gets through because it rates highly on TagCloud and search engines. But, as Friedman points out, evil men like Osama bin Laden found equal opportunity on the Web. Therein lies a danger to professional communicators who may be significant targets for at least communications attacks, but who may not know their challenger's identity, status, or legitimacy—and neither will the public.

The good news here is that as companies begin to see all communications venues as related to a big picture, such as the CVFCC, they can work to achieve whatever balance is lost to emerging media and increased decentralization. For example, as corporate intranets move to become the primary preferred source of information about the corporation, we might disenfranchise the first-line supervisors who control the employees that most determine the success of client relationships

through their influence on customer satisfaction. The other good news is that technology is providing holistic instructions so that those working in remote corners can better understand their role amid overarching strategies.

Newfangled communications programs must include tactics to balance the innovator and broker roles with the monitor and coordinator roles, or they risk blinding the company to the first-line supervisor's unique ability to identify and navigate around roadblocks. Manager input is as vital as manager buy-in to corporate vision. Similarly, an overly directive approach will abuse disconnected workers with less sense of belonging or history than the older gold-watch crowd.

If the future sounds confusing, it is. It is only through a holistic look at communications that program strengths and weaknesses will be properly gauged across an overly extended enterprise. It is only through an academic framework such as the CVF and new CVFCC that increasingly splintered practice will have meaning and relevance. So students should learn these theories well, and put their AOL Instant Messenger in the BRB (be right back) mode while reading this book. You're already years ahead of us older folks in terms of social networking. This book is even more important for you, as future corporate communicators.

The Takeaway

I have written about String Theory, the debate over evolution, and a management theory called the Competing Values Framework. And I have shown some implications that the CVFCC holds for the broad communications process as I understand Belasen's ongoing work. I saw a number of early manuscript versions of this book, and each successive iteration's progress has been stunning. How far his theory has progressed in such a short period of time is truly awesome. I suspect the story gained a few more wrinkles before he submitted the version you are about to read. I can only guess.

From here I will let Belasen explain the CVFCC in all its intricacies. My role has been to make you aware of its significance—why undergraduate and graduate students alike will want to pay close attention to this new framework, why working communications professionals will want to return to the classroom to get up to date on the CVFCC, and why former MBA candidates who fled graduate school to found dot.com start-ups will want to reinvest some of their IPO earnings to learn the new fundamentals of business and business communications. A lesson in balancing brokering innovation in terms of electronic commerce with business process normalization in terms of promised delivery of goods—what has been called *balancing bricks and clicks*—might have saved their now-defunct companies.

Students in the fields of management and now communications have quite an advantage over their counterparts in other academic departments. We have a deceptively simple framework, an intelligent design that is both evolutionary and predictive. Rapid change ahead will make this basic understanding of the communications process invaluable. Take the time to learn this because it can be used to explain complex relationships, identify myriad sources of influence, plan complex strategies, and measure sophisticated competencies in an increasingly complex world.

How does one diagram explain so much? Likely because the CVFCC taps into something quite natural in the way of management. Perhaps our four forces align with the four forces of String Theory that manage nature. We won't really know until the field of physics comes to better terms with its potential field theory. Alas, poor Einstein is best known to the current generation as the facial model for Yoda, the Master Jedi Knight in George Lucas' *Star Wars* movies. I'm sure Lucas wanted to portray a

sensitive Yoda as both an alien and the ultimate hope for humanity. Einstein was always an optimist despite a harrowing life of ethnic persecution, professional ridicule, and personal difficulties. He escaped to his own world of planets and competing values, and probably would have liked his portrayal on film.

But does not the CEO's setting of sales quotas reflect a strong force and the soothing voice of human resources a weaker one? Is not gravity that which holds us all to the standard of earth while electricity lights the darkness, beckoning us to broker the unknown? Although Belasen makes no attempt at answering the greater questions of the cosmos in this book, he does much to fuse decades of a splintered communications academia, unifying important voices toward an astonishingly simple reality we have danced all around but never understood in Einstein's absolute terms. So perhaps communications is rocket science after all. Who knew? Here is a gift to those who study or use communications on a daily basis: May the four forces be with you.

Notes

1. Denis Brian, Einstein, a Life, p. 426, John Wiley & Sons, New York, 1995

2. Brian, op. cit., p. 1061.

3. Brian, op. cit., p. 243.

4. http://superstringtheory.com/basics/basic4.html.

5. R. E. Quinn, J. Rohrbaugh, "A spatial model of effectiveness criteria: Towards a competing values approach to organizational analysis," *Management Science, 29*, pp. 363-377, 1983.

6. Brian, op. cit., pp. 240-241 (photo caption).

7. F. Scott Fitzgerald, *The Crack Up*, New York, 1945.

8. A. Belasen, *Leading the Learning Organization*, SUNY Press, New York, 2000.

9. Thomas L. Friedman, *The World is Flat*, Farrar, Strauss and Giroux, New York, 2005, p. 345.

PART A

Why a New Book on Corporate Communication?

1

Corporate Communication as a Field of Study and a Community of Practice

The Missing Link of Corporate Communication as a Field of Study

A quick glance at the titles published in the *International Journal of Corporate Communication*, by far the most credible source of articles and reviews in the area of corporate communication, is both revealing and puzzling. The majority of the topics cover everything imaginable that connotes internal communication, external communication, or both. The variety and range of topics compiled in the journal and the content areas are so wide and mutually exclusive that one can easily confuse the field with its subsets. The topics range from image management, reputation, stakeholder analysis, public relations (PR), investor relations, customer relations, government relations, marketing management, corporate citizenship, crisis management, media relations, and corporate advertising to corporate identity, employee relations, internal communication, management

communication, organizational communication, corporate culture, change, core values, and managing climate. Notably, each writer had a different audience in mind, and each article was aimed at mapping out different parts of the construct space of corporate communication. While most corporate communication researchers and executives could benefit from the use of an integrated and more systematic framework of corporate communication, unfortunately the academic field of corporate communication is scattered, divergent, and lacks coherence. Van Riel (1995), a prominent researcher and a prolific writer in the area of corporate communication, concludes that "the confusion concerning the central concepts of corporate communication has not been resolved" (p. 24).

An earlier reviewer of this book commented: "There is really no definitive text which is able to address the diversity of this field within a coherent theoretical framework." The two volumes written by Michael Goodman epitomize this problem. The first volume, *Corporate Communication: Theory and Practice* (1994), was aimed at clarifying definitional issues as well as identifying professional practices of corporate communication. *Corporate Communication* offers a close look at the growing professional practice of corporate communication and provides a discussion of critical functions. As a discipline, corporate communication is more art than science, but its body of knowledge is as old as rhetoric itself. Its theoretical foundation is interdisciplinary, drawing from language and linguistics, anthropology, sociology, psychology, management, and marketing. Its practice within contemporary corporations is seen as a strategic tool to lead, motivate, persuade, and inform numerous audiences inside and outside the organization. The objective outlined in the book is to "explore further corporate communication as a professional practice and an academic discipline" (p. xiv). In the first chapter Goodman goes on to define the intellectual boundaries of the field: "As a focus of academic study, corporate communication can be considered in the large context presented here, or it can be seen as an art of public relations" (p. 1). He then goes on to include the context: "Given the business environment, the more encompassing definition works well in both the applied context of the workplace, as well as within the context of academic study" (p. 2). Unfortunately, the rest of Goodman's book falls short of providing a solid theoretical basis or systematic procedure for building positions, presenting arguments, or integrating the various corporate communication topics. The value of his book, however, is in providing numerous academic views, stories, and case histories written by different experts in the field.

Goodman's companion volume, *Corporate Communications for Executives* (1998), sheds more light on the strategic context of corporate communication: "As an executive function, corporate communication is a strategic tool to lead, motivate, persuade, and inform numerous audiences inside and outside the organization. This book . . . further explores corporate communication as an executive and managerial practice" (p. xiv). Whereas the first volume was geared

more toward academic discipline, its companion largely focused on practice. Then again, the total meaning of corporate communication has remained unchallenged, at least in the eyes of the readers in the field. Around the same time, Oliver (1997) rightfully concludes in her introductory words to her own book that "the challenge for higher education and training research and development lies in the encapsulation of excellence from the patchwork parts to produce a definitive whole which is greater than the sum of its parts, and which is capable of regaining lost academic momentum to meet future management, student and practitioner needs" (p. 13).

Corporate Communication as a Community of Practice

What is the reason for the many conceptualizations of corporate communication? Why is there such disagreement over the definition and much debate over the intellectual boundaries of corporate communication? Why has writing about corporate communication models and organizational practices been so fragmented, noncumulative, and in such disarray, breeding different conceptions that are often incoherent and at best incompatible with one another? Why are a plethora of models used with arbitrary variables, unclear relationships, and multiple and diverse audiences? The short, simple answer is that communication is no longer the exclusive domain of PR or marketing departments. Other functional areas within the organization play an important role in decision making and implementation of policies that affect internal and external stakeholders. As organizations become increasingly large, they also tend to become more bureaucratized and standardized, relying on functional departmentation as the primary mode to organize labor and achieve economies of scale. Growth in size is normally followed by a greater formalization and standardization of organizational communication as a means to enhance internal consistency as well as achieve greater levels of uniformity in organizational responses. However, the proliferation of communication products (e.g., policies, procedures, memos, internal documents, brochures, newsletters, press releases, annual reports) across the functional units takes on a life of its own. Each functional department develops customized methods of communication and uses specialized language with unique syntax, form, style, and substance orientation to address its audience. Let's look at some examples.

The finance department deals with communication directed toward shareowners and institutional investors. The personnel department advertises positions externally and internally; develops codes and procedures to deal with the implementation of selection, training, evaluation, and compensation of employees; and is responsible for disseminating information about government policies and corporate compliance. The legal department handles the communication dealing with business law and regulations, public affairs, industry structure, environmental issues, and financial transactions. In addition to staff units, which provide services to the rest of the organization, most organizations have an operating core staffed by line units that do the basic work of the organization. Like the staff units, line units tend to be organized around occupational skills and technical areas of expertise. These units (e.g., engineering, purchasing, production, marketing) also use specialized language to enhance their operating efficiency and connect well with their customers. The marketing department, for example, interacts with wholesalers, distributors, and retailers and uses advertisements in print and electronic media, direct mail, and various methods of telemarketing to promote the goods and services of the organization.

Although the differences among these functional units and departments are important in delineating their distinct roles and responsibilities, enabling in-depth knowledge and skill development, they also become inhibitors of communication within and outside the organization. Functional areas develop their own standards and operating procedures for dealing with internal and external communication while treating other functional areas as nonrelevant, rendering the communication across functional lines ineffective. The very same differences that yield efficiencies and economies of scale within the functional departments also breed communication inefficiencies across units and lines. These differences are punctuated by idiosyncratic jargon, specialized meanings, and communication channels and messages that are tailored uniquely to the needs and interests of the clients, internal and external, served by the functional area. On the one hand, the personnel department uses relational and persuasive written messages to motivate new recruits to meet performance expectations creatively and often at "all costs"; on the other hand, the legal counsel staff use rational and conclusive messages to inform employees about the legal consequences associated with product liability laws. These communication activities are essential for the proper functioning of the organization, but they also underpin the proliferation of various corporate communication channels and functions.

Attempts to Integrate the Field of Corporate Communication

During the 1990s, several noteworthy books were written on the subject of corporate communication (Argenti, 1994; Oliver, 1997; Van Riel, 1995). While all of these books advanced the need for a broader, integrated view of the field of corporate communication, each one approached the field from a very different perspective, usually by focusing on a particular function. Oliver, for example, describes the "fragmentation of the discipline" and the "subsequent credibility gap" (pp. 11–12) as the main reasons for the shift that she advocates toward a more systems-oriented approach, which combines both internal and external organizational communication with functional and strategic approaches to corporate communication. Rather than offering a unifying framework in which the different parts of corporate communication could be presented uniformly and systematically, she divides the field into four mainstream categories by level (individual, group, operational, and strategic) and concludes the book by tying the strategic planning process to organizational communication plans and practices. Oliver's integrated communication planning model, adapted from Van Riel (1995), was then linked with a stakeholder analysis to highlight the significance of internal and external forces shaping the communication plans of the organization and igniting reactive and proactive public relations responses. The function of public relations quickly became the essence of Oliver's message, as captured in her indispensable recommendation to researchers of corporate communication. Researchers, she points out, must "incorporate the body of knowledge from the discipline of public relations into their corporate communication interdisciplinary research" (p. 205).

The Challenge to Identify the Construct Space of Corporate Communication

Surprisingly, lobbying for a more holistic and integrated approach to corporate communication has given rise to the emergence of PR as the most significant element of corporate communication. A PR unit as an important function of external communication has also become synonymous with corporate communication. It is important to note that corporate communication cannot be reduced to any one particular model. Instead, it must be promoted holistically— as a gestalt that brings together groups of researchers to provide direction for future research. There must be a greater willingness to tackle communication problems from a broader perspective infused with multiple viewpoints and enriched by diverse areas of expertise. Van

Riel (1995) punctuates the broader view as a necessity: "The holistic perspective of corporate communication preeminently makes it an area for special attention, which can be meaningfully positioned within the interdisciplinary research and educational field of management" (p. 23). The challenge for future researchers is to identify the construct space of corporate communication both as an interdisciplinary academic field of study that draws on a broader range of specialties bound by principles and theoretical and methodological issues and as a community of practice in which individuals and groups with similar occupational skills share common goals and interests associated with corporate communication. These groups form informal networks and social links within and around organizations aimed at promoting shared understanding, common values, and principles across their practices. They, too, are looking for guidance that informs their views and interpretations of events around them in a way that is consistent with the overarching goals of the organization. As Argenti (1994) observes, "more and more companies have come to realize the importance of a unified communication function" (p. vii).

Weick's (1979) concept of loosely coupled social systems is particularly useful in clarifying how the structure of multiple networks of communication operates. Since functions within the larger system of corporate communication tend to vary circumstantially, the system resembles a loosely coupled subsystem with dynamic patterns of interaction in a network of relationships. These loosely coupled functions and the individuals within them are different from the traditional loosely coupled systems, which are relatively uncoordinated. Individuals and groups playing different roles involving corporate advertising and advocacy programs, customer relations, media relations, and so on are relatively interdependent. Presenting the framework of corporate communication as a loosely coupled system is consistent with Argenti's (1994) view of corporate communication "as a combination of a strong, centralized, functional area . . . plus a network of decentralized operatives helping to keep communications consistent throughout the organization while adapting the function to the special needs of the independent business unit" (p. 57). Argenti goes on to describe how the tension that exists in a centralized structure with embedded semiautonomous groups is typically resolved functionally:

> As we begin to look at each of the different aspects of the function, we will find that some of these activities are already handled through another functional area. For example, the investor relations (IR) function could be in the treasury department, the employee relations (ER) function within the personnel department, and the customer relations (CR) function within the marketing department. All of these activities require communication strategies connected to the central mission of the firm. And . . . each of the activities can be classified as a sub-function of the corporate communication function itself. (p. 57)

Professionals with specialized skills who operate in a matrix-like structure with selective vertical and horizontal decentralization typically perform these activities and functions. While the power to control most of the line decisions is dispersed across the specialized areas (e.g., customer relations, government relations), the central office of corporate communication retains the responsibility to coordinate and integrate the different functions to achieve a unified and coherent organizational response.

Overhauling the Field

There is certainly a need for rescuing the field of corporate communication not by merely reinventing it, as Argenti (1994) suggests in his seminal work, but by overhauling the field as a practice and as an important academic discipline. With that in mind, Goodman (1994, 1998) deserves some praise for pioneering some of the early work on modern corporate communication. By focusing on particular characteristics of corporate communication, Goodman highlights the need to make explicit the theoretical, empirical, and practical value of each as well as the need to recognize tradeoffs among academicians and practitioners. Furthermore, by segmenting the field into diverse topical areas, he also indirectly creates the need for identifying a universal framework that streamlines the field and presents it as a uniform and consistent base of knowledge.

Van Riel's (1995) triangle of marketing communication, organizational communication, and management communication is one such framework. Marketing communication is an umbrella for a wide range of external communication, including advertising, sales promotion, direct mail, sponsorship, and so on. Organizational communication has a much broader appeal that includes public relations, public affairs, investor relations, employee relations, corporate advertising, and scanning. Management communication includes traditional aspects of supervision; administration, such as planning, organizing, coordinating, and controlling; and leadership, such as developing shared vision and mobilizing support for that vision through trust and empowerment. According to this schema, the overarching goal of corporate communication is threefold:

1. Increase the harmony among these three functional areas to maximize the fit between corporate strategy, organizational identity, and external image.

2. Sustain the effort to institutionalize the corporation through branding and legitimization.

3. Facilitate the coordination of communication activities for optimal implementation of policies and decision making.

Van Riel's (1995) definition of corporate communication implicitly underscores the importance of using a stakeholder approach: "Corporate communication is an instrument of management by means of which all consciously used forms of internal and external communication are harmonized as effectively and efficiently as possible, so as to create a favorable basis for relationships with groups upon which the company is dependent" (p. 26). This definition, however, does not provide sufficient direction for enabling researchers and practitioners to grasp the total meaning of corporate communication. Corporate communication transcends the areas of specialty of communication practitioners (e.g., advertising, direct marketing, media relations) and cross-functional boundaries to harness the strategic interests of the organization as a whole (Cornelissen, 2004).

The Need for a Theoretically Based Organizing Framework

Corporate communication as an academic field and as a community of practice must be broad enough to allow for the integration of ideas and the development of agreement among theoreticians, researchers, and practitioners. It also needs to be specific enough to allow for differentiation of distinct contributions to the field. The organizing framework should reflect the paradoxical nature of corporate communication where unity and variety, consistency and creativity are practically recognized and academically accepted. The value of each contribution to the field, at minimum, must be assessed against the dual criteria of theoretical significance (from the researcher perspective) and functionality (from the practitioner perspective). The importance of any addition to the field can therefore be judged based on (a) unity and thematic focus (Does understanding crisis

management advance knowledge of corporate communication? Does it belong to corporate communication?), and (b) usefulness and relevance to stakeholders (Are technological innovations for revitalizing corporate culture crucial for the practice and functioning of corporate communication from the perspective of employees, investors, customers, or suppliers?). This last question is particularly important for contextualizing corporate communication and for sensitizing the organization to claims and demands by different stakeholders. As Oliver (1997) rightfully points out, a stakeholder approach reminds communication executives, professionals, and academicians that the conduct of corporate communication involves public accountability both internally and externally.

Summary

Chapter 1 discusses the need for a more integrated approach to corporate communication. Corporate communication as a field of study and community of practice encompasses multiple functions. Corporate communication also responds to a large number of specialized and general stakeholders in a number of important areas, including employees, customers, financial markets, and government regulations. It is argued that both researchers and practitioners could benefit from the use of an organizing schema that considers the interdependencies across the functions and responsibilities of corporate communication as well as brings greater coherence to the field.

Review Questions

1. Do you agree with the statement that understanding corporate communication requires an organizing schema that considers the interdependencies across the functions and responsibilities of corporate communication?

2. What are the advantages and disadvantages of having an integrated approach to corporate communication?

3. Why is contextualizing corporate communication and sensitizing the organization to claims and demands by different stakeholders important for organizational effectiveness?

PART B

Strategic Corporate Communication: An Integrated View

2

Competing Values Framework for Corporate Communication

Drawing on Quinn (1988) and Belasen (2000), the Competing Values Framework for Corporate Communication (CVFCC) was developed primarily to address concerns over the wide dispersion of the field and the need for greater focus in attending to important stakeholders. Although existing conventions of corporate communication (e.g., media relations, public relations, customer relations) have broadened our thinking about the scope of corporate communication tasks and responsibilities, both internally and externally, there is still a need to explore the context of corporate communication as a unified, highly interdependent function.

A key point of the CVFCC is that, whereas corporate communication functions are often perceived as fundamentally opposing, contradictory, and exclusive of one another, in reality they are complementary and mutually inclusive. Organizations are expected to use regulative systems to achieve uniformity and coherence of their internal communication practices and procedures. They are also expected to use innovative systems and become more responsive and adaptive to external communication networks and important stakeholders. The CVFCC highlights the fact that corporate communication executives and professionals operate under the burden of contradictory and often inconsistent expectations. Responding to these expectations is vital for building a strong identity and sustaining a credible organizational image.

The competing expectations appear as polar opposites on two juxtaposed dimensions with incompatible values (see Figure 2.1). The vertical dimension ranges from decentralized networks of communication to centralized structures of communication, and the horizontal dimension stretches from external communication to internal communication. Essentially the CVFCC can be thought of as a compass. The first dimension, the vertical axis, represents expectations for organizational flexibility as a goal on the north pole, and expectations for organizational control as a goal on the south pole. This spectrum represents the organization's need to provide a predictable and stable work environment versus the organization's need to be flexible, dynamic,

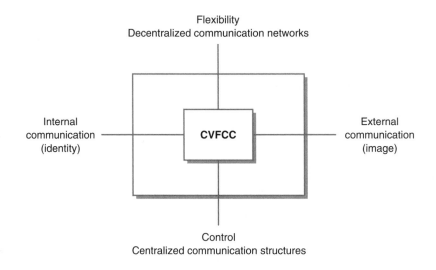

Figure 2.1   Competing Values Framework for Corporate Communication: Dimensional Qualities

and responsive to human needs and changes in the external environment. The second dimension, the horizontal axis, represents expectations for internal consistency on the west end and expectations for external adaptation on the east end. This spectrum represents the belief that organizations need to be able to manipulate, monitor, and measure internal tasks while simultaneously being responsive to the demographic changes, global economic events, government regulations, and competitors' behaviors and actions in the external environment.

The internal and external foci of corporate communication reflect the relationship between corporate identity and corporate image. The external endpoint of the CVFCC represents positioning, differentiation, rivalry, and image. Markwick and Fill (1997) define corporate image as the totality of stakeholders' perceptions of the way an organization presents itself, either deliberately or accidentally. Corporate identity has a direct effect on organizational image. Identity refers to the organization's presentation of itself to its various stakeholders and the means by which it distinguishes itself from other organizations. As such, corporate identity is the outward presentation of an organization. Consistent

impression of positive corporate image results in positive corporate reputation (Alessandri, 2001). Corporate identity is like a DNA blueprint, which is unique to that particular organization. Corporate identity tells both the internal and external stakeholders what the organization is about, what it does, and which strategies it adopts for its business. Organizational goals, mission statements, values, names and logos, as well as rituals and ceremonies help to shape corporate identity, and corporate identity can be divided into two levels: surface and deep structure (Alessandri, 2001). The visual elements such as logos and names comprise the identity that is visible to the public and stakeholders; an organization's structure, behaviors, and values are the elements that exist below the surface but are still very important in shaping corporate identity.

Communication Perspectives

The juxtaposition of these two dimensions forms quadrants that reflect important sociological paradigms (Burrell & Morgan, 1979) and communication perspectives that constitute the construct space for corporate communication (see Figure 2.2). These perspectives of communication compound the field and make the task of identifying solutions to internal and external communication problems very difficult because no one set of concepts and assumptions can be used exclusively. Collectively these perspectives define the domain of corporate communication.

Functionalism focuses on the process and measurement of communication performance, roles, and behaviors aimed at responding to regulatory, market, and information constraints and challenges. Communication tends to be directive and centralized, with managers relying on promotional message orientations. There is a focus on external image, goals and strategies, performance credibility, and accountability.

Interpretivism focuses on the flow and meaning of structured communication, hierarchy culture, rules of behavior, and codified decisions aimed at regularizing the system of interactions. Communication tends to be normative and hierarchical. There is a focus on internal identity, coordination, symbolic convergence, compliance systems, uniformity, and accountability.

Radical humanism focuses on the messages of relational-interpersonal communication and centering on dynamics of human communication. Communication tends to be decentralized and informal. There is a focus on internal identity, culture, core values, shared beliefs, commitment, concerns for human resources, and participation of individuals in problem-solving communications.

Radical structuralism focuses on the goals of transformational-institutional communication and centers on the alignment of communication activities with the external requirements of the environment through innovative and informative systems of communication. Communication tends to be decentralized and external. There is a focus on external image, products and markets, branding, and reputation management.

The functionalist approach is based on the belief that social structures have discernible purposes, or functions, that are reflected through and contain human action, whereas the interpretive approach is based on the belief that

human constructs ultimately reside in and are manifestations of human thought. In communication theory, the functionalist paradigm draws on the principles of scientific management and economic models of rationality. The interpretive paradigm has its roots in the behavioral models of bounded rationality and in the notion that uncertainty and limited time to deal with complex issues give rise to implicit and explicit decision-rules. Structures and processes can be expressed as the results of codified rules, which simultaneously constrain and facilitate actions while also symbolizing organizational commitments. The interpretive approach views organizational control as binding members through normative systems by creating an image of the organization and how its subjective realities are socially constructed (Fairhurst & Putnam, 2004). Effective organizational leaders present the world with images that grab members' attention and interest. They use language in ways that allow members to see leadership not only in a decision-making role, but also as a series of moments in which language images build upon each other to help members construct a reality to which they must respond (Fairhurst & Sarr, 1997). J. R. Taylor and Van Every (2000), for example, illustrate the importance and impact of both text and conversation on organizing. They show that both the contexts of a particular interaction and the new information brought to that interaction assist in maintaining the intersubjectivity of the world. They demonstrate that both text and conversation are embedded within one another. Moreover, an agency can convey an identity and a voice through textualization, and through back propagation, conversation can contribute greatly to the evolution of an organization.

The question that functional researchers and communication specialists attempt to answer is essentially a managerial question: How can an organization use communication to be more efficient? One of the metaphors used in functional theory illustrates communication as traveling through a pipeline. Managers put a message into the pipeline and send it down

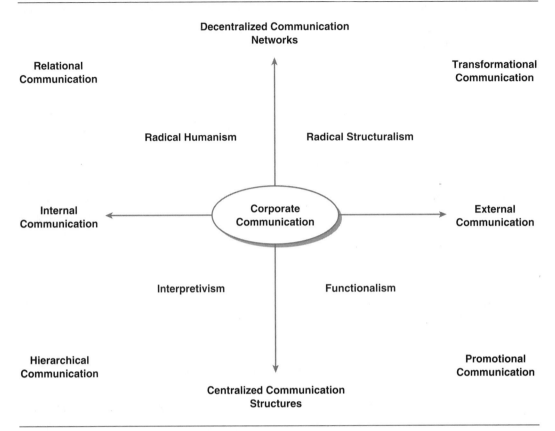

Figure 2.2   Competing Values Framework for Corporate Communication: Perspectives and Message
Orientations

through the organization to the employees. Any trouble has to do with the message or the channel. Organizational scholars and consultants work to understand how that communication travels downstream and upstream and the remedies available for improving the process. Interpretive scholars, however, try to understand how organizational members make sense of their world; they do so primarily through qualitative research, often in the form of ethnographic study, that is, how the world around the members changes and how members develop interpretations and make sense of that world (Cheney, 2002). Radical humanism and radical structuralism, on the other hand, fall under critical theories of organizational communication.

Critical researchers try to uncover the political power structure that often is under the surface of much interaction in any human system. They focus on power relationships, dynamics of dominance, oppression, and how members might emancipate themselves (Deetz & Mumby, 1990). Corporate owners and managers dominate workers by the commodification of their skills and employment, as well as through active consent or hegemony. Once a group has established its sectional interests as universal, discredited any contradictions to its interests, and reified the symbols that it espouses, other members of an organization are controlled or dominated, either through active or manufactured consent or through the dominant ideology. One example of this is the documentary *Roger and Me*, a film produced by Michael Moore that tracks the exit of General Motors (GM) from Flint, Michigan. GM was founded in Flint, was the top employer for many years, and for these reasons created and maintained the dominant ideology in the city—an ideology that established its own interests as universal to residents. Moore's film is an ethnography that shows repeatedly how GM and its macro actors discredited opposing ideological views, and how Flint continually reified itself as the birthplace of the automobile (e.g., through creation of the car museum). Moore portrays a community that, even during the worst of times in layoffs and heightened crime, continues to be dominated by the GM ideology that had been planted over 50 years before.

Functionalism

Functionalism employs quantitative research methodology for measuring and evaluating the efficacy of communication systems, structures, processes, and goals—why members behave and interact in a particular manner and what the means are to align communication behaviors with stated goals. The purpose of the functional approach is to develop outcomes and benchmarks as measured by the rate of optimal flow of communication. A functionalist, for example, would map out the flow of communication within formal organizational structures, identify communication leaks and breakdowns, and highlight possible strategies for improvement. The following are some of the questions that a functionalist would ask: What are the communication needs of the organization? Does the communication system have the elements required to help support the mission and goals of the organization? How well are the formal and informal systems of communication working? What are the efficiency and effectiveness of specific communication networks? Are existing communication media compatible with the communication needs of the organization?

There are two main features of the functionalist approach. First, humans are a product of their environment. In other words, functionalists instill the abstract of organizations into concrete forms, claiming that the physical structures precede human activity. Second, the functionalist approach contains a managerial bias. There is a strong focus on a top-down, unilateral model of communication, with the main purpose of transmitting information about tasks. This focus is due to the functionalist perspective's strong emphasis on efficiency. The functionalist approach is also closely related to technical rationality, which encompasses the ideas of prediction and control—management employs tactics in order to control the means of production to warrant predictable outcomes. Similarly, the functionalist approach would claim that managers utilize control systems to enhance organizational efficacy and viability. In this view, managers are responsible for scanning the external environment and initiating structures and actions to obtain predictable outcomes.

Interpretivism

The interpretive approach fits well into the lower left quadrant of the CVFCC model and varies immensely from the functionalist approach. In contrast to functionalists, who believe that human activity occurs as a result of physical structures, interpretivists claim that structures originate from human interaction. In other words, organizations are the abstract set of social relationships centered on tasks and goals rather than on the physical structures; organizations are socially constructed systems of shared meanings. The interpretive approach is also less management oriented than the functional approach and less biased in that it views organizational control as binding members through the application of normative systems of communication, which create a shared vision about common practices, expectations, and interpretations. The interpretive approach is closely related to practical rationality, which is grounded in human interest and interpreting intersubjectively constructed meanings. Similarly, the main goal of the interpretive approach is to understand subjective experiences and how shared meanings are created through social interaction.

For the interpretivist, organizational communication can be extracted out of themes that appear as patterns. The interpretivist explores meaning and symbols, metaphors and rituals to unlock the mystery of how behaviors are enacted and how organizational shared reality is constructed with codified decision-rules and procedures that keep the social system unified and coherent. Functionalists evaluate the use of individuals and groups, whereas interpretivists are more concerned with how employees create normative systems of social interactions using unified norms of behaviors (Smircich, 1983). Despite these differences, the two perspectives share a common viewpoint: Both see organizational ideology as a legitimate force that uses formal, transactional communication systems to influence employees' social reality. Group members interact and share stories and fantasies from past events or about the future and become more cohesive through the process of symbolic convergence (Bormann, Cragan, & Shields, 1994). Symbols are used mostly to establish faith and trust, but also to construct the fantasy or the identity of the organization. They enable one to see how these symbols can be manipulated by managers and leaders, and in turn are used to frame organizational reality into a perceived consensus.

Although the two perspectives, functionalist and interpretivist, evolved from diverse needs, they do seem to have a common purpose that is dependent on both efficiency and stability. Putnam (1983) and Weick (1983) further elaborate on the diversity of these fields of study, but give greater explanation to the methods and application of both. Micro/macro, subjective/objective, determinism/voluntarism, and innovation/regulation are just a few of the aspects that are in opposition to one another. Whether one is looking from the "inside" or the "outside," a new point of view is made evident using a myriad of lenses. With this newfound philosophy, other schools of thought that are vital to the research of organizations have emerged. Critical

researchers, for example, emphasize the importance of the human component in modern organizations. They highlight that practical interests cannot be ignored and that collective intelligence is essential to the success of the organization as well as the individual. It seems as though the naturalistic research of the interpretive movement has shifted to critical research, in the sense that it is now investigating not only how we interpret organizational reality but also why we internalize the ideologies.

Critical Approaches

Both radical humanism and radical structuralism follow from critical theories of human communication that set out to explain communication behaviors and dynamics from the perspective of power relationships. Members initiate and react to communication based on perceptions of themselves, of others, and of the world. They use words that reflect their status, personal style, interests, and relationships to internal networks. To radical structuralists, communication relationships are the product of power differences and inequalities embedded in the design of the organizational structure. Radical humanism, on the other hand, focuses on consciousness or viewing human ideas as being imprisoned within ideological processes dominated by powerful actors; the potential for change is seen as dependent upon making organizational members aware of patterns of dominance. Radical structuralism, on the other hand, is grounded in the antagonisms between structural relations, not consciousness; reality is not changed by the consciousness of people but by the binding together of the contradictions that transform existing social systems into new forms (Burrell & Morgan, 1979).

Self-Efficacy

The critical approach's primary goal of emancipation could be used to clarify how and why managerial messages symbolically dominate and unobtrusively continue to control employees by cultivating managerial goals and initiatives (Deetz & Kersten, 1983). Seen as human relations ploys and indirect means of enacting control, the values and motives of management infiltrate the minds of members and the very essence of how people function within organizations. Employees' minds become saturated with managerial ideals of how to organize and stifle the means of self-control and empowerment. Members are motivated to examine the deeper structures of values systems in order to free themselves from suppression. This deeper structure, and not the surface structure, forces people to think hard about the values and consequences of power and empowerment. Often people operate under a false consciousness and are led to believe that they are empowered, when, in fact, they are not empowered. This context stresses the importance of self-efficacy as it relates to personal and interpersonal relationships that influence one's feelings of empowerment. Self-efficacy is composed of four subcategories: enactive attainment (the experience of mastering a task, which leads to feelings of confidence and achievement), verbal persuasion (communication from coworkers or supervisors to convince an individual that he or she is capable of successfully completing a task), vicarious experience (observation of another's mastery of a task, which can persuade an individual to master the same task), and emotional arousal (the surfacing of positive emotions and the elimination of negative emotions surrounding one's perceptions of work and situations; Chiles & Zorn, 1995).

Communication as Organizing

Radical structuralists question the basis for shared meaning and the appropriateness of consensus. Changes in the environment are inevitable. How we adapt to these changes is of great concern. According to Weick (1979), ecological change is what allows us to recognize the

details that would normally go unnoticed. The organizing method we choose to employ distracts us from the very things that might make sense. This is truly evident in the concept of enactment, in which an isolation of specific ecological change tends to manifest itself. The issues that we choose to isolate and further analyze in a sense limit our scope of the real occurrence to which we are subjected. What we choose to bracket for further analysis causes us to avoid many of the details that are vital to the organizing process. When organizing, we do not look outside the box, but rather we create the box.

Ecological change and the process of enactment are the cause and effect of each other. Adaptation or enactments inevitably involve change to an environment, and this change will cause more change. It is a cyclical process that continues to perpetuate. What we choose to enact and why has a direct impact on what we select and what we choose for retention. Selection is the process whereby we attempt to determine what is going on and to make sense of the raw data so we can in turn create a sense of reality that enables us to interpret some form of organization. There are many complications in the selection process. For instance, there are usually multiple features of ecological change that derive from the raw data, and enacted interpretations of the past can have a bearing on future recovered data. This is similar to notions of sunk costs, defensive routines, and inactive inertia that hinder change and instead promote existing structures of communication and power (Belasen, 2000). Habit and time constraints often limit the scope of the search for information, selection, and interpretations. Change, in effect, is a self-limiting process. The competing tension between change and stability punctuates the constant struggle between the polar opposites, with radical structuralism embracing change and interpretivism emphasizing socialization processes through norming and self-regulation. How can an organization determine what data are more relevant? How can an organization make progress if policy and decision makers rely merely on past interpretations?

The memories we choose to retain are a product of our selection; enactment and retention are in constant struggle with one another. This is the premise of the CVFCC. There are always competing values or needs that are necessary for successful corporate communication. The values may be competing, but they are complementary when used on balance. We need enactment because we need change in order to develop, but we also need guidance from the past to develop efficiencies. Weick (1979) recommends using partial constraint on the present in order to assure a balance between variety and repetition. The knowledge that we do retain will be stored in the form of causal maps to be used in future activities. Once an organization has stored its data, members are left wondering what they should do with this newfound information. Radical structuralism is important because there is always a need for shaking up existing structural arrangements and adapting to new system requirements. Looking at an organization as a means of oppression, or as an evolutionary process, allows researchers to gain new insight. Apollo 13 is a good example.

Apollo 13

By breaking down the Apollo 13 experience into evolutionary steps, for example, one can see how organizing processes impact an organization, especially in times of crisis. The Apollo 13 crisis forced NASA to deviate from its routine and/or expectations and enabled the organization to embrace new ideas that were vital to resolving the crisis (Tompkins, 1990, 2005). The ecological change for the Apollo 13 lunar mission occurred when the pilot conducted a routine procedure, stirring the oxygen tanks, which caused an explosion that depleted the crew's oxygen. The NASA crew on the ground began to enact the experience by selecting and choosing what

they would look at in order to determine what exactly was going on: Was it a mechanical error, an electrical malfunction, a cabin pressure issue, or something else? Ground control managers, along with NASA employees at the consoles in Mission Control, were in a sense bracketing the various possible issues at hand in order to further examine their possible roles in the malfunction. It was not until the commander recognized gas spilling into space and the pilot looked at the corresponding gauges that they realized that it was an oxygen issue. It was interesting to see all the other possibilities that ground control chose to look at in order to resolve the issue. When one thinks about it in this light, it makes one wonder whether or not they would have reached a conclusion about what was occurring without the observation of the crew. Would they have realized what was going on in enough time to fix the malfunction and save the crew? Considering the fact that everyone involved was racing against time, without the crew's immediate observation, they probably would have all perished. Once the crew and ground control were aware of the issue, they had to figure out what to do about it and how.

During the Apollo 13 crisis, selection occurred in the middle of the process of organizing the response to this crisis. With the problem identified, NASA had to select which issues could be employed to resolve the crisis. This was especially apparent in terms of ground control's meeting to discuss the various interpretations of what course of action they thought would be most reasonable in resolving the problem. What ground control chose to interpret as reality and reasonable courses of action was in conflict with their past experiences and previous knowledge of shuttle capabilities. They had to abandon the flight plan and devise a new plan to use the command module in a way that had never been attempted. Interpretive, functionalist, and critical approaches were all blended in an effort to find a solution. Ultimately, NASA combined the four quadrants and achieved success. There was clearly observable tension among the staff who did not want to deviate from the norm, but at the same time, people were ultimately willing to go beyond the realm of their standard organizational practices in a direction to which NASA was not accustomed. They tested not only the limits of the technology but also the limits of NASA in terms of reorganizing in times of crisis. They were forced to look and think outside the box. There were conflicts regarding which options were necessary for selection and which options were necessary for retention. Because the staff were forced to look at things in a new perspective and enact and select new interpretations, the retention process was in direct opposition to the organization's memory. This situation occurs quite frequently, which is why organizations need to be both flexible and stable in terms of retention. Although we cannot let the past blind us to future options, we have to be able to rely on the past in order to be efficient. An organization is a tightrope act—people need balance in order to stay on top.

High-Reliability Organizations

Effective corporate communication executives develop awareness of the contradictions that exist among the four sociological paradigms and have the behavioral complexity to deal with paradoxes. Behavioral complexity allows them to master contradictory behaviors while maintaining some measure of integrity and credibility (Denison, Hooijberg, & Quinn, 1995). A leader must be able to employ the radical humanist, radical structuralist, interpretive, and functionalist quadrants simultaneously. A leader must be

able to understand marketing, financial, organizational, and managerial communications. Indeed, effective leaders must fulfill multiple and interdependent roles such as those relating to interpersonal, information-processing, and decision-making issues. They also must design the work of the organization, monitor the internal and external environment, initiate change when desirable, and renew stability when faced with disturbance. This speaks to the five hallmarks of high-reliability organizations (HROs) discussed by Weick and Sutcliffe (2001): preoccupation with failure, reluctance to simplify interpretations, sensitivity to operations, commitment to resilience, and deference to expertise. An HRO is an organization whose rate of failure is linked to its mortality rate. Nuclear power plants, aircraft carriers, fire departments, emergency rooms, and airlines are examples of organizations that cannot afford to fail—otherwise someone might die. Awareness is the key.

Most of us do not work on aircraft carriers or in nuclear power plants. Why, then, do we concern ourselves with HROs if they are the exception, rather than the norm, in today's marketplace? By examining the practice of HROs, Weick and Sutcliffe (2001) discovered commonalities that might offer insight into how other companies can catch errors early, before they become catastrophic; contain the errors, when possible; and rebound afterward. When HROs fail to invoke any, or all, of these hallmarks, the consequences can be devastating. Examples of failure can be seen in the Mann Gulch disaster in 1949, the Tenerife air disaster in 1977 (Weick, 1990), and the Challenger disaster in 1986. A study of the Mann Gulch disaster indicates a collapse of the first hallmark of an HRO—preoccupation with failure. Underestimating the situation they were entering, smoke jumpers in the mountains of Montana were unprepared for the fire that engulfed and killed them. They were confident that they were facing a "10 a.m. fire"—one that they believed to be of such little significance that it would easily be contained by

10 a.m. This is the sort of expectation that leads to overconfidence and, in the case of HROs, can lead to dire consequences. The smoke jumpers at Mann Gulch were not preoccupied with failure; they assumed success and, as a result, perished. Weick and Sutcliffe note that HROs need to be constantly vigilant in considering what could go wrong. The notion of resting on one's laurels has no place in this sort of organization because it can ultimately result in critical errors that cannot be contained. By being participative according to the radical humanist quadrant of the CVFCC, employees are more likely to report errors and, by employing the functionalist and radical structuralist quadrants, to environmentally scan for possible errors. Managers should utilize the interpretive quadrant by being aware of the employees' perceptions on regulations of error reporting.

The second hallmark of HROs is the reluctance to simplify interpretations. Complex organizations benefit from diversity of knowledge; bringing diverse perspectives to a project or challenge creates the opportunity to look at a situation from many angles, thus minimizing the exposure to risk. The collective mind is a mass of many viewpoints, with an eye on a shared objective, that is heedful of possible obstacles to this objective. Weick and Roberts (1993) use an aircraft carrier as an example of this concept. On an aircraft carrier, every sailor has a specific, defined task to perform, and he or she is fully aware that his or her performance of this task is critical to the mission's success. Together, the sailors share a mission-critical collective mindset, heedful of the importance of each cog in the process. This situation falls into the two quadrants of the CVFCC centralized communication: functionalism (Is the information conclusive, decisive, and action oriented?) and interpretivism (Does the communication seem practical, realistic, and informative?). Ultimately there needs to be an understanding of how and when we communicate, as well as what we should do and say, and why. Collective minds and collective intelligence are necessities in an HRO.

Sensitivity to operations is the third hallmark of an HRO. A shared truth in corporations is that if you really want to know what's going on in the unit, you should ask the secretary. The same is true for first-line supervisors and HROs. Managers and executives may see the big picture, but the people who spot the little errors that can potentially escalate into larger problems are in operations. This hallmark touches on all four of the CVFCC quadrants: humanism, by knowing the channels of communication and organizational members; functionalism, by understanding the informational systems; structuralism, by understanding what's happening now; and interpretivism, by understanding the daily discourse within the boundaries of organizational communication. One must embrace all four of the CVFCC quadrants to have a true understanding of sensitivity to operations.

Whereas the first three hallmarks of HROs deal with anticipation of the unexpected, the fourth and fifth concern methods of containment of the unexpected. The first of these containment strategies, and the fourth hallmark of an HRO, is a commitment to resilience. HROs do not have the luxury to wallow in failure. They have to be prepared to quickly bounce back from failure. They have to constantly ask, "If something goes wrong, how can we work around it?" Externally, structuralism and functionalism take precedence. One needs to be innovative once the unexpected has occurred. Damage control needs to be taken not only internally but also externally. Stakeholders need to know that an organization can rebound, that the incident has been contained, and that revenue will not be negatively impacted. Internally, humanism and interpretivism need to be applied in order to achieve internal consistency.

Both the Tenerife and Mann Gulch examples show a breakdown from which the organizations could not rebound. Much of this had to do with the expectations of each group. In Tenerife, the tower was not expecting the KLM jet to take off. When the jet did take off, the staff in the tower did not know what to do or how to rebound. In

Mann Gulch, the smoke jumpers were not expecting a fire that large, and they were unprepared to react resiliently when their expectations were not met. The fifth hallmark of an HRO is the deference to expertise; hierarchy is abandoned in the face of adversity. The person with the most knowledge is the person who takes control of the situation. As one might expect, this might mean a series of different "commanders." An HRO would encourage this changing of the guard in return for a diminished or contained error. The Tenerife air disaster is an example of failure to embrace this hallmark. The disaster resulted from a number of small errors that escalated to a catastrophe due to the KLM flight crew's failure to communicate. As the revered, experienced pilot of the KLM jet prepared to take off, the copilot and flight engineer failed to repeat their concerns to the pilot or the tower. As a result, their reluctance to assert themselves ultimately resulted in the loss of 583 lives. The key to the fifth hallmark is balancing all four of the quadrants: humanism (Do all organizational members react the majority of time based on self-perception and the perceptions of others? Do they perceive themselves as the experts?), structuralism (How does power play into the perception of who is the expert?), interpretivism (Concerning regulations, how do organizational members view themselves in relation to one another? Who is the expert?), and functionalism (Is communication in the hands of the executive suite, or are there legal ramifications regarding delegation?). The more one looks at HROs and their five hallmarks, the more it becomes evident that the CVFCC embraces much of the communication systems needed to deal with diverse organizational situations.

Loss of life is the ultimate consequence in the actions, or failure to act, of any HRO. The safety of its employees and others affected by its activities is always at the forefront of an HRO's responsibilities. NASA is an organization that prides itself on its concern for safety. How then, one might ask, on January 28, 1986, did it fail on such a grand scale? Why did seven astronauts lose their lives in an explosion that could have

been avoided? The answer lies in NASA's failure to heed the five hallmarks of an HRO. Was NASA preoccupied with failure? No, in fact, quite the reverse—NASA was desperately preoccupied with success. Believing that the rewards from a few successes will outweigh the losses from many failures, top executives often blame failed projects on taking calculated (i.e., rational, reasonable) risks in uncertain situations (e.g., consumer markets, business markets, global markets, nonprofit and governmental markets). A success-oriented culture is sustained with inertia and slack until a key assumption—growth—disappears from the equation. Take Cisco Systems as an example. After recording more than 40 straight quarters of growth, Cisco failed to stop its slide in 2001 (its shares lost 88% of their value in one year). Executives are less likely to make optimal decisions after long periods of success, and NASA was no different.

The space program was being assaulted by Congress for its failure to successfully launch a shuttle. The president wanted an opportunity to broadcast this launch as evidence of a successful space program and wanted to use it as an occasion to inspire schoolchildren everywhere by sending the first teacher into space. The pressure was on. NASA management responded by proceeding with the program and ignoring any discussion of failure. Did NASA show a reluctance to simplify interpretations? Unfortunately, no. NASA management did not want differing viewpoints—they wanted one. And the viewpoint they wanted, regardless of the consequences, was that "all systems are go." NASA did not want to look at complex issues that might delay the launch from occurring on schedule. Was NASA sensitive to operations? In the case of the Challenger, operations were ignored in deference to management's objectives. NASA officials did not want to hear about o-rings or see charts involving obscure data and calculations. They wanted a timely launch. Did NASA demonstrate a commitment to resilience? Its interest to proceed with the countdown overrode all else. Even when presented with information that most HROs would consider vital to the mission, and a clear indication that more attention had to be given to the situation, NASA management refused to change its expectation that the launch would go as planned. Did NASA officials defer to expertise? This is the area of their greatest failure. Instead of deferring to the expertise of their engineers, they forced the engineers to think like managers. This action did not defer to expertise—it disabled it. NASA failed on all five counts. Officials were not mindful. They were not heedful. Along with millions of people around the world, I watched as the Challenger lifted off the launchpad and then exploded into a cloud of smoke. It has been two decades since the Challenger disaster. It remains one of those moments for which everyone can recall where he or she was when it happened. That is what happens when HROs fail.

Communication Systems and Goals

The domain of corporate communication comprises the four communication perspectives discussed earlier along with communication systems, each with one or more organizational goals. The innovative communication system sustains the ability of the organization to adapt to change. Communication tends to be decentralized and external. There is a focus on external image, products/markets, branding, and reputation management. The keyword is *transform*, and the key question is: "To what extent is the communication insightful, mind stretching, and visionary?"

The informative system relates to the mission of the organization to perform productively and meet shareholders' expectations by implementing corporate-wide communication strategies that maximize their returns on equity. This system centers on the process and measurement of communication performance, communication roles, and communication behaviors relating to regulatory, market, and information constraints and challenges. Communication tends to be directive and centralized, with managers relying on promotional message orientations. There is a focus on external image, goals and strategies, performance credibility, and organizational accountability. The keyword is *perform*, and the driving force follows the question: "Is the communication conclusive, decisive, and action oriented?"

The regulative system reflects the flow and meaning of structured communication, internal process culture, rules of behavior, and codified decisions aimed at regularizing the system of interactions. Communication tends to be normative and hierarchical. There is a focus on internal identity, coordination, symbolic convergence, compliance systems, uniformity, and control. Within a regulative system, the hierarchical communication maintains the flow and dissemination of administrative communications across organizational lines. The keyword is *conform*, and the key question is: "Does the communication seem practical, realistic, and informative?"

The integrative communication system focuses on relational and interpersonal communication as well as the dynamics and interactions of social groups. Communication tends to be decentralized and informal. There is a focus on internal identity, culture, core values, shared beliefs, commitment and concerns for human resources, and participation of individuals in problem-solving communication. This system maintains formal structures and informal networks of communication within the organization and creates opportunities for revising and realigning social networks with the organization's mission and goals. The keyword is *reform*, and the key question reflects on individuals and groups as important corporate stakeholders: "Is the communication discerning and perceptive of the receivers' needs?" These communication systems and goals are displayed in Figure 2.3.

Balancing Competing Tensions

The key to effective corporate communication is striking a balance among the four perspectives

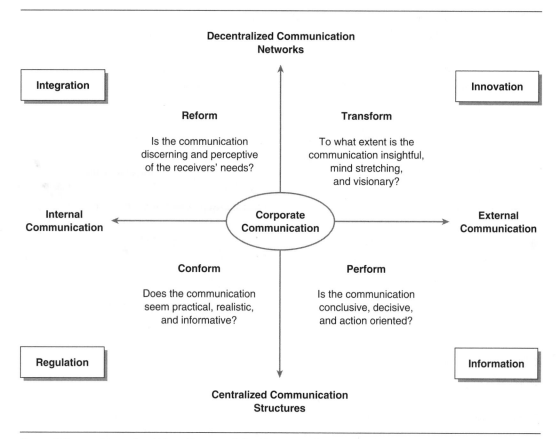

Figure 2.3   Competing Values Framework for Corporate Communication: Systems and Goals

and communication systems. An important objective is to recognize the unique interests and objectives associated with each domain while developing a response that considers the interdependence among all four areas of corporate communication. Rather than marginalizing or dismissing individual perspectives, this framework illustrates the relative value and qualities of individual perspectives using a broader, contextual view of communication. In addition, the CVFCC allows for the simultaneous consideration of promotional, transformational, relational, and hierarchical orientations of corporate communication (Belasen, 2000; Rogers & Hildebrandt, 1993). For example, the innovative communication system deals with transformational communication roles and activities in which network architects and brokers use

corporate advertising and public relations to advance the image and reputation of the corporation for better alignment with external constituencies. At the same time, hierarchical forms of communication are needed to divert attention to internal consistency and the need to stabilize and integrate the system. Hierarchical communication relies on the formal flow of communication and reporting relationships to disseminate directives. Although this form of communication tends to limit the creativity needed to address external concerns such as the media, it has enormous value in sustaining order and stability and in preserving the organization's institutional memory. Similarly, employing relational communication and paying attention to employees' communication needs via teamwork and collaborative efforts may foster commitment and a sense of belonging, as well as promote the construction of shared reality and the social identity of organizational members. However, this approach might breed further ambiguity and reduce some certainty, essentially contradicting the goals of speed, clarity, and decisiveness, the underlying communication goals manifested in the roles and activities of promotional communication. Radical structuralism, radical humanism, interpretivism, and functionalism are not only competing with but also nourishing to one another. It is understood that there needs to be a compromise among the values, but that all are deeply embedded within one another and are dependent on each other in order to establish a comprehensive and applicable model of corporate communication.

Summary

Chapter 2 provides the rationale for using the CVFCC, which was developed primarily to address concerns about the wide dispersion of the field and the need for greater focus in attending to important stakeholders. Although the existing conventions of corporate communication (e.g., media relations, public relations, customer relations) have broadened our thinking about the scope of corporate communication tasks and responsibilities both internally and externally, we still need to explore the context of corporate communication as a unified, highly interdependent function. The key to effective corporate communication is striking a balance among the four perspectives on communication. A leader must be able to employ the radical humanist, radical structuralist, interpretive, and functionalist quadrants simultaneously. A leader must be able to understand marketing, financial, organizational, and managerial communications. And a leader must be able to design the work of the organization, monitor the internal and external environment, initiate change when desirable, and renew stability when faced with disturbance—all of which is in alignment with the five hallmarks of high-reliability organizations: preoccupation with failure, reluctance to simplify interpretations, sensitivity to operations, commitment to resilience, and deference to expertise.

Review Questions

1. Discuss the value of the CVFCC as an integrative framework both conceptually and practically.

2. Explain the emphasis on interdependence among the primary functions of corporate communication.

3. Discuss the differences between the critical and interpretive approaches. Illustrate your points by providing some examples.

4. What is the significance of developing a high-reliability organization (HRO)? Discuss the roles of different corporate communication personnel in enhancing the strengths of HROs.

5. Using the five hallmarks of HROs (preoccupation with failure, reluctance to simplify interpretations, sensitivity to operations, commitment to resilience, and deference to expertise), compare two organizations (preferably within the same industry) and determine which organization is more effective and why. What is the predominant system of communication (see Figure 2.3) used by each organization?

Satellite Systems

It was 9 AM and time for the staff meeting, but the VIP wasn't there. Satellite Systems Vice President and General Manager Bill Curtis noticed that this meeting was different from the usual weekly affair. He could see each manger was dressed a little sharper, and the coffee was being served in "real" cups. The participants from the different departments in the satellite uplink company were going through their wallets, showing each other their cards. One suggested that before starting they pledge allegiance to the plaque on the wall. After twenty minutes the VIP from corporate came in. He was Robert Vallet, CEO of the communications holding company. He was dressed like a CEO, or at least a Wall Street banker. Lean in appearance, he also had the reputation for being lean on risk. "A bottom-line man," Curtis had heard Vallet call himself.

Today's meeting did not have the usual agenda of business-related items. Instead, Robert Vallet stood and talked about the greatness of the company, the bright future of the organization, and the pride each manager should feel. The group of twenty managers listened politely and intently. They did not want to disagree or take issue. Vallet did not invite the other fifty technical workers in the company. Bill Curtis had suggested inviting them, but Vallet had said he wanted to meet with the "movers and shakers" and not a bunch of technicians. To Bill, who was an engineer by training, these technical workers were the heart of the company. He knew that the technicians and staff workers were talking about the "bigwig" meeting and that whatever information they did not get soon would be fabricated by the grapevine anyway.

Vallet continued to talk, but Curtis was only half listening. Only the day before, over lunch, Curtis had reviewed the state of the company with this same group. Most had agreed that morale was at an all-time low. "It's like the soup of the day around here," said one experienced and senior technical manager. "We get a new program every six months that is supposed to make us better people and create a better company. But it's really just window dressing. They don't want to address the real issues." Another technical manager complained that the organization had not caught up with the technology. She said, "They want a one-size-fits-all program in this company, but the reality is that we are very different than our sister divisions. They are really show biz with a little technology built in. We are truly a technology company. Our success is based on how well we stay on or create the leading edge. If we fall behind, our customers are gone in 90 days."

Bill's mind wandered as he thought about the frustrations of his people. He could think of five or six "effectiveness programs" that had come from corporate over the last six years. Though "required," they had no apparent relevance to the company's circumstances or conditions. In addition to these half dozen programs, he knew there were others he was forgetting. This new program that Vallet was pushing, however, seemed to have more emphasis than the others—perhaps because Vallet himself was relatively new and did not have a real history with the firm.

Overall, Bill was proud of his division. Despite the problems of a rapid, ever-changing technology, he believed his group had adapted well. Most of the competition had gone under or merged in the last few years, leaving Satellite Systems smaller and more agile than the remaining bunch. Bill liked to think they were closer to the clients' needs than their competitors. In fact, Bill knew most of their major clients on a first-name basis. He was not above going to lunch with one of his account managers who was meeting with a client. Contrary to what some of the managers felt about this practice initially, Bill's presence usually made the account managers feel important, showing they were on a first-name basis with the vice president. And the clients felt more important, too.

In the conference room Vallet talked about the corporate-wide values program. He said he believed it had been a great success. He said the company had come to represent the values of fairness, honesty, and integrity to the customer and the employees: "We are a people company and we are proud of it." As part of the program, headquarters issued plaques to every division with the values statement inscribed. The CEO said he was glad to see that there was a plaque in this very room. Bill Curtis scanned the room. On the faces of all, he could see the outward evidence of that sense of pride, but he knew it was not genuine.

(Continued)

(Continued)

Bill knew, for example, that the conference room white board usually covered that plaque—except when there was a corporate visitor. Then there were the cards. As if on cue, CEO Vallet continued by asking each of the employees to hold up the "values card" that each was expected to carry in pocket or purse. Twenty out of twenty managers held up their cards. Bill had to smile wryly, knowing that the grapevine from other divisions was working. They had been warned at Satellite Systems to expect that the CEO would ask to see the cards. Some had dug through their desks to find the unused card. Bill himself had to borrow one from his secretary.

"I believe if we keep these corporate values before us, we will treat our people better and have a better company!" Vallet paused for effect, and it was something less than he expected. There was polite applause, however, and then the CEO sat down. Bill rose and asked if there were any questions. That, he felt, was at least a polite gesture. He did not really expect any questions and silently prayed that there would be none. Wouldn't you know, though, that one of the younger, outspoken sales managers piped up. "We've spent a lot of time on a new uplink system this year, and now we learn that it won't be online until the middle of the fourth quarter. Our customers simply aren't buying because they can't see it working yet. Because of that," he stumbled a little, apparently realizing he was now getting to the sticky spot, "because of that, sales revenues are down. What should we do?"

This particular issue had been the major, most hotly debated topic of the last five staff meetings at Satellite Systems. Members of the sales force were concerned because they were losing needed commissions, but everyone agreed fully that if they could just get the new system online, there would be plenty of commissions and plenty of work to go around. Meanwhile, it was not just rumored: the company admittedly was borderline in the red. Robert Vallet rose to his full CEO height and responded directly to the brave questioner: "If you can't sell this thing, then we will get someone who can!" There were no more questions.

Case Questions

1. Analyze and evaluate Satellite Systems from the interpretive, critical, and functionalist approaches.

2. What would your recommendations be according to each approach?

SOURCE: From Hammond, Scott C., Satellite Systems, in *Communicating in Organizations: A Case Book*, 2nd ed., Gary Peterson (ed), Allyn & Bacon, Boston, MA, 2000. Reprinted with permission.

3

External Image, Internal Identity

Crafting the strategy that shapes the image and identity of the organization is probably the most important responsibility of corporate communication staff. Image helps the organization to differentiate itself from others, and identity enables the organization to integrate itself from within. Strong identity evolves into ideology that helps pull organizational members toward the vision of the organization. And strong image helps companies manage the adaptation and retention processes. When the image and identity are in agreement, the organization as a whole is externally adaptive and internally cohesive. When image and identity are not managed properly, constituents are confused, and the credibility of the organization tends to diminish. The linkage between identity and image can be strengthened via intense integration, coordination, and monitoring activities across different areas of corporate communication functions (e.g., investor relations, media relations, employee relations, government relations) and based on different communication approaches (e.g., financial, marketing), as shown in Figure 3.1. Although the functions of corporate communication are only briefly described in the following sections,

they are discussed at length in chapters 5–8. Chapters 9–11 provide a thorough review of the four communication approaches and related theories and topics.

The value of the Competing Values Framework for Corporate Communication (CVFCC) is in providing a broader and integrative interpretation of corporate communication environments by addressing diverse stakeholders such as reporters, marketers, competitors, customers, investors, regulators, employees, and managers. Shaping and sustaining the image of the organization is a challenge that requires a broad, strategic view of organizational environments. Kiriakidou and Millward (2000), for example, discuss the importance for an organization to have a *strategic fit*, which entails auditing the organization's desired identity (management's vision and mission) and the actual identity (what the organization is and how it frames the mindsets and behaviors of its members) to reveal the potential gaps between the two. Doing so, in turn, shapes the reputation of the organization. Image is the mental map that constituencies have about the organization. Effective image management requires corporate communication managers to act as if they are

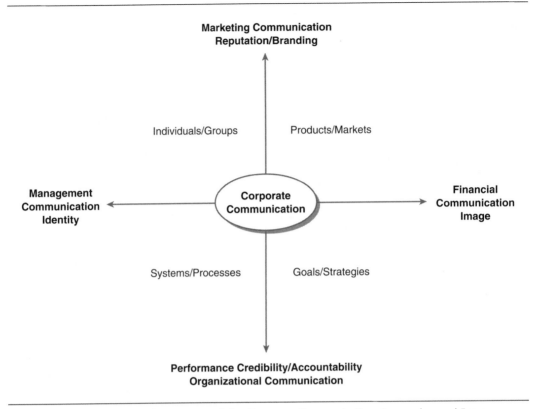

Figure 3.1   Competing Values Framework for Corporate Communication: Approaches and Focus

paranoid managers—constantly scanning the external environment and sorting through the multiple images that are formed perceptually by diverse stakeholders. The goal is to address possible weaknesses and vulnerabilities and guard against suboptimization. In addition to building positive image and reputation for an organization, sustaining and managing an organization's identity is important in helping corporate identity adapt to a constantly changing environment.

When image aligns with identity, an organization is widely accepted by the public; it is recognized implicitly and explicitly, and, in effect, is institutionalized. Retention by the environment is then facilitated through branding and legitimization. Leading companies in different industries successfully manage the institutionalization process through strong identity programs and credible image. Verizon, for example, began a significant brand name campaign in the spring

of 2002, describing the company as "helping customers make progress every day." Its brand name was associated with a positive, uplifting message, centered on accumulation of events that might otherwise be overlooked, rather than groundbreaking or historic events. IBM's experiment with the World Jam and the creation of "gravity centers" with information brokers acting as communication conduits or communication links is an example of a company that is in the midst of updating its identity. IBM has a very strong corporate communications department and seems to be doing very well. As of 2002, it was listed as the number two company in the Holmes Report.

Another successful example is the Japanese department store Sogo, which established a strong corporate identity in order to integrate its employees effectively through rituals and ceremonies. For instance, employees need to call out the company's slogan and sing the company's song together in the morning before they begin work. They also bow 90 degrees to welcome their customers. Because of distinctive characteristics such as these, Sogo presents the public image of employee solidity and a reputation of putting customers above everything else. These characteristics are embedded within Sogo's corporate identity; thus, corporate identity is significant in constructing the company's external image and affecting its reputation. As much evidence has revealed, a reputable organization has a competitive advantage and, therefore, sustaining and managing corporate identity seems to be an inevitable and valuable part of organizational strategic planning.

Integrated Corporate Communication

As Figure 3.1 illustrates, marketing and management communication is the dominant communication link between the brand image and the identity fabric of the organization. Financial and organizational communication, on the other hand, is the dominant communication link between organizational goals, strategies, and operators who are expected to embrace the mission and vision of the organization. Marketing and financial communication addresses the outside view of the corporation, with much attention given to managing external stakeholders (e.g., customers, investors). Management and organizational communication, on the other hand, responds to the need to link key interfaces (e.g., systems, structures, processes) and operators internally and align the corporate sociotechnical system. This integrated view of corporate communication is also consistent with Markwick and Fill's (1997) analytical framework for managing corporate identity and aligning resources with organizational goals and strategies.

Viewing internal and external communication as connected functions shifts the focus of corporate communication to answering questions about how an organization can communicate consistently to its many audiences in a way that represents a coherent sense of self. That sense of self is needed to maintain credibility and reputation inside and outside of the organization through strong organizational identity and positive external image. Corporate identity is projected to stakeholders using a variety of cues and represents how the organization would like to be perceived. Through delivering a planned message to target audiences, an organization's particular objective is more likely to be achieved. One such planned message would be the corporate identity program, which consists of two parts: the organization's visual identity, including the design and graphic associated with an organization's symbol of self-expression, and the corporate mind and behavior, such as organizational values and actions that are embedded in organizational culture (for more on this topic, see chapter 11). Before embarking on a plan, managers should take into consideration both the organization's original identity and its current identity. As shown in chapter 13, this process could start with audits that measure the current cultural profile of the organization and compare it with a desired cultural profile. Understanding an organization's past allows managers to identify strengths and weaknesses in the current identity and improve weaknesses in the corporate identity program (Van Riel & Balmer, 1997).

Sustaining and Managing Identity Programs

There are four important elements that should be considered in sustaining and managing an effective corporate identity program:

1. SUSTAINING AND MANAGING AN ORGANIZATION'S MIND IDENTITY AND BEHAVIOR IDENTITY THROUGH INCREASING INTERACTION WITH AN ORGANIZATION'S STAKEHOLDERS. An organization's mind identity is the set of values and philosophies that are believed by everybody in the corporation. The

behavior identity is the actions that an organization takes in order to distinguish itself from others. In the corporate identity program, both mind identity and behavior identity are significant enough to be recognized. In an attempt to consummate both, there must be increasing interaction with the organization's stakeholders to create and nurture a sense of positive corporate identity. To allow communication with an organization's stakeholders, both internal and external perception programs are needed. The target audience of an internal communication program is the company's employees. One of the most important messages to deliver in the internal program is to create and define the company's values and beliefs to the employees who will thus have a clearer sense of what it means to be a member/employee of the organization (Goodman, 1998). Examples of this kind of internal perception program include employee orientation and two-way communication between manger and employees. From these communication programs, employees will establish confidence and trust in the company, which eventually results in increasing the company's competitiveness through employees' better job performance. Moreover, interacting with employees through internal communication programs enables a manager to determine an organization's negative identity. As Markwick and Fill (1997) suggest, employees' view of corporate identity can be seen as a barometer of customers' opinions and as a catalyst for change and implementation. External communication also is significant in shaping public perception about an organization; it is usually associated with public relations and generates media attention. Examples of external communication programs include corporate-sponsored literacy and outreach programs, which promote the image of good citizenship.

2. SUSTAINING AND MANAGING AN ORGANIZATION'S VISUAL IDENTITY. According to Goodman (1998), corporate image is part of the overall makeup of corporate identity and goes hand in hand with the organization's graphic design. Logos, letterhead, and house style are examples of visual identification of an organization. Because of its role in communicating about the organization to its stakeholders, symbolism has been assigned a great deal of importance (Van Riel & Balmer, 1997). For example, a company's logo is expected to present the basic tenets of corporate identity as well as its meanings to the stakeholders. A logo's design is based on the company's letter name, captures stakeholders' attention in the company, and reinforces positive reaction via the visual stimulus (Goodman, 1998). Hence, the shape, use, and color of the logo are all important elements to be considered in an organization's identity program.

One example that illustrates the importance of logo design is Samsung's 1993 identity program. The objective of the program, according to Samsung's (1995–2007) official Web site, was to "strengthen competitiveness by bringing the attitudes and behavior of all employees in line with Samsung's desired perception by the public" (¶ 1). Samsung redesigned its logo in an attempt to change its image of second- or third-rate products to become a world leader in its business areas. The new logo was crafted in English to symbolize its global presence throughout the world. It incorporated an elliptical shape to convey a message of innovation and change. The letters "S" and "G" both partially break out of the oval, showing Samsung's desire to be one with the world and to serve the society as a whole. Moreover, Samsung chose blue as the color of its logo to suggest the organization's reliability and stability, and at the same time to exude a feeling of warmth and intimacy with its stakeholders. The design of the new logo has been successful in communicating and reinforcing the company's corporate identity with stakeholders. Before implementing its identity program, Samsung gave the impression that its products only sold in discount stores and Wal-Mart. To change this negative brand image, the company's redesigned logo created a nonverbal message to reinforce the company's qualities of reliability and innovation.

As a result of its corporate identity program, Samsung has become one of the world's leading corporations in the electronics industry, especially in mobile phones.

3. UNIFYING THE COMPANY'S MIND, BEHAVIORAL, AND VISUAL EXPRESSION THROUGH A CONSISTENT AND HIGH-QUALITY APPLICATION OF PROGRAM STANDARDS. The mind, behavioral, and visual expressions of an organization must be designed and applied consistently across the functions of corporate communication. Visual expression includes the use of similar symbols, consistent typography, and standardized colors (Alessandri, 2001). A positive corporate identity and image can be developed and perpetuated via internal programs and those directed at the public. Applications of visual identity include different means of communication such as print advertising, letterhead, brochures, stationery, checks, and business forms (Goodman, 1998).

Consistency and standardization are keys in the unifying application of corporate identity; a corporation's identity should be consistent and consecutive. For example, the contents or techniques of advertisements, such as those used by Disneyland, may be boundlessly variable, but the main idea and character should be consistently conveyed. Although different advertisements are presented every year, the main idea that Disneyland communicates to its audience is its "happy family," and the character it uses is always Mickey Mouse. Because of the repeated application of the same expression, Disneyland's corporate identity is recognized throughout the world. From this example, we can see that consistent and standardized application is essential in creating and unifying an organization's corporate identity.

Boyd (2003) provides an example of the importance of keeping a message consistent across diverse constituencies. He demonstrates how the use of a metaphor can be a method for building identity and image with multiple stakeholders. Metaphors let messages for different audiences reinforce a single identity of the organization and the issue at hand; they unify internal and external stakeholders. The case Boyd discusses involved a merger between two companies and a hostile takeover attempt by a third party. The companies involved needed to gain the support of various stakeholder groups, and Boyd's study focused on the media campaigns the companies used to gain support. The two merging companies used a war metaphor throughout the whole campaign. They tried to show that the third company was launching a war against them by attempting a hostile takeover, and they kept their messages consistent. They used the media to send their messages through advertisements, articles, and commercials. They addressed how a hostile takeover would impact all stakeholders, not just shareholders.

According to Boyd (2003), the use of the war metaphor damaged the takeover company's image. The company was portrayed as aggressive, irrational, forceful, and savage, and the two merging companies were seen as victims in need of support from the stakeholders. The third company sent out a number of different messages, but none were consistent, which may be why it failed to achieve the hostile takeover. Boyd's example shows how a consistent message can get all stakeholders to identify with the organization and its goals. It also shows the importance of targeting both internal and external stakeholders.

4. AUDITING THE IDENTITY PROGRAM AND REVIEWING THE CORPORATE IDENTITY CONTINUOUSLY. Assessment must be made during and after implementation of the corporate identity program. To audit the effectiveness of the actions taken by management, it is necessary to look at the program's objectives and evaluate whether the expected outcomes have been reached and properly communicated (see chapter 13). Even though the identity program may be successful at the moment, the designed corporate identity might not fit the organization forever. Because the corporation and its environment are both perpetually changing, corporate identity needs to be reviewed for possible updates.

Primary Functions of Corporate Communication

The overall value of the CVFCC is that it provides a fuller view of corporate communication in which a dynamic interplay of complementary and often competing orientations takes place. The framework supports the notion of communication systems that are both independent and interdependent. It offers an integrated view in which the relative value of each perspective is not mitigated by the value of the other perspectives. The CVFCC affords an excellent opportunity to describe these perspectives while weighing the tradeoffs among the perspectives to enrich the analysis. The framework is therefore a representation of four perspectives on communication that are highly interdependent. As Figure 3.2 illustrates, these perspectives are also aligned with the four primary functions of corporate communication.

The framework is particularly useful in helping communication researchers and practitioners form a better understanding of the scope and range of communication activities that affect the organization both internally and externally. Moreover, it promotes the development of communication responses that consider the objectives and consequences of employing different messages when addressing different audiences. These functions and their subareas must be balanced and managed strategically. Thus, the CVFCC integrates communication perspectives, messages, and skills across the different areas. These areas are outlined below and treated thoroughly in chapters 5–11:

1. **Marketing communication** concentrates on *media relations*, corporate advertising, issue management, public relations, community relations, customer relations, and reputation management.

2. **Financial communication** covers *investor relations*, image management, legal communication, executive communication,

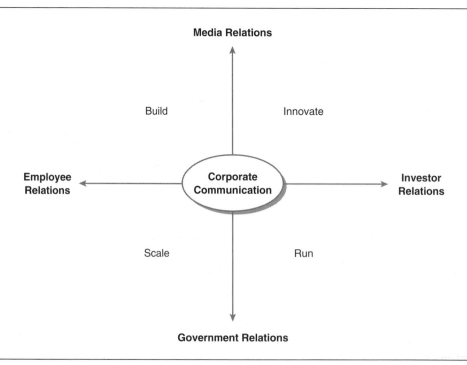

Figure 3.2   Competing Values Framework for Corporate Communication: Functions

strategy communication, external affairs, performance management, and crisis management.

3. **Organizational communication** focuses on *government relations*, field communication, administrative communication, codification and integration, and compliance communication.

4. **Management communication** centers on *employee relations*, culture and change communication, site communication, human resource management, and social identity communication.

Media Relations

Media relations (MR) is characterized by outward communication serving to advance the corporation's goals. One of the main concerns of the MR function is keeping up with current trends in the market. The organization must stay current in order to determine which opportunities are worth pursuing and which are not. In addition, a concern for this section of the CVFCC is to determine how customers will be won over. Essentially, the MR function engages in corporate advertising, a form of advertising different than product advertising because it involves promotion of the entire organization. Corporate advertising is an extremely important factor in retaining customers. As Goodman (1998) asserts, getting the media to provide press for your corporation is almost universally the goal of any MR plan. The main question to ask in this sector is "To what extent is the communication insightful, mind stretching, and visionary?"

The purpose of MR is to build a positive reputation and encourage branding of the organization's name in the marketplace. The corporation intends to portray the characteristic of innovation to its constituents, hopefully strengthening its image as perceived by external stakeholders. A current environmental issue that exemplifies the relevance of corporate communication in this area is the acceleration of product life cycles. This trend is particularly evident in fluid markets such as consumer electronics, in which companies with high visibility and a strong reputation have a competitive advantage because their brand name adds value to their products by reducing uncertainty in the minds of customers, retailers, and distributors (Balmer & Gray, 2000). This example drives home the significance of corporate communication by showing what effective corporate advertising can accomplish.

Attracting new customers and retaining current ones are two essential goals pursued by corporate advertisers to help support the financial goals of the organization. It is therefore in the organization's interest to direct corporate messages through various media, such as television, newspapers, magazines, radio broadcasting, and the Internet. Essentially, the organization wants to get as much press as it can. Examples of outlets used to deliver messages in the MR subenvironment include press releases, interviews with reporters, and distribution of corporate brochures. Much of the work of MR staff is done by boundary-spanning personnel who act as a buffer between the organization and the environment, screening out things not relevant to the corporation. Boundary spanners, such as market sensors or customer relations staff, relay to the organization information about current trends and changes in the environment. Boundary spanners also develop strong and sustained working relationships with reporters, contacting them in a timely manner with news and updated information.

Employee Relations

Employee relations (ER) focuses primarily on internal communication and identification issues. Identity is understood as the visual manifestation of a company's reality as seen in corporate actions, symbols, sagas, and jargon. However, image can be understood as a product of identity. Therefore, even though the ER function may not deal directly with managing external communication, it is nonetheless a factor in determining image. Essentially, corporate communication in this environment is aimed at integrating the organization from within, using a broad range of communication activities and products that are receiver centered. According to the CVFCC, the main question to ask in this quadrant is "Is the communication discerning and perceptive of the receivers' needs?"

The task of corporate communication in the ER function is to strengthen the organization's reputation and credibility in the eyes of the internal stakeholders by emphasizing the values of the organization, its strong culture, and its congruent communication systems. The key to staying competitive in today's volatile markets is the ability to attract and retain a skilled and motivated workforce. Attracting and retaining high-caliber personnel play a prominent role both formally and informally in communicating the organization's identity to the outside world (Balmer & Gray, 2000).

The predominant form of communication used by ER staff is interpersonal and relational in nature. In targeting employees, corporate communication ER staff must take into account the diversity and complexity of the corporation's workforce. Different types of people respond to different kinds of messages. Therefore, from a CVFCC perspective, having knowledge of employee needs is extremely important. In addition, the current trend of telecommuting and outsourcing makes reaching employees with corporate communication messages an even more complex task. Management must now figure out how to measure things like productivity from employees who are telecommuters or working in outsourced companies. Corporate communication in this segment must also address the concerns of union members, if relevant, and their respective unions, as necessary.

A variety of message types are exchanged in the ER quadrant of the CVFCC, and a great number of techniques are used for the actual delivery. These techniques range from individual meetings to company-wide seminars. Seminars and retreats are a good way to build a solid reputation and positive corporate identity because they bring together many employees in one place, thus making it easier to deliver a consistent message across the board. Other examples of message delivery methods include print and electronic newsletters, local area networks, intranet, and various mail lists. The more employees identify with their organization, the more likely they are to show a supportive attitude toward it, accept its premises, and make decisions that are consistent with organizational objectives (Stuart, 2002).

Government Relations

Government relations (GR) is characterized by internal organizational communication aimed at achieving compliance through regulative systems and processes. The goal is to increase accountability through accurate information about the organization while adhering to certain system and governmental standards. Activities in this environment are aimed at communicating the company's position on particular issues, strengthening organizational credibility, and fostering a positive organizational identity. An effective corporate strategy cannot be realized if credibility is tarnished. Communication in the GR function is more centralized and internally oriented than in the other functions, but nonetheless has implications for corporate image. One current environmental issue that exemplifies the importance of corporate communication in this sector is deregulation. Many organizations have a blurred public image as a result of deregulation in their particular industry (Balmer & Gray, 2000). Corporate communication addresses this issue by modifying the public personas of these companies; it provides a rationale for what information should be communicated about the corporation and why. By regulating the company's processes and adhering to ethical standards, the corporate communication department helps to portray the company as a good corporate citizen. By communicating social responsibility internally, the corporation can project accountability and a positive image to its stakeholders.

Corporate communication in this function also addresses the issue of society's growing demand for high levels of corporate responsiveness and ethical standards. Corporate communication staff works with regulators to make sure relevant information is processed and supplied to the people who need it. To maintain ethical standards and establish accountability, it is necessary to have a workforce that internalizes the importance of complying with ethical standards.

Investor Relations

Investor relations (IR) sets out to provide present and potential investors with an accurate portrayal of a company's performance and prospects. The communication that occurs in this function is financial in nature, aimed at promoting the credibility of the organization. IR is also concerned with achieving organizational goals and economic reasoning, or publication of the methods for getting returns on investments. IR is an important corporate communication function because it projects the organization's financial strengths and creates a corporate message that legitimizes the existence of the corporation. Another issue that exemplifies the importance of corporate communication in IR is dealing with mergers, acquisitions, and divestitures. Such moves might result in a gap between a company's image and its true identity, especially when assimilation processes (as in merged companies) go astray. IR staff must therefore be familiar with sociocultural dynamics as well as how to influence the level of congruence between the different parts of the organization.

Developing trusting relationships with security analysts and the financial community is important for effective delivery of key corporate messages. The target audience for IR personnel is largely made up of stakeholders such as venture capitalists and financial media reporters with influence over the financial success of the organization. Messages can be addressed to the business press and various analysts in the investment community. Some companies, however, may find it beneficial to bypass analysts and go directly to institutional fund managers at financial firms such as banks, insurance companies, and major investment organizations with specific messages. The types of messages and the means for delivering them may include direct mail aimed at analysts or highlighting the organization in the financial media through advertising and promotional campaigns. Specifically, IR may handle the production of financial publications, annual reports, and other such documents required by the Securities and Exchange Commission, stock exchanges, and shareholders. The aim of corporate communication in the IR function is to enhance business results and stock market evaluations. The person responsible for corporate communication in IR may be the communication executive, the financial director, the company's press secretary, or a mix of all three (Dolphin, 2003). It is also important to note that many companies create autonomous departments to handle IR, and some even hire outside consultants.

The Communication Process

Communication involves the exchange of purposeful messages between senders and receivers. Directors of corporate communication, unit managers, and staff specialists from various corporate communication departments such as MR, IR, GR, and ER create messages that target specific audiences or receivers. Receivers are internal and external target audiences that may include reporters, investors, analysts, regulators, and employees. When receivers require senders to provide more information or to clarify some aspects of the message (e.g., when MR staff fends off criticisms from investigative reporters about alleged advertising mishaps), they also act as senders. Thus, an overlap in communication roles between senders and receivers occurs in an exchange system that provides both sides with opportunities to record, inform, reinforce, or challenge the intent of the message.

The communication process is contextual, circular, and dynamic. Contextual factors include the interests, motives, and values of the communicators. Feedback loops and simultaneous exchanges between multiple players (e.g., MR personnel and reporters) make the communication process both dynamic and circular. The exchange of communication through positive or negative feedback allows both sides to adjust the communication, make necessary corrections, and align their expectations. Often referred to as the S-R (sender-receiver or stimulus-response) process, Figure 3.3 illustrates the nonlinearity of the communication process.

A typical process is often filtered through "noises" or barriers that need to be dealt with or overcome before a meaningful outcome can be obtained. Examples of barriers that might hinder the achievement of acceptable outcomes include hidden motives, gaps in expectations, incompatible values, cultural differences, mistrust, or lack of credibility. Other barriers include language and the use of complex metaphors, intended or unintended ambiguity, misinterpretations, and misunderstandings. The challenge for the communicators is to conduct the communication constructively and persuasively until a mutual understanding is reached. Effective flow of communication occurs when senders and receivers are engaged in a meaningful exchange of feedback that considers the objectives of both sides. When encoding (senders' expressions of thoughts) and decoding (receivers' interpretation of messages) are in sync, the communication process is effective.

Although chapters 11 and 12 include illustrations of different message orientations and diverse communication roles, it is important to remember that the communicator's focus is on attainable outcomes and target audiences. For example, the target audience for IR includes analysts and stockholders, and that of ER includes employees and trade associations. The key is to compose the appropriate message by figuring out *what* the objectives of the communication are, *who* the audience is, and *how* (e.g., verbal, visual) and *when* the message should be delivered. The selection of suitable channels

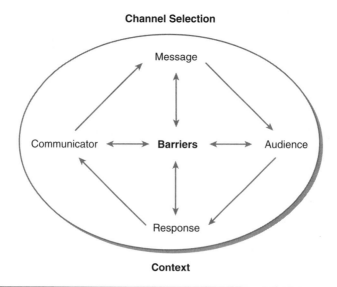

Figure 3.3   The Communication Process

is also important. A concerned regulator will require the GR staff specialist, for example, to compose a formal written report that accurately addresses the facts and details of a particular compliance procedure. ER staff, on the other hand, may choose to supplement a newsletter with an informal presentation that is interactive and entertaining. In selecting the right channel of communication, the goal is to reduce the noise, increase trust and credibility in the engagement, and ultimately gain the attention of the audience.

The main challenge is to recognize the need to gain the trust and mutual respect of the parties involved in the communication. As you read this book, you will learn more about the importance of this process. Communicators on both sides of the spectrum develop trusting relationships when they move toward convergence and when messages are composed clearly and coherently. As you will see in chapters 5–8, the challenge for corporate communicators is to balance the competing tension that is often generated between the functions of corporate communication and their divergent audiences.

Summary

Chapter 3 sets the stage for linking the primary functions of corporate communication both internally (identity) and externally (reputation).

Viewing internal and external communication as connected functions shifts the focus of corporate communication to answering questions of how an organization can communicate consistently to its many audiences in a way that represents a coherent sense of self. That sense of self is needed to maintain credibility and reputation inside and outside of the organization through strong organizational identity and positive external image.

In most contemporary corporations, media relations (MR), employee relations (ER), government relations (GR), and investor relations (IR) are interrelated and form the whole of the corporate communication system. Internally, ER and GR ensure that the company's sociotechnical system functions well; externally, IR and MR present the company to the market. IR and MR are dedicated to creating a good reputation and enhancing the corporate image in the eyes of the public, whereas ER and GR concentrate on corporate identity, ethics, socialization processes, compliance systems, and social responsibility initiatives. It is important for each of these functions to establish clear objectives and work collaboratively to achieve consistency across diverse corporate communication goals and messages. Strategically, the functions of corporate communication are both independent and interdependent, operating as a matrix structure, as illustrated in Figure 3.4. The matrix exemplifies the role of corporate communication as an

Functions of Corporate Communication (Centralized structure)	Departments (Decentralized operatives)				
		Human Resources	*Finance*	*Marketing*	*Legal*
	Media Relations			○	
	Investor Relations		○		
	Employee Relations	○			
	Government Relations				○

Figure 3.4   Corporate Communication as a Matrix

all-inclusive department with cross-functional lines. The circles represent corporate communication functions that draw on functional departments for resources.

This network of highly interconnected operatives requires close proximity to the strategic apex of the organization. Pushing corporate communication to the top is necessary for developing coherent corporate messages and communicating these messages to diverse organizational stakeholders. Therefore, corporate communication should be appreciated and treated as an integral part of the top management function. A close relationship between communication directors and upper management aids in developing strategies to deal with issues management and to maintain a logical and clear decision-making process (Cornelissen, 2004).

Review Questions

1. The different functions of corporate communication reflect the need to respond to multiple organizational constituencies. Give examples of such constituencies and discuss the importance of creating a consistent image across these constituencies.

2. Discuss the usefulness of the CVFCC in addressing interconnectivity across internal and external communication systems and functions.

CASE STUDY

Starbucks Coffee Company

Starbucks, generally considered the most famous specialty coffee shop chain in the world today has over 6,000 stores in more than 30 countries, with three more stores opening every day (*Fortune*, 2003). Many analysts have credited Starbucks with having turned coffee from a commodity into an experience to savor. Starbucks' objective has always been to emerge as one of the most recognized and respected brands in the world. Since it made its IPO (initial public offering) in 1992, Starbucks had been growing at a rate of 20 per cent per annum and generating profits at a rate of 30 per cent per annum. Starbucks has always felt that the key to its growth and its business success lies in a rounded corporate identity, a better understanding of customers and a store experience that would generate a pull effect through word of mouth. Howard Schultz, Starbucks' founder and chairman, had early on in the company's history envisioned a retail experience that revolved around high-quality coffee, personalized, knowledgeable services and sociability. So, Starbucks put in place various measures to make this experience appealing to millions of people and to create a unique identity for Starbucks' products and stores.

Schultz felt that the equity of the Starbucks brand depended less on advertising and promotion and more on personal communications and word of mouth. As Schultz put it: "If we want to exceed the trust of our customers, then we first have to build trust with our people. A brand has to start with the [internal] culture and naturally extend to our customers. . . . Our brand is based on the experience that we control in our stores. When a company can create a relevant, emotional and intimate experience, it builds trust with the customer . . . we have benefited by the fact that our stores are reliable, safe and consistent where customers can take a break" (*Business Week Online*, August 6, 2001). Schultz regarded the baristas, the coffee makers in the stores, as his brand ambassadors.

Starbucks looked upon each of its stores as a billboard for the company and as a contributor to building the company's brand and reputation. Each detail was scrutinized to enhance the mood and ambience of the store, to make sure everything signaled "best of class" and that it reflected the personality of the community and the neighborhood. The company went to great lengths to make sure the store fixtures, the merchandise displays, the colors, the artwork, the banners, the music and the aromas all blended to create a consistent, inviting, stimulating environment that evoked the romance of coffee, and signaled the company's passion for coffee.

By the late 1990s, consumers associated the Starbucks brand with coffee, accessible elegance, community, individual expression and a "place away from home." And in 2001, brand management consultancy Interbrand named Starbucks as one of the 75 true global brands of the twenty-first century. Starbucks' identity and positioning as "a socially responsible purveyor of the highest quality coffee [that is] offered in a unique retail environment" has thus led to a respected and strong reputation with customers, industry analysts, communities and other stakeholder groups.

Starbucks has always been concerned about its image and reputation, and rightly so. One of the possible ways of growing for Starbucks was to distribute its coffee through supermarkets, airlines (e.g., United Airlines) or fast food chains such as McDonald's and Burger King. But such alliances and alternate distribution chains carry significant risks for the brand and its reputation. Starbucks has built its distinctive reputation around a unique retail experience in company-owned stores. And customers could perceive the brand differently when, for instance, they encountered it in a grocery store aisle—an environment and channel that Starbucks did not control.

Case Questions

1. Consider the risks for Starbucks in forming product alliances with other companies or adding alternative distribution chains. What rules of thumb can you suggest, particularly from the viewpoint of Starbucks's corporate identity and the strong reputation that the company enjoys?

2. Reflect on the corporate identity of Starbucks in the coffee shop market. To what extent do you feel that this identity is unique, authentic, and competitive in this marketplace?

3. "If we want to exceed the trust of our customers, then we first have to build trust with our people. . . . [A] brand has to start with the [internal] culture and naturally extend to our customers" (Howard Schultz, Starbucks founder and chairman, quoted in Stanley, 2001, ¶ 2). Use the CVFCC to evaluate the significance of Schultz's assertion. Which functions of corporate communication play a role in brand management? Clue: Consider the relationship between internal and external communication.

SOURCE: From Cornelissen, J., *Corporate Communication Theory and Practice*, pp. 80-81. Copyright © 2004, London: Sage Publications, Ltd.

4

Identity, Reputation, and the Functions of Corporate Communication: A Strategic View

Corporate communication is an integral part of the strategic management process in which organizational mission and goals are communicated explicitly to various stakeholders, including employees. When key organizational leaders define what the company is about, they are forced to clarify and find common agreement on what the organization's values are and what differentiates it from other organizations. The end result provides focus and direction for all organizational members. Yamauchi (2001) argues that corporate philosophy is encapsulated in an organization's vision. Formulating a philosophy of what management hopes the company will one day become is a requirement for organizational success. Corporate philosophy (or mission) energizes employees; it builds common ground between the company and its employees. It helps unify a company by producing a co-creation of values so that workers can achieve organizational goals and maintain strong internal and external relationships. Internalizing a corporate mission also helps employees develop a sense of identification. Communication helps to create an image that conveys the company's vision or mission and reflects the interests of the organization. Employees want to feel that they are making a unique contribution to the goals of the organization; this can be achieved through integration and identification programs in which employees assimilate organizational core values and align their interpretations of how the organization sustains its operations with the overall strategy and vision.

Corporate communication is valued for its strategic input into decision making and the overall corporate strategy, not just for its operational excellence in managing communication resources and programs that are already deployed within the organization (Cornelissen, 2004). The following questions provide a starting point for developing communication strategy (Clampitt, DeKoch, & Cashman, 2000):

- With whom will executives communicate?
- How will employees and executives communicate?
- When will employees and executives communicate?
- Where will employees and executive communicate?
- Why should executives communicate?

So what is strategic corporate communication? It is the central, integrated, externally oriented framework of how the organization intends to obtain its stated objectives (Hambrick & Fredrickson, 2001). Thus, strategy serves as the basis for organizing, implementing, and evaluating communication activities within and outside the organization. Effective communication strategy links the mission and goals of the organization with its markets ("What business will we be in?"); clarifies the means to achieve the stated objectives ("How will we get there?"); and identifies the unique characteristics (e.g., corporate identity, reliability of service, reputation) and core competencies of the organization that help differentiate

it from its competitors ("How will we win over customers?") and the sequence of activities, timing, or staging (e.g., pursuit of early wins, building credibility) to achieve growth ("What are our moves, and how will we obtain our returns?"). Strategies are altered based on changes in the environment, competitors' responses, and new choices and initiatives made by top executives (Hambrick & Fredrickson, 2001). Creating appropriate messages and choosing the right communication channels to deliver them can help companies align their goals with the interests of key stakeholders (see Figure 4.1).

The integrated approach to strategic corporate communication allows for a number of benefits, including greater consolidation of communication disciplines, increased coordination from a corporate perspective, more input into executive decision-making processes, and adoption of a more consistent form of message composition and channels (Cornelissen, 2004). Above all, it leads to the rise of the centrally located corporate communication figurehead. Taken together, this model and its benefits suggest the centrality of

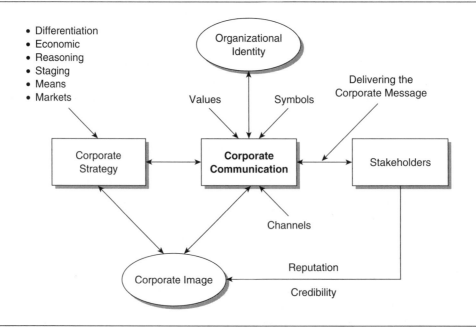

Figure 4.1   Linking Strategy and Communication

corporate communication and the importance of using stakeholder analysis to advance the strategic goals of the organization.

Corporate communication that is linked to strategy has particular characteristics that differ from past conceptions of PR. First, current research emphasizes that corporate communication must be connected to top management due to the importance of bringing an outside perspective to executive decision making. CEOs who hire investor relations executives as merely peripheral staff members do so at their own peril.

Second, effective corporate communication often employs a two-way symmetrical model of exchange with stakeholders (see chapter 12). The one-way model is often adopted because many PR professionals come from the field of journalism and are trained in the public information model of generating unidirectional messages (Gordon & Kelly, 1999). The two-way model, on the other hand, seeks feedback from stakeholders toward the goal of mutual understanding (Plowman et al., 1995).

Third, strategic planning seems to be synonymous with proactive planning and the initiation of communications. In 1991 the New Zealand government implemented a radical restructuring of its social services, including the privatization of its state-owned public hospitals, which were converted into 23 Crown Health Enterprises (CHE), and the creation of an internal market with purchasers (four regional health authorities) separated from providers. Interviews with chief executives of CHEs suggested that provider units were seeking a wider role than originally envisioned, with an interest in the health care needs of their populations and the initiation of some purchasing on their behalf. The purchasers, on the other hand, saw a much more limited role for the CHEs, subjecting them to attacks from politicians, medical organizations, community groups, and media (Barnett & Malcolm, 1997; Comrie, 1997).

In her study of two similar CHEs over a 3-month period, Comrie (1997) found that proactive press relations were more likely to yield positive news stories (75% of the time) than were reactive activities or mere responses

to media requests for comment. Of the two provider units, MidCentral and Health Waikato, described by Comrie, MidCentral was more proactive in issuing media releases, initiating phone calls to reporters, holding conferences, and attending pubic meetings. During the 3 months, MidCentral received more newspaper coverage overall than Health Waikato, and 65% of news stories about MidCentral were the result of proactive activities. Health Waikato had nearly 25% fewer of its stories result from proactive strategies. Generally, the more input that provider units (CHEs) had in a story, the more likely it was to be neutral (presenting both sides of an issue) or positive. Strategically developing and maintaining favorable relationships with the press can impact positive coverage and increase the likelihood that the press will present an organization's side of the story. Establishing this relationship in advance of crises gives companies more control in protecting their image.

Gotsi and Wilson (2001b) noted the important role employees have in influencing corporate reputation. Organizational actions and outcomes often lead to conflicting reputations, such as doing well in the marketplace but not having a good workplace climate and satisfied employees. Employees deal directly with the organization's external stakeholders and can be influenced by their feedback. Conversely, employees are able to influence stakeholders by projecting certain images to them. For instance, employees can affect an organization's reputation negatively if the internal messages and values they perceive are not consistent with the values and messages directed toward outside constituents. On the other hand, if the corporation's values and messages are consistent, employees can be the best resource for advocating the company's reputation. Moreover, if an organization adopts a proactive strategy with the media and consumers, its reputation is more likely to be positive. However, if the media and consumers must seek out information regarding the corporate actions and outputs independently, the likelihood that the organization will be portrayed negatively in the news media is relatively high.

Effective marketing communication, PR strategies, and media relations help shape a corporation's identity and affect its reputation. Maintaining a good reputation allows companies to differentiate in a saturated market. Excess capacity and cutthroat competition often force companies to emphasize branding and service reliability in which corporate reputation significantly influences customer loyalty and retention (Caudron, 1997). In addition, knowing where the company stands on public issues and identifying the factors influencing its current reputation are important corporate communication goals. When an organization maintains a proactive and accountable communication strategy with various media outlets, corporate reputation and credibility tend to increase. Corporate reputation is the result of communication strategies, activities, and products that intersect with the fields of marketing and management communication. Reputation is both the cause and effect of a dynamic relationship between organizational members and external stakeholders (e.g., customers) in which either one has the ability to influence the other. A corporation's social performance and image are key factors in influencing reputation and attractiveness (Turban & Greening, 1997). As Figure 4.2

shows, shaping public attitudes toward an organization can help increase trust and enhance organizational credibility. In turn, the public image of an organization affects the viability of the organization over time. As Goodman (2001) suggests, integrity and credibility are the pillars of strategic communication.

The government also has a role in shaping the reputation of organizations; it enacts regulations and laws to which corporations must adhere. Socially responsible organizations that choose to go above and beyond the guidelines specified by regulatory requirements usually enjoy a better reputation. Moreover, organizations that provide shareholders with updated financial information that is open and honest enjoy a better perception of organizational credibility. A system of accountability allows investors to be confident in the organization, which improves its reputation. Likewise, investors will likely flee organizations that hide financial deficits and lack measures of accountability. The loss of credibility might also hinder new prospects and produce an unfavorable reputation among future investors. Arguably, the boundaries that separate internal and external communication are ambiguous and therefore must be managed interdependently

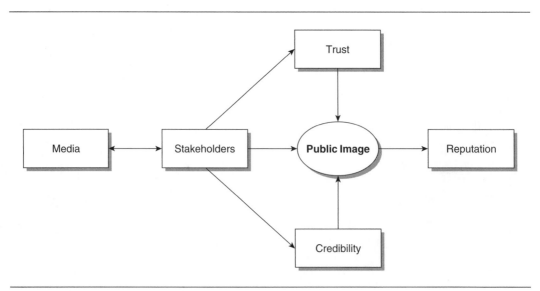

Figure 4.2   Media and Corporate Reputation

(Cheney & Christensen, 2001; Corley Cochran, & Comstock, 2001). Organizations need to maintain credibility both inside and outside the organization. Since employees are important internal stakeholders, management needs to focus attention on the firm's identity or image as it is presented to the employees. At the same time, management must communicate a good public perception as well. Many internal stakeholders are influenced by the messages delivered by or filtered through the external environment (Corley et al., 2001). Thus, in the early stages of strategic planning, the dynamic relationship between internal and external communication programs should be taken into consideration.

GE: Managing Image and Corporate Identity

Organizations and their environments are changing continuously, so organizations need to reexamine their corporate identity over time. For example, General Electric (GE) historically dealt with only one area of business, but as the company changed over time, it evolved into one of the largest diversified multinational companies in the world. According to *Fortune*, "GE makes 65-cent light bulbs, 400,000-pound locomotives, and billion dollar power plants. It manages more credit cards than American Express and owns more commercial aircraft than American Airlines" (Kjellerup, n.d., ¶ 1). In such a situation, it is necessary for GE to simultaneously sustain and manage its "original" and "new" corporate identity to avoid any confusion about the company's messages both internally and externally.

Keeping a consistent image across different constituencies is a nearly impossible task. How do you bridge the gap between extreme stakeholders' views or competing demands without confusing stakeholders or tarnishing the credibility of the organization? GE's internal restructuring during 2002–2003 significantly reduced the number of people employed in its Power Systems division in Schenectady, New York, demoralizing the local community that once maintained strong ties with the company. And GE's image was tarnished by its intense fight against dredging and the blitz of ads it placed in print and electronic media opposing the Environmental Protection Agency ruling on that topic. These corporate ads backfired when the local community and the media highlighted GE's inconsistent communications and lack of accountability by using the company's new motto, "We bring good things to life," sarcastically. Establishing an accurate corporate identity helps people understand who a company is, what it does, and what value it adds to the community. For this reason, GE, one of the world's business leaders, changed its identity in the 1980s based on its true facts and its development needs. This case application provides a pertinent example of how important it is to define a strong positive corporate identity to grow the company. In the early 1980s, General Electric Company was already positioned as the number one or number two diversified multinational business in the United States. However, its logo, which included the company's name, gave people the impression of "electrical business" only. In 1985, management reexamined the corporate identity and decided to reshape it to reflect the company's true identity.

Richard Costello, the manager of Corporate Marketing Communications, who was in charge of reshaping the company's identity, assigned the case to corporate identity consultant Landor. To address the reality of the corporation, Landor recommended that in its external and internal communication, the company no longer call itself General Electric, but simply GE, and the highest level of competency was added to the business name to make it concise and lean. Using such concise competency terms as GE Aerospace and GE Plastics, the company hoped to build awareness of its diversity. A similar logic was applied internally to simplify functional titles, which supported the company in becoming less bureaucratic. Also, Landor's research showed that perceptions of GE were high in terms of reliability but fell short in terms of dynamism and innovation. So the new identity system maintained the image of reliability and improved perception of its innovation and dynamism. Figure 4.3 shows the evolution of GE's identity. This change broadened the awareness of GE's diversity, so that people would have a more accurate perception of the company. It maintained GE's image of reliability and improved perception of its innovation and dynamism. The new identity also unified the company's visual and verbal expression through a consistent and high-quality application of the contemporary program standards.

When the corporate identity of GE changed, so did the corporate image. Because corporate image reflects the totality of stakeholders' perceptions, it must be managed responsibly. Chairman and CEO Jack Welch established the Identity Advisory Council to help Landor set up interviews with various stakeholders and provide the visual materials for the audit program. In addition, GE held a seminar with 40 to 50 of its major suppliers and got them to begin working with the system to help keep the program on track. In so doing, GE created an organizational identity that incorporated both internally held values and external expressions of these values. Landor delivered to GE's division heads a two-volume manual documenting all the standards that were now linked to the new identity. Supported by a communications manager who had participated in the development of the program through the Advisory Council, each business began implementing the standards of the new corporate identity system. After the Advisory Council had communicated the guidelines internally, it took on the challenge of implementing the program with external suppliers. To make the corporate identity program work well in the real market, they made sure that it did not get out of line from a financial perspective and got people to feel comfortable with and take ownership of it. Landor continued to work with GE on identity system maintenance, monitoring the implementation of the identity system and maintaining it over time.

When GE changed its logo to reflect the new identity, it wanted to sustain its corporate reputation. Reputation is the reflection of an organization's public image; it is a reflection of the historical, accumulated effects of previously observed identity cues and organizational experiences. The new identity system retained the GE monogram, a 100-year-old symbol that reflects consistency and reliability, and communicated GE's emphasis on dynamism and

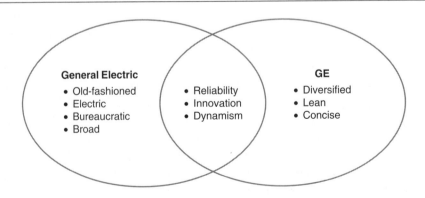

Figure 4.3   Transforming GE's Identity

innovation. Goodman (1998) states that a logo builds corporate image by giving a nonverbal message that reinforces the company image in the mind of the viewer. GE spent tremendous energy delivering a logo that represents its new identity while preserving its image. The new GE monogram not only maintained the company's corporate tradition and spirit, but promoted its innovative and dynamic corporate environment. The newly designed identity program was a huge success; it helped improve the company's awareness and external image. As a result, GE's revenues grew from $25 billion in 1980 to $134 billion in 2003.

Target: Managing Corporate Reputation

The Target Corporation is an example of a company that has differentiated itself from the competition by promoting a unique image and positive reputation. "Expect more of everything: More great design, more choices, more convenience, more service and more clothes, housewares and designer-created items that you'll never find anywhere else. And pay less. It's as simple as that" (Target.com, 2007, ¶ 1)—this is Target's promise to its customers as disseminated in the Philosophy and Values section of the company Web site. Target's slogan of "Expect more. Pay Less." projects the corporate image of an upscale discount retailer. Although the terms *upscale* and *discount* may seem paradoxical, through its innovative and creative marketing strategies, Target has successfully integrated these competing values into its corporate image. Through its innovative marketing and branding strategies and its favorable corporate reputation, Target has differentiated itself from its competition. None of Target's key competitors, Wal-Mart, Kmart, or Kohl's, enjoys the image of an upscale, trendy, and chic retailer. The niche that Target has carved out for itself is as a classy, low-cost alternative to superstores, especially for customers who would not shop at

Wal-Mart. The average Target shopper has a family income over $50,000 a year compared to $30,000 for the average Wal-Mart shopper (On Target, 2004).

So how has Target managed to project itself as being classier and trendier than its competitors? One particularly innovative strategy was to hire high-profile fashion designers such as Michael Graves, Cynthia Rowley, and Isaac Mizrahi to design low-cost product lines to be sold exclusively in Target stores. Currently, these designers can be seen in Target's television ads describing their innovative take on high fashion. These television spots serve a dual function of promoting Target's trendy new products and promoting Target itself as a trendy place to shop. Indeed, the majority of Target ads serve as brand builders. Since the 1990s, Target has used "a sort of 'pop art' advertising that mixes music, imagery and color" (T. Howard, 2001, ¶ 1). According to Schlosser (2004), "Target settled on a marketing style that more closely resembled Andy Warhol–inspired pop art than the drab price-focused ads of its competitors" (¶ 11). Target's advertising projects the "Expect More" component of the company's slogan, and weekly newspaper flyers deliver the "Pay Less" promise. Target Advertising Director Nancy Carruth affirms this: "Pay less is always our Sunday insert. On TV it is really brand awareness we are showing. And we're showing it's a hip, fun and entertaining place to shop" (T. Howard, 2001, ¶ 8). J. P. Morgan senior analyst Shari Eberts agrees, stating that "advertising is a really important part of what helps differentiate Target from Wal-Mart. It is more of a fun, fashionable image that helps drive people into the stores. Target is much more about developing the brand and the image" (T. Howard, 2001, ¶ 12). It is important to note that Target attempts to live up to its advertised image of being a trendy store; for example, many Target stores feature a Starbucks as opposed to the generic hotdog and popcorn stands often located at its competitors' locations.

Target's innovative, image-building app- roach earned it *Advertising Age*'s Marketer of the Year honors for 2000. *Advertising Age* praised Target not only for its finely honed populous marketing but also for its widely recognized red-and-white bull's-eye logo as an effective advertising icon in a class with those of McDonald's arches and Nike's swoosh. Target has used a variety of innovative tech- niques to flood the public with its logo, one of which occurred in February 2004 when "thirty-five clones of Target's mascot, a white bull terrier named Bullseye, invaded New York City's celebrity-filled Fashion Week" (Schlosser, 2004, ¶ 20). Publicity stunts such as this have helped Target create buzz about the upscale retailer while actually spending less on adver- tising than its competitors. In 2003 alone, Sears spent $627 million, Wal-Mart $467 million, and Target $442 million on U.S. television, print, and Internet ads. Whose logo stands out?

Target seeks to differentiate itself not only through its image as a trendy and innovative organization but also through a strong rep- utation as a charitable and philanthropic corporation. Target's corporate responsibility statement begins with words from Chairman and CEO Bob Ulrich:

Being committed to the social, economic and environmental health of the communities we serve is a key part of Target's heritage, a cornerstone of Target's strategy and vital to our long-term success. . . . Today, Target continues to work hard to enhance the communities we serve. We are actively engaged in programs that benefit families and young children through our donations of more than $3 million each week; we endeavor to design stores that complement and protect the environ- ment in which we operate, even as we continue to grow; and we strive to adhere to the principles of integrity and strong corporate governance that have guided our business conduct and perfor- mance for decades (Target.com, 2006b, ¶ 1–2).

Indeed, *Forbes* ranked Target as the most charitable organization in 2004. Target donated

2.1% of its 2003 earning compared to 1.3% for Nationwide, *Forbes*' second most chari- table organization (Moyer, 2005). Along with donating a large portion of its cash earnings, Target is engaged in several national partner- ships with philanthropic organizations such as the American Red Cross, the Breast Cancer Research Foundation, and the Family Literacy Foundation. Recently, in partnership with the Tiger Woods Foundation, Target began the Start Something Program, designed to teach children leadership skills and achieve their dreams. On March 20, 2006, Target broke records when it donated $15.6 million to schools across the country as part of its Take Charge of Education program.

Clearly, Target is a charitable and humani- tarian organization. But it should be pointed out that Target also makes an effort to ensure that the public knows this information. The company's Web site lists all of its charitable activities in great detail and provides press releases detailing its latest donations and partnerships with humanitarian organizations. Furthermore, Target is likely enjoying the enormous amount of negative press being directed at its rival, Wal-Mart. Wal-Mart's pub- lic image issues, coupled with Target's strong presentation of its image as a charitable, good- neighbor organization, allow Target to further differentiate itself from its competitors. However, no corporation is invincible, and Target is no exception. During the 2004 holi- day season, Target made the decision to ban Salvation Army collectors from operating out- side of its stores, because the company has a no-solicitation policy, and it stated that it could no longer make an exception for the Salvation Army because of a dramatic increase in solici- tation requests (E. B. Smith, 2004). Target faced criticism for this decision, and some specu- lated that the company "might have decided it could take a harder line with the Salvation Army because its shoppers tend to be more affluent than the impoverished families the Salvation Army serves, and more affluent than customers at competing retailers that kept the kettles in place" (E. B. Smith, 2004, p. 5b).

The organization's upscale and trendy image could have been transformed into one of arrogance and snobbishness; however, Target seems to have dealt with this issue both creatively and effectively. During the 2006 holiday season, in the wake of Hurricane Katrina, Target and the Salvation Army formed a partnership to provide relief to the victims. Visitors to Target's online store could purchase a variety of items for hurricane victims that would be delivered by the Salvation Army. Major George Hood, the national community relations and development secretary for the Salvation Army, stated that "this is an important partnership with Target to help the people of these areas begin to rebuild their lives. With their assistance, we are enabling thousands of Gulf Coast families and people all across the country to begin that process" (Target.com, 2006a, ¶ 4).

An analysis of Target reveals that it seems to understand the importance of having both a strong image and a strong reputation. Target's reputation as a charitable, caring organization has allowed the company to stay relatively off the radar of groups that have strongly criticized many of its competitors. Target has successfully taken a unique approach to discount retailing and marketed itself in a way that sets it apart in the marketplace.

McDonald's: Promoting the New Image

McDonald's is the leading global foodservice retailer with more than 30,000 local restaurants serving nearly 50 million people in more than 119 countries each day. [It] is one of the world's most well-known and valuable brands and holds a leading share in the globally branded quick service restaurant segment of the informal eating-out market in virtually every country in which it does business. (McDonald's, 2005–2006, ¶ 1–2)

McDonald's is now in a position to once again rule the market of fast food, but some years ago it faced serious problems. Without a consistent marketing strategy—rather, leaving the creation of its image to the local restaurant owners—it had become notorious for lacking focus, being out of touch with the culture, stifling ideas in bureaucracy, and creating a subpar work environment (Arndorfer, 2005). The company fought the bad sales figures and stock prices with a new marketing campaign whose trademarked slogan is "I'm lovin' it." However, the campaign is more than simply a series of new, continuously produced commercials. McDonald's itself calls it, in a press release, a "brand campaign." According to a press release (McDonald's, 2003), the new campaign—designed by the German advertising agency Heye & Partner—is unique in the history of McDonald's because it is not only the first marketing endeavor entirely invented and produced outside the United States but also the first campaign that unites all restaurants under a single brand message.

The expectations connected with the new campaign, as well as the goals that the company hopes to achieve, are high. According to Larry Light, McDonald's executive vice president and global chief marketing officer, "it's a new way of thinking about and expressing our worldwide brand appeal to the consumer. . . . We will communicate a consistent brand message while at the same time capturing the spirit, music and flavor of each local country" (Ragan's PR Intelligence Report, 2003, The Execution, ¶ 2, 6). According to Light, McDonald's "I'm lovin' it" campaign is a key ingredient in the company's new marketing approach, intended to invigorate, revitalize, and energize the McDonald's brand worldwide. Called Rolling Energy, this approach involves McDonald's first-ever integrated global 2-year marketing calendar that will provide consistency in messaging and communication to customers and employees. The Rolling Energy program features a variety of integrated marketing activities, including promotions, media planning, new products, merchandising, and internal marketing. This campaign serves the function of sustaining and managing the organization's visual identity because it promotes not only the products but also the image and the organization itself. The campaign consists of putting the slogan "I'm lovin' it" on the company's products and initially releasing five television commercials that depict young people in everyday situations enjoying McDonald's food. The campaign also used Justin Timberlake as a prominent representative of the new message, portraying the characteristics of innovation in the form of a modern and trendy star.

In the spring of 2004, McDonald's faced a major crisis when it was indirectly blamed for the obesity of thousands of Americans (and fast-food consumers worldwide) when the movie *Super Size Me* was released. The documentary shows creator Morgan Spurlock—who ate only McDonald's food for 30 days—consuming more than 5,000 calories each day without exercising. The consequences for his health were disastrous, and the movie resulted in a great deal of bad publicity for McDonald's. The company's response was to start a new initiative, called "Go Active," which was aimed at highlighting McDonald's intent to promote a more balanced, active lifestyle. McDonald's signed successful athletes such as tennis players Venus and Serena Williams to promote its Go Active program. The company also adjusted its menu by eliminating the "super-size" option altogether, and it introduced more salads and low-fat chicken sandwiches as alternatives to its expansive hamburger selection. In addition, McDonald's gave away "stepometers" in the hopes of motivating people to track their daily fitness activity, and even proactively started a campaign that sought to make the nutrition facts about the food available at a standard McDonald's restaurant more readily attainable (in conjunction with the 2006 Winter Olympic Games, the company launched a Nutrition Information Initiative to provide nutrition facts directly on the food packaging). Another step toward creating a better image concerning health risks was to sponsor major sporting events, including the Olympic Games (through 2012) and soccer events such as the European Championship (EURO 2004) and the 2006 World. McDonald's also developed sponsorships for sporting events at many (predominantly American) schools.

In connection with the promotion of a healthy lifestyle (and consequently, corporate image) the "I'm lovin' it" strategy was elastic enough to allow regional adjustments (both nationally and internationally) while still presenting an underlying, unified message to stakeholders. For example, some restaurants in Germany went so far as to change the dominant colors from the traditional red and yellow to green, white, and gray to give a more healthy and stylish impression. Together with a series of commercials launched in 2005—which starred internationally recognized supermodel Heidi Klum as a spokesperson—McDonald's acknowledged the strong trend in Germany toward fitness food and a healthy lifestyle, and used it in the campaign.

A good and open relationship with the press, especially following the *Super Size Me* crisis, made it possible for McDonald's to get a number of articles and stories published, which showed that its food does not necessarily lead to obesity and other health problems and can actually help individuals lead a healthier lifestyle and possibly even lose weight. Several groups attempted to repeat the experiment demonstrated in the movie, but had different experiences and results. The newly created image differentiated McDonald's from its direct competitors, Wendy's and Burger King, and thus enabled McDonald's to get a bigger market share and become even more recognizable as a brand. The combination of the efforts taken resulted not only in an image that is arguably stronger now than it was before the crisis, but also, together with the "I'm lovin' it" campaign, in the rise of sales figures—from 6.4% in 2003 to 9.6% in 2004, after a decline in the previous years (MacArthur, 2006). Proving that the ad campaign was a successful strategy for image improvement, McDonald's experienced a significant decrease in its employee turnover rate (Arndorfer, 2005). Plans for television commercials to portray the pride felt by McDonald's employees (a visual manifestation of internal identity) are already in the works.

Further promoting corporate reputation is the fact McDonald's has been active in the community for years. Since 1974, the Ronald McDonald House program has provided homes away from home for families of critically ill children (coincidentally, it is also the primary recipient of Southwest Airlines' charitable donations). Additionally, McDonald's engages in several regional community programs and actions, including neighborhood beautification initiatives, education and youth development programs, and local/regional sporting events. The company is especially interested in charities that benefit children and stresses the McDonald's World Children's Day, which is celebrated in its restaurants all over the world. The company prides itself on raising money for children and ultimately aims to create broader awareness of children's issues. In addition, McDonald's stresses the company's commitment to environmental protection, and its homepage lists a number of awards that the company has received from numerous environmental protection groups. Particular emphasis is placed on the responsible treatment of natural resources such as water and energy, as well as the proper means of waste disposal. The company has also researched reusable material for packaging because excessive waste of the paper used in its product packaging has been a constant point of criticism over the years.

Not only does McDonald's engage in various charities, but it also provides emergency support in the event of catastrophes such as Hurricane Katrina and the tsunami in Southeast Asia. Often, the money raised among employees or in restaurants is donated to children, as was the case with the tsunami relief (the organization donated $500,000). And when Hurricane Katrina hit New Orleans in 2005, McDonald's donations provided not only money for the reconstruction of destroyed areas but also free food at restaurants in the vicinity of destroyed neighborhoods and refugee camps. This kind of engagement connects the organization with the community by creating or invoking the image of the good neighbor.

Effective Communication Strategies

The many forms of media relations and formative research activities typically used to design effective marketing communication strategy aimed at enhancing corporate communication can be grouped into the acronym SMART (Bruning & Ledingham, 2000):

1. Scan—Identify and segment target groups; audit the existing perceptions of key public members.

2. Map—Develop a strategic plan that integrates the mission and goals of the organization and the interests of its key stakeholders.

3. Act—Conduct a pilot study and take the steps necessary to adjust the plan to match the values and needs of key public members.

4. Roll out—Implement the revised strategic plan with the larger population.

5. Track—Monitor the effects of organizational activities on public perceptions, and use the information gathered to reassess organizational initiatives and direct and control the implementation of a marketing communication strategy.

Dionisopoulos and Crable (1988), however, discuss a different strategy for influencing media discourse. In the aftermath of the Three Mile Island nuclear accident, when a coolant pump failed and citizens had to be evacuated from the area around the plant, the danger of nuclear power became salient for reporters and for Congress. This atmosphere led to inaccurate information and an increasingly fearful public. The nuclear power industry employed definitional hegemony to change the rhetoric surrounding nuclear power "establishing new frames of reference for interpreting 'relevant' information and thus, influencing the discussion in ways designed to have a policy impact" (Dionisopoulos & Crable, p. 136). By changing what was being discussed in relation to the accident, the industry was able to control the information and use it to lessen the crisis. First, the Nuclear Regulatory Commission questioned the credibility of the media and accused them of providing inaccurate or inflammatory information about the accident and the safety of nuclear power. Next, the industry emphasized the guarantee of future safety and refocused attention on the importance of nuclear energy to the country's future fuel needs. When the industry's credibility and very existence were threatened, it was able to change the reactive dialogue surrounding an accident and introduce proactive discourse to manage it. The industry strategically disarmed existing media messages and replaced them with more proactive communication.

A government organization can use the media to its advantage as well, and perhaps none used media relations strategy better than the Federal Bureau of Investigation (FBI) when it was headed by J. Edgar Hoover. Gibson (1997) describes how the FBI built its public persona by ruthlessly cultivating media relationships. Hoover perpetuated the myth not only of himself as a great leader and lawman and but also of the power of the agency through an intense publicity campaign spanning 50 years. One part of the campaign was establishing mutually beneficial relationships with the media; Hoover allowed certain cooperative journalists to view case files in exchange for writing positive stories. The *Chicago Tribune* and the FBI were so intertwined

that raids were often scheduled to coincide with the newspaper's deadlines. Perhaps even more insidious, Hoover was able to extend his influence to other parts of government. FBI ghostwriters sometimes contributed to the content of congressional speeches. FBI book authors Watters and Gillars (cited in Gibson, 1997) claimed that, although it was common for Congress to be supplied with speech material from government agencies, only the FBI provided material solely glorifying its leader. The FBI used a propaganda-style model, and its PR machine painstakingly planned and carefully administered its messages to create and control the hero image of the FBI and specifically Hoover. Today, however, the media would be unwilling to participate in such an arrangement, and the public would likely question the motives behind this type of one-way asymmetrical campaign.

External Communication

Gordon and Kelly (1999) found that hospitals that developed managerially oriented PR departments that use two-way symmetrical communication with external stakeholders were more likely to enhance organizational reputation than departments that use more traditional means of communication, such as periodical press releases. External communication based on promoting values rather than products helps organizations to improve their image and increase their credibility.

Crooke (1996) supports the position that the function of corporate public relations and media relations should involve the promotion of corporate image and external affairs rather than marketing products and services. Credibility problems arise when the press identifies the corporate spokesperson as someone fulfilling a marketing function for the company, a situation that communications consultant William N. Curry says enhances the skepticism and cynicism that journalists have for corporate spokespersons. Furthermore, according to Curry (cited in

Crook, 1996), "you end up with a lack of credibility because the suspicion on the part of the press is that companies misbehave to increase their profits and that, if you're in the marketing department, your job is to sell the product, not the truth" (p. 9). Clearly, a corporate PR professional who has been identified by the media as a marketing representative loses the credibility that is needed to advance the corporation's reputation. *Fortune's* America's Most Admired Companies is a prime example to support this point. The companies on this list have the best reputations in America, but they also continue to please their stockholders. For example, in 1998 Microsoft was ranked second on the list after having generated $11.3 billion in revenue in 1997 and averaging a 29% return to stockholders (Stewart, 1998). Corporate PR professionals must be careful when trying to sell a product to the media; they must maintain the credibility necessary to manage and improve the reputation of the corporation. Companies with high visibility and a strong reputation have a competitive advantage in fluid markets because their respected names add value to their products by reducing uncertainty in the minds of their customers, retailers, and distributors (Balmer & Gray, 2000).

Creating a consistent image is a very challenging goal that requires a strong culture and the branding of an organization's name through effective corporate advertising on one hand and a strong identity program on the other. Starbucks initially built its brand with limited advertising and plenty of PR, sometimes through stories published in national magazines but primarily through field communications to establish brand awareness backed up by the development of strong organizational identity based on principles of corporate citizenship. The concept of *negotiated accountability* (Ospina, Diaz, & O'Sullivan, 2002) implies that corporate communication personnel are required to communicate organizational information consistently to both external and internal audiences. To do so effectively, corporate communication staff and executives must be familiar with and knowledgeable about aspects of internal and external organizational environments; they have to cope well with pressures coming from all four functions of corporate communication: marketing, financial, organizational, and management.

Summary

Chapter 4 discussed the need for a more holistic approach to corporate communication by highlighting strategic communication issues and concepts. Internal and external priorities include responsibility to investors, relations with the media, company culture, and relationships with government and regulatory agencies—areas covered by the Competing Values Framework for Corporate Communication (CVFCC). Organizations must attend to the needs of their stakeholder groups through strategic corporate communication in order to build image and identity and maximize credibility. Communication should co-create an image that conveys a company's vision or mission, reflects its interests, and encourages employees to feel that they are making a contribution and a real difference within the organization.

Review Questions

1. What is the value of strategic thinking and acting for corporate communicators?

2. Discuss and illustrate the relationship between image and reputation.

3. Evaluate the importance of the SMART principles for corporate communication. Illustrate your answer with pertinent examples.

The Power of Symbols: Creating Corporate Identity at Agilent Technologies

In March 1999, technology icon Hewlett-Packard announced its intention to split into two separate companies. The Silicon Valley giant, citing the difficulty of growing its $47 billion revenue stream and the challenges of competing with smaller and often more nimble competitors, announced a plan to separate its original instrument, test and measurement, and medical equipment product lines from the newer computer and imaging businesses. The surprise announcement was generally well received by customers, stockholders, and Wall Street analysts. Many of the company's 23,500 employees, however, were anxious.

A significant challenge to the leadership team chosen for the new company revolved around the celebrated company culture known to employees as "the HP Way." Long known as a pioneer in progressive management philosophies, including management by objective, profit sharing, and flextime, Hewlett-Packard boasted an extremely loyal set of long-term employees. These employees had grown accustomed to consensus decision making and the often-bureaucratic infrastructure that sometimes hampered the organization's ability to compete in the fast-moving new economy. The leaders of the new company were faced with the need to quickly and effectively communicate the vision of their new enterprise. What cherished elements of the old days would remain intact? What new values needed to be instilled?

In July 1999, just four months after the announcement of the split, the new company was named Agilent Technologies. The name was derived from the notion of agility. The connection to Hewlett-Packard heritage was made clear by the tagline, "Innovating the HP Way." Further, a starburst logo, representative of a burst of insight, was unveiled. The leadership team at Agilent Technologies effectively used myriad symbols to communicate core values, vision, and purpose. The new CEO, Ned Branholdt, told employees, stockholders, and customers that Agilent Technologies would emphasize three core values: speed, focus, and accountability. The company vision (save lives and help people communicate) and purpose (we make the tools for people who make dreams real) were widely communicated. The company name, logo, and initial marketing campaign were meticulously crafted to communicate the new company's identity. Internal and external communications were consistent in tone and presented the same core values, vision, and purpose. At each major milestone of the transition, employees participated in ceremonies laden with symbolic meaning. Gifts and stock option grants were given in an effort to motivate and energize employees. The popular Hewlett-Packard culture was not abandoned, as the Innovating the HP Way tagline illustrated, but the new core values began to create a distinct identity for the new company taking shape.

The leaders at Agilent Technologies successfully completed the transition by defining the transformed company culture through the use of symbols. In a matter of months, the results were apparent. Organizational behavior began to change, aligning employees with the new company's well-articulated ideals and values. The thoughtful management of organizational communication reaped a huge reward. Employees at Agilent Technologies rallied behind the new organization, embracing the new corporate identity with the same enthusiasm they had exhibited for their former employer, Hewlett-Packard.

Case Questions

1. Describe this change in terms of strategic communication planning.

2. Why was it important that the employees leaving Hewlett-Packard for the new company have a clear sense of the vision and purpose of Agilent Technologies?

3. Think of an organization with which you have been affiliated that has done a very good job or a very poor job of communicating core values, vision, and purpose. How closely do you identify with this organization? How important are core values, vision, and purpose in building a strong sense of organizational identity?

SOURCE: From Michael Z. Hackman and Ross Campbell, "The Power of Symbol." In Shockley-Zalabak, P. S. (2006), *Fundamentals of Organizational Communication: Knowledge, Sensitivity, Skills, Values.* New York: Pearson/ Allyn & Bacon. Reprinted with permission.

PART C

Functions of Corporate Communication

5

Media Relations

Diverse communication roles and activities are also important in obtaining corporate communication goals across the four areas. Media relations (MR) requires communicators to be creative, inspiring, and adaptive in establishing a professional and productive relationship with the press. Maintaining such a relationship is an ongoing effort that must be nurtured carefully so an organization is able to paint a certain picture of events that are occurring to or around it. Corporate communicators need to bring a creative approach to disseminating information to the press or media channels, keeping in mind how that information will affect the image of the organization. Creating an open relationship with the media allows corporate communicators to serve as a resource that the media can turn to before going public with a story. According to Shockley-Zalabak (2006), MR specialists have an important responsibility

to become familiar with the nature of the various media and to understand the needs of the press and their range of approaches. From newspapers to magazines, the Internet to network or cable television, each medium has its own style, scope, and audience. . . . The media relations specialist can increase the likelihood of press coverage by understanding journalists' needs and providing them with information that is timely, interesting, newsworthy, and presented in a straightforward and usable format. Knowing the various media and their methods and approaches can be invaluable in effectively establishing press contacts and managing media relations efforts. (p. 365)

Although MR appears in the CVFCC diagram at the north pole, it is also well connected to the other corporate communication functions (i.e., investor relations, government relations, and employee relations). This connection occurs through roles and activities that signify the main focus of MR (see Figure 5.1) in a way that complements the roles and activities of the other functions. MR is like "a busy highway with traffic traveling in both directions between journalists and public relations practitioners, and the rules of the road are observed as courtesies rather than enforceable regulations" (Lamb & McKee, 2005, p. 88). Ultimately, organizations depend on the media to expose their target audiences to their corporate messages and advertising. Media specialists are able to utilize this outlet in order to improve efficiency, establish credibility, confine targets, and develop relationships.

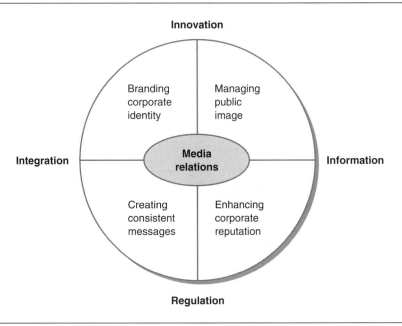

Figure 5.1   Media Relations Activities Across the Competing Values Framework for Corporate
Communication

The combination of goals and efforts aimed at consumer and media target groups creates several important roles for MR staff, including reputation manager, issue manager, and publicist.

Reputation and Media Relations

It is vital that organizations obtain some sort of competitive advantage to distinguish themselves in the marketplace. In addition to tangible assets such as cash, equipment, and real estate, companies leverage nonfinancial assets or intangible assets to achieve competitive advantage. Intangible assets such as patents, skills, knowledge, brand name, professional intellect, and reputation are unique capabilities that are not easily imitated and therefore help differentiate the company from other firms. Intangible or intellectual assets are now the major value drivers of many business enterprises and are considered tradeable assets;

experts agree that they make up more than 80% of the corporation's market value (Kurz, 2000). These assets contribute immensely to firms' sustained performance. Firms with good reputations, for example, have been found to sustain superior financial performance over time (Roberts & Dowling, 2002). Corporate reputation consists of a stakeholder's overall evaluation of a company over time, an evaluation based on direct experience with the company, any other forms of communication and symbolism that provide information about the firm's actions, and/or comparison with the actions of other leading rivals (Gotsi & Wilson, 2001a). Hutton, Goodman, Alexander, and Genest (2001) illustrate the rising trend among scholars and practitioners to refer to the concept of corporate reputation as important strategic differentiator. For instance, a trade publication, *Reputation Management,* and a new journal, *Corporate Reputation Review,* recently described the emergent value of reputation management in the field. However, it was suggested that the overall direction of reputation management might still be in the assessment stage. Research found that although most companies find the management of their reputation important and regard it as one of the key functions of public relations (PR), they have difficulty controlling, measuring, and defining it. Frost and Cooke (1999) note that the way organizations manage their communication with key stakeholders determines the strength of their reputation. An organization's reputation consists of many different images that each stakeholder may possess. And stakeholders may influence, as well as be influenced by, an organization's reputation.

According to Strenski (1998), the function of corporate PR professionals has broadened and gone through an evolution from issue management to reputation management. As Warren Buffet, CEO of Berkshire Hathaway, was heard saying, "losing reputation is a far greater sin for an organization than losing money" (Hutton et al., 2001, p. 249). Buffet's sensitivity for corporate reputation landed his company a position on *Fortune*'s respected list of America's Most Admired Companies. Jackson (1997) states that reputation is the "real deal," and image is something that is false and can backfire. Once the public has a negative experience with a company, previous images of that company are likely to fade and be replaced by that experience. DeLapp (1996), for example, discusses the need for reputation management in the public school system. Even though this is not an economic organization, in order for schools to survive, they must have a solid reputation within the community.

Managing a corporate reputation through MR is important especially because society sees the world through the lenses of the mass media (Ihator, 1999). In a study conducted by Hutton et al. (2001), reputation management was identified as the most common role for PR in large-scale corporations. Of the survey respondents, 96% identified MR as the most common function of corporate communication budgets. The survey also found that MR expenditures correlate with reputation. Organizations with a large portion of their PR budgets devoted to reputation management tended to have stronger reputations than those companies that focused primarily on marketing and sales. Charitable actions and philanthropic endeavors by corporations and a proactive approach to PR were also found to benefit an organization's reputation. This finding is echoed by Goodman (2001), whose study of *Fortune*'s most admired companies "indicated a positive, statistical relationship between what a corporation spends on its 'foundation activities' and its permutation ranking" (p. 118). Furthermore, "the more companies focused on 'managing relationships with non-customer publics' or 'reputation management' as their guiding communication philosophy, the more likely they were to have a strong reputation" (Hutton et al., p. 255).

Corporate reputation is the reflection of an organization over time as seen through the eyes of its stakeholders and expressed through their thoughts and words. The dilemma is that the many stakeholders of an organization may develop different or conflicting views of the same company's image. One challenge of the MR role as reputation manager is to market the goals and objectives of an organization in a way that aligns different stakeholders with a powerful and consistent image. More specifically, MR specialists develop reputation strategies for consumer and media targets as their guiding communication philosophies (Gotsi & Wilson, 2001b). One way to implement reputation strategies is through corporate advertising. According to Goodman (1998), the purpose of corporate advertising is to create a desired image of the organization in the minds of a particular group. In the case of MR, the target group would be customers and the media. Corporate advertising can be accomplished through establishing company logos, slogans, and jingles. Nonverbal messages have the strength to reinforce organizational image in the mind of the audience members; typically, these images are conveyed via television, print media, and radio. Perhaps the best example of a successful corporate logo is the golden arches of McDonald's, a visual symbol that has become deeply ingrained in American culture and is recognized internationally. Corporate advertising can also feature issue advocacy, which hints at the MR role of issue manager (Goodman, 1998).

Enhancing Public Image Through Issue Management

The second role that MR staff and professionals fulfill is that of issue manager, which enables them to identify and plan for issues that potentially could develop into crises. Coombs (1999) identifies issues management as a process that embodies identification, planning, responding, and evaluation. Renfro (1987) suggests that issues could be anticipated and identified through boundary spanning and anticipatory action. Understanding organizational environments and public demands provides MR staff with the chance to predict the outcome of issues and prevent crises. Once possible sources of crises have been identified, MR staff specialists can develop a plan to reduce the risks of the issue. Typically, the action step is to communicate the organization's position on the issue to concerned stakeholders. It is imperative that customers and media have a clear understanding of the organization's viewpoints. Distorted or false perceptions may damage organizational reputation and lead to a loss in profit. Specifically, MR staff must determine what messages need to be portrayed, when they will communicate them, and what media channels they will utilize to disseminate the information. After implementing the issue management strategy, it is important to evaluate the success or failure of the outcome by comparing the actual results of the strategy to the desired resolution of the issue. Success is determined by how closely the actual and desired outcomes are matched. Evaluations are important because issues are cyclical in nature; determining the success or failure of an issue management strategy can help MR staff better

plan how to tackle similar issues in the future (Coombs, 1999).

Branding the Image and Identity

MR staff, professionals, and directors are also identified with the role of publicist. In this role, media directors are able to accomplish several tasks. As mentioned previously, they are able to utilize media resources to disseminate messages about organizational goals, activities, and outputs. Likewise, media channels make it possible to strategically align stakeholders with a corporate image and reputation. Overall, dealing with the media provides MR staff with the opportunity to fulfill their other two roles: reputation manager and issue manager.

Corporate advertising promotes the overall image of the organization by influencing key stakeholders' attitudes about the overall wealth and long-term financial viability of the company. This form of corporate advertising can stimulate interest among potential investors as well as market analysts. The goal is to create public awareness of the company to legitimize its financial status and business performance. Identity, on the other hand, is the visual manifestation of the company's reality as expressed by the company's actions, symbols, rituals, ceremonies, sagas, and jargon. Strong identity acts as a powerful prism through which organizational members interpret and evaluate information about the organization. Unlike image, identity remains virtually unchanged until the organization undergoes a paradigmatic shift. When such change occurs, members are expected to follow a different ideological path, that is, use a different set of constructs that describe what is central, enduring, and distinctive about their organization.

The transition from one paradigm to another is often characterized by a state of crisis or identity crisis. In a dynamic environment where markets, products, and customers shift quickly from one brand to another, the organization, through its corporate communication unit, must take measures to update its corporate strategy or realign it with the new system requirement. Effective integrated marketing communications (IMC), for example, uses a multichannel, integrated strategy that communicates with a single voice to the organization's various customers. Matching messages to consumer needs and integrating communications into a single clear and understandable message are important ways to increase the chances that marketing messages will be desirably processed (Shockley-Zalabak, 2006).

Public Relations and Media Relations

PR is a management function that establishes effective two-way lines of communication, understanding, acceptance, and cooperation between the organization and its public stakeholders. In addition, PR staff oversees external affairs, responds to public opinions, generally scans the environment for potential threats, and informs management about emerging issues. A fundamental task of PR, however, is to enhance the motivation, ability, and opportunity of all stakeholders to process its messages. Leeper and Leeper (2001) observed that effective PR facilitates internal and external relationships and leads to greater organizational stability. The main function of corporate PR, however, is to enhance organizational reputation (Hutton et al., 2001; L. Smith, 1996; Strenski, 1998). In many organizations PR and media relations (MR) are therefore integrated. MR consists of two roles: originator and facilitator of news (Lee, 1998). Communicating with the media is an important organizational function, because as Goodman (1998) notes, contemporary business is awash with media. Good relations with the press often offer the opportunity to set the record straight or put the facts into a clearer, more objective context. The responsibilities of corporate PR professionals must focus on ethics

and honesty, thus enabling them to establish credibility with the media in order to manage the corporation's reputation and image.

Openness and accessibility are important PR strategies. Allowing news media access to organizations enables reporters to understand and articulate organizational interests while positively influencing external perceptions and corporate image. MR directors are therefore encouraged to provide accurate facts and statistics, which helps strengthen the arguments on behalf of the organization while eliminating opportunities for the press to misconstrue information. Building credibility into communication with the media develops a long-term relationship that benefits both the organization and the press: The press meets its deadlines and completes its assignments, and the organization receives fair media assessments. A good strategy is to always take into account the audience of the media outlets. The media can be used to the advantage of organizations if the MR division strategically utilizes these outlets to shape messages to its target audiences. Goodman (1998) advises against "off the record" and "no comment" policies; they almost always make the organization look like it has something to hide; which is the exact opposite of what MR attempts to accomplish.

Corporate PR professionals serve as the public face of the corporation when they interact with the media. They must advocate for their organization. This advocacy must include the truth, and these professionals should be prone to disclosing, not withholding, information (Seitel, 1994). Corporate PR professionals must be conscious of their role and that maintaining an open and honest relationship with the media is reflective of the corporation they represent. Furthermore, when interacting with the media, Kitto (1998) argues that corporate PR professionals are responsible not only for being open and honest with the media but also for speaking with one voice, especially in times of crisis. If reporters suspect that a corporation is trying to withhold information, they will only dig deeper.

When public safety is involved, it is the responsibility of the PR staff to tell the truth and tell it fast (Goodman, 1998). If this objective is accomplished, fear is minimized because the general public is informed, and the news only makes headlines once. By speaking with one voice and relaying information in a timely manner, corporate PR professionals can establish credibility with the media.

Despite the fact that the media may skeptically view corporate PR professionals as the gatekeepers of information, they continue to rely on them for information from within the corporation. It is therefore the corporate PR professionals' responsibility to establish mutually rewarding relationships with the media (Ihator, 1999). Cheney and Christensen (2001) describe the transformation of externally focused PR practices to ones that focus on internal audiences as well. They argue that PR practices must be integrated, that is, the organization must communicate at least somewhat consistently to its various audiences in order to maintain credibility and legitimacy. The use of PR planning councils, which include representatives from each major department of the organization, can also help achieve consistent message across the organization. Council members would be responsible for seeking out stories and keeping the media informed continually about the organization's mission and goals. Ensman (1993) advocates the use of personal stories and human-interest features as effective PR strategies. Stories and features may include achievements, successes, humor, quotations, milestones, information about interesting people connected with the organization, and photo opportunities. A survey of 225 top U.S. business journalists highlighted some of these challenges. It found that mistrust of corporate PR professionals is widespread. Approximately 46% of the journalists surveyed believed that PR personnel do not tell the truth most of the time (Crooke, 1996). For this reason it is imperative for corporate PR professionals to build and maintain relationships with the media that are based on credibility and integrity.

Johnson & Johnson

Johnson & Johnson's handling of the Tylenol-tampering incident is a good example of corporate PR functioning in a transparent and open way. In 1982, Johnson & Johnson's Tylenol medication held a 35% portion of the U.S. over-the-counter analgesic market, which accounted for 15% of the company's profits. Unfortunately, a terrorist activity shocked the nation. An individual laced the drug with cyanide, and seven people died as a result. A nationwide panic ensued as people speculated how widespread the contamination might be. Johnson & Johnson took strong and immediate actions by recalling all Tylenol capsules, making its top management available to the press, and using the press and ads in newspapers to reassure the public that the company's products were safe again. The cost of the crisis was considerable. The company's market value fell by $1 billion when the crisis first hit, which does not even take into consideration the loss from the destroyed merchandise. However, the PR department did an excellent job in damage control, and Johnson & Johnson quickly recovered. Within 5 months of the disaster, the company had recovered 70% of its market share for the drug. Within the next year, the share price increased by 50% over its precrisis market value. This incident, and Johnson & Johnson's response to it, furthered the company's image as a credible and responsible organization. During the crisis, the company communicated openly with the media and set up a national hotline to keep the lines of communication with the public open. Ihator (1999) supports the argument that Johnson & Johnson's openness and transparency during the Tylenol incident furthered its relationship with the public and the media. In fact, the substance and spirit of effective corporate PR is summarized in the company's credo: "responsible to the communities in which we live and work and to the world community as well" (Johnson &

Johnson, 1907–2007, ¶ 4). This sentiment was echoed at a business ethics summit in 2001, when Michael Coates, CEO of Hill and Knowlton Canada, stated that a corporation must live and breathe its code of conduct, rather than just create one that sits on the shelf in the office. It should express the code of conduct through mission statements that reinforce ethical behavior patterns and effective communication.

Public Relations and Investor Relations

Industry experts say that although PR and investor relations (IR) don't always overlap in terms of external audiences, these two venues of corporate communications must make sure to always work in conjunction (Petrecca, 2002). The cooperation of PR and IR officers is especially important during a crisis. PR officers should frequently exchange information with the IR staff, stay informed of the financial changes of the market, and react to the public's needs. At the same time, IR officers need to provide timely financial information to current and potential investors to attract investments. In Johnson & Johnson' case, there was an immediate reduction in the price of stock when the crisis first hit. This reaction from investors was transmitted from the IR department to the PR department, and then the PR officers went into action, working hard to rebuild consumer confidence and helping the company regain its market value (Kaplan, 1998). Later on, a recovery of the market share was reflected in increased revenue and earnings. IR officers immediately reported those numbers to the investors to boost their confidence.

Another example of a successful comeback is Martha Stewart Living Omnimedia. An insider trading scandal in 2004 forced Martha Stewart to resign her position as CEO. To make matters worse, she was subsequently sentenced to a 6-month prison term. It is amazing to see how much influence one person can have on such a big company; investors felt so betrayed and uncertain of the future of Martha Stewart Living Omnimedia that their first reaction was to sell their shares of stock. The company's stock price dropped from more than $20 to only $7 per share during the investigation of Stewart. To prevent a corporate collapse, Stewart admitted her fault and stood strongly against the media. After her sentencing hearing, she spoke outside the courthouse and said she would be back. She encouraged her supporters to continue buying her products when she was in prison, and while incarcerated she wrote open letters to the public. What Stewart and her company did greatly changed the perceptions and attitudes of the public, particularly the investors. Many Americans came to believe that the media unjustly targeted her. As soon as she went to prison, the stock price began to rise, and after she completed her 6-month term, the stock price peaked at $30 per share. Effective IR and PR strategies enabled Martha Stewart Living Omnimedia to overcome the crisis, to move forward in a healthy and upwardly mobile manner, and to further develop.

The Corporate Spokesperson

MR skills can be understood in terms of a problem-solving model that lays out a plan for projecting change of any kind to stakeholders. Developing a message to project a certain image of the organization requires a communication plan that integrates the interests and values of multiple parties. This plan includes problem/issue identification, goal formulation/program development, execution, and outcomes assessment. The most common visual figure in MR is the corporate spokesperson, whose role is to represent the voice within the community. It is important for that person to know how to present information and to know how much information should be released. The company wants the press to spin a story in its favor. When dealing with issues management, the corporate spokesperson needs to provide the community with enough information to reduce ambiguity and to rationalize the organization's actions (Troester, 1991). The earlier an organization recognizes an issue, the better chance it has of influencing the outcome. By recognizing that an issue exists, the organization has the opportunity to gather information and tackle the issue before it escalates. The organization then has time not only to decide what stance it wants to take on the issue in order to create a message but also to choose a spokesperson to deliver that message. The spokesperson must communicate with internal as well as external stakeholders. Internal stakeholders should be informed before the external ones because they are members of the organization. If they are not informed, it may cause them to distrust the organization, especially if they read something in the newspaper before hearing from the organization. By reading it in the paper or seeing it in the news media, the internal stakeholders would begin to feel detached from the organization, which could lead to a damaged corporate identity. Internal stakeholders would begin to see the organization in a negative light.

It is crucial for an organization and its spokesperson to develop a good relationship with the media. Yet the relationship between corporate PR professionals and the media is complex, due to the growing cynicism of journalists who do not trust big corporations or their spokespeople, who are routinely viewed as spin doctors and gatekeepers of information (Crooke, 1996). Sometimes, however, fostering a relationship with the media is pulled to the extreme, resulting in unintended consequences unless steps are taken to restore accountability and credibility in the exchange. C. Howard (1995) cites an example in which it was an acceptable practice for companies that had operations in Mexico to pay the Mexican journalists under the table for good press. The corporate PR director of one large corporation, however, refused to pay for press under the table, and the corporation still managed to receive good press without compromising its

ethics. Similarly, in Moscow, it is common for a company to purchase advertising in order to attain news coverage. Despite this practice, journalists and corporate PR professionals need to trust each other to function effectively.

Being honest with reporters does not mean an organization must provide the press with every detail. The organization must form a strategy to deal with the press that might include partial openness and incomplete disclosure (Troester, 1991). It may not need to disclose something that may be too damaging for its image as long as it discloses enough information to satisfy the community's need for information. During an interview with the press, if the spokesperson is uncertain of an answer to a question, he or she should tell the reporter that the answer will be supplied within a reasonable period of time and get back to the reporter with an answer as soon as possible. Innovation is required as a communicator walks the fine line between giving enough information for the organization's issue to be properly understood by the media and public, and giving away too much, which could result in disadvantaging or even harming the company. The art of formulating such media messages takes on a creative nuance that works its way into preparing for media interviews, training spokespersons, employing winning communication strategies, and using the CEO as spokesperson. Advances in technology, Internet resources, and more efficient uses of communication channels have extended the scope of PR. PR staff have a variety of techniques available to them to pretest the effectiveness of messages, increase responsiveness to stakeholders, and mobilize public support.

Summary

Chapter 5 connected reputation with image. Diverse communication roles and activities are important in achieving corporate communication goals across the four areas of the Competing Values Framework of Corporate

Communication. Media relations requires communicators to be creative, inspiring, and adaptive in establishing a constructive working relationship with the press. Maintaining such a relationship is an ongoing effort that must be taken seriously because it can provide an organization with a certain amount of control in portraying its business to the press.

Review Questions

1. Compare the roles of reputation manager, issue manager, and publicist in profit and not-for-profit organizations. Are they similar? Dissimilar? Why?

2. Discuss different means for corporate advertising. How effective are they in creating a desired image of the organization in the minds of a particular group? Use examples to illustrate your answer.

3. What is the significance of maintaining a good relationship with the press? How do corporate communication officers achieve this goal?

CASE STUDY

Adolph Coors Company

Shirley Richard returned from lunch one April afternoon in 1982 and found a message on her desk that Allan Maraynes from CBS had phoned while she was out. "God, what's this?" was all she could say as she picked up the phone to discuss the call with her boss, John McCarty, vice president for corporate public affairs. Now in her second year as head of corporate communications for the nation's fifth-largest brewer, Richard was well aware of the Adolph Coors Company's declining popularity—a decline that she partially blamed on an ongoing conflict with organized labor. But the conflict was hardly breaking news, and she was almost afraid to ask why CBS was interested in the company.

Richard found out from her boss that Maraynes was a producer for the network's news program, *60 Minutes*. Reporter Mike Wallace had already phoned McCarty to announce plans for a *60 Minutes* report about the company. Program executives at CBS were aware of accusations of unfair employment practices that the AFL-CIO had raised against Coors and wanted to investigate the 5-year battle between the brewery and organized labor. Once McCarty explained the message from Maraynes, Shirley Richard sank into her chair.

She had spent the last year working hard to understand organized labor and its nationwide boycott of Coors beer, and she was convinced that the company was being treated unfairly. She believed the union represented only a small subset of Coors's otherwise satisfied work force. But Richard also doubted whether the facts could speak for themselves and was wary of the AFL-CIO's ability to win over the media. She was well aware of Mike Wallace's reputation for shrewd investigative reporting and was reassured to some extent that the program would portray the company fairly. On the other hand, *60 Minutes* was considered by many corporations as anti–big business, and Richard had no idea how corporate officials would respond under the pressure of lights, camera, and the reporter's grilling questions. McCarty and Richard met with the two Coors brothers to discuss the network's proposal and to determine whether producer Maraynes should even be allowed to visit the Coors facility. Company president Joseph ("Joe") Coors and Chairman William ("Bill") Coors were skeptical of the prospect of airing the company's "dirty laundry" on national television. But McCarty was interested in the opportunity for Coors to come out into the public spotlight. Richard had already calculated the enormous risks involved in granting interviews with Wallace and filming the Coors plant and employees and knew the Coors brothers' reservations were warranted.

(Continued)

(Continued)

Richard was frustrated by growing support for the boycott and because her own strategies to deal with the problem had been unsuccessful. She believed the interview with CBS might only exacerbate an already difficult situation. Her own public relations effort had been an attempt to portray the circumstances as she believed them to be: good management harassed by disgruntled labor organizers. She was convinced that her job was not an effort to cover up Coors's employment practices. "PR doesn't make you into something you're not," Richard stated. "You can't whitewash." Richard debated how the company should handle the proposal from CBS, realizing that the communications strategy could seriously affect the corporation's public image. Any decisions about approaching *60 Minutes* would also have to be approved by the Coors brothers. Richard felt uncertain about how much control she would ultimately have over the communications strategy. Joe Coors, an ardent conservative and defender of private enterprise, would undoubtedly resist an open-door policy with the network. At the same time, Richard wondered if she should attempt to convince the management of this traditionally closed company to open itself to the scrutiny of a *60 Minutes* investigation or whether the best defense would be a "no comment" approach. But with no comment from Coors, anything organized labor was willing to say on camera would go uncontested.

History of the Adolph Coors Company

The Coors brewery was established in 1880 by Adolph Coors, a Prussian-born immigrant who came to the United States in 1868. Having trained as an apprentice in a Prussian brewery, 22-year-old Adolph Coors became a foreman at the Stenger Brewery in Naperville, Illinois, in late 1869. By 1872, Coors owned his own bottling company in Denver, Colorado. With his knowledge of brewing beer and the financial assistance of Joseph Schueler, Coors established his own brewery in Golden, Colorado. His product was an immediate success. In 1880, Adolph Coors bought out Joseph Schueler and established a tradition of family ownership that was maintained for almost a century. The company continued to operate during Prohibition, switching to production of malted milk. During Prohibition the Coors Company also expanded with the development of new manufacturing operations. A cement manufacturing facility and a porcelain products plant were essential to the company's survival during the 17 years of Prohibition. Its brewing operations flourished again when alcohol was legalized in 1933. Famous for its exclusive "Rocky Mountain spring water" system of brewing, the Adolph Coors Company soon became something of a legend in the beer industry. The Coors philosophy was one of total independence. A broad spectrum of Coors subsidiaries combined to create a vertically integrated company in which Coors owned and managed every aspect of production: The Coors Container Manufacturing plant produced aluminum and glass containers for the beer; Coors Transportation Company provided refrigerated trucks to haul the beer to its distribution center as well as vehicles to transport coal to fuel the Golden brewery; Coors Energy Company bought and sold energy and owned the Keenesburg, Colorado coal mine that was expected to meet the brewery's coal needs through the end of the 20th century; the Golden Recycle Company was responsible for ensuring a supply of raw materials for aluminum can production. By 1980, the recycling plant was capable of producing over 30 million pounds of recycled aluminum a year. Other subsidiaries fully owned by Coors included Coors Food Products Company, Coors Porcelain Company, and the American Center for Occupational Health.

The Coors Mystique

A certain mystique surrounding the Golden, Colorado brewery and its unique unpasteurized product won the beer both fame and fortune. Presidents Eisenhower and Ford shuttled Coors to Washington aboard Air Force jets. Actors Paul Newman and Clint Eastwood once made it the exclusive beer on their movie sets. Business magazines lauded Coors as "America's cult beer." As Coors expanded its distribution, the mystique appeared irresistible; Coors moved from 12th to 4th place among all brewers between 1965 and 1969 with virtually no advertising or marketing. Part of the Coors mystique was attributed to its family heritage. For over a century of brewing, company management had remained in the hands of Adolph Coors's direct descendants. Reign passed first to Adolph Coors, Jr., then to his son William Coors. In 1977,

Bill Coors turned over the presidency to his younger brother Joseph but continued as chairman and chief executive officer. The company's newest president, Joe Coors, was a well-known backer of right-wing causes such as the John Birch Society; a founder of a conservative think-tank, the Heritage Foundation; and a member of President Ronald Reagan's so-called "Kitchen Cabinet." The family name was closely associated with strong conservatism by consumers, labor, and the industry.

The Coors Company was built on a tradition of family and, even after going public in 1975, remained an organization closed to active public relations. Bill Coors recalled that his father, Adolph Coors, Jr., was a shy man, and throughout its history the company was reluctant to attract any public attention. In 1960, the sensational kidnapping and murder of brother Adolph Coors III focused the public eye on the family and the business, but Coors maintained a strict "no comment" policy.

The Nature of the Brewing Industry

From the mid-1960s through the 1970s and into the 1980s, the brewing industry was characterized by a shrinking number of breweries coupled with a growing volume of production and consumption. In 1963, Standard and Poor's Industry Surveys reported 211 operating breweries. Ten years later that number had dropped to 129, and by 1980 there were only 100 breweries in operation. On the other hand, per capita consumption of beer rose from 15 gallons a year in 1963 to 19.8 gallons in 1973. By 1980, per capita consumption had jumped to 24.3 gallons a year. Until the mid-1970s beer markets were essentially local and regional, but as the largest breweries expanded so did their share of the market. Combined, the top five brewers in 1974 accounted for 64% of domestic beer production, up from 59% in 1973. Previously strong local and regional breweries were either bought by larger producers or ceased operations. A notable exception, however, was the Adolph Coors Company, which dominated the West. Until 1976, the company's 12.3 million-barrel shipment volume was distributed only in California, Texas, and 10 other western states. Coors's share of the California market alone was well over 50% in 1976. Coors dominated its limited distribution area, capturing at least 35% of the market wherever it was sold statewide. The Coors Company ranked fifth in market share throughout the 1970s trailing giants Anheuser Busch, Joseph Schlitz, Phillip Morris's Miller, and Pabst, all of which had much broader distribution areas. Competition for market share among the top five brewers was intense during the 1970s and led producers to more aggressive attempts to win consumers. According to compilations by Leading National Advertisers, Inc., advertising expenditures for the first nine months of 1979 were up 37% from the previous year for Anheuser-Busch, 18% for Miller, 14% for both Schlitz and Pabst, and 78% for Adolph Coors.

Marketing and Distribution at Coors

Industry analysts criticized the Coors Company's sales strategy for stubbornly relying on its product's quality and image rather than marketing. In 1976, the Coors mystique appeared to be losing its appeal to strong competitors—for the first time since Prohibition, Coors could not sell all of its beer. The company finally responded to competition by intensifying its marketing and development operations. Between 1976 and 1981, the company attempted to revive sales by adding eight new states to its distribution. In May of 1978, Coors began to market its first new product in 20 years: Coors Light. In 1979, Coors began the first major advertising campaign in its history to defend itself against aggressive competitors such as Phillip Morris's Miller Brewing Company and Anheuser-Busch. The company's 1981 annual report pictured Coors's newest product—George Killian's Irish Red Ale—along with a newly expanded package variety designed to "keep pace with consumer demand." The Coors Company went public in 1975, but investors did not fare well as stock prices declined for the rest of the decade. Coors entered the market at a share price of $31 but by 1978 had fallen to $16—a loss of about 50% for the first public stockholders. Net income, according to the company's annual report, was $51,970,000 in 1981, or $1.48 per share. That figure reflected a 20% drop from $64,977,000, or $1.86 per share, in 1980.

(Continued)

(Continued)

Management-Labor Relations at Coors

During pre-Prohibition years, breweries, including Coors, were entirely unionized. In 1914, the first vertically integrated industrial union in the country established itself at Coors. When the country went dry, Coors remained viable through alternative operations, but the workforce still had to be reduced. Coors offered older workers employment but fired younger employees. A strike of union employees resulted and remained in effect until 1933 when Prohibition was repealed. The company, however, continued to operate without a union until 1937 when Adolph Coors, Jr., invited the United Brewery Workers International (UBW) into the Coors Company. In 1953, the company experienced an abortive strike by the UBW to which a frightened management immediately gave in. In 1955, Coors's organized porcelain workers struck because their wages were less than those of brewery workers. Although the plant continued to operate, all of Coors's unionized workers engaged in a violent strike that lasted almost four months. The union ultimately lost the battle 117 days after the strike, when workers returned to the plant on company terms.

Negotiations over a new union contract in 1957 ended in a stalemate between labor and management, and workers again decided to strike. For another four months, workers were torn between paternalistic and small-town personal ties to management and the demands of the union. Bill Coors, who was then the plant manager, recalled that during the strike, management had wanted to show the union it was not dependent on union workers. Coors hired college students during the summer of 1957 as temporary replacements for the striking brewers. When the students left, the picketers were threatened by management's vow to hire permanent replacements and returned to the plant. The strike was a clear defeat of the union's demands and ultimately left international union leaders with an unresolved bitterness toward Coors. Back in full operation by the fall of 1957, Coors management believed it had won complete control. By the end of the 1950s, 15 local unions were organized at Coors. Management tolerated the unions, but claimed they did not affect wages or employment practices. The Coors family firmly believed that good management removed the need for union protection and that management could win workers' loyalty. In 1960, the plant's organized electricians went on strike but failed to garner the support of other unions, and the plant continued to operate with nonunion electricians hired to replace the strikers. Similar incidents occurred with Coors's other unions. A 1968 strike by building and construction workers ended with Coors breaking up 14 unions. By 1970, Coors's workforce was predominantly nonunion. A contract dispute between Coors's management and UBW Local 366 erupted in 1976. Workers demanded a 10% wage increase and better retirement benefits. After more than a year of negotiations, union officials rejected management's compromise offer, which labor contended would erode workers' rights. In April of 1977, over 94% of UBW workers voted to strike. Production at the plant continued at 70% of normal capacity, however, and management boldly announced plans to replace striking workers. In defense of the union, AFL-CIO officials declared a nationwide boycott of the beer until a new contract settlement was reached. But within five days of initiating the strike, 39% of the union members crossed the picket lines to return to work.

In 1978, Coors management called an election for decertification of UBW Local 366. Because more than a year had passed since the strike began, National Labor Relations regulations restricted striking union members from voting. Only workers remaining at the plant, including "scabs" hired across the picket lines, could vote on whether to maintain the UBW Local. In December of that year, Coors employees voted a resounding 71% in favor of decertifying the Local UBW. Since 1957, the Coors brewery had been a "closed shop," in which workers were required to pay union dues if they were to benefit from union action. But company officials called the 1978 decertification vote a victory for the "open shop," wherein workers could enjoy union benefits without paying dues as members. Union officials, frustrated over the lack of a new contract and the decertification vote, publicly charged Coors with "union busting." In fact, according to AFL-CIO officials, the UBW was the 20th Coors union decertified since the mid-1960s. Management consistently argued that employees simply rejected union organization because they didn't require it; good management eliminated the need for a union to protect workers. But organized labor maintained that all 20 unions had been "busted" by votes called while members were on strike and scabs were casting the ballots. By the end of the decade, only one union representing a small group of employees remained active at Coors.

Nationwide Boycott

The AFL-CIO was determined not to be defeated by the ousting of the UBW Local from the Golden plant. In defense of the union, AFL-CIO officials declared a nationwide boycott of Coors beer until a new contract settlement could be reached and soon began to claim that their efforts had a significant effect on sales. In fact, 1978 figures reported a 12% profit decline for the brewery during fiscal 1977 and predicted that 1978 figures would fall even lower. Corporate officials conceded the boycott was one factor influencing declining sales but refused to admit the drop was consistent or significant. The defeat of the Coors local brewers' union fueled the boycott fire, but the protest focused on issues beyond the single contract dispute begun in 1977. The other issues of protest related to Coors's hiring practices. Labor leaders claimed that a mandatory polygraph test administered to all prospective employees asked irrelevant and personal questions and violated workers' rights. In addition, the protesters claimed that Coors discriminated against women and ethnic minorities in hiring and promotion. Finally, boycotters argued that Coors periodically conducted searches of employees and their personal property for suspected drug use and that such search and seizure also violated workers' rights. The boycott galvanized organized labor as well as minority interest groups that protested in defense of blacks, Hispanics, women, and gays. The boycott's actual effect on sales was the subject of dispute. Coors's sales had begun to fall by July 1977, just three months after the boycott was initiated. Some analysts attributed the drop not to protesting consumers, but rather to stepped-up competition from Anheuser-Busch, which had begun to invade Coors's western territories. Despite a decline, Coors remained the number-one seller in 10 of the 14 states in which it was sold. Labor, on the other hand, took credit for a victory at the end of 1977 when Coors's fourth-quarter reports were less than half of sales of the previous year for the same period. Dropping from $17 million in 1976 to $8.4 million in 1977, Coors was faced with a growing challenge. There was no doubt that management took the AFL-CIO protest seriously and began attempts to counter declining sales through more aggressive advertising and public relations.

Federal Lawsuit

The AFL-CIO boycott gained additional legitimacy from the federal government. In 1975, the federal Equal Employment Opportunity Commission had filed a lawsuit against Coors for discrimination in hiring and promotion against blacks, Mexican Americans, and women. The suit charged Coors with violating the 1964 Civil Rights Act and challenged Coors's hiring tests, which the EEOC said were aimed at revealing an applicant's arrest record, economic status, and physical characteristics. The lawsuit stated that the company used "methods of recruitment which served to perpetuate the company's no-minority male workforce."

In May of 1977, one month after the initiation of the AFL-CIO boycott, Coors signed an agreement with the EEOC, vowing that the brewery would not discriminate in hiring. But according to media reports, Coors still refused to admit any past bias toward blacks, Mexican Americans, and women. Coors said it would continue a program begun in 1972 designed to increase the number of women and minorities in all major job classifications. Striking brewery workers refused to sign the agreement, although the Coors's Operating Engineers Union entered into the agreement. David Sickler, the principal organizer of the AFL-CIO boycott against the Adolph Coors Company, was the former president of the company's Local UBW. David Sickler had been employed by Coors for 10 years, acting as a business manager from 1973-1976. Sickler left the plant in 1976 to take a job with the AFL-CIO in Montana. In April of 1977, the AFL-CIO decided to put Sickler in charge of coordinating the national boycott against Coors. Sickler moved to Los Angeles, where he also served as director of the Los Angeles organizing committee and the subregional office of the AFL-CIO. Sickler initially resisted the AFL-CIO's request to put him in charge of organizing the

(Continued)

(Continued)

boycott. He believed that his past employment at the company made him too close to the situation to offer a fair position on the issues at stake. But the AFL-CIO felt that Sickler's tenure with Coors made him an ideal choice; according to Sickler, his personal reports of abuse by the company in hiring and employment practices were shared by numerous Coors employees and were the central issues of the boycott. Sickler contended that when hired by Coors, he had been subjected to questions on a lie detector test regarding his personal life and sexual preference. In addition, he reported the company's practice of searching individuals or entire departments for suspected drug use. Despite corporate officials' insistence that the accusations were false, Sickler was convinced that Coors employees were generally "unhappy, demoralized."

Coors management was determined to fight back against the boycott, and filed a breach of contract suit against the Local 366. The company charged that any boycott was prohibited under contract agreements. Management also made clear to the public its outrage over the boycott, as chairman Bill Coors began to speak out in the national media. In a 1978 interview with *Forbes* magazine, Coors stated about the AFL-CIO: "No lie is too great to tell if it accomplishes their boycott as a monument to immorality and dishonesty." Earlier that year, Bill Coors defended the company against charges of being antiunion. A *New York Times* report on the dispute quoted the CEO as saying: "Our fight is not with Brewery Workers Local 366. Our fight is with organized labor. Three sixty-six is a pawn for the AFL-CIO; that's where they're getting their money."

Corporate Communications at Coors

The 1977 boycott forced company officials to re-examine the area of corporate communications. Because labor leaders set out to "destroy the company," Bill Coors, now chairman and chief executive officer of the company, believed management must relate its side of the story. "There was no lie they wouldn't tell," the CEO recalled. "No one knew about Coors, and we had no choice but to tell the story." In 1978, John McCarty, a fund-raiser at Pepperdine University, was hired as the vice president for corporate public affairs. McCarty brought to Coors expertise in minority relations and set out to repair the company's damaged reputation among minority groups. McCarty established a staff of corporate communications officers. The division was organized into four branches under McCarty's leadership: corporate communications, community affairs, economics affairs, and legislative affairs. In response to the boycott and declining sales, McCarty enlisted the expertise of J. Walter Thompson's San Francisco office to help the company improve its corporate image. Coors launched what analysts termed a strong "image building" campaign in 1979, with messages aimed at ethnic minorities, women, union members, and homosexuals. The theme throughout the late 1970s was clearly a response to labor's accusations against the company: "At Coors, people make the difference." Another component of the new image campaign, according to media reports, was to condition company managers to project charm and humility in dealing with reporters. Coors executives participated in a training course designed to help them overcome a traditional distrust of the media.

Shirley Richard

Shirley Richard was hired along with McCarty in 1978 to direct the company's legislative affairs branch but was familiar with the Coors Company long before joining its staff. From 1974-1978, Richard worked on the Coors account as a tax manager for Price Waterhouse. One important issue for the Coors account, Richard recalled, was the deductibility of lobbying expenses and charitable donations. As part of her job, Richard became involved in the political arena, helping Coors set up political action committees. When Richard decided to leave Price Waterhouse in 1978, she asked Coors's vice president of finance for a job and was hired to head the legislative affairs department, a position she held until 1981. Richard recalled her first year with the company as a time when Coors was "coming out of its shell"; Phillip Morris's purchase of Miller Brewing Company meant increased competition for Coors and a demand for more aggressive advertising. In 1975, the company sold its first public stock. The bad publicity from the

1977 strike and its aftermath combined with greater competition led to a serious decline in sales and disappointed shareholders. Clearly, the Coors mystique alone could no longer speak for itself and an aggressive public relations campaign was unavoidable.

One year before the *60 Minutes* broadcast of the Coors story, Richard became Adolph Coors Company's director of corporate communications. In that position, she managed 25 people, covering corporate advertising, internal communications, distribution communications, training programs, and public relations personnel.

Confrontational Journalism

The challenge of CBS's *60 Minutes* to any company under its investigation was formidable. The 14-year-old program was consistently ranked in Nielsen ratings' top 10 programs throughout the 1970s. Media critics offered various explanations for the success of this unique program, which remarkably combined high quality with high ratings. A *New York Times* critic summarized the sentiment of many within the broadcast profession when he called *60 Minutes*, "without question, the most influential news program in the history of the media." The program had earned its popularity through consistently hard-hitting, investigative reporting. Executive Producer Don Hewitt proclaimed *60 Minutes* the "public watchdogs." In his book about the program, Hewitt recalled, "I became more and more convinced that a new type of personal journalism was called for. *CBS Reports*, *NBC White Papers*, and *ABC Close-ups* seemed to me to be the voice of the corporation, and I didn't believe people were any more interested in hearing from a corporation than they were in watching a documentary." Stories revealing insurance executives taking advantage of the poor with overpriced premiums, companies polluting streams and farmlands by irresponsible dumping, or physicians gleaning profits from unnecessary surgery had all worked to rally public support and faith in CBS as a sort of consumer protection agency.

The program's success in uncovering scandal was due in large part to the aggressive and innovative technique of Mike Wallace. Wallace had been with the program throughout its history and was responsible for shaping much of the *60 Minutes* image. His reporting was always tough, sometimes theatrical, and was commonly referred to within the media as "confrontational journalism." Wallace had a reputation in broadcast circles and among *60 Minutes* viewers for making the sharpest executives and politicians crumble. But the program was not flawless. Hewitt admitted he had made mistakes, and one of the most glaring cases against *60 Minutes* was a story about the Illinois Power Company.

In November of 1979, *60 Minutes* broadcast a story about cost overruns at a Clinton, Illinois nuclear power plant, a story that included some obtrusive inaccuracies. Illinois Power was not to be victimized by *60 Minutes* and produced a videotape about the program, portraying it as antibusiness and antinuclear. Hewitt admitted that the company's defense had worked. "Five years after Illinois Power took us over the coals for that story, the plant is now seven years behind schedule and more than two and a half billion over budget. Have we reported that? I'm afraid not. You see, their bean ball worked."

Allan Maraynes was assigned to produce the Coors segment. His experience with *60 Minutes* was highlighted by some significant clashes with big business. He had produced stories on the Ford Pinto gasoline tank defects, Firestone tires, and SmithKline. Maraynes was alerted to the Coors controversy when *60 Minutes* researchers in San Francisco told him they suspected bad things were happening at Coors. The research group told Maraynes that the AFL-CIO was calling Coors a "fascist organization," which sounded to the producer like good material for a story.

Maraynes first flew to California to interview David Sickler. "We said we were setting about to do a story explaining that a fascist state exists at Coors," Maraynes recalled about his conversation with Sickler. "If it's true, we'll do it." Maraynes wanted Sickler to give him as much information about the boycott as he had. Maraynes wanted the angle of the story to be a focus on case histories of the people who had experienced Coors's unfair treatment.

(Continued)

(Continued)

April 1982

With the phone call from Maraynes, all of the pressures from David Sickler, the AFL-CIO, and the boycott were suddenly intensified. Shirley Richard had worked hard in the last year to focus public attention away from the boycott, but now her efforts to project a positive corporate image were threatened. Thinking ahead to the next few months of preparation time, she felt enormous pressure in the face of such potentially damaging public exposure. Shirley Richard was not naive about Mike Wallace or the power of television news to shape a story and the public's opinion. Richard, along with other Coors executives, believed that the company was not at fault, but that did nothing to guarantee that its story would be accurately portrayed in a *60 Minutes* report. Mike Wallace himself had voiced the reason for a potential subject to fear the program's investigative report. In an interview with *The New York Times*, Wallace stated: "You [the network] have the power to convey any picture you want." Richard knew that a big corporation's abuse of employees was just the kind of story *60 Minutes* was built on, and she didn't want Coors to be part of enhancing that reputation, especially when she believed organized labor had fabricated the controversy about Coors. Given Mike Wallace's desire to get the story, Shirley Richard guessed the company would automatically be on the defensive.

It was clear that *60 Minutes* was determined to do the story, with or without cooperation from Coors. Richard wondered, however, whether an interview with Mike Wallace would do the company more harm than good. On the other hand, she considered the possibility that the company could somehow secure the offensive and turn the broadcast into a final clarification of Coors's side of the boycott story. Richard was clearly challenged by an aggressive news team, and she was uncertain about cooperation from the conservative Coors brothers. Even if she could convince them that an open door was the best policy, would corporate officials be able to effectively present the facts supporting Coors's position? The national broadcast would reach millions of beer drinkers, and Richard knew that the *60 Minutes* report could either make or break the future success of Coors beer.

Case Questions

1. Should Shirley Richard encourage or discourage the Coors brothers to go on *60 Minutes*?

2. What kind of research should she do?

3. What would her communication objective be if Coors agreed to the interview? If they did not do the interview?

4. What suggestions would you have for improving media relations at Coors?

5. Use Figure 5.1 to examine other corporate communication problems that Richard should focus on.

SOURCE: From Argenti, P. A., *Corporate Communication*, copyright © 1994, McGraw-Hill. Reprinted with permission.

6

Investor Relations

In contemporary organizations, the responsibilities of investor relations (IR) staff are far more important than merely keeping record of corporate financial information. A survey conducted in 2005 shows that 65% of the Fortune 500 companies have a dedicated IR department, 27% report that IR is handled by the finance/treasury department, and 7% have IR managed by the communications/public relations department (Laskin, 2006). The National Investor Relations Institute (NIRI) defines investor relations as "a strategic management responsibility that integrates finance, communication, marketing and securities law compliance, to enable the most effective two-way communication between a company, the financial community and other constituencies, which ultimately contributes to a company's securities achieving fair valuation" (Vahouny, 2004, p. 34). Although IR appears on the right side of the CVFCC horizontal dimension, it is also well connected to the other corporate communication functions (i.e., media relations, government relations, and employee relations). This connection occurs through roles and activities that signify the main focus of IR in a way that complements the roles and activities of the other functions. IR staff specialists focus primarily on enhancing organizational credibility in financial markets. At the same time, they are expected to support the overall corporate communication effort to align internal communications and identity programs with external affairs and the public image of the organization. All of these efforts call for multiple tasks and communication responsibilities that are initiated at the local level (e.g., decentralized operatives, departments, specialized units) and that are well synchronized at the centralized level. System stability and employee commitment are therefore important elements in the attainment of successful IR outcomes. IR roles and activities appear in Figure 6.1.

The goal of IR is to help both the investor and the analyst enhance their understanding of the firm's earning potential and how the firm plans to reach that potential. According to Verchere (1991), IR involves, above all, a planned approach to shareholder communication. There are four essential steps to having an effective IR program. First, the current perception of the firm needs to be assessed. The IR department does this by surveying and collecting information about how analysts and the public perceive the company. Analysts are important stakeholders for IR, and a long-term relationship with them must be maintained. Second, people who have a position in an IR program need to be familiar with the firm's financial, legal, and ethical issues. IR professionals must be effective internal and external communicators who work closely with the CEO and CFO and provide information to the public. Third, IR specialists need to align their views with those of the CFO. They must ensure that the stock price is appropriate. They must limit fluctuation of the stock price. And they must fully understand the investment needs of their stockholders and build and maintain a strong relationship with them. Last, an IR department needs to share stockholder feedback with upper management and, in line with the organizational mission, clarify and develop the means to attain the overall IR objectives. They must communicate the firm's ideas for future growth and be able to balance the different messages to create a reliable picture of where the company stands in the present and its goals for the future.

Stakeholders

An IR program is critical to any firm. For a firm to be profitable it must have an effective IR program to address financial issues. There are many key stakeholders that have to be addressed, and they include the following:

STOCKHOLDERS. The IR department addresses the general public when announcing issues pertaining to the company, but the real goal is to legitimize organizational decisions and actions. The IR department therefore must maintain an open and honest relationship with investors. IR has to act in a credible way not only externally but also internally. There are two types of stockholders: the general public (external) and employees (internal). Employee stockholders are important to a company for several reasons. Those who remain with a company for a long time become

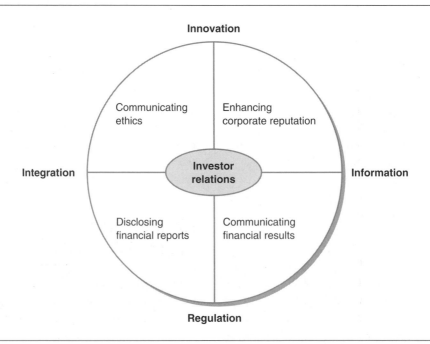

Figure 6.1   Investor Relations Activities Across the Competing Values Framework of Corporate Communication

more positive in their attitudes toward the company, and investing in company stock gives employees a sense of ownership and a feeling that "we're all in this together" (Nichols, 1989, p. 113).

FINANCIAL MEDIA. IR practitioners must make sure to keep the financial media informed of the firm's financial status. This in turn keeps the public informed so they can evaluate the firm and buy stocks. If the IR department does not keep the financial media informed, they will find other ways to obtain the financial information, a situation that can harm the firm if the information the media gets is inaccurate. It is better for the firm to have the IR department keep the financial media updated so they will report accurate financial results to the public. According to Tim Metz, a reporter for the *Wall Street Journal,* of all the creatures in the financial jungle, none is quite as dangerous as a financial journalist coming up on his or her deadline without the company's side of the story (Nichols, 1989). A firm that ignores the media or responds with "no comment" is destined to shape stockholders' opinions in a negative way. If a firm runs into problems, the CEO and CFO need to be accessible and visible. For example, in the fall of 1986 Avon notified its investors of a problem with growth due to new government regulations. The president of Avon outlined the problem and discussed the steps that the company would take to combat the problem and to increase profit. Later, when the news hit, stock prices fell but then stabilized and began to climb shortly afterward. Another example of the importance of making top management visible in a crisis is Johnson & Johnson's reaction to the Tylenol poisonings in the United States on two separate occasions. These incidents could have been detrimental to the company, but both times the company took strong and immediate action. It recalled all Tylenol capsules, made its top management available to the press, and used the press and ads in national newspapers to reassure the public that the company's products were safe again.

Johnson & Johnson's stock price dropped at first, but once the company announced that it was taking all Tylenol capsules off the market, the share price recovered. Not only did the share price return to what it had been, but within the next year it increased by 50%.

FINANCIAL ANALYSTS. The IR program of any firm must make sure to maintain a long-term relationship with analysts. Firms see analysts as being able to influence the price of their stock and affect the performance credibility of the company. Analysts appreciate when companies are forthcoming about a negative situation. Analysts believe that doing so shows that the company is credible and will impact what happens with the stock price. What financial analysts say about a firm determines whether or not people will buy its stock. If the analysts show a pattern that the firm is credible in the long term, stockholders will take that into account and may decide to hold on to the stock through any hard times (Nichols, 1989). IR staff should be in touch with analysts on a regular basis to make sure that current market issues are addressed, and they should make sure to release information selectively and only after prioritizing the risks (i.e., mistrust in a company's disclosure practices) associated with partial disclosure. IR staff specialists also need to maintain ongoing relationships with media relations staff. IR practitioners need to keep the media relations department aware of the company's financial issues so that they can relay that information accurately to the press.

Working With Financial Analysts

Investor relations, loosely described, refers to the means a company uses to report and distribute fiscal information to its shareholders. IR is a strategic corporate marketing activity, combining the disciplines of finance and communication, which provides present and potential investors with an accurate portrayal of a company's performance and prospects. Conducted effectively, IR can have a positive effect on a company's total value relative to that of the overall market and a company's cost of capital (Brown, 1995). The IR function is an essential component of a total corporate communications strategy and should be used to improve the financial reputation of a corporation. Communicating fiscal information to stockholders effectively increases stockholders' confidence, attracts new investors, and helps improve the company's reputation.

IR requires that a communicator be a taskmaster and possess the competency to engage in promotional communication efforts, which if handled correctly and honestly can help improve the company's financial position. Being a taskmaster involves setting up organizational dialogue to facilitate understanding of financial expectations and a long-term outlook. IR staff provide coordinated information to investors and analysts in order to reflect a complete, unified message about the organization's financial outcomes and vision for the future (Goodman, 1998). Communicators involved in IR must work with the intent of managing analysts' expectations and correcting misconceptions in the investor and analyst communities (Rao & Sivakumar, 1999). Therefore, to promote and package relevant organizational information most efficiently, they must understand the frameworks that different analysts use. According to Lang and Lundholm (1996), financial analysts are integral parts of the capital market, providing earnings forecasts, buying and selling recommendations and other information to brokers, money managers, and institutional investors. Although direct disclosure of financial information to investors is a major activity of IR officers, their contact with financial analysts also accounts for a substantial part of their daily activity. Typically, financial analysts get information directly from the companies and make predictions and recommendations to investors based on their professional knowledge and experiences, but it is also prevailing conduct for

companies to exercise discretion in disclosing information to analysts. Different analysts may make varied forecasts based on information gained from sources other than the company itself, rather than on differences in interpretation of common information provided by the company (Lang & Lundholm, 1996). So the situation demands that corporate communicators be able not only to engage in effective communication with the investor and financial community but also to attract new and retain current investors who will align themselves with the values projected in the company's communications (Rao & Sivakumar, 1999).

Managing Stockholder Confidence

One important goal of IR staff is to manage stockholder confidence through effective press releases and ongoing communication. The software giant Oracle provides a good case example. By keeping customers and investors happy, Oracle's CFO Jeffrey Henley received the 2000 CFO Excellence Award for Managing External Stakeholders. Although Oracle had a history of inconsistent marketing communication, its IR efforts received top marks from analysts throughout Henley's tenure. And although Oracle investors may occasionally get nervous, they are rarely uninformed. Maintaining stockholders' confidence no longer lies solely in regulatory improvements. Therefore, when communicating financial results, companies must strategize by asking such questions as "How and when do we do and say it?" Companies have learned that they must communicate financial results to investors in a timely, conclusive, and decisive manner, and that financial information should be readily available. As Ferris and Newman (1991) rightfully recognize, in an era when a company's financial position is often discussed in the popular press, there is a growing need for interdependence between IR and other corporate communication professionals.

Lack of transparency creates asymmetry between communication activities and policies (e.g., a no-comment policy) and stockholders' knowledge about outcomes (e.g., net cash flows). When financial results are reported to a company's stockholders, this asymmetry is reduced. Open communication with stockholders should be the number one goal for IR personnel. In fact, CEOs should often be the ones who communicate the company's performance and financial results to the stockholders. Companies must release pertinent information that stockholders have the right to know in a timely manner. Financial results should be communicated in a consistent, conclusive, and concise way, and in a manner that shows the company is proactive and responsive. Consistent and responsible communication with stockholders reduces any asymmetry that might harm relationships with them.

A significant amount of research has studied the issue of communicating financial results to stockholders. Gibbins, Richardson, and Waterhouse (1990) define financial disclosure as "any deliberate release of financial information, whether numerical or qualitative, required or voluntary, or via formal or informal channels" (p. 122). In terms of financial disclosure, external demands, which require the release of financial information, generally come from the capital market or the product market. However, due to scandals such as the one surrounding Enron, which have received intense media coverage, managers now realize that keeping investors informed of the company's financial status has important effects on organizational reputation.

Financial Reporting

Dye (1998) discusses the importance of *what, where, when, how,* and *why* in responding to questions of financial reporting. He specifically highlights the disclosure of financial information in financial reports. Although one can recognize that financial reports are necessary for communicating

financial results, a company should also use many more channels to keep stockholders informed of its financial status (e.g., a company's Web site, press releases). Because Dye discusses the communication of financial information solely through the use of financial reports instead of through multiple media, he does not include a *who* question. Therefore I add the question "Who should communicate the financial results of the company?" to emphasize the responsibility that CEOs must assume in shaping a culture of excellence, transparency, and accountability to earn their investors' trust. Corporate communication departments should recognize this and work with the CEO to keep him or her updated on which strategies he or she should use. In other words, the CEO should not simply disclose financial results to the company's stockholders; he or she must present him- or herself in a way that shows high commitment to performance credibility and ethical standards. In return, stockholders will trust the leadership of the company and show confidence in the company's directions.

Former Southwest Airlines CEO James F. Parker recognizes the importance of maintaining the confidence of stockholders. Parker remains in the public eye and maintains a high level of communication with the public. He is often asked to be a keynote speaker at conventions around the nation, and at these engagements he reveals his knowledge of Southwest's financial situation, its creative operative marketing and operations strategies, and its plans for future growth. Known for his creative and democratic ways of leading the company, Parker shows his dedication to the organization and, in turn, stockholders maintain their trust in him and in their investments.

Another *who* question to consider is "Who should help identify disclosure issues?" Research has shown that external consultants and advisors can help direct most of the disclosure process, which is particularly helpful to small firms (Gibbins et al., 1990). Bringing in external resources, such as external auditors, adds credibility to disclosures, which helps maintain investor confidence. This is another strategy that should be recognized and utilized by corporate communicators.

Dye's (1998) *what* question regarding financial reporting involves information about a company's financial conditions that should be considered for external dissemination. Although it is mandatory for companies to release their numerical financial information, there are other aspects of financial conditions that a company may decide to keep quiet. Investors might perceive timely disclosure of information to be an important sign of a decision maker's openness and honesty. On a symbolic level, it reflects the company's consideration of investors' needs; on a practical level, it is critical in order for the investors to make ongoing decisions. However, CEOs may be reluctant to release timely information to the outside world for reasons including the diminishing power of the CEO, the reluctance to report poor performance, a significant amount of time and money spent on gathering feedback, and so on. As a result, most companies with publicly traded stocks disclose information selectively (Sapienza & Korsgaard, 1996).

Companies have economic incentives to both disclose and withold information (Gibbins et al., 1990). A company may decide not to release information because of the potential economic advantages the information may hold. Richardson (2001) highlights this concept in discussing the issue of discretionary disclosure, which claims that the level of disclosure is affected by the costs of disclosure. For example, a company in a highly competitive market has a research and development department that discloses a project in the making. Once the company feels secure that the project will yield a considerable profit, the company may decide to withhold certain information. A company must report its numerical financial results and should disclose information about current and future projects, but only to the extent that valuable information will not be revealed to competitors.

The question about *where* the information should be released involves multiple channels, not just quarterly and annual company reports. Many organizations maintain constant updates on their Web sites so that investors and other interested parties can view the information at their convenience. Southwest Airlines, for example, has an Investor Relations link on its About page that offers information regarding corporate governance, news releases, quarterly earnings, and financials. Canon also places links to its investor relations department directly on its Web site for quick access.

The answer to Dye's (1998) question about *when* financial information should be disclosed seems to be inconclusive. Gibbins et al. (1990) found that the timing of disclosing financial information varies from firm to firm. Although some of variation may be issue related, some is undoubtedly a matter of choice. More important, the answer to the *when* question is: in a timely manner. Investors hold stock in the company and are therefore entitled to know about the company's financial situation. Once a company has financial information that stockholders would want to know, and the company knows the information to be true and conclusive, it should be disclosed.

On the matter of *how,* Dye (1998) asks, "How should the information be recorded: at historical cost, at market value, based on estimates, discounted?" (p. 149). A better question to ask is "How should the information be *presented*?" The answer seems to be in a consistent, conclusive, and decisive manner that shows the company is action oriented.

The financial results of a company should be communicated consistently. Imagine what would happen if a company produced conflicting information in more than one type of media. Stockholders would be left confused, and the ethical value of the company would lower. Gibbins et al. (1990) refer to this issue as *support of redundancy*. Positive redundancy occurs when management disseminates the information through multiple outlets directed at various audiences. The results of their study reveal that many companies locate a subset of information to be revealed for some recipients, instead of producing inconsistent information for different recipients. The financial status of a company should also be revealed in a way that shows the company is taking an active approach in communicating the information to its stockholders. Gibbins et al. discuss this in terms of what they call *opportunism*: "a managerial predisposition to behave in a particular way, but through active stances in which disclosures are seen as opportunities to reap specific benefits by managing the disclosure process" (p. 130). Finally, when communicating financial results to stockholders, companies should take an active approach in being sure the information that is presented is conclusive and decisive. In other words, it should include all the information a stockholder has the right to know. If a company holds back and does not reveal the information in full, it risks the liability of being seen as unethical if the unknown information is disclosed to the public at another time and/or by another source.

Dye's (1998) final question of financial reporting asks, "Why should the information be included in financial reports?" (p. 149). The answer should ensure that stockholders experience consistency in knowing exactly when they will have hands-on access to certain information. Another issue in this category is why financial results should be presented to investors. One obvious reason is the need to comply with regulatory and institutional requirements through disclosure. Disclosure is affected by legislation, standards, and regulations, which apply to a company contingent upon laws under which the company was chartered, the sources of capital used, the size of the company, and the existence of product market regulation (Gibbins et al., 1990). The strategies presented above must be employed in an ethical and honest manner. In a time when company stockholders are increasingly judgmental of the actions of a company, corporate communication departments must work with those in charge of IR to ensure consistency and reliability in managing the company's reputation. Having a good reputation adds strategic value to the company and can yield superior financial performance (Roberts & Dowling, 2002).

Investor Relations and Corporate Reputation

Within the past 10 years, the concept of IR as a discipline has transformed itself. Whereas in the past it was largely considered a bookkeeping activity and/or clerical work, it is now seen as a critical element in corporations (Brown, 1995). The IR function and the company's ability to share information with the public are what set the standard for how corporate communications are employed. The manner by which the organization chooses to communicate has a dramatic impact on its capacity to appeal to new investors and keep existing investors satisfied. Brown identifies one way that companies can communicate nonverbally how much importance they place on their investor relations function. A recent NIRI survey revealed that 52% of IR positions report to the CFO and 35% report directly to the president or CEO. This placement of IR within a company (i.e., accountable to CEO, CFO) is a direct reflection of how much weight the company places on IR. How high the IR department is positioned is a clear indicator of the degree to which a company is concerned that this function be closely connected to upper management, specifically the CEO or president. Having the IR officer in touch with upper management sends a direct message to stockholders. It allows the IR officer to be in the same frame of mind as the executives and greatly increases investors' assurance that their investments are highly valued. Hence, IR programs are now considered to be an integral part of an organization's total corporate communication strategy (Dolphin, 2004).

A proactive approach to dealing with investors helps to enhance the image of the organization. If companies report information to their stockholders not because they want to, but just to report it, this could be viewed a reactive approach. A proactive approach is simply translated into the organization's ability to disclose company information; the more a company makes investors aware of its existence, business, and strategies, the more likely it is to increase the attractiveness of its stock. Stockholders select and invest in organizations that they are familiar with and that are transparent. It is the investors' right to know how their money is being used, and efficiently communicating this will have a positive effect on stockholders' confidence. Effective companies divulge information in a straightforward manner rather than waiting until after the fact to report news to investors (Prickett, 2002). One option to consider is the Web as an efficient outlet that can give investors access at any time to fiscal information regarding the company. Even though this idea raises security concerns about Web access revealing company information to competitors, it would directly increase investor confidence.

Corporate Social Responsibility

At the center of accurate financial reporting is corporate social responsibility (CSR) reporting, which is designed to provide stockholders with key information, such as about the fiscal and social performance of the company (Coleman, 2004). Organizations are realizing the importance of such a method of reporting and the impact it has on communicating effectively to their stockholders. Companies should treat reporting like a tool and use it as a means to communicate performance and translate information so that investors can understand it. Increasing visibility through ethical reporting and CSR statements helps a company reveal both its positive and negative characteristics to investors and greatly increases its credibility and stockholders' confidence. Another aspect of IR that has the ability to influence stockholders is the company's annual statement. Seen as part of

the umbrella of corporate communication, and thus IR, annual statements are effective tools to communicate financial results and strategic intents to stockholders (Clarke & Murray, 2000). Rose and Thomsen (2004) contend that the company could also use its balance sheets, income statements, or other key figures to communicate financial status and decisions to stockholders. Reporting financial performance in this open and voluntary manner enables a company to enhance its corporate reputation. The annual statement also has the ability to make a positive first impression on an interested stockholder. Prior to selecting a company to invest in, interested stockholders often evaluate a company's reputation. As Jackson (1997) points out, reputation has more to do with direct experience than projected images, so constituents are more likely to trust and uphold a company's reputation. Indeed, a company's previous and future involvement in financial gains and/or losses will be the force that improves or worsens its reputation (Rose & Thomsen, 2004). Thus, it is essential that organizations take advantage of this resource and incorporate it into their strategic planning. The company that chooses not to focus and sustain its reputation will not only suffer in the marketplace but lack employee commitment and attractiveness to future applicants and investors.

Financial Performance and Corporate Reputation

A company's reputation can serve as an indicator of the company's status and/or success, and reputation plays a significant role in attracting new investors. Reputation is a reflection of a company's past investments and requires time to build. Hence, a company with steady and continuous investments over time will build a solid and quality-driven reputation (Roberts & Dowling, 2002; Sabate & Puente, 2003). From this perspective, the connection between investor relations, financial performance, and corporate reputation could be seen as following a cyclical pattern. As previously discussed, the IR department is not only the strategic tool that keeps current investors satisfied and informed about financial information but also the means to lure and attract new investors. Essentially, the IR function is the company's legitimate and most direct voice to use in speaking to investors, stockholders, and the public. It is the responsibility of the IR function to handle the distribution of a company's financial information (e.g., financial performance, profits and losses). Thus, following Rose and Thomsen's (2004) work, the synergistic effect of IR and financial performance creates the framework for a favorable corporate reputation.

Corporate communicators become transmitters of the investment story—one that orchestrates an organizational niche in order to separate itself from the heavily saturated and competitive market. The messages should establish positive relations with investors and help the organization develop new equity that serves as a type of corporate advertising to represent the organization's values and goals. This type of corporate promotion is essential especially in light of the growing interest to respond to bottom-line pressures. Miller (1988) suggests that the Value Exchange Perception Process, as applied to IR by communicators, provides a way to evaluate the needs of different levels of constituents. This framework is especially helpful because a corporate communicator's actions can have an impact on potential investors who are considering equity in the company. Members of the organization's stockholder groups often have diverse needs, and their value systems reflect such complexity. Effective communication with these groups must be constantly attuned to and in line with their needs. Beyond the more explicit reasons for a communicator to be a good taskmaster in delivering appropriate promotional tactics is his or her influence on shareholder loyalty.

Investor Relations Success Story

In May 2002, San Antonio-based Argonaut Group, Inc. engaged Pierpont Investor Relations to assist in its initiative to build and drive the company's IR function. More than 4 years later, Pierpont continues on as IR counsel, helping Argonaut Group provide shareholders with an outreach program as good as, if not better than, most of its peers.

With assets totaling $3.6 billion, Argonaut Group, Inc. (NasdaqGS: AGII) is a national underwriter of specialty insurance products in niche areas of the property and casualty market.

Business Challenge

At the outset of the engagement, Argonaut Group was in the midst of restructuring its business. As it completed strategic acquisitions, a geographic shift of business, and a complete overhaul of its management

(Continued)

(Continued)

team, the company felt it was time to share its progress with Wall Street. The financial community's perception of Argonaut Group, however, lingered in the past due to its total lack of communication during the transition.

Objectives

Pierpont recommended that Argonaut Group's IR program be designed to achieve the following objectives:

- Increase awareness of Argonaut Group's investment potential among key financial audiences.
- Increase demand for Argonaut Group stock by elevating the quality and breadth of the existing audience.
- Optimize Argonaut Group's valuation based on its performance in relation to the performance of its peers.
- Elevate the effectiveness and reach of the current messages being given to the financial community.
- Broaden the network of sell-side analysts following the company and writing reports on Argonaut Group.
- Increase awareness of the company with buy-side analysts and portfolio managers through participation in investor conferences as well as one-on-one and group meetings.

Strategies

To elevate and broaden the financial community's perception of Argonaut Group, Pierpont formulated the following communication strategies that would leverage the company's improved outlook for consistent growth and profitability:

- Increase the frequency of communication to existing and prospective investors.
- Communicate the company's plans for growth, and validate management's ability to execute those plans, by conveying the progress and results of the company's turnaround activities.
- Implement quarterly earnings calls to keep stockholders and research analysts informed of progress.
- Target institutional investors in Argonaut Group's peer group to broaden its investor base.
- Target the smaller institutions and money managers who invest in small-cap companies.
- Participate in fee-based investor conferences until invitations are extended by banking firms.
- Schedule one-on-one and group meetings with targeted buy-side analysts and portfolio managers.
- Target the retail market by developing relationships with sell-side analysts and investment bankers.
- Create, and drive traffic to, best-in-class investor relations Web site.

Results

Four years into Argonaut Group's Wall Street outreach program, the company maintains a sophisticated IR presence and continues to increases its awareness in the financial community. Major program accomplishments include (1) increasing the number of sell-side coverage analysts from one to six, (2) presenting at numerous investor conferences, including major insurance industry conferences geared toward professional investors in the sector, (3) conducting half a dozen road shows from coast to coast, and (4) implementing a best-practices investor relations Web site that facilitates effective communication with the company's key financial audiences. The outreach effort also connected Argonaut Group with Raymond James & Associates, which became the company's lead investment banker for two oversubscribed secondary stock offerings. Market demand for Argonaut Group's stock has quadrupled since the outreach program began, and the company's market capitalization is now more than $1 billion, up from a low of $189 million in April 2003. In 2005, Argonaut Group produced the highest total shareholder return in the property/casualty insurance industry.

SOURCE: Reprinted with permission from Michael Russell, SVP and general manager, Pierpont Investor Relations, 9606 North Mopac, Suite 850, Austin, TX 78759, and Matt Shaw, vice president, Council of Public Relations Firms.

Financial Ethics

Ethics is no longer an individual issue, but an organizational one as well, because the organization's behavior (actions) is constantly under watch by its constituents. Ethical behavior must be encouraged throughout the organization by employing organization-specific integrity strategies that focus on commitments, values, daily functions, and role models. Bowie (1998) discusses the need for organizations to take a more proactive stance with regard to ethics. Organizations that abide by ethical standards are less opportunistic, which in turn leads to more productivity and greater profitability. A company that is known for its high ethical standards will have high profits because the more trusted that company is, the more likely it is that people will want to do business with it. Ethical behavior helps companies by reducing business costs (i.e., costs associated with dealing with failures) and building trust among internal and external stakeholders. When there is trust within a company, customers, employees, and suppliers are less likely to act in their own best interest. The need for IR to maintain and manage the flow of information to these audiences is fundamentally important (Verchere, 1991). It is the responsibility of IR staff specialists to make sure that annual and quarterly reports are produced in a timely and accurate manner. Annual and quarterly reports from years past should also be made available so financial growth can be seen. Also, newsletters should be utilized to keep investors and analysts abreast of what is going on in the company; they should include articles about the firm, new financial information, press releases, and messages from both the CEO and the CFO (Nichols, 1989). Now with greater access to the Internet, many firms have a link on their homepage to provide investors with crucial information from financial reports, press releases, and so on. For example, the Key Bank Web site's IR link connects to analysts, dividend history, e-mail alerts, financial reports, presentations, news releases, and stock price. There is also a link that one can click on to request information. This is just one example of how IR programs have expanded to meet the needs of their stakeholders.

Summary

Chapter 6 shifted the emphasis to financial markets and stockowner communications. The area of investor relations requires a communicator to be a taskmaster and to possess the competency to manage promotional communication efforts, which if handled correctly and honestly can help improve a company's financial position. The role of taskmaster involves setting up organizational dialogue to facilitate understanding of financial expectations and the long-term corporate outlook. This promotional ability combines the information provided to investors and analyzers in order to reflect a complete, unified message of an organization's financial outcomes and vision for the future.

Review Questions

1. Discuss the IR role of taskmaster in facilitating understanding of financial expectations and long-term corporate outlook.

2. Check the Web sites of at least two companies that offer links to their IR functions, and describe their similarities and/or differences.

3. Call the IR unit of a publicly traded company and ask for information about how financial results and projections are communicated to stockholders. Evaluate the effectiveness of the means of communication used by that IR unit.

4. Discuss the importance of *who, what, where, when, how,* and *why* in responding to questions about financial reporting.

The Press and the Stockholders

Linda Thomas and Brad Youngren were almost speechless. Their meeting with Jane Bevins, president of Ostern Corporation, was not what they had expected. They had known there was big trouble but nothing as complex as this problem and with so many issues. Linda and Brad sat down to determine what to do next. It would be only a matter of hours before the press would be calling. They had to figure out how to approach public announcements and get more specialized information to their stockholders as well. Linda called Ostern's corporate attorneys and asked for an emergency meeting. She and Brad began to make a list of all their options.

As communication professionals in the Corporate Communication/External Relations department of Ostern Corporation, a publicly traded midsize medical software manufacturer noted for its excellent software programs for hospitals and medical practice offices, Linda and Brad were challenged to handle the public announcements of a serious earnings loss, the firing of a popular senior vice president, and the filing of a major lawsuit against Ostern. In their tenure at Ostern, a situation like this one had never happened. Until recently, sales growth had averaged 200% a year, with the most recent year-end figures topping $1 billion. Stock prices had increased 40% since the first public stock offering, and confidence was high in the company's future. Linda and Brad were faced with determining how to use past credibility to help with the present situation.

Jane Bevins had laid it on the line. Mike Mitchell, the senior vice president in charge of software development, had taken shortcuts with Hospital Manager 05, a major upgrade of the Manager Programs used by over 2,000 hospital systems throughout the country. Worse yet, conversion to the upgrade, which had begun in the last quarter and was continuing, had created serious trouble in some 500 hospitals. Software flaws were creating major scheduling and inventory mistakes as well as billing errors. Interwest Hospitals, the largest chain of hospitals using Hospital Manager programs, had notified Jane that it would file a lawsuit against Ostern asking for damages due to problems with the upgrade. If that were not bad enough, Jane told Linda and Brad that her internal investigation indicated that Mike had subcontracted work on the upgrade to vendors in which he had substantial personal investments. Vendors who had helped with the original release of Hospital Manager were not even contacted for bids to work on the revisions. Jane cautioned that this information must not be used publicly, but she wanted Linda and Brad to know that she had no choice but to instantly terminate Mike. The lawsuit from Interwest was to be filed on Monday, and Monday was also the day to release the most negative quarterly earnings figures in Ostern's history. Jane told Linda and Brad she believed a loss in one quarter, although not desirable, was not the major problem. What the public would learn was that Ostern had a loss, had fired a senior vice president, and was to be sued by its most important customer. Jane asked Linda and Brad to return later in the day to discuss options and approaches to handling the press, detail how to communicate with stockholders, and recommend processes for internal announcements to management and employees.

Case Questions

1. What are the key issues in this case?

2. Discuss Linda and Brad's options for dealing with these issues.

3. Develop a communication plan to help Ostern deal with its stockholders.

4. Use Figure 6.1 to evaluate the effectiveness of the communication plan to help Ostern restore its credibility and reputation.

7

Government Relations

Government is a special stakeholder for corporations because of the unavoidable interdependent and multifaceted relationships between these two parties. The ultimate objective of government relations (GR) is to develop a more effective relationship between business and government. Companies spend a large amount of their corporate communication budget to deal with this special stakeholder every year, which is a reflection of the importance of GR (Hutton et al., 2001). In fact, most Fortune 500 companies have a formalized GR function in place. Government establishes the legal framework within which commercial activity is conducted, but it also imposes limits on market relationships. The Environmental Protection Agency (EPA), for example, acting under authority granted by Congress, insists that businesses limit or avoid pollution even when it is costly for them to do so. Government is also expected to be the friend of business, protecting it from foreign competition and supplying advice on markets, technical assistance, and possibly cheap loans. And business is dependent on government to maintain sound economic conditions, generally defined as acceptable levels of inflation and unemployment. Moreover, government is a customer, but a customer of a special type—one

that can be persuaded to buy a product not only through a combination of the usual commercial skills but also through political pressure. In the meantime, business is an important supplier of resources to government. To take an obvious example, tax policy creates many opportunities for interaction between business and government. Businesses pay taxes equivalent to about 10% of total income and profits in the United States. And due to society's dependence on the business sector to attain macroeconomic goals such as growth in employment and national income, firms play a legitimate role in the public policy process by advocating particular policies (Shaffer, 1995).

Externally Derived, Internally Enforced

Regulations originate from the external environment but require compliance oversight, which is an internal function. This dual requirement intersects the two parts of the bottom half of the CVFCC. Although the GR function appears at the south pole of the CVFCC diagram, it is also well connected to the other corporate communication functions (i.e., investor relations, media

relations, and employee relations). This connection occurs through roles and activities that
signify the main focus of GR in a way that complements the roles and activities of the other
functions. These roles and activities appear in
Figure 7.1. Regulations require compliance
through new rules and controls as well as internal communication aimed at training and edu-
cating employees about the new rules, norms of
behavior, and values. At the same time, GR
specialists help organize the corporate effort to
reduce compliance costs, on one hand, and
develop proactive strategies to improve external
affairs and the reputation of the company, on
the other. For example, the Occupational Safety
and Health Administration's (OSHA) role "is
to assure the safety and health of . . . workers
by setting and enforcing standards; providing
training, outreach, and education; establishing
partnerships; and encouraging continual
process improvement in workplace safety and
health" (OSHA's Mission, n.d., ¶ 1). Employers
are expected to comply with OSHA's directives

by providing a safe and healthy workplace for
their employees. Employers also have leverage
in reducing the effects of regulations, creating
favorable consequences for their companies, or
prolonging the implementation of regulatory
requirements.

Micro Air® Sends Alert on New OSHA Ruling

Micro Air Clean Air Systems sent a news
alert on March 1 [2006] to its distributors
announcing the new OSHA ruling regarding
Hexavalent Chromium. The long-awaited ruling
was announced on February 28 in the *Federal
Register*. In the alert, Micro Air spokesman Jim
Orr stated, "The final PEL (permissible exposure
limit) went from 52 micrograms to 5 micrograms,
a tenfold decrease in allowable exposure. The
effective date of the ruling is June 1, 2006, with
a four year time limit for manufacturers to implement engineering controls that comply with the
ruling." The standard will be published in accord
with the timetable established by the U.S. Court
of Appeals for the Third Circuit which in April

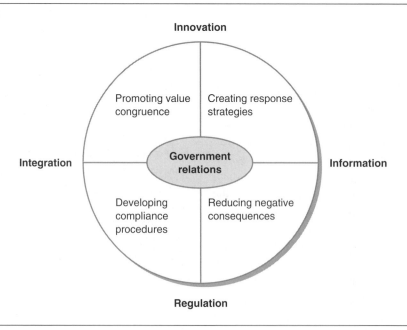

Figure 7.1   Government Relations Activities Across the Competing Values Framework of Corporate
Communication

2003 ordered OSHA to promulgate a standard governing workplace exposure to hexavalent chromium. The new standard lowers OSHA's permissible exposure limit (PEL) for hexavalent chromium, and for all Cr(VI) compounds, from 52 to 5 micrograms of Cr(VI) per cubic meter of air as an 8-hour time-weighted average. The standard also includes provisions relating to preferred methods for controlling exposure, respiratory protection, protective work clothing and equipment, hygiene areas and practices, medical surveillance, hazard communication, and recordkeeping. Jonathan L. Snare, acting assistant secretary for occupational safety and health, stated, "OSHA has worked hard to produce a final standard that substantially reduces the significant health risks for employees exposed to hexavalent chromium. Our new standard protects workers to the extent feasible, while providing employers, especially small employers, adequate time to transition to the new requirements." Hexavalent chromium compounds are widely used in the chemical industry as ingredients and catalysts in pigments, metal plating and chemical synthesis. . . . The major health effects associated with exposure to Cr(VI) include lung cancer, nasal septum ulcerations and perforations, skin ulcerations, and allergic and irritant contact dermatitis.

SOURCE: http://news.thomasnet.com/companystory/479665. Copyright © Micro Air.

Policy Fields

It is useful to examine the quality of business-government relations through the lenses of policy fields. The first type of policy field is *distributive*—benefits are solicited by and awarded to specific public groups, and the cost is dispersed across the entire population. The second is *regulatory* (e.g., environmental protection, price control)—organizations are monitored by existing policies. The third is *redistributive*—wealth is simply transferred from one population to another (e.g., Medicare, subsidized housing). The last is *constituent*—state management and the "rules of the game" are set.

D. W. Taylor (1990) suggests that industries that find themselves more affected by the receiving, positive ends of distributive or regulatory policies will have more satisfactory business-government relations. Companies that are affected more by redistributive and constituent polices will not be satisfied with the state of their government relations. Therefore, GR personnel should assess the type(s) of policy fields that pertain to their organization and take measures to ensure a healthy, working relationship with the relevant governmental agency. Involvement is crucial, as is constant monitoring of the regulatory environment. Otherwise, it is easy to involuntarily fall into a negative relationship with the government and risk being "regulated out."

Market failures often breed regulatory actions. These regulations set limits on how corporations can conduct business. Costs of compliance in nearly all areas of business are quite high and have been continuously climbing over the past 25 years, with exceptions in the late 1970s and early 1980s. In 1992 the cost of complying with government regulations in the United States exceeded $500 billion for the year (Winston, Crandall, Niskanen, & Klevorick, 1994). Research shows that government decisions regarding regulations can be influenced by interest groups, public opinion, and voting patterns (Gerber & Teske, 2000). For business to prevent unexpected changes and control the amount of money that will be spent on keeping the costs of meeting regulations from rising even higher, it must be able to manipulate these factors. This can be achieved through the use of corporate constituents and other key stakeholders. The story of how firms rushed to win government support for assault on new laws and regulations passed after the Enron and WorldCom scandals is a case in a point.

Businesses Seek New
Protection on Legal Front

Frustrated with laws and regulations that have made companies and accounting firms more open to lawsuits from investors and the government, corporate America—with the encouragement of the Bush administration—is preparing to fight back.

Now that corruption cases like Enron and WorldCom are falling out of the news, two influential industry groups with close ties to administration officials are hoping to swing the regulatory pendulum in the opposite direction. The groups are drafting proposals to provide broad new protections to corporations and accounting firms from criminal cases brought by federal and state prosecutors as well as a stronger shield against civil lawsuits from investors. Although the details are still being worked out, the groups' proposals aim to limit the liability of accounting firms for the work they do on behalf of clients, to force prosecutors to target individual wrongdoers rather than entire companies, and to scale back shareholder lawsuits.

The groups hope to reduce what they see as some burdens imposed by the Sarbanes-Oxley Act, landmark post-Enron legislation adopted in 2002. The law, which placed significant new auditing and governance requirements on companies, gave broad discretion for interpretation to the Securities and Exchange Commission. The groups are also interested in rolling back rules and policies that have been on the books for decades. To alleviate concerns that the new Congress may not adopt the proposals— regardless of which party holds power in the legislative branch next year—many are being tailored so that they could be adopted through rulemaking by the S.E.C. and enforcement policy changes at the Justice Department.

The proposals will begin to be laid out in public shortly after Election Day, members of the groups said in recent interviews. One of the committees was formed by the United States Chamber of Commerce and until recently was headed by Robert K. Steel. Mr. Steel was sworn in last Friday as the new Treasury undersecretary for domestic finance, and he is the senior official in the department who will be formulating the Treasury's views on the issues being studied by the two groups. The second committee was formed by the Harvard Law professor Hal S. Scott, along with R. Glenn Hubbard, a former chairman of the Council of Economic Advisers for President Bush, and John

L. Thornton, a former president of Goldman Sachs, where he worked with Treasury Secretary Henry M. Paulson Jr. That group has colloquially become known around Washington as the Paulson Committee because the relatively new Treasury secretary issued an encouraging statement when it was formed last month. But administration officials said Friday that he was not playing a role in the group's deliberations. Its members include Donald L. Evans, a former commerce secretary who remains a close friend of President Bush; Samuel A. DiPiazza Jr., chief executive of PricewaterhouseCoopers, the accounting giant; Robert R. Glauber, former chairman and chief executive of the National Association of Securities Dealers, the private group that oversees the securities industry; and the chief executives of DuPont, Office Depot and the CIT Group.

Jennifer Zuccarelli, a spokeswoman at the Treasury Department, said on Friday that no decision had been made about which recommendations would be supported by the administration. "While the department always wants to hear new ideas from academic and industry thought leaders, especially to encourage the strength of the U.S. capital markets, Treasury is not a member of these committees and is not collaborating on any findings," Ms. Zuccarelli said. But another official and committee members noted that Mr. Paulson had recently pressed the groups in private discussions to complete their work so it could be rolled out quickly after the November elections. Moreover, committee members say that they expect many of their recommendations will be used as part of an overall administration effort to limit what they see as overzealous state prosecutions by such figures as the New York State attorney general Elliot Spitzer and abusive class action lawsuits by investors. The groups will also attempt to lower what they see as the excessive costs associated with the Sarbanes-Oxley Act.

Their critics, however, see the effort as part of a plan to cater to the most well-heeled constituents of the administration and insulate politically connected companies from prosecution at the expense of investors. One consideration in drafting the proposals has been the chain of events at Arthur Andersen, the accounting firm that was convicted in 2002 of obstruction of justice for shredding Enron-related documents; the conviction was overturned in 2005 by the Supreme Court. The proposals being drafted would aim to limit the liability of auditing firms and include a policy shift to make it harder for prosecutors to bring cases against individuals and companies.

Even though Arthur Andersen played a prominent role in various corporate scandals, some business and legal experts have criticized the decision by the Bush administration to bring a criminal case that had the effect of shutting the firm down. The proposed policies would emphasize the prosecution of culpable individuals rather than corporations and auditing firms. That shift could prove difficult for prosecutors because it is often harder to find sufficient evidence to show that specific people at a company were the ones who knowingly violated a law. One proposal would recommend that the Justice Department sharply curtail its policy of forcing companies under investigation to withhold paying the legal fees of executives suspected of violating the law. Another one would require some investor lawsuits to be handled by arbitration panels, which are traditionally friendlier to defendants.

In an interview last week with Bloomberg News, Mr. Paulson repeated his criticism of the Sarbanes-Oxley law. While it had done some good, he said, it had contributed to "an atmosphere that has made it more burdensome for companies to operate." Mr. Paulson also repeated a line from his first speech, given at Columbia Business School last August, where he said, "Often the pendulum swings too far and we need to go through a period of readjustment." Some experts see Mr. Paulson's complaint as a step backward. "This is an escalation of the culture war against regulation," said James D. Cox, a securities and corporate law professor at Duke Law School. He said many of the proposals, if adopted, "would be a dark day for investors."

Professor Cox, who has studied 600 class action lawsuits over the last decade, said it was difficult to find "abusive or malicious" cases, particularly in light of new laws and court decisions that had made it more difficult to file such suits. The number of securities class action lawsuits has dropped substantially in each of the last two years, he noted, arguing that the impact of the proposals from the business groups would be that "very few people would be prosecuted." People involved in the committees said that the timing of the proposals was being dictated by the political calendar: closely following Election Day and as far away as possible from the 2008 elections.

Mr. Hubbard, who is now dean of Columbia Business School, said the committee he helps lead would focus on the lack of proper economic foundation for a number of regulations. Most changes will be proposed through regulation, he said, because "the current political environment is simply not ripe for legislation." But the politics of changing the rules do not break cleanly along party lines. While some prominent Democrats would surely attack the pro-business efforts, there are others who in the past have been sympathetic. People involved in the committees' work said that their objective was to improve the attractiveness of American capital-raising markets by scaling back rules whose costs outweigh their benefits. "We think the legal liability issues are the most serious ones," said Professor Scott, the director of the committee singled out by Mr. Paulson. "Companies don't want to use our markets because of what they see as the substantial, and in their view excessive, liability."

Committee officials disputed the notion that they were simply catering to powerful business interests seeking to benefit from loosening regulations that could wind up hurting investors. "It's unfortunate to the extent that this has been politicized," said Robert E. Litan, a former Justice Department official and senior fellow at the Brookings Institution who is overseeing the committee's legal liability subgroup. "The objectives are clearly not to gut such reforms as Sarbanes-Oxley. I'm for cost-effective regulation."

The main Sarbanes-Oxley provision that both committees are focusing on is a part that is commonly called Section 404, which requires audits of companies' internal financial controls. Some business experts praise this section as having made companies more transparent and better managed, but many smaller companies call the section too costly and unnecessary. Members of the two committees said that they had reached a consensus that Section 404, along with greater threat of investor lawsuits and government prosecutions, had discouraged foreign companies from issuing new stock on exchanges in the United States in recent months. The committee members said that an increase in stock offerings abroad was evidence that the American liability system and tougher auditing standards were taking a toll on the competitiveness of American markets. But others see different reasons for the trend and few links to liability and accounting rules.

Bill Daley, a former commerce secretary in the Clinton administration who is the co-chairman of the Chamber of Commerce group, expects proposed changes to liability standards for accounting firms and corporations to draw the most flak. But he said that the changes affecting accounting firms are of paramount importance to prevent the further decline in competition. Only four major firms were left after Andersen's collapse.

Another contentious issue concerns a proposal to eliminate the use of a broadly written and long-established anti-fraud rule, known as Rule 10b-5, that allows shareholders to sue companies for fraud. The change could be accomplished by a vote of the S.E.C.

John C. Coffee, a professor of securities law at Columbia Law School and an adviser to the Paulson Committee, said that he had recommended that the S.E.C. adopt the exception to Rule 10b-5 so that only the commission could bring such lawsuits against corporations. But other securities law experts warned that such a move would extinguish a fundamental check on corporate malfeasance. "It would be a shocking turning back to say only the commission can bring fraud cases," said Harvey J. Goldschmid, a former S.E.C. commissioner and law professor at Columbia University. "Private enforcement is a necessary supplement to the work that the S.E.C. does. It is also a safety valve against the potential capture of the agency by industry."

SOURCE: From Labaton, Stephen, "Firms Rush to End Reform," in *New York Times:* October 29, 2006 Copyright © (2006) by the New York Times Co. Reprinted with permission.

Importance of Government Relations

What accounts for the high variance of GR across organizations? And what determines the relative importance of GR within organizations? Large capital-intensive companies, particularly those operating in highly regulated environments, require more time and effort to develop contacts, knowledge, and credibility than is the case for high technology or retail firms. Highly regulated industries demand more attention from organizational legal staff, but GR units have also proliferated in less-regulated industries displaying highly interdependent organizations. The factors that most influence the significance of GR in an organization are size and industry. Other factors, such as a company's stage of development, the philosophy of the CEO, and a company's level of centralization have also been found to influence the importance of the GR function both internally and externally (Meznar & Nigh, 1995; Shaffer & Hillman, 2000). There is also a relationship between the type of organizational structure and the degree of importance that GR units are granted. Companies organized geographically typically have more elaborate GR due to the need to respond to diverse markets and locations, whereas a unitary structure that is predominantly functional with extensive support staff places less importance on GR primarily because of overlapping roles.

During the 1980s, when the rate of regulation was quite high, companies struggled to manage their GR departments to either anticipate new regulatory requirements or take steps to reduce compliance costs through lobbying and other initiatives. Earlier researchers investigated several GR factors to determine which had the greatest influence on corporate strategic planning. They found that public affairs has the greatest influence on corporate policy "when it identifies public issues for corporate attention, and least influence when it prepares a narrative for future social/political tends" (Dickie, 1984, p. 17). The level of internal GR influence on corporate policy also varies among industries—the utilities and service industries have strong GR influence, and energy and technology industries have weak influence. Industry regulation was found to affect internal influence of GR: The most influential departments were those in companies in highly regulated industries. This finding was corroborated by the fact that the companies most active in public affairs were those in highly regulated industries. Companies with centralized corporate communication allowed a more direct link between GR personnel decision authority centers, whereas larger, diversified companies used more decentralized operatives at the business level. Although there are many differences among organizations that require different GR strategies, there are also similarities regardless of company size and industry. GR professionals fulfill boundary-spanning roles, simultaneously monitoring and scanning the external environment while supporting executive decision-making processes with pertinent information. These roles require proximity to decision authority centers as well as permeability and resiliency that allow top-ranked boundary spanners to detect change and use information in strategic planning sessions. Not surprisingly, a large number of GR professionals are at the vice-president level or higher, and most report directly to the president or CEO.

Altria

The size of an organization and the industry to which it belongs are highly influential in determining how much emphasis is placed on the GR function. Large, mature companies in highly regulated industries not only invest more than other companies in their GR staff and activities, but the public affairs functions also generate more influence internally and externally in these types of companies. One example is Altria, the parent company of Philip Morris USA, Philip Morris International, Philip Morris Capital, and Kraft Foods, Inc. Philip Morris USA and Philip Morris International had been the largest and most profitable tobacco companies in their markets. As such, they enjoyed great financial success, but along with their success came criticism. Until 2003, the companies mentioned above were recognized as members of the Philip Morris Companies. However, amid increasing criticism from the public, a surge in antismoking campaigns and regulation, price wars, and becoming the target of landmark tobacco lawsuits, the board of directors at Philip Morris approved changing the holding company's name to Altria. The name change was partly a result of the inadequate handling of GR by the Philip Morris Companies. In the years leading up to changing the name to Altria, federal regulators faced challenges from the public to increase regulation on tobacco products. Tobacco companies were accused of having misleading product labeling and an unsatisfactory level of awareness of the effects of smoking, and lawsuits against these companies, most notably Philip Morris, began to emerge. In response to this crisis, Philip Morris chose to defend itself against the government and the public, finding medical experts to attest to limited negative health effects of smoking. By doing so, the company alienated the public by denying any role in deaths and illness caused by smoking. The effects of the ensuing lawsuits and continued denials scarred the company's image. With stocks and public opinion of the company declining from 2002 to 2003, changes had to be made, beginning with the name.

As a large company in a highly regulated industry, the Philip Morris Companies' GR staff had engaged more in buffering activities than proactively adopting regulatory changes (Meznar & Nigh, 1995). Presently, however, the structure of Altria and the Philip Morris

Companies reflects a change that places more importance on its GR activities. Altria has two senior vice presidents in charge of GR, along with a political action committee and separate teams handling federal and state issues. The company has also supported the involvement of Philip Morris USA and Philip Morris International in the Framework Convention on Tobacco Control, which is shaping further regulation on the tobacco industry (Altria Group, 2007a).

In addition to taking a more proactive role in regulation (and making that involvement public), Altria has made available on its Web site more company information dealing with government and federal issues. Not only does it provide information about how to quit smoking, but it also provides information on past and current litigation in which its companies are involved. Making such information available can help to repair the company's image in the long run (and help it comply with the government). Although Philip Morris has made a complete financial comeback from its 2002– 2003 slides, the company's image has taken longer to repair. By implementing a new stance on sharing information with the public, diversifying assets, and shifting the corporate focus to responsible truth in advertising, Altria has taken steps to shift attention away from the tobacco companies and focus on being the holding company of several successful brands such as Kraft Foods. No longer relying on a dominant product, Altria now promotes its "marketing excellence and innovation, performance and financial strength, commitment to responsibility, compliance and integrity, and dedication to people" (Altria Group, 2007b, ¶ 1).

American Red Cross

Meznar and Nigh (1995) organize the main functions of GR professionals into two main categories: *buffering* and *bridging*. Buffering involves shielding the core business of organizations from external interferences. Bridging, on the other hand, is a proactive approach by which organizations adapt to the external environment. Large-scale organizations are less vulnerable to environmental fluctuations and would therefore buffer their core businesses from external interferences. Smaller, less-resourceful organizations would create interdependencies to manage their environments. A firm's engagement in bridging activities is most closely linked to the philosophy of top management. Those organizations with a commitment to proactive strategies for reducing environmental uncertainty are more likely to bridge. The American Red Cross is one example.

The American Red Cross is a nonprofit tax-exempt, charitable institution. Unlike nongovernmental agencies such as the Girl Scouts of America, the Red Cross works closely with government agencies, such as the Federal Emergency Management Agency, during times of major crisis. "It has the legal status of 'a federal instrumentality,' due to its charter requirements to carry out responsibilities delegated to it by the federal government" (Federal Charter of the American Red Cross, n.d., ¶ 1).

The fundamental principles of the International Red Cross and Red Crescent Movement are humanity, impartiality, neutrality, independence, voluntary service, unity, and universality. Since its incorporation in 1905, the American Red Cross has been the nation's premier emergency response organization. Today it offers services in six areas: domestic disaster relief; community services that help the needy; support and comfort for military members and their families; the collection, processing, and distribution of life-saving blood and blood products; educational programs that promote health and safety; and international relief and development programs. According to the organization's Web site, "each year, in communities large and small, victims of some 70,000 disasters turn to . . . the nearly one million volunteers and 35,000 employees of the Red Cross. Through more than 800 locally supported chapters, more than 15 million people gain the skills they need to prepare for and respond to emergencies" (American National Red Cross, n.d., ¶ 3). While the Red Cross strives to become a partner and a leader in mobilizing communities to help prevent, prepare, and respond to disaster and other life-threatening emergencies, it also aims to strengthen the financial base and infrastructure needed for improving its service-delivery system. For the fiscal year ending June 2004, the Red Cross took in $3.2 billion, and its expenses amounted to $2.9 billion; for the same year, fund-raising costs totaled 18% of related contributions (American Red Cross Charity Report, 2005).

Most of the coordination of legislative and regulatory initiatives with government agencies at the local and national levels occurs through the organization's government relations (GR) group, which consists of a senior associate of grassroots advocacy and outreach, an officer of government relations and the Hurricane Recovery Program, a vice president of government relations and public policy, a director of government relations, a senior director of federal relations and partnerships, a senior associate of state legislative relations, a senior director of state government relations, a senior associate of Senate relations, a senior associate of federal relations and partnerships, a senior associate of House relations, an executive assistant, and a legislative assistant (American National Red Cross, 2006). The size of this group and the type and level of positions signify the weight that the Red Cross places on its relationships and interaction with government agencies. This group's responsibilities include coordinating and developing policy positions articulated by Red Cross staff serving on external task forces and committees, developing testimonials and responses to executive and legislative branches, and taking proactive stands in meeting or exceeding regulatory requirements or in carrying out the mission and goals of the organization.

Regulations and Boundary Spanning

Corporate GR is a boundary-spanning function. It requires that the public affairs professional incorporate information from outside sources that may affect the business. It also requires that positive information about the business be communicated to stakeholders in order to gain political allies. Because government and business tend to have competing interests, it is important to maintain positive relations with government officials in an effort to gain influence during times of disagreement. One way to achieve such a relationship is for the company or individual high-ranking executives to make large contributions to political campaigns. These contributions, which political candidates may depend on during campaigns, are used as a way to influence politicians not only to prevent the passage of regulations that are damaging to business but also to promote legislation that is otherwise beneficial. However, because of regulations placed on the amount of political contributions a business can give, other ways of preventing unwanted regulations must also be utilized.

Some options for dealing with pending regulations include filing lawsuits, hiring lobbyists to convey the company's interests, making contributions to (or against) political campaigns, and joining or creating political action committees or grassroots movements to influence specific elected officials. However, corporations can also generate support for or against a political cause by recruiting third-party advocates from stakeholder groups such as stockholders, suppliers, community members, and industry associations

(Gerber & Teske, 2000). These stakeholders can be won over through mailing lists, television commercials, or newspaper advertisements to gain support for a cause. Studies show that shareholders consider business executives to be credible sources of information and, when exposed to public policy information regularly from a company, tend to adopt similar opinions on political issues. It is not unusual for a large corporation to spend millions of dollars every year in an attempt to control government. Businesses formulate information-based strategies and create coalitions of third-party corporate advocates to fight government regulations (Belasen, 1988). The more individuals and groups an organization can recruit, resources it can access, money it is able to spend, access it has to influential people, and people committed to its goals, the more politically powerful it is and the more likely that legislators and other government officials will consider the proposal being made by the business (Wakefield & Coleman, 2001).

Corporate communicators have the opportunity to control their regulatory environments, often through private interdependence in which companies self-regulate or mutually adjust to each other. A system of self-regulation, albeit under government supervision, provides another means of vesting authority in parties connected through a value chain (Eisner, 2004). One example is the beer and beverage industries' adaptation to the Returnable Beverage Container Law in New York (Belasen, 1988). Both industries employed various lobbyists to either revert or reduce the effects of the bottle bill on the distribution systems. When all efforts failed and they were forced to comply with the new regulation, the industries took full advantage of the inconsequentiality of law enforcement by adapting measures such as passing on the cost of collection to retailers. The industries used corporate advertising, issue management, and strong political campaigning to influence the direction of the law. Eventually, they had to realign their distribution system and use private interdependence to comply with the regulatory requirements.

When initiating external communication, such as creating support for a cause, it is important to be educated about the constituencies' views and beliefs. Audiences should be targeted with literature or advertisements that are appealing to that group. What may produce a positive response from one person or subgroup may result in a negative response from another. A corporation may encourage a specific subgroup (e.g., constituents of an influential legislator) to target a certain prominent person and create constituent education programs to motivate people to think the way the corporation does. Most people have a favorable response to corporate constituency building, are willing to support the business, and in many instances actually want to be involved in the campaign (Baysinger, Kein, & Zeithaml, 1985).

Organizations are not always on the defensive end of government regulations, though. Rather than waiting for government to impose regulations, some businesses anticipate changes and adopt new rules before they are legally required. In certain cases this may be due to market repositioning or jumping industries (i.e., moving from one industry to another). Boundary spanners may come up with ideas that fulfill requests made by corporate constituents. For example, a business invents a new safety feature for cars and is the only company that manufactures it. If the government eventually requires the device in all cars, the business stands to make a profit from the purchase of this safety equipment. Such a proactive approach can also be seen in the way many businesses deal with environmental issues by creating environmentally friendly internal policies. Such policies help strengthen relations with government as well as community members. These examples illustrate how corporate external affairs and government regulations achieve integrative solutions. Ultimately, compliance with regulations is much less expensive than noncompliance, and many times businesses simply adopt regulations without a fight. Although there are sometimes clear distinctions between internal and external issues, there are occasions when business and government work together and lines begin to blur. NASA and the U.S. Department of Defense enjoy just such a high level of interdependence.

Interdependence

Figure 7.2 depicts a simplified model of the interdependence of nongovernmental organizations (NGOs) and government agencies. When government uses its authority to implement public policies through processes of legislation and regulation, the main response from corporations is adaptation. Conversely, when government develops public policies, corporations act as interest groups and attempt to influence policy development. A corporation should both adapt to and influence public policy. Corporate managers should become more aware of and concerned with government and politics, and

at the same time increasingly motivated to influence government policies favorably. Organizations adapt to environmental uncertainty through internal realignment. The eventual effectiveness of organizations depends largely on the degree to which they are able to adjust and modify internal structures and processes to accommodate regulatory requirements (Shaffer, 1995). The good communication that builds a positive, favorable image in the eyes of government agencies must continue. Maintaining the highest standards for propriety and ethical behavior is the best approach to developing a reputation for honesty and integrity. An organization's public reputation and social legitimacy are important intangible assets; as one government officer says, "We trust those companies that we respect, so we grant them the benefit of the doubt" (Shaffer & Hillman, 2000, p. 176). By establishing a positive identity,

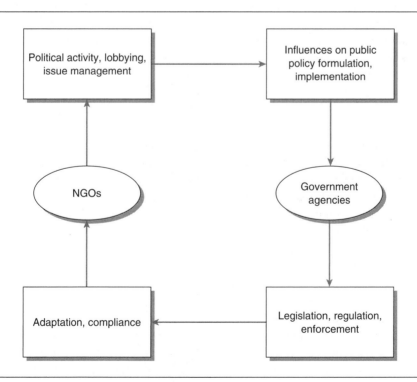

Figure 7.2   Interdependence of Business and Government

corporations may enhance their legitimacy and reputation in the eyes of government and other external constituents, which is effective when adapting to government regulations.

Shaping Favorite Policies Through Issue Management

Issue management, a long-term strategic management practice, is an important aspect of GR. Through this practice, organizations identify significant changes or issues that may affect them and make long-term strategic decisions that may involve changes in policy and practice (Shaffer & Hillman, 2000). The fact that so many issues appear first as areas of public concern and then move on to inspire government legislation and regulation enables companies to anticipate and identify the major stages of the issue management process. This anticipation of likely future government requirements gives corporate managers a good chance to make proper decisions. Because most of the issues that have an important impact on corporations are defined by outside participants, corporations initially focus on their only option—responding and reacting to issues already defined. Issue management places emphasis on corporate involvement in the issue-defining process (Renfro, 1987). The corporation should move from externally driven reactions to new laws and regulations, to internally focused proactive strategies. The mission of management should be to change an organization's future from one that happens *to* it to one that happens *for* it.

Issue management makes it possible for organizations to shape government policy on issues that affect them, rather than to just adapt to policy changes. But the problem now is how to start? The first and most important step is to make sure that GR staff specialists take a more proactive stand in dealing with regulatory requirements. Fixing the situation after the government has written the law or regulation is very difficult— much more difficult than monitoring the

situation from the start and getting involved early so that the government considers the organization's particular interests. Being proactive is cheaper, too. Trying to identify and change issues before they influence government policy and legislation is what preventative issue management advocates—in other words, being proactive all the time. So major American corporations are becoming increasingly proactive in the management of their external legal environment, and plan to become even more so in the future (Theaker, 2001). Moreover, one of the techniques used most commonly in carrying out issue management campaigning is lobbying, which includes persuasion tactics and political activities to influence legislative and regulatory policies as well PR efforts aimed at supporting government-business relationships (Shaffer, 1995). Organizations are increasingly using lobbying techniques to present their case to government and stakeholders. Lobbying can be either defensive, designed to abolish or amend an existing law, or offensive, aimed at pushing the authorities to create a law. Therefore, GR is related to media relations, and the two functions should interconnect well in order to develop the corporation's strategies. Much of lobbyists' efforts are directed toward making sure that their case is covered in the media in an appropriate manner to influence the public. Public perception of an issue increases proportionately to the amount of attention given to that issue by the media. By simply paying attention to an issue and neglecting others, the media affect public opinion. The public agenda then influences the political agenda.

The experience of Unilever demonstrates that improving the effectiveness of GR involves a more proactive and collaborative approach on the part of the business enterprise. Successful corporate executives must anticipate and respond to government issues and opinions that are important not just for their constituents (e.g., customers, suppliers, employees) but also to corporate decision-making processes. Unilever, through its subsidiary companies such as Bird Eye Walls, Gorton's, and Findus, is the largest buyer of fish in the world. In early 1996, Unilever was warned of a proposed campaign by Greenpeace that would highlight decreasing global fish stocks. Greenpeace was planning to target the company and criticize its fish-buying practices, which Greenpeace felt were contributing to the problem. To avert this attack, Unilever established a partnership with the World Wide Fund for Nature, the largest environmental campaigning group in the United Kingdom, to form the Marine Stewardship Council (MSC) to determine the sustainability of every fishery in the world and issue certification of those that were judged to meet strict criteria (Constance & Bonanno, 2000). Unilever then committed itself from 2000 onward to source all its fish from MSC-certified fisheries only. Instead of a negative attack, the strategy resulted in the following headline in the *Financial Times* on February 22, 1996: "Unilever in Fight to Save Global Fisheries." By taking initiative, the company became associated with the solution rather than the problem, simultaneously building its authority on global fisheries policy and protecting its brand and future business.

Supplier Relations

The area of supplier relations requires corporate communication staff to be dependable and reliable in analyzing and running communication programs effectively (Reynolds, 1995). This area has become increasingly important because of government's increased influence on domestic issues as well as the ever-changing role of companies in international business operations (Sharon, 1990). With such fluid combinations of business groups and constituents, it is paramount that corporate communicators follow suit with a flexible, rapid communication repertoire that can develop a communication system around the supply chain of the organization. Communicators must be able to tap into the

skills (e.g., negotiation, facilitation, consensus building) that enable such systems to be coordinated, and they must develop familiarity with the inside workings of the industry, regulatory concerns, and technical standards and procedures. The catalysts of GR programs are often the result of a misstep or violation of a new law or regulation; the organization must then react to and deal with the situation at that moment. Corporate communicators can enhance their competencies in assessing what information is most important with respect to how such government regulations affect the operations and strategy of their corporation. They can do so by utilizing a consultant or firm to assist with the type of regulation pertaining to their organization, joining industry trade associations, and reading newsletters to keep up on industry news.

Summary

Chapter 7 focuses on business-government relationships and regulatory environments that require compliance and greater control and accountability. GR is best understood as a form of long-range planning applied to the legal or regulatory environment of an organization. GR staff should be aware of and adapt to government regulations and monitor the legal/regulatory environment in order to provide input for the strategic decision-making process and to promote public policies favorable to the organization's success. Organizations should operate under notions of transparency, which allow an open flow of information and input. Proper communication is required to nurture a team-like relationship with government agencies, thereby helping companies create an atmosphere of quasi self-regulation. A win-win relationship is the ultimate result of such a partnership: The government gains a constant flow of accurate information, and organizations gain more control over their changing legal environments.

Review Questions

1. Corporate government relations is a boundary-spanning function. Explain.

2. Use Internet resources to confirm (or disconfirm) the finding that companies operating in highly regulated environments have elaborate structures of government relations staff.

3. Use examples to illustrate the point that complying with regulations is much less expensive than noncompliance and the fact that businesses often simply adopt a regulation without fighting it.

CASE STUDY

The Anti-trust Case Against Microsoft

In March 1998, Bill Gates, chairman of Microsoft Corporation, went to Congress to answer charges that Microsoft had become a high-tech monopolist, stifling its competitors in the market for application software. In dramatic testimony before the Senate Judiciary Committee, Gates vigorously asserted that Microsoft's success was not the result of any anti-competitive practices, but of its ability to innovate. "At the end of the day," he concluded, "what really counts is building great software."

Microsoft's adversaries would have none of it. James Barksdale, CEO of Netscape Communications, Gates' main competitor in the Internet browser market, turned to the Senate audience and asked how many of them used personal computers. Most members raised their hands. "How many of you have a computer with Internet Explorer?" he added, referring to Microsoft's browser. Most of the same hands went up. "That is a monopoly," Barksdale stated.

The background to this confrontation was an ongoing anti-trust investigation of Microsoft by federal regulators. Just four months earlier, the Justice Department had charged that the company violated an earlier agreement by requiring computer makers to install Internet Explorer (IE) on their computers as a condition of licensing Microsoft's popular Windows 95 operating system. In response, Microsoft agreed that IE was simply an enhancement of Windows, not a separate product, so no antitrust laws had been broken.

The Senate hearing and the Justice Department's actions were just the latest salvos in a long series of government antitrust skirmishes with Microsoft, dating back to the early 1990s. Many believed that this ongoing dispute was an important test of antitrust laws in the new knowledge economy, where dominance of cyberspace was as important as dominance of oil supplies or rail lines had been a century earlier.

Microsoft Corporation is one of the success stories of the information age. Founded in 1975 by Gates, a computer wiz who dropped out of Harvard, the company first made its mark by developing MS-DOS, an operating system that directs a computer's inner workings. When IBM adopted MS-DOS for use in its personal computers (PCs), the program quickly became the industry standard. Microsoft later introduced an improved operating system, Windows, and branched out into applications software, developing word processing, spreadsheet, and other desktop programs, as well as Internet Explorer. By the late 1990s, Microsoft controlled 85% of the market for all PC operating systems and was pulling in revenues of $5 billion a year. Gates himself was the wealthiest person in the country.

Government regulators and some of Gates's competitors believed that Microsoft used its dominance in operating systems to hurt its rivals in the applications business. For example, Microsoft could use its advance knowledge of upcoming changes in Windows to get a head start on developing compatible word processing or spreadsheet software. Or Microsoft could deliberately design features into its operating systems that would make them incompatible with competitors' products. Adobe Systems, a maker of Microsoft's typefaces, for example, complained that Windows had been designed so that Microsoft's own typefaces would run at twice the speed of Adobe's products.

The government was also concerned about Microsoft's purchase of competing companies. In 1995, Microsoft abandoned a plan to buy Intuit, a maker of personal finance software programs, after the government threatened an antitrust suit. Two years later, the government launched investigations into Microsoft's acquisition of WebTV, a company that made equipment allowing viewers to cruise the Internet using a television, and of its investment in Apple Computer, a longtime rival.

In response to its critics, Microsoft insisted that it did not fit the monopolistic mold. High-tech industry differed from old-line manufacturing industry, transportation, and utilities because there were few barriers to entry. All that was needed to compete in software was brains, entrepreneurial zeal and a good idea. "In the computer software industry," Gates noted, "rapid and unpredictable changes constantly create new market opportunities and threaten the position of existing competitors."

Moreover, the company argued, government efforts to restrict the company would be poor public policy. The software industry was a major provider of jobs, growing two-and-a-half times faster than the U.S. economy overall in the 1990s. Microsoft's dominance of operating system software helped the United States balance of trade and contributed to the emergence of the United States as a world technology leader.

The outcome of the ongoing dispute between Microsoft and its critics would be critical to antitrust enforcement into the new century, many believed. "Justice is taking a stand here," said one industry analyst. "It will be a watershed event no matter which way it goes." Commented Senator Orrin Hatch (R-Utah): "I think the current antitrust laws are adequate. But understanding how these crucial high technology markets work [and] whether competition and innovation are being fostered or inhibited is a very important issue for our economy and our society."

Case Questions

1. In what ways have Microsoft's actions promoted public interest? In what ways have they harmed public interest?

2. Why did the Department of Justice believe that Microsoft had violated U.S. antitrust law? Do you agree or disagree with government antitrust regulators?

3. What is the best solution to Microsoft's market dominance: (a) breakup into smaller companies, (b) strict legal enforcement of applicable antitrust laws, or (c) increased competition from innovative rivals?

4. The basic antitrust laws were written in the late 19th or early 20th century, an era when the economy was dominated by manufacturing firms and business competition was primarily national or regional in scope. Do you think these laws are relevant to the situation of Microsoft and other high-technology companies that emerged in the late 20th century? If not, in what ways should antitrust policy be changed to better fit today's society?

8

Employee Relations

One of the main points that the literature makes about employee relations (ER) is the need to sustain organizational credibility and legitimacy by linking identity programs with external communication. Cheney and Christensen (2001) suggest that those involved with external communication functions must communicate regularly with internal constituents about matters such as symbols of pride and motivation, relevant audiences and environments, market analysis, and perceptions about the organization's external information. Leaders must communicate a clear vision and take responsibility for maintaining a high level of awareness of the organization's vision, goals, and values. Maintaining a good community relationship by eliciting feedback and promoting dialogue is the key to building trust in the organization (Belasen, 2000; Gore, 1994; Kearns, 1996; Ospina et al., 2002).

Cheney and Christensen's (2001) research also confirms that many organizations are starting to consider their employees as part of their overall marketing communication and, therefore, part of their efforts to communicate the organization's preferred self-image. This self-image can be mitigated by employees' communication with outside constituents. Self-image or

identity is, in part, how organization members imagine that their organization is seen by outside constituents. Marketing communication can link internal and external audiences around identity, and a strong corporate identity can raise employees' motivation while inspiring confidence among external target groups (Van Riel, 1995). Top management must form a consensus on core values and organizational purpose as well as furnish a consistent view of organizational mission (Scott & Lane, 2000). In doing so, top management has the responsibility to reinforce the core values to everybody in the organization and reaffirm positive aspects of the organization to various stakeholders. Moreover, managers should constantly review the organization's corporate philosophy and determine whether there is any need to update the corporate identity program. Strong identity programs are associated with longevity, satisfaction, and personal commitment to organizational goals, values, and philosophy.

Although the ER function appears at the left side of the CVFCC diagram, it is also well connected to the other corporate communication functions (i.e., investor relations, media relations, and government relations). This connection occurs through roles and activities that

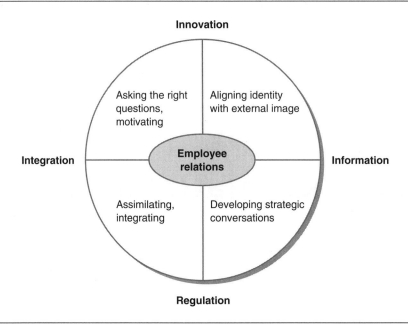

Figure 8.1   Employee Relations Activities Across the Competing Values Framework of Corporate
Communication

signify the main focus of ER in a way that complements the roles and activities of the other
functions. These roles and activities appear in
figure 8.1. Conforming to regulatory requirements, addressing identification issues, developing identity programs, and managing the
reputation and credibility of the organization
are important activities that bring together
employees, management, and key organizational
stakeholders. As discussed in chapter 11, creating consistent corporate messages that are supported by employees and sustained through the
culture of the organization is greatly facilitated
when management uses strategic conversations
and participative approaches with employees.

Aligning Identity
With External Image

Employees are central to understanding the
views held by organizational stakeholders. As
discussed in chapters 3 and 4, employees have a

strong impact on an organization's desired and
actual identity. A strong identity program increases
personal commitment to organizational goals
and values. Employees need to understand, facilitate, and commit to the organization's identity
(core values) in order to become advocates of
corporate goals and values. Once their attitudes
and beliefs coincide with those of the organization, a positive reputation is projected to other
stakeholders through direct and indirect communication with employees. As discussed
throughout this book, such internal and external
communication also underscores the role of
ethics in building and sustaining the organization's image and reputation.

Achieving a consistent organizational identity
can be helped by a strong vision coupled with a
clear mission and corporate philosophy that are
supported by employees. Establishing a mission
statement is the first formal act of creating an
organization's identity (Goodman, 1998). The
written mission statement provides a foundation
for organizational goals, behaviors, values, and

beliefs. A mission statement, however, must reflect the consensus among powerful constituencies about the core values and directions of the organization. Because multiple constituencies often have competing views about the direction of the organization, the mission statement must retain some sense of strategic ambiguity. It needs to be crafted as a political statement that helps legitimize the value proposition of the organization. As such, the mission statement rejects the notion of an objective reality; instead, it provides organizational constituents with a mental map that guides them toward the values and goals developed by top management. It also allows constituents to identify with such values and goals based on their subjective interpretations and experiences, while still believing that they are in agreement with the organization as a whole.

Markwick and Fill (1997) suggest that corporate communication directors manage identity by promoting organizational symbols, behaviors, and elements of self-expression. The organization's identity directly influences the organization's image. As mentioned earlier, external stakeholders have different images of the same organization based on their distinct exposure to the identity cues of the organization. For instance, corporate stockholders (the investor relations stakeholder) and customers (the media relations stakeholder) may have different perceptions of the same organization because they have been exposed to different messages, behaviors, and norms, which could take the form of annual reports, logos on letterhead and interoffice memos, and television commercials. Top executives and corporate communication directors who want to influence the images held of their organization can only do so through maintaining a consistent organizational identity.

Strategic Conversation

Strategic conversation is communication that takes place across boundaries and hierarchical levels and concerns the group mandate or organizational vision, critical strategic themes, and values that can help achieve desired outcomes (Clampitt, Berk, & Williams, 2002). Four main components are needed for strategic conversations:

1. **Open communication**—leaders sharing all types of information throughout the company and across all levels

2. **Listening**—the skill of grasping and interpreting a message's genuine meaning

3. **Discernment**—the type of listening by which a leader detects unarticulated messages hidden below the surface of spoken interaction

4. **Dialogue**—active sharing and listening through which people explore common ground and grow to understand each other and share a worldview

When initiating strategic conversations, communication champions use a variety of channels and forms of message composition to persuade and influence members, establish credibility, build goals on common ground, make compelling arguments, and connect emotionally with others. A channel is a means by which a communication message is carried from sender to receiver. Leaders have many channel options to choose from when communicating, including face-to-face interactions, telephone conversations, e-mail, instant messaging, the Web, the company's intranet, memos, addressed and unaddressed documents, and formal reports. These channels are classified based on the richness of information conveyed and whether the message is routine or nonroutine. Channel richness refers to the amount of information that can be transmitted during a communication episode and is determined by the ability to (a) handle multiple cues simultaneously; (b) facilitate rapid, two-way feedback; and (c) establish a personal focus for the communication (Trevino, Daft, & Lengel, 1990). The high-paced environment of corporate communication often requires extensive reliance on electronic communication despite the accompanying risk of losing human touch, which is the richest and by far most effective medium of communication.

Asking the Right Questions Rather Than Giving Solutions

Belasen (1999) suggests that solutions to adaptive challenges reside not in the executive suite but in the collective intelligence of employees at all levels, which underscores the importance of shared knowledge within an organization and its impact on the success and survival of organizations that are faced with conflict or change. Collective intelligence is a byproduct of the facilitation of organizational memory, learning, and the reframing of organizational knowledge-sharing strategies. For an organization to learn, it must be able to acquire new knowledge and update its memory with that knowledge. Organizational memory helps sustain the common beliefs and core values of the organization through the construction of shared reality and the development of organizational culture (Belasen, 2000). Boje (1995) further explores the concept of organizational memory by studying the impact of storytelling as a means for developing direction and cohesion within an organization. Michael Eisner, the former CEO of the Walt Disney Company, often employed the use of organizational memory as well as his innovation and relational communication skills to achieve organizational goals and meet the needs of both internal and external stakeholders. By reframing questions and organizational memory, managers can implement needed change without losing their organizational sense of identity.

When managers adopt a participative style in leading employees, they may find it easier to build trust and confidence in employees, establish norms for effective communication, and create a following that is loyal and supportive of the change effort (Belasen, 1999). Involving others in decision making that might shape the direction of working relationships and affect outcomes of work enhances employee commitment and positively effects productivity. Reframing is influenced by radical humanism; the way managers as well as employees ask questions is constantly being re-examined and tested.

Motivating Employees

The area of ER requires a communicator to be a motivator and to possess the relational communication behaviors and competencies that go beyond writing and editing the company newsletter. Wright's (1995) survey of communication executives demonstrated the significance of employee communication and personal relationships, especially at times of downsizing: the key to success in ER involves motivating employees and building relationships rather than disseminating information through formal channels. Communicative efforts to restore employees' trust and commitment are maximized when they occur in tandem with action. Ironically, despite these executives' perceptions, many organizations are still pursuing more traditional avenues such as employee newsletters and videos over relation-based activities. Corporate communication directors can use motivation to pitch such new activities as they develop a coaching and empowering style of management that draws more on quality of work life than on financial rewards. New tasks could include assisting with program development that fosters two-way communication, utilizing computer-mediation initiatives to receive feedback and distribute informational updates, and monitoring employee groups to make sure that communicative efforts are successfully heard and/or understood. Johnson (1992) details the elements of such motivating program development for employees, noting that a key factor is the face-to-face component. In the role of motivator, a corporate communicator needs to keep moving forward in order to bring employees together and provide them with relevant information that focuses on future activities and outcomes.

Corporate philosophy (or mission) energizes employees by building common ground between the company and its workers. Organizational mission helps to unify a company by producing a co-creation of values so that workers can achieve organizational goals and maintain strong internal and external relationships. Internalizing a corporate mission also aids employees in identifying with the organization; employees want to feel that they are making a meaningful contribution to the organization. The most productive organizations are ones in which individuals clearly understand the vision of the organization and their contributions to that vision (Belasen, 2000). Not only is it important to have a vision, but strong culture also needs to be sustained and core values articulated well. Organizational culture comprises the set of values, beliefs, understandings, and way of thinking shared by members. Culture provides employees with a sense of identity and commitment to a set of values and beliefs. Sharing implicit and explicit values encourages consistent alignment between employees and management. Encouraging effective vertical communication (i.e., superior-subordinate) helps facilitate understanding across hierarchical levels and align the organization in a means-ends chain of objectives.

Integrating and Assimilating Employees: The Role of Culture

Strong culture guides employee behavior as well as the organization's response to external demands and service to customers. When the environment changes frequently, the culture of the organization should embrace the values of agility and quick response as well as give rise to emergent networks of communication alongside flexible forms of structures and teamwork to match the needs of the environment. An important ER objective is to sustain a strong culture that provides effective internal integration and external adaptation. ER staff specialists commonly organize important events and ceremonies to celebrate employee accomplishments; storytelling and rituals that reinforce core values and reconstruct the shared meaning for employees often follow these ceremonies. Effective organizational leaders know how to communicate goals using symbols and metaphors that help connect employees with the current organizational ideology.

Cameron and Quinn (1999) developed a model for assisting managers and other change agents in making sense of their organization's culture. The model allows for a comprehensive cultural assessment that maps out the cultural profile of a target organization along the lines of four culture types (which are consistent with the dimensions and quadrants of the CVFCC): clan, adhocracy, market, and hierarchy. The predominant cultural type of an organization is identified by surveying employees' attitudes toward dominant organizational characteristics, leadership, management of employees, core values, strategic emphasis, and criteria of success. Cameron and Quinn's methodology, which includes a theoretical framework and a validated instrument, allows for the systematic diagnosis of an organization's predominant current and preferred cultures. Systematic cultural diagnosis is a necessary precursor to implementing effective change efforts. Assessments of organizational culture are useful because they help managers and organizations adapt to the demands of external environments and enhance organizational performance. An adaptation of Cameron and Quinn's model appears in Figure 8.2.

The *hierarchy* culture is characterized by a formalized and structured workplace. Rules and procedures govern organization members' actions. Leaders are good coordinators and organizers who help maintain a smooth-running organization. Value is placed on stability,

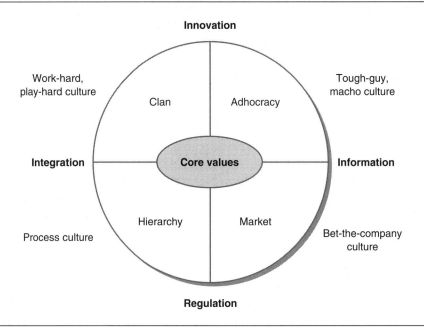

Figure 8.2   Four Types of Organizational Culture

SOURCE: Based on Cameron, K. S., & Quinn, R. E. (1999). *Diagnosing and Changing Organizational Culture*, New York: Addison-Wesley. Reprinted with permission.

predictability, and efficiency. The organization is oriented toward internal concerns and is kept together by formal rules and policies. The *market* culture is characterized by a focus on the external environment and transactions with external constituencies, including investors, business partners, and regulators. The organization is a results-oriented workplace. Leaders are hard-driving producers and competitors. Value is placed on competitive actions and meeting goals and targets. The glue that holds the organization together is an emphasis on winning. The *clan* culture is characterized by a workplace that is supportive and interactive. The organization dominated by a clan culture is like an extended family to members. Leaders act as and are thought of as mentors and even parental figures. The glue that holds the organization together is loyalty and tradition. Value is placed on individual development, high cohesion, morale, teamwork, and consensus. Success is

defined in terms of the internal climate and concern for organizational members. Finally, the *adhocracy* culture is characterized by a dynamic, entrepreneurial, and creative workplace. Organizational members are risk takers. Effective leadership is visionary, innovative, and risk oriented. Commitment to innovation is the glue that holds the organization together. Value is placed on being on the leading edge of new knowledge, offering products and/or services, being ready for change, and meeting challenges. Success means producing new and original products and services.

These types of culture are also consistent with Deal and Kennedy's (1982) typology, which is based on the dimensions of risk tolerance and feedback and rewards. Deal and Kennedy's cultural types parallel the CVFCC quadrants and are featured on the outside of the circle in Figure 8.2. The *work-hard, play-hard* culture fits with the clan culture and is characterized by a high commitment to work goals and an exchange of meaningful feedback about results and positive rewards. The *tough-guy macho* culture fits with the adhocracy culture, in which change and uncertainty lead to higher levels of risks (and stress, too!) and rapid feedback is needed to respond to the changing environment. The *process* culture fits with the hierarchy culture, in which a stable flow of feedback comes through procedures and formal communication. Because this culture thrives on stability and predictability, the flow of feedback is slow, and the rewards in this low-risk work climate are quite low. The *bet-the-company* culture is characterized by high risk factors and slow feedback and therefore fits the market culture. The organization goes through transitions in an attempt to reposition itself in the market, the goals and strategies are often long term, and the results (feedback) are often not known sometimes until the very last minute.

Mapping Culture in the Training Organization

The Training Organization (TO) employed 141 people in 2003 and had gross revenue of nearly $22.5 million. The mission of the TO is to bring the resources of training and development programs to federal, state, and local government agencies as well as colleges, universities, unions, foundations, and private organizations so they can develop their workforce through education, research, and evaluation. Since its inception in 1976, the organization has secured funding in excess of $298 million to help its partners meet their workforce development needs. The TO conducted more than 2,700 educational activities in 2002 and served a participant enrollment of close to 24,000. Of the 141 employees at the TO, approximately 134 provide professional services; the remaining employees serve in administrative roles. A director and two associate directors run the TO, each responsible for overseeing three of the organization's six middle

(training unit) managers. A third associate director is responsible for general administrative operations, including oversight of human resources, information technology, finance, and evaluation. Each of the six middle managers is responsible for one of the training units within the organization and supervises as many as 25 employees. The structure of the organization seems to indicate a narrow span of control. There are only three managerial levels, and divisions are aligned primarily in a vertical (silo) structure wherein communication and directives come predominantly from the top down. The goal of the communication audit was to examine the effectiveness of the communication processes currently in place and assist the TO in becoming a more effective organization.

Overall, the cultural diagnosis showed that all three organizational levels (though to varying degrees) preferred that the organization move away from the hierarchy and market culture types toward the adhocracy and clan culture types. Because the current cultural profile of the organization is rated as emphasizing the market culture type by top executives, and the hierarchy culture type by middle managers and first-line supervisors, all three levels demonstrated a belief that the organization requires a cultural shift in order to meet future challenges (see Figure 8.3 and Figure 8.4 for the current and desired profiles, respectively).

Cameron and Quinn (1999) emphasize the importance of reaching a consensus among managers and employees and having open lines of communication to accurately map out the cultural profile. Considering the results presented, one can see that organizational members, though not currently at consensus, have similar ideas for where their culture is and where it should be. But because there is some discrepancy between how top executives and the other two management levels view the current and preferred organizational culture, it is important for organizational members to decide what it would mean for their organization to move toward or away from a particular culture type.

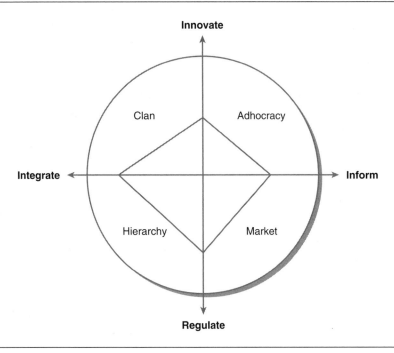

Figure 8.3   The Current Cultural Profile of the Training Organization

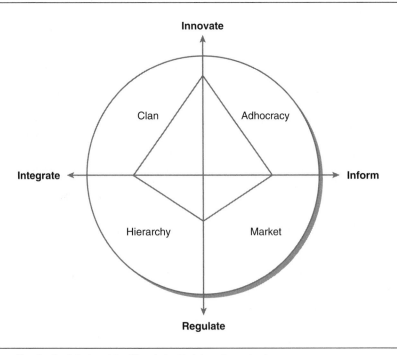

Figure 8.4   The Desired Cultural Profile of the Training Organization

More specifically, members of the TO also received the following suggestions:

- Review the organization's mission statement. Modify the mission statement to include the value of creativity within the organization. This may inspire individuals to look onward and outward and realize the importance of their individual contributions to organizational effectiveness.
- Create horizontal linkages across organizational lines. Establish task forces or other cross-functional units in an attempt to minimize the "silo effect" currently in place at the organization.
- Increase the value of participation. Allow more participation in the decision-making process. This should result in decentralization and a shift away from the hierarchy culture.
- Reward risk takers. Managers should inspire employees to come up with new ideas by developing high-risk tolerance. This will help develop trust in management.
- Celebrate and reward even the smallest employee improvement or success story. This will give employees a sense of worth and inspire more creativity and increased motivation among employees.

Avoiding the Trap of Knowing-Doing

Matching what managers say to what they do is critical for effective communication. Without a match of values in formal channels with values of practice, employee communication may be subject to "smart talk" that is difficult to understand, let alone realize. If what is said and what is done are communicated as different things, the hidden message that managers send will contradict the official message that is conveyed to employees. As a result, employees will have an adverse attitude toward change, begin to lose company loyalty and commitment, and start to feel insecure and confused about their work environment, consequently lowering employee satisfaction, morale, and retention. Instead, managers should convey their intentions and ideas through action and by communicating facts. When a change requires employees to do their job differently, that information must be delivered face to face, first in discussions among top executives and first-line supervisors, and then in conversations between the supervisors and employees (Larkin & Larkin, 1994). The right type of talk can inspire and guide intelligent action. Organizations that successfully create a culture that negates smart talk share five characteristics (Pfeffer & Sutton, 1999):

- They have leaders who know and do the work.
- Their leaders have a bias for plain language and simple concepts.
- Their leaders frame questions by asking *how*, not just *why*.
- They have strong mechanisms in place to make sure decisions are implemented.
- They believe that experience is the best teacher, and they view the process of doing as an opportunity to learn.

A significant amount of communicating practices and change in organizations is accomplished through the leadership of the CEO. Young and Post (1993) suggest eight principles of effective internal communication:

1. Having a chief executive who is a communication champion and manages by walking around

2. Having stated values and values in use that match consistently

3. Ensuring commitment to two-way communication by paying attention to upward communication

4. Emphasizing face-to-face communication

5. Sharing responsibility for employee communications

6. Communicating good and bad news—if reporting bad news is culturally valued and supported, then high ratios of bad news to good news will not hurt employee morale; in fact, reporting bad news in a timely and accurate fashion increases the credibility of good news

7. Knowing customers, clients, and audiences by paying attention to sender-receiver perceptual differences; communication staff must understand organizational issues, job demands, and how communication efforts affect all parties

8. Supporting employee communication activities

Positive Communication Relationships

Research shows that when employees can voice their concerns about work situations, employee dissatisfaction tends to decrease, and retention increases. When employees have the opportunity to speak out, they feel a sense of trust and openness, and they value their affiliation with the organization. Thus, organizations that provide employees with such opportunities (e.g., grievance committees, suggestion boxes, employee-management meetings, feedback programs) strengthen the relationships employees have with their managers. Employees expect managers to communicate not only what is happening but also why and how it is happening. Timeliness of information is important, too; employees want to receive current information and be updated regularly on changes and revisions to policies or instructions. Managers should communicate continuously and link the big picture with local issues and concerns. Employees want to know how the big decisions might affect their current work and job responsibilities.

Spencer (1986) studied turnover rates in hospitals and found a positive relationship between employee retention and employees' freedom to voice concerns. One could suggest that improving relations by providing mechanisms for open communication among employees can strengthen employees' perceptions of the organization's commitment to them. As Ledingham and Bruning (1998) conclude, positive communication relationships create win-win situations across organizational stakeholders. Other corporate communication products, activities, and perks aimed at effective employee relations include sign-on bonuses, paid training, on-site child care and laundry services, tuition reimbursement, flexible work week/flextime schedules, employee-of-the month ceremonies, free tickets to plays and sporting events, and holiday and service awards celebrations (Caplan, 2005; Challenger, 2006; Dominiak, 2006).

Retaining the best employees is an important goal of human resources (HR) and ER directors alike. If an employee has highly marketable skills, he or she may look elsewhere for more appealing compensation or even be recruited by a headhunter. HR departments face major challenges in recruiting and retaining employees; to foster better employee relations, HR must continually find ways to motivate, stimulate, and empower employees. To accomplish this objective, many corporate communication departments implement products and activities (i.e., perks). Such programs are important because they have the potential to create an empowered, loyal, and committed workforce. They can also help organizations build a positive image and a reputation as a desirable place to work, which is consistent with the objective of any corporate communication ER department. So how do ER staff foster good relations with employees? Some of the main tasks of ER include the following:

- Keeping managers informed of personnel policies
- Informing all employees about changes within the corporation

- Making sure that updated contact information is available
- Ensuring that training is available for staff as needed or as a way to increase a skill set

One organization that has been highly successful in employing and retaining a self-motivating workforce is the Costco Wholesale Corporation. According to a profile in *Workforce Management*, "treating employees well is as much . . . a part of the Costco way as the concrete floors and unadorned cinder-block walls of its warehouses and the fresh salmon fillets it sells by the truckload" (Rafter, 2005, ¶ 10). In addition to offering some of the best wages and benefits in the retail industry, Costco rewards employees with bonuses and other incentives. It promotes from within, encourages workers to make suggestions and air grievances, and gives managers autonomy to experiment with their departments or stores to boost sales or shave expenses as they see fit. As a result, Costco has an extremely low turnover rate compared to its competitors, and low turnover helps a corporation realize cost savings in the form of less training and more on-the-job hours.

Message Orientations

Rogers and Hildebrandt (1993) suggest that each quadrant in the CVFCC represents a different message orientation with significant parallels and polar opposites: relational, transformational, hierarchical, and promotional. Together, the four quadrants and their characteristics form a framework that illustrates some of the potential conflicts or competing values that a manager may experience in face-to-face or written communication. An adaptation of this model appears in Table 8.1.

In the field of business communication, conventional rules tend to stress power writing and focused results (i.e., the end product), and build on informative and persuasive messages. A typical management directive is evaluated on seven criteria (the seven Cs); the message is expected to be complete, concise, considerate, clear, concrete, courteous, and correct (Rogers & Hildebrandt, 1993). The effectiveness of written communication is thus judged more in terms of its impact (Did the message accomplish its intended objective? Was the stated goal clear enough? Persuasive?) and less in terms of the process of writing (Was the argument well presented? Supported with evidence? Well documented? Mind stretching? Stimulating?). A good example comes from planning and goal-setting theories (e.g., management by objectives). The primary emphasis of these theories is on the development and articulation of clear goals and objectives that are SMART: specific, measurable, assignable, realistic, and timely. And although the literature on developing management skills tends to emphasize the importance of active listening, interpersonal communication, and public speaking skills, it is clear that writing skills and message formation are also important.

Managers must consider not only the explicit messages (i.e., substance) but also the intrinsic characteristics of the source of information both upstream (where it comes from) and downstream (where it goes). A successful ER staff specialist who has been promoted to an administrative position can use the CVFCC diagnostically to adjust his or her message orientation based on systematic feedback received from supervisors, peers, and subordinates. The diagnostic model also can be used to identify the *collective* (predominant) approach used by corporate communication staff.

Mapping Message Orientations

The mapping process focuses on written and spoken managerial messages and communication transactions at four levels: relational, transformational, promotional, and hierarchical. The sample for this study was a health-care provider with an elaborate administrative system that

Table 8.1   Primary Message Orientations and Characteristics

Innovate

Relational	Transformational
Purpose: establish credibility, rapport, trust	**Purpose**: challenge receivers to accept mind-stretching vision
Medium and tone: conversational, familiar words; inclusive pronouns; personal examples; honesty	**Medium and tone**: visionary, charismatic, vivid, colorful metaphors and symbols; oral delivery; enthusiastic, emphatic, unorthodox written communication
Focus: receiver-centered	
Examples: informal chats; cafeteria talks; reflective listening; personal, supportive communication; reinforcing feedback	**Focus**: idea-centered
	Examples: CEO speech, written strategic plan, smart talk
Hierarchical	Promotional
Purpose: provide clear directions to receivers	**Purpose**: promote an idea, sell a product or service, persuade receivers
Medium and tone: neutral, precise words; procedural, controlled, sequential, standard constructions; factual accuracy; structural rigor; logical progression; realistic presentation; conventional documents; concrete examples; lists; tables; audit reports	**Medium and tone**: decisive, engaging, original, supported by credible evidence, prepositional, assertive, declarative, vivid examples, sense of urgency
	Focus: argument-centered
Focus: message-centered	**Examples**: sales presentations, recommendations to senior managers, press releases, directives
Examples: policy statements, procedural specifications, rules	

Integrate (left)   *Inform* (right)

Regulate

SOURCE: Based on Rogers, P. S., & Hildebrandt, H. W. (1993). Competing values instruments for analyzing written and spoken management messages. *Human Resource Management Journal, 32*(1), 121-142; Alan T. Belasen (2000). *Leading the Learning Organization: Communication and Competencies for Managing Change*, p. 61, SUNY Press. Reprinted with permission.

included several managerial levels, professionals, and support staff. The goal of this assessment was to identify possible blind spots and misalignment between intended managerial communication and the context within which the message has been created and delivered. Using a survey methodology, responses were compiled in a spreadsheet, and the average was calculated for both "now" and "preferred" responses (see Table 8.2).

The average scores for Now (current) and Preferred (desired) were plotted onto a spider graph (see Figure 8.5) consisting of 12 axes, each representing one of the message orientation characteristics listed in Table 8.2. (Four of the message features—aware; innovative; practical, realistic, informative; and accurate—span two of the message orientations and mark the main axes of the graph). These 12 axes form quadrants, each representing one of the CVFCC categories.

Table 8.2   Results of Message Orientations

Message Orientation	Characteristic	Now	Preferred	Perceptual Gap
Relational-Transformational	Aware	5.85	6.42	0.57
Transformational	Emphatic	4.54	5.23	0.69
Transformational	Insightful	4.54	5.58	1.04
Transformational-Promotional	Innovative	3.81	5.12	1.31
Promotional	Engaging	4.15	5.27	1.12
Promotional	Action-oriented	5.23	5.54	0.31
Promotional-Hierarchical	Practical, realistic, informative	4.91	6.13	1.22
Hierarchical	Organized	5.19	6.42	1.23
Hierarchical	Precise	4.77	6.31	1.54
Hierarchical-Relational	Accurate	5.08	6.31	1.23
Relational	Plausible	5.20	6.28	1.08
Relational	Honest	5.15	6.38	1.23

By plotting the Now responses and the Preferred responses onto the same profile, we can easily look at the two and suggest areas of improvement for the organization based on perceptual gaps that exist between how employees view messages and how they prefer the messages to be.

Generally, when using the CVFCC, researchers focus on scores in which the difference between the averages of Now and Preferred total two or more points. Any perceptual gap of less than one point is typically dismissed because the characteristic is seen as already being close to its ideal state. Figure 8.5 shows that the respondents seemed to be happy with the overall state of messages in their organization as reflected in the average score of 4.87 (Now), as compared with 5.95 (Preferred). The respondents in the sample viewed the relational and hierarchical orientations to be generally more important than the transformational and promotional orientations. This may be because these orientations are responsible for establishing credibility, generating trust, ensuring factual accuracy, and encouraging realism, all of which are necessary message features in the business environment of the health-care institution.

It appears that the respondents were expressing a desire to receive the best possible directions for completing the tasks assigned to them. The respondents seemed to be saying that although the organization was currently doing a good job in presenting hierarchical messages (4.98 out of 7), there was room for improvement because these types of messages are so important. The respondents felt the most drastic change in the hierarchical orientation was needed with regard to the "Precise" characteristic (representing a 1.54-point gap between the Now and Preferred scores). In the relational category, "Honest" and "Accurate" each produced a gap of 1.23 points. Although both received high scores in the Now column (5.15 and 5.08, respectively), they were each perceived as crucial to the employees. The promotional quadrant, on the other hand, involves messages that use facts and credible evidence to support arguments in favor of the ideas being promoted and might be quite creative in order to hold the attention of the message receiver. Promotional messages are centered on prepositional, assertive, declarative, or up-front recommendation statements. These messages are fashioned to persuade the message receiver to take action on the subject being promoted. Although the employees' overall assessment of the promotional quadrant showed little need for

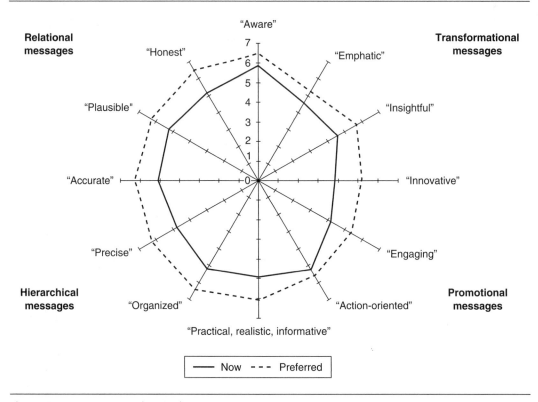

Figure 8.5 Current and Desired Message Orientations

improvement, the message feature that had the most significant request for change was "Innovative."

Most of the communication at the health-care institution is transmitted electronically, through e-mail, intranet, or memos. These methods of communication may contribute to the perception that vivid words, colorful seman-tics, and symbolic comparisons (all indicative of transformational communication) are of less importance. These types of communication fea-tures may be hard to convey through electronic means, or they may be viewed as inappropriate in the business setting. However, in looking more closely at this orientation, "Emphatic," "Insightful," and "Innovative" drew particularly low scores on the Now scale. In fact, "Innovative" drew the lowest score of all 12 fea-tures in both the Now (3.81) and Preferred (5.12) responses. The relatively large perceptual

gap (1.31, the second highest of all features) signals a strong need for change.

In addition, the reliance on e-mail over face-to-face communication made it difficult for feedback to remain current. Free-flowing two-way communication is beneficial to supervisors and subordinates alike: Subordinates get clear information and have the opportunity to pro-vide feedback, and supervisors gain employees who have a stronger sense of belonging and are therefore more committed to the organization. The area within the hierarchical quadrant that employees indicated needed the most improve-ment was "Precise." Face-to-face communica-tion could also be beneficial in sending more precise messages because it gives employees the opportunity to ask questions and receive feed-back more quickly and thoroughly than via electronic communication. The organization's employees said that e-mail provides them with the information about what is going to happen, but seldom explains why. It is also important for supervisors to remember that different people are better with different types of messages. For instance, some people learn better through oral instruction and others through written instruction; therefore, it is essential that both types of communication be used to reach all members of a team. Even if messages are originally sent via e-mail, they could be reinforced through face-to-face communication. If it is not feasible for all employees to meet personally with managers, it might be possible to have representatives conduct personal meetings with management and report back to others in a face-to-face setting. Two-way communication between managers and subordinates in this institution was insignificant and typically occurred only during performance appraisal meetings. Although publications such as bulletins, newsletters, and memos are useful and informative, relational messages may be improved if management delivers some messages to lower level employees in person. First-line supervisors also reinforced this idea by stating that people become upset at times because information from upper levels takes so long to reach them. This type of delay is attributed to a lack of communication across organizational lines, in this case between the first-line supervisors and the middle managers.

A Diamond Model of Interactions

An effective communication system encourages positive relationships between employees and employers and employees and customers (see Figure 8.6). Information sharing is the main tool that enhances the relationship between employers and employees; information empowers employees to do their jobs better and more effectively. It is important to open the channels of communication to allow employees to ask questions and be informed. Gathering information from employees makes employers aware of their personal needs

and helps employees get satisfactory solutions to their problems. Communicating a company's shared vision and establishing a shared mission with employees also foster employee commitment; they feel a stronger sense of job satisfaction when they agree with the overall direction of the company and when they are involved in shaping decision-making processes. There are two aspects of sharing information: (1) gathering information from employees about their needs and expectations, and making that information usable, and (2) sharing information that the employees need and getting their feedback.

Employees' needs and expectations typically evolve around their personal goals and interests as well as their career and professional goals. For employees who want better development in the workplace, the employer could provide work that best suits an individual's particular interests. For those employees who have personal difficulties, the employer could offer some flexible policies regarding work and family issues. When the employer recognizes and responds to employees' needs for greater balance in their lives, employees develop loyalty for the organization that respects them as individuals, not just as workers. This process of gathering information can be conducted through periodical surveys and face-to-face interviews.

What kinds of information do employees need? They need to receive feedback about how well they meet expectations—relevant information feedback about personal performance, company performance, organizational goals, and managerial attention to employees' job concerns. Different types of information can have different effects. Knowing how managers evaluate performance gives employees a sense of whether they meet managerial expectations. The company should try to make information accessible and up to date and can do so through various means, including conducting weekly meetings, updating information databases, offering information on employee manuals, and encouraging informal interaction between employers and employees.

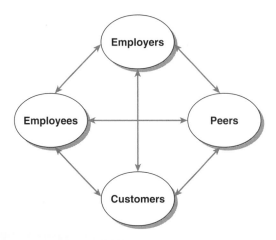

Figure 8.6   Diamond of Interactions

Enhancing employee productivity through opportunities for job rotation requires cooperation between employees in different departments. Coworkers need emotional and technical support from each other in order to realize their career goals. Employers can improve relationships between coworkers through company-wide activities such as camping trips. As relationships improve, the level of communication will increase. Employers should also reward teamwork by recognizing the efforts of all employees who contribute to a successful project. Doing so fosters a cooperative spirit among coworkers. In addition, employees can assess their own performance from communication with customers and improve the quality of their work accordingly. Managers can contribute to this improvement by providing more opportunities for employees to communicate with clients using formal and informal channels, including banquets after finishing a project.

Managing for Organizational Integrity: The Social Contract With Employees

By creating a supportive work climate, managers strengthen ER and the organization's reputation. A social contract with employees can be built into the behavioral expectations and code of ethics that guide managerial decisions, and it can serve as the governing ethos for all members of the organization. Effective ethical guidelines complement the quality-control system by establishing acceptable norms of behavior that are consistent with organizational policies and operating procedures. First and foremost, corporations need to keep their employees active, engaged, and involved. Such initiatives as total quality management, quality circles, and open lines of communication (horizontal, vertical, and diagonal) keep employees honest and engender loyalty and a sense of personal commitment. Second, companies need to practice exemplary leadership and encourage personal responsibility in their employees. Leadership is not bound by organizational levels; everyone has the potential to lead, and leadership means taking personal responsibility for actions. When employees are given opportunities to account for work results, they are more apt to think twice before they act. Third, companies need to build ethics into the fabric of their organizations. Establishing a code of ethics that all employees, including management, must follow is a good starting point. This code of ethics should be integrated into the company's mission statement and permeate daily decision making. Employees should be trained, and ethical policies and procedures should be enforced. A whistle-blower's hotline could be used to discourage unethical behavior. An ethics officer or an ombudsman can be appointed to oversee and enforce ethics and policies, as well as to discipline offenders. As a final defense, independent audits should be conducted to review all company books. Fourth, companies must adhere to social responsibility. They must cultivate internal and external trust.

Organizational stakeholders should develop trust in the strategic intent and the efforts taken by the organization to meet its ethical goals. Stakeholders need to buy in, too, in order to engender loyalty and commitment. According to Sharp Paine (1994):

> Managers must establish compliance standards and procedures; designate high-level personnel to oversee compliance; avoid delegating discretionary authority to those likely to act unlawfully; effectively communicate the company's standards and procedures through training and publications; take reasonable steps to achieve compliance through audits, monitoring processes, and a system for employees to report misconduct without fear of retribution; consistently enforce standards through appropriate disciplinary measures; respond appropriately when offenses are detected; and take reasonable steps to prevent the occurrence of similar offenses in the future. (p. 110)

Companies that operate with an integrity strategy model of leadership in mind—that is, the conception of ethics as the driving force of their enterprise—hold themselves to a more robust standard. The integrity strategy is broader, deeper, and more demanding than legal compliance. It almost ensures that a corporation will survive common pitfalls that result from ethical gaps. Leaders cannot have a narrow and personal focus on the goals they want to accomplish, but rather they need to take into account how their decisions will affect everyone involved. Establishing a strong corporate culture means having an important purpose, a predetermined plan, decision-making processes, people with

integrity, and a place where people can share preconceived notions of correct behavior.

Although the first important step involves establishing all of these things, it is even more important to follow through and enforce what has been established. When human risk is involved, corporations need to create goals that are not only in compliance with the minimum legal standards but also above and beyond the legal limits and what is expected of them from stakeholders. Setting higher standards helps to create not only a culture of socially responsible behavior but also a higher degree of respect and integrity from the corporation's stakeholders. *Corporate accountability* has become an important catchphrase due to recent scandalous behavior from top corporate executives, and the sooner corporations emphasize the importance of accountability in their social systems, the better these organizations will function in the long run.

FedEx

Federal Express (FedEx) is an organization that appears to have an effective ER communication system that values, motivates, and empowers employees. The company's culture, core values, and decision-making processes were created and revolve around employees, and it expects every employee to work hard and give 100% every day. In return for employees' hard work, FedEx implemented and created programs aimed at empowering and rewarding them. In 2006, *Fortune* and the Great Places to Work Institute (2007) recognized the company as one of *Fortune*'s "100 Best Companies to Work For." FedEx was also recognized as one of the 10 most diversified companies. Its founder and CEO, Frederick Smith, attributed the recognition his company received to FedEx's People-Service-Profit (PSP) philosophy, which represents the culture, vision, goals, and mission of the ompany. The first *P* represents the importance of motivating and empowering employees;

S represents FedEx's commitment to high reliability in service quality; and the second *P* represents the belief that when the company puts employees first and lives up to their expectations, profits should follow (FedEx, 1995–2007).

The programs that FedEx implemented for employees include the following:

- Survey Feedback Action is a program for employees to give and receive feedback from their managers; it is conducted every April. It operates both horizontally and vertically through the company.
- Leadership Evaluation and Awareness Process is a program to improve leadership and retention within the organization; it evaluates and encourages employees who want to move into management positions.
- Bravo Zulu and Golden Falcon Award are recognition and reward programs that acknowledge the actions taken by employees who provide outstanding service to customers.
- An Open Door program allows employees to submit questions or complaints about any work-related issue. Employee submissions are routed by the ER department to the proper management member, who must respond to the employee within 2 weeks.
- Communication channels (print and broadcast programming) are in place to share information with employees.

It can be argued that staff responses to such initiatives can positively affect the achievement of an organization's goals, which underscores the use of different communication channels in addressing employees' concerns and influencing the pattern of interactions within an organization.

Summary

Chapter 8 completes the circle of corporate communication functions, as depicted by the CVFCC, by covering important employee relations issues. ER staff specialists use strategic communication across organizational lines to help incorporate various perspectives and inform employees about initiatives and policies that might affect their quality of work life. This function has become especially critical in the face of the equivocal future of many employees' jobs and the state of the economy since the early 1990s; the demands on employees have increased significantly, and the need to address, value, and retain employees is more important than ever.

Review Questions

1. Explain how corporate philosophy (or mission) can help energize employees. Search the Internet for examples of corporate missions, and identify the similarities and differences among them. What is the main purpose for crafting a mission statement?

2. Trace the communication products and activities of ER departments in one or two organizations. Describe the focus and importance of these communications.

3. Suggest ways to foster better ER in organizations. How would you reduce a potential conflict between hidden and official messages?

4. How is the CVFCC helpful in explaining the variety of ER roles and activities?

Hanover Software

Jan Barry, a recent graduate of the Tuck School at Dartmouth, was driving home from work in her Q45 listening to more depressing news about layoffs at a major computer firm. She had just left a meeting with her boss, Bob Morse, the vice president of human resources at Hanover Software. "Jan, we are going to have to let some of the old-timers go. I'm hoping that the CEO will buy my plan for a voluntary severance and early retirement package. We should be able to smoke out some of the deadwood in this company as well."

Now a billion dollar-operation, Hanover Software had never laid off anyone in the 10 years of its existence. As the director of employee communications, Jan would be responsible for telling employees about the new policy within the next couple of days. As she looked at the beautiful Southern California Hills surrounding the freeway, many thoughts were going through her head. How should she frame the issues involved for all employees? Should she get the people in corporate communications involved? Who would be the best person to release the information? What about communications with other Hanover constituencies?

Hanover Software Background

Hanover was started by Madeline Bernstein, a brilliant, young UCLA graduate, following her graduation from college in 1983. With only $10K in capital borrowed from her father, Bernstein had built the firm up into a billion-dollar powerhouse through the development of two successful software products. One was called Passages, a spreadsheet used by virtually everyone with an IBM personal computer. The other major product, called Keystone, was a piece of software that Bernstein herself had created especially for the investment banking community.

As the business grew, Bernstein gradually turned the day-to-day operation of Hanover over to professional managers, preferring young MBAs from top eastern business schools. But the original group of employees, mostly men in their mid-50s, still represented the bulk of senior management at Hanover.

By the early 1990s, analysts were predicting that the software industry in general and Hanover in particular were ready for consolidation. Many of Hanover's competitors had trimmed the workforce repeatedly since the stock market crash in 1987. But Bernstein felt that keeping all of her employees happy through good times and bad was more important than anything else.

In a speech that Bernstein delivered to all of Hanover's employees in 1991, she outlined the company's philosophy toward employee turnover: "You, the employee of Hanover, are the most important asset we have. Despite the difficult times this company faces, you have my assurance that I will never ask you to leave for economic reasons. This is not General Motors!"

Corporate Communications at Hanover

That company relied on a small staff of public relations professionals to handle its communications efforts. All of the various activities that could be decentralized (such as employee communications, investor relations, etc.) were housed in the appropriate functional areas. This developed naturally as the company grew to become one of the largest software developers in the United States.

The young owner/chairwoman/CEO enjoyed lots of attention from the press as a result of her meteoric rise in the business world and her association with prominent Hollywood celebrities. She relied on an outside consultant, Todd McEwen, to handle her own public relations; he also had a tremendous amount of influence over the communications department of the company itself.

(Continued)

(Continued)

The vice-president of corporate communications, Cary Blandings, was actually one of the several employees who would be affected by the current plan to trim the workforce. He had been hired early on as a favor to Bernstein's father. Blandings had spent 25 years at the *Los Angeles Times* before signing on at Hanover. The problems associated with Blandings made the communications effort more difficult for both Jan Barry and the outside counsel advising her through the process.

The VSI and Early Retirement Program

Although the CEO was very much against the two programs that were about to be implemented, she had been convinced by both Morse, the head of human resources, and her board of directors that something had to be done right away or the company itself would be at risk. The way the programs would work, several senior managers would be told about the generous voluntary severance or early retirement packages and asked to avail themselves of the appropriate plan. Thus, a director who had received less than stellar performance appraisals for two consecutive years would be a prime candidate for voluntary severance while a vice president approaching 60 would be offered the retirement package. Although both of these programs were "voluntary," the supervisors responsible for identifying candidates were urged to get the right people to sign on immediately.

Communicating About the Plans

Barry reported to work the following day and was asked to attend a meeting with her boss, Bob Morse, Bernstein, and Todd McEwen. "Well, Jan, how are you going to pull this one off?" joked Bernstein. "Quite honestly, Madeline, given your position on this issue, my feeling is that you need to get involved with the announcement tomorrow," responded Barry.

As the discussion progressed, however, it was obvious to Jan Barry that she was the one that her boss and the head of the company wanted to take the heat. After two hours, Bernstein looked at Jan squarely in the eye and said, "This was not my idea in the first place, but I know that we have no choice but to adopt the voluntary severance packages and early retirement plans for Hanover Software. Unfortunately, I need to leave the country for a conference in Brasilia the day after tomorrow. You and Bob are going to have to run with the ball this time."

Jan looked over at Bob. He was gazing at a drawing on Bernstein's wall. It was a picture of someone poised to lose his head during the French revolution. Somehow the tableau seemed very appropriate to the current situation.

Case Questions

1. Evaluate the CEO's decision to leave the country and delegate the announcement about the voluntary severance and early retirement to Barry.

2. Use Figure 8.2 to describe the culture at Hanover Software.

3. What are Barry's options? Draw on Table 8.1 to develop a communication plan that supports these options using appropriate message orientations.

4. Use the CVFCC (in Figure 8.1) to examine the steps that Barry should take to proceed with implementation.

SOURCE: From Argenti, P., *Corporate Communication*. Copyright ©1993, New York: McGraw-Hill. Reprinted with permission.

PART D

External and Internal Communication

9

Marketing Communication and Corporate Advertising

Marketing communication is the collective theme for all communication functions used in adding persuasive value to marketing or delivering products to customers (Kitchen & De Pelsmacker, 2004). Marketing communication occupies the north pole of the CVFCC, and although its predominant emphasis is on markets and products, it also overlaps with key management communication interfaces (see Figure 9.1). Thus, marketing communication has an important role in driving the corporate message both externally and internally as well as aligning corporate image with social identity. In many ways, marketing communication supports the institutionalization of the organization by rationalizing its existence through corporate advertising and by legitimizing the outputs of the organization through branding management. Organizations can institutionalize corporate identity through various management communication initiatives, such as newsletters and magazines, employee surveys and taking action as a result of the feedback, a structured training program, clarification of roles and responsibilities, the development of links with management to hear information face-to-face,

and informal opinion leaders and local managers who deliver messages externally and validate information internally at workplace sites. These initiatives may encourage a two-way communication process. For this reason recent developments in the field have also included the use of Integrated Marketing Communication (IMC).

Integrated Marketing Communication

Schultz and Kitchen (2000) developed a four-stage integrated marketing communication (IMC) model that includes (a) tactically coordinating generic promotional activities, (b) more specifically tailoring communication to customers' needs by redefining the scope of marketing communications, (c) applying segmentation strategies to the application of information technology and databases, and (d) scanning and monitoring performance outcomes and linking financial and strategic goals. Although most firms use their capabilities to attain the goals of a and b, very few are operating at the more progressive stages of c and d. According to Duncan (2002), IMC is a

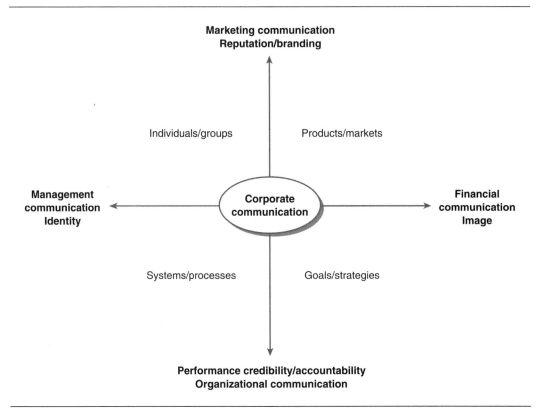

Figure 9.1   Competing Values Framework for Corporate Communication: External and Internal Perspectives

process for managing the customer relationships that drive brand value. More specifically, it is a cross-functional process for creating and nourishing profitable relationships with customers and other stakeholders by strategically controlling or influencing all messages sent to these groups and encouraging data-driven, purposeful dialogue with them. Kitchen and De Pelsmacker (2004) suggest that IMC become a strategic driving force while it is being implemented.

Southwest Airlines

An excellent example of IMC in action is Southwest Airlines. Its emphasis on customer service tailored to the individual customers and their problems or questions does much to differentiate the company from its

competition. Its self-proclaimed customer-oriented messages appear everywhere:

> Call us traditional, but we elect to steer clear of the chat-style, respond-on-demand, quick casual format and focus on meaningful Customer dialogue. This is not because we don't care. It's because that style counters our . . . commitment to Customer Service. Our Customers deserve accurate, specific, personal, and professionally written answers, and it takes time to research, investigate, and compose a real business letter. We answer every letter we receive in the order it arrives, and we streamline in order to keep our costs low, our People productive, our operating efficiency high, and our responses warm and personal. (Southwest Airlines, n.d., ¶ 10)

Whereas its competitors "farm out" ticket sales to popular travel sites like Orbitz and

Expedia, Southwest does not ask that users seek airfare from anyone but the company itself. Customers can purchase tickets either over the phone or through Southwest's Web site, which typically offers "Web fare" discounts on a continually updated basis. Additionally, customers using the DING application are notified electronically of upcoming airfare deals. This application is a marked difference from the competition, in that Southwest literally sends airfare prices to a consumer's computer desktop, versus the consumer having to actively shop for the best deals, potentially visiting half a dozen different travel sites in the process.

Visitors to Southwest's media Web site can read about what sets the company apart from the competition in the "SWA in a Nutshell" memo. They can learn about how founders Herb Kelleher and Rollin King essentially formulated the plan for the business on a cocktail napkin, and how they've been operating profitably for 35 consecutive years. Readers can learn about "positively outrageous service" (e.g., vice presidents helping ramp agents load bags). And they can discover that Southwest Airlines has been included on *Fortune*'s list of America's Most Admired Companies since 1997. Readers further learn that

> besides being smart, efficient, and dedicated, Southwest Airlines' 31,000+ Employees are "required" to be one more thing—FUN! Humor is an essential element of Southwest's success and this attitude comes straight from the top. Herb Kelleher, our Fun-LUVing, off-the-cuff Chairman of the Board, has (among other things) dressed up like Elvis, given out whiskey with airline tickets, and settled an industry dispute with an arm-wrestling competition. It is from such unique leadership that our extraordinary corporate culture has evolved, and the motto "We take the competition seriously, but we don't take ourselves seriously" has been fully embraced. Employees routinely dress up and decorate offices for holidays, tell silly jokes, and even *sing* in-flight instructions to our customers. (SWA in a Nutshell, n.d., p. 1)

Sustainability

Marketing communication has significantly increased in value as global markets have become more interdependent, with companies using creative distribution channels to reach their customer bases. In addition, rapid change and having to respond to multiple stakeholders has led many companies to scale up their MR activities, intensify their PR efforts, and use extensive corporate advertising and direct marketing to manage their brand image. Although PR and marketing communication are viewed as distinct corporate functions, they also have many important similarities and complementary relationships, primarily cultivating favorable perceptions toward the corporate image among key audiences and stakeholders. Indeed, PR has emerged as an interactive medium of communication, promoting mutually beneficial relationships between an organization and its various stakeholders. These relationships must be sustained through open and symmetrical communication aimed at building a strong public corporate image.

Issue Management and Corporate Advertising

A common means used by marketing and PR experts to proactively advance the company's interests is *issue management*. It is an effective way for organizations to expose their identities to the public and tackle issues that the public considers important. More important, it is a way for an organization to deal with issues that have the potential to affect the organization negatively. Thus, the purpose of issue management is to enable the corporation and its surrounding environment to live in harmony. The passive dimension of issue management is to avoid the occurrence of public policies that are hostile to the corporation's operating goal, and the active dimension is to implement public policies that are beneficial to the corporation's development.

Propagating the issue is crucial because it allows the corporation to create an accurate picture for the public and attain the support it needs for its action. Issue management involves four steps: (1) defining and collecting competitive intelligence about the issue, (2) identifying and analyzing the sources of the issue, (3) drafting the strategy and taking action, and (4) evaluating the result (Heath & Nelson, 1986). Corporate communicators often use advertising to propagate their viewpoints about the focal issues among different stakeholders (Heath, 1997). Corporations can manage an issue through advertisement and often through the agenda-setting function of media. The common assumption of agenda setting is that mass media have the ability to influence the visibility of events in the public's mind; therefore, mass media can determine what people think and worry about.

Through advertising, a corporation may convince the public that it has a positive attitude toward important issues and generate public concern about issues that are positively related to its corporate identity. For example, the mission statement of The Body Shop is "To passionately campaign for the protection of the environment, human and civil rights, and against animal testing within the cosmetics and toiletries industry." The company positions itself against animal testing in its advertisements and makes great efforts to convince consumers that using animals to test cosmetics is cruel and detrimental to the environment. As a result, reading The Body Shop's advertisements causes consumers to think about the issue of animal testing. The Body Shop is a good example of highlighting a specific issue, which will be a benefit to the corporation, and gaining public attention for the issue by a continuing advertising strategy. Another good example is Tatung Company, which was founded in 1918 and headquartered in Taiwan. From 1951 to 1953, the company made a series of advertisements to convey the idea that the best way to enrich the country is by encouraging the industrialization of the private sector. This public issue forced the

government of Taiwan to raise customs duties on foreign products in order to protect local industries. In 1962, diplomatic relations between the United States and Taiwan broke, and the people in Taiwan passionately embraced patriotism. At that time, Tatung Company used the slogan "Native goods are the best" to persuade the public that using native goods was a kind of patriotic action. It successfully advertised the issue and led its business through a remarkable recovery as the public began a shift toward consumption of domestic products. Both The Body Shop and Tatung Company are examples of successfully exerting the media's agenda-setting power to make particular issues emerge. Corporations can use advertising to create public concern about an issue, and once the issue is under the spotlight, more and more media will report the issue and reinforce the public's concern.

PR and Corporate Advertising

Marketing communication integrates a number of organizational interfaces, including surveying and using the psychology of consumer behavior to design creative messages that influence buyers' perceptions, and it uses advertising to enhance the company's reputation and credibility. PR, on the other hand, mediates between the press and management but also uses corporate advertising as a form of "paid PR" to augment the positive image of the organization. PR staff use advocacy advertising, corporate newsletters, public opinion surveys, and media outlets to publish the official stand of the organization and legitimize its activities. PR staff specialists strengthen the outside-in perspective of an organization through its managed relationships with various internal and external stakeholder groups (Gaywood, 1997). Singh and Smyth (2000) point out that PR is increasingly being viewed as a strategic management function, as evidenced by the fact that 60% of senior PR staff (who participated in a survey conducted by the authors) reported directly to the CEO, managing director, or chairman.

Some companies, however, outsource their external affairs to PR agencies that specialize in relationship management—the function that uses communication strategically. Others handle the relationship management function through MR units, which focus on the increasingly integrated fields of marketing, advertising, PR, broadcast management, and other marketing communication practices and strategies such as media planning, media buying, evaluation, and execution.

Nonprofit Organizations

Nonprofit organizations provide goods and services when government often fails to respond to particular groups' preferences or meet constituents' demands. Nonprofits have fund accounting, budgetary control, and financial reporting requirements that are different from those used by commercial entities or for-profit organizations. For example, when donors or sponsors give large sums or contributions with restrictions that outline how the money should be allocated, nonprofits establish fund accounting with tracking and reporting systems to ensure that the associated funds are redistributed according to the specific requirements. Nonprofits have social and legal obligations to act in good faith and in the best interests of their sponsors and clients. Failure to demonstrate that restricted funds have been redistributed appropriately may have legal ramifications (e.g., termination of executives) and negative consequences, including a tarnished image and drying up of funds. Adhering to greater accountability and ethical behavior can help nonprofits increase their credibility and gain access to financial resources to support their activities. The large number of nonprofits competing for the allocation of scarce resources makes the task of sustaining a positive image and securing funds to support their activities enormously important. Although nonprofits often partner with the government (see the discussion about the American Red Cross in chapter 7), they also

seek to influence the government's plans and priorities through political activity, issue management, lobbying, advocacy, and persuasion.

Judd (2001) contends that nonprofit organizations face competition for funds, volunteers, and customers. The key marketing challenge, therefore, is how the organizations differentiate themselves to gain a competitive edge. Promoting their goods or services is particularly challenging when responding to diverse constituents with different interests and needs (see more in chapter 12). Advertising may not be the best marketing tool to use because the organization's constituents might consider it to be unethical and manipulative, or the organization may have limited finances or be unable to use advertising because of its laws or charter. Henley (2001a) agrees that it is more difficult to "sell" the work of nonprofit organizations, which is why a solid plan is required for successful marketing communication. Akchin (2001) suggests that the majority of nonprofits have not adopted a comprehensive marketing approach; instead they perform one or more marketing activities. A survey conducted in 1999 by the Maryland Association of Nonprofit Organizations (2002) illustrates that, although there are people in nonprofit organizations who are in charge of many marketing tasks, their marketing responsibilities are secondary to other priorities, and few have received formal marketing training. These organizations often view the marketing function in narrow terms, such as promotions.

The literature makes several noteworthy points about PR within nonprofit organizations. The first point addresses the importance of having a PR plan, but research shows that there is an overall lack of knowledge about communication concepts, campaigns, and campaign evaluation. Therefore, nonprofits need to educate employees and volunteers. The second point is that nonprofits do not make the most efficient use of their resources to promote themselves. Ensman (1993) recommends that organizations seek out personal stories and human-interest features to keep the media continually informed and for use in promotional materials. Much of the literature on PR discusses the nonprofit organization's relationship with its donors. The literature stresses how important it is for an organization to be knowledgeable about its donors in order to target prospects and direct relevant messages and literature to them. Nonprofits must find new ways of communicating with donors (for example, three out of every four baby boomers are online, suggesting that Web sites and e-mail are the new-fashioned means of progressive communication). One of the chief concerns that donors and the general public have about nonprofit organizations is the question of accountability. Organizations need to create dialogue with their public about this issue. Considering the negative publicity surrounding the American Red Cross involvement in the distribution of funds after the September 11, 2001 catastrophic terrorist attacks, organizations need to educate their public about their operational realities and respond quickly to media inaccuracies, misrepresentation, and misunderstanding (Carson, 2002).

Managing Organizational Constituencies

Gwin (1990) argues that stakeholder analysis is fundamental to marketing communication. The relationships with constituent groups are less formal in nonprofit organizations than in for-profit organizations. The nature of the nonprofit organization determines which constituent group is more relevant. A nonprofit's constituents or stakeholders include donors, service users, government regulators, managers, staff members, and volunteers. In practice, there is a hierarchy of importance among the constituent groups, but one person may belong to a number of stakeholder groups, and each group has different needs and demands. Developing a marketing plan involves listing an organization's constituent groups and researching their needs. Then, based on these needs, the organization

can develop strategies to simultaneously satisfy more than one group. The more focused the strategies, the better the marketing to the groups. Radtke (1998) suggests that a particular strategy is only effective if the organization has a relationship with or understanding of the intended audience. Researching an audience involves reviewing the media and relevant publications, such as census data, annual publications, questionnaires, interviews, and focus groups. Building a profile of an organization's audience gives that audience a human face and contributes to more effective message development. Henley (2001a) breaks down the constituent groups into internal and external stakeholders and recommends investigating an organization's competitors as well as its constituent groups. Furthermore, he argues that the organization's relationship level with its constituents is an important gauge, that is, the degree to which a group feels connected with the organization affects how receptive it is to the organization's marketing messages. See chapter 12, Stakeholder Analysis, for an extended discussion about organizational responses to constituent groups and further guidelines and tools for developing effective organizational responses to constituents' issues and concerns.

Marketing Communication in Nonprofit Organizations

Gallagher and Weinberg (1991) observe that nonprofits often have to market simultaneously to two different audiences: users and sponsors. They recommend that nonprofits take a proactive marketing stance (e.g., successful nonprofits anticipate and influence the direction of change, rather than passively letting change happen). Being proactive involves regular and systematic scanning of external and internal environments, for example, within the context of a marketing audit. An audit identifies user expectations or, more informally, monitors user interactions with staff members. Once an organization is aware of user expectations, it can decide whether it can meet the demands, in line with the organization's mission, and formulate communication strategies to modify expectations, if needed.

Henley (2001b) further proposes an integrated approach to marketing as the means to take advantage of limited resources. The first step is to have a board-approved written marketing communication plan, which sets out the organization's mission and specific marketing objectives and action points. This should be a working document that is used with members, staff, volunteers, and donors as a reference guide and an evaluation tool. The goals of the marketing plan are to increase the organization's connection with its constituents and to find the best opportunity to communicate its message. Some issues for nonprofits to consider when drawing up a marketing plan include which types of media are most appropriate to use with their audience; whether to communicate directly to constituents or through the mass media, volunteers, or opinion leaders; action timelines; and the budget, including cost-effective and creative ways to stretch the budget.

Marketing to Employees in Nonprofit Organizations

An effective marketing audit raises awareness of donors or sponsors' interests and needs in most organizations, especially in nonprofits. Gallagher and Weinberg (1991) note that sponsors often expect performance measures that are meaningful to them, but not necessarily meaningful to the nonprofit organization. Therefore, a nonprofit must work with donors or sponsors to raise their awareness of the organization's long-term goals and inform them about its plans to meet short-term goals. Judd (2001) argues that one of the ways that a nonprofit can differentiate itself from other organizations is to view its internal stakeholder groups (employees, board members, and volunteers) as a distinctive element of its

marketing activities. Many organizations are beginning to regard their employees as part of their overall marketing communication or part of their efforts to communicate their preferred self-image. The achievement of customer focus as a broad marketing goal is impossible unless people involved with the organization see themselves as being there to serve the customers. The organization's self-image of being customer focused can be contradicted by its internal constituents' messages to outside constituents (Cheney & Christensen, 2001). Therefore, the organization needs to institutionalize customer relations and promote concern for customers among all the people within the organization. Judd suggests that this can be achieved through recruitment, selection, and training of employees, board members, and volunteers, as well as developing customer-oriented performance standards to evaluate and reward people. Radtke (1998) argues that the only way for a marketing communication plan to be successful is if it has 100% buy-in from the entire organization. The language that an organization uses to persuade its internal constituents must resonate with them and their concerns; they need to see the connection between the marketing communication plan and the organization's mission, goals, and objectives.

E-Channels for Nonprofit Organizations

Online marketing opportunities have significance for marketing communication in nonprofit and public sector organizations alike. According to Baker (2001a, 2001b, 2001c), the most effective organizations on the Web engage Web site users in open dialogue and involvement, which can lead to lasting relationships. Baker recommends turning *visitors* to an organization's Web site into *friends* by, for example, producing online newsletters, conducting surveys and polling, asking for feedback on the site's content, asking people to share the content with a friend, creating an online membership program with benefits, providing a calendar of events, and highlighting testimonials. And Henley (2001a) suggests that e-mail is a practical and efficient way to maintain communication with constituents. However, Baker cautions that it would be necessary for the organization to respond quickly to e-mails (e.g., within 24 hours) to sustain good relationships. Wagner (1998), however, argues that nonprofit Web sites are neither eye-catching nor interactive enough due to the lack of funding and Web development skills. Wagner concludes that if nonprofit organizations want to develop a dialogue with their key public, they must think about how to raise the interactivity of their Web sites. Further development of information and communication technology (ICT) is needed in the public sector, for example, if Web sites are to be effective tools in federal and local governments' service delivery to citizens. Moon (2002) contends that government agencies are only at the early stages of *e-government*; only a small number have a proactive and strategic plan for the development of ICT, and relatively few have introduced active two-way communication with citizens or implemented service and financial transactions for citizens using ICT. For nonprofit organizations, two-way dialogue with potential donors requires interactive technology interface with donors, and not simply a "donate" button on an organization's Web site. Nonprofits need to invite public comments, questions, and criticisms about accountability to build donor confidence, and there is no reason this could not occur via the Internet.

Marketing Communication and Ethical Advertising

Ethics is an issue that has plagued the advertising industry for years. Advertisements inappropriately targeting children, bait-and-switch tactics, deceptive and misleading ads, and the use of *puffery* or exaggerated praise to attract potential buyers are common practices for making otherwise ordinary objects seem extraordinary. Although closely monitored by the Federal Trade Commission (FTC), advertising agencies continue to use subtle and unethical means of enticing their customers. The question is, do the creators of these advertisements have a social responsibility to create ethical ads?

It is interesting to note that the advertising industry as a whole, due to its protection under the First Amendment, has no industry-wide code of ethics. It does, however, abide by a code of conduct set forth by the Council of Better Business Bureaus (CBBB), which oversees, and takes action in response to, complaints registered by consumers. But the process is more punitive than preventative. Agencies are given free reign to create unethical ads; however, if someone complains, the ad may be destroyed. The FTC Act of 1914 gave the FTC full responsibility for regulating deceptive advertising and creating standards regarding acceptable and unacceptable advertisement, but CBBB does monitor all advertisements directed toward children. Advertisements are no longer merely ordinary testimonials displaying the product and its uses. Now, advertising agencies try to create ads that are "edgy" and memorable. Techniques such as using sex to market beer (Jernigan, 1997) have become increasingly popular, and with that newfound popularity has come much intense controversy. Key (1973) argues that advertisers use *subliminal seduction* to hide images within advertisements to influence potential buyers. The term *subliminal* refers to something that is below the threshold of consciousness; consumers register images of certain products in their minds and these images shape their preferences and purchasing decisions. They do so without realizing that they have seen the images, and advertisers take full advantage of this method to promote companies' agendas.

Although closely monitored, advertising agencies often find themselves the subject of increased criticism, and perhaps the most intense criticism involves the methods they use to entice customers, especially kids. Children's advertising is rightfully held to a different, higher standard. Attempts to deceive and persuade children to purchase unsafe or adult-intended products are illegal and immediately generate controversy and negative feelings. Yet young children, the hyper-consumers of the future, are increasingly the target of advertising and marketing because of the amount of money they spend themselves, the influence they have on their parents' spending (the nag factor), and the money they will spend when they grow up. In the United States the regular monthly allowance for a child between the ages of 7 and 12 is $29.10; children are earning more disposable income as time goes on. No wonder companies are trying everything they can to make their products appealing to children (Beder, 1998). A few years ago the only products that advertisers tried to sell to kids were toys and cereal. Now some car manufacturers are targeting children with online vehicle ads because of the influence that children have over their parents. Although completely banning online advertising to children is impossible, companies should have to adhere to regulations in order to get information to and from children (Lovstrom, 1998). Studies have shown that children simply do not have the capacity to understand the meaning of the advertisements. Until age 8 they cannot interpret the ads and therefore should not be targeted so aggressively.

Inappropriately targeting children in advertisements is not only unethical but can also be illegal. Perhaps the most famous case of unethical child advertisements is that of Camel cigarettes' Joe Camel campaign. Rather than look intrinsically at the already dangerous nature of its product, RJR Nabisco decided to capitalize on the fact that youth smokers were among its best customers. From this controversial truth was born a clever new advertising campaign starring Joe Camel as a cool cigarette-smoking mascot. As soon as the new campaign was kicked off, sales of Camel cigarettes rose significantly (Wayne & Connolly, 2002).

Boudreaux (1995) presents an interesting argument against puffery, stating that, although it is considered unethical by nature, the lawyers' claims about it are far more unethical. In other words, lawyers who help people file suit against illegal uses of puffery to sell products are the ones reaping the benefits of the situation. To prove that the practice is illegal, the plaintiff must prove that the advertisement itself is factually misleading the consumers it targets. Perhaps Boudreaux's most interesting claim is that if a law eliminated puffery altogether, product innovation would lessen significantly. He states that well-known products always have an advantage in the marketplace over new emerging products, so new products often resort to puffery in order to gain recognition and buyer approval. According to Boudreaux, if this advertising practice were illegal, people would not pay attention to new products and would remain comfortable with their old products; thus would product innovation as we know it disappear. When approached from this angle, is the elimination of puffery unethical?

Boudreaux's (1995) views on the frivolous nature of the lawsuits against puffery are reasonable. In this day and age, people sue one another and corporations excessively. Obviously if a claim is substantial and the advertising slogan used to sell a product does in fact violate law, then the claim should be made. The problem lies in that fact that most advertising claims are used to draw attention to the product, and any reasonable person knows this. By bringing suit against companies for such campaigns, people are only contributing to the already exorbitant compensation for their lawyers. Thus an unethical situation within another unethical situation is created. Should these lawyers take advantage of a situation in which the case is difficult to prove and the claim is clearly settlement driven?

Boudreaux's (1995) claim about these lawsuits resulting in the end of innovation has some truth to it as well, but one suspects that this claim is somewhat exaggerated. However, the facts supporting it cannot be ignored. People do always look to the product they feel most comfortable with. In order to rock the boat, advertising agencies must creatively attract those buyers who are so set in their ways. In addition to positioning and product placement, the advertising campaign is what really gets the product on the customer's radar. Puffery has been around for years, and although false product usage claims such as "cures cancer" are illegal, saying the product is new and "the best" is not. It is done to catch the eye of the consumer rather than to mislead him or her. If puffery were eliminated altogether, there is a chance that people might be enticed less and remain with their traditional product choices, thereby hindering innovation. The other side of this argument, though, is that most people do not buy products based strictly on the claims of greatness proposed by the advertisers. Any product of great importance, such as a new drug or an expensive appliance, is generally recommended by a doctor or salesperson. The decision to buy is probably researched more intensely, and a simple claim made by the company trying to sell the product is not always trustworthy. We should have more faith in the consumers' intelligence and allow a little puffery to remain in the advertising industry to prevent declines in product innovation and reduce frivolous litigation.

Advertising is a necessary element in society. Although more important to the companies attempting to sell products to consumers, advertisements act as a bridge between companies and consumers. Without advertising, the buying public would have difficulty comparing products and knowing when new products are introduced to the market. Yet unethical practices within the industry are destroying the trust formed between businesses and consumers. Trust requires that consumers have confidence in organizational promises or claims made to them (McCord & Richardson, 2000). By using deceptive advertising techniques, such as using illegal puffery or designing entire campaigns to inappropriately target underage customers, advertisers are slowly destroying that trust. With each unethical action comes a detrimental reaction not only to the company the advertisements promote, but to the advertising agencies themselves. If trust is lost, ads will be overlooked and doubted, and the system as we know it will fail. By being more aware and socially conscious, advertisers can restore trust and regain a positive reputation.

Summary

Chapter 9 describes marketing communication, which has significantly increased in value as global markets have become more interdependent with companies using creative distribution channels to reach their customer bases. Rapid change and having to respond to multiple stakeholders have also led many companies to scale up their MR activities, intensify their PR efforts, and use extensive corporate advertising and direct marketing to manage their brand image.

Review Questions

1. Provide examples that illustrate how corporate communicators use advertising to propagate their viewpoints about important issues.

2. Discuss how matching messages to consumer needs and integrating communication into a single clear and understandable message help increase the chances that marketing messages meet their objectives.

3. Examine ways to increase more ethics and accountability in corporate advertising.

4. Use examples to show how nonprofit organizations use Internet resources to communicate with external audiences.

Wal-Mart and Its Communications Strategy

From the beginning the Wal-Mart retail firm and its founder, Sam Walton, have been enormously successful. Sam Walton opened his first Wal-Mart discount store in 1962, the company became a public company in 1970, SAM's Club was rolled out in the 1980s and became super-centers in 1990s. Today, Wal-Mart is the largest retailer in the world and easily topped the latest Fortune 500 list of the world largest corporations in 2003.

Wal-Mart's success and its exemplary growth first and foremost within the US market has been attributed to the large size US market, founder Sam Walton's inspirational leadership, an associate-focused organizational culture, a capacity for reinvention and innovation, low cost operations, vendor partnering, an efficient logistics system, extensive internal communications, continuous merchandising, a customer service orientation and competitor inattention. But, one important and previously overlooked cause for Wal-Mart's phenomenal growth seems to be its communications strategy, which is linked to its corporate mission and identity of serving customers and the communities in which the company operates, and also enables it to reach its market objectives and cancel out opposition to its aggressive low cost strategy.

Wal-Mart is exemplary of the low-cost competitive strategy, and it has fine-tuned the low-margin, high-inventory turnover and volume selling practice that comes with it. Volume buying enables lower cost of goods, and the key, according to Sam Walton, "is to identify the items that can explode into big volume and big profits if you are smart enough to identify them and take the trouble to promote them." Wal-Mart demands vendors forgo all other amenities and quote the lowest price. And its retail strategy for capturing market share involves an aggressive carpet bombing campaign in which an area is chosen and competitors are challenged and eventually driven out by its low-cost strategy. The mega-retailer's low-cost strategy is, according to Thomas Zaucha, president of the National Grocers Association in the US, alarming enough to call "saturation bombing." Zaucha explains that "they [Wal-Mart] have the ability to come into a market with their super-centers, with their neighborhood markets, with their traditional Wal-Marts, and with clubs. I think there is a growing concern that not only do we have the potential for concentration, we have he possibility of [monopoly] power." "They are re-structuring the industry," according to David Rogers, a market consultant; "When you put that amount of store space in, you have to take an equivalent amount of floor space, and that is going to happen through store closings, isn't it? That's the brutal truth." The latest industry surveys in the US indicate that of all recent bankruptcies of supermarket chains, eight out of nine were heavily influenced by Wal-Mart's expansion strategy.

Of course, with such an aggressive low-cost market strategy, one would expect the Wal-Mart Corporation to run into fierce opposition from citizens, communities, the industry and the US government. But the retail giant has not, because of its sophisticated communications strategy that connects the retailer symbolically to the dominant ideologies of American life. Through the imagery of frugality, family, religion, neighborhood, community, and patriotism, Wal-Mart locates itself centrally on Main Street of a nostalgic hometown. This symbolism and imagery, carried through in all its advertising, in-store promotions, and staff communications, not only positively dispose shoppers but also "decouple" Wal-Mart from unfavorable outcomes of its low-cost strategy and its market success. These consequences include local retailers being forced out of business, small town opposition, accusations of predatory pricing and allegations about products being sourced from overseas sweatshop suppliers. It is noticeable in this regard that Wal-Mart, a hard-hitting low-cost firm, has received fairly little public opposition and shuns the limelight in recent anti-global demonstrations (that have instead targeted such companies as Starbucks and Shell).

In other words, Wal-Mart is able to couch its low-cost market strategy in terms that not only fit with its own customer-focused corporate identity but also are acceptable to consumers and the general US public—with language such as "Our aim is to lower the world's cost of living," "Our pledge . . . to save you more," "Our commitment . . . to satisfy all your shopping needs"—and that appease opposition to

(Continued)

(Continued)

it. This is done, as mentioned, by referring to retail symbolism of saving, family, America and patriotism, and community and hometown. Advertising flyers, for instance, present "plain folks" (as opposed to professional models), apparently ordinary people including Wal-Mart "associates," spouses, children, parents, pets, suppliers and customers, and devote an inordinate amount of space to community-oriented and patriotic topics, delving in places into philosophical monologues about American enterprise, friendly customer service and other topics. The general public that is exposed to such flyers is, because of its nostalgia and patriotism, likely to be favorably predisposed to them.

Stephen Arnold, a professor at Queens School of Business (Canada), and his colleagues observed that the symbolic presentation of Wal-Mart might be different from the objective reality. That is, Wal-Mart projects an innocent, homespun image of a happy community involving vendor "partners," associates and customers. The extremely rich weave of cultural-moral symbols upon which this interpretation is based, however, may have as much to do with Wal-Mart's communication strategy and its quest for legitimacy as it does with a true and profound community spirit. For example, in lieu of the "vendor-partner" persona, aspiring Wal-Mart suppliers wait long periods before meeting a buyer and are then squeezed aggressively for the lowest prices. Many goods, apparel in particular, do not display a "Made in the USA" label, and "Buy American" signs are found situated embarrassingly on racks of imported products. Furthermore, some have alleged that the goods are sourced at overseas sweatshops and that the low prices are a consequence of child labor. Newsgroups and Web sites have sprung up for disgruntled former Wal-Mart associates to vent their unhappiness (e.g., http://www.walmartworkers.com, http://www.walmartsuck.com). Wal-Mart is regarded by some as a wolf in sheep's clothing, and its communications strategy, which is closely linked to its corporate mission and has also successfully supported its low cost marketing strategy, may in such a view have been the instrument for constructing and legitimizing the sheep's costume.

Case Questions

1. What communications strategy has Wal-Mart followed? Would an alternative strategy have been more successful?

2. Why has Wal-Mart been so successful on this account, while other large firms with aggressive low-cost market strategies have been subject to public scrutiny and outrage?

SOURCE: From Cornelissen, J., *Corporate Communication Theory and Practice.* Copyright © 2004, London: Sage Publications, Ltd.

10

Financial Communication and Corporate Social Responsibility

The primary objective of financial communication is to promote the value, credibility, and reputation of the organization in order to achieve a favorable market image about its financial strength. Institutional investors and analysts receive a company's communications regularly, which help them evaluate the company's earning potential and its intention to materialize its potential and attain short- and long-term goals. This means producing and distributing financial reports and analyses regularly through annual meetings and quarterly distribution of mandatory reports, answering shareowners' questions and concerns, addressing long-term strategic issues with major institutional investors, and sending information to securities analysts and other Wall Street parties. The most direct objective of investor relations (IR) personnel is to limit stock price volatility and ensure that the stock price and the firm's market capitalization are appropriate for the earning prospects, the industry outlook, and the economy. Strategically, decision makers and communication directors must identify the complex set of values that are important to

institutional and individual investors and balance the corporate scorecard (e.g., financial and human assets, strategies and goals, systems and structures) with communication activities central to corporate growth and survival.

Whereas externally, IR personnel need to develop long-term relationships with influential shareowners and analysts, internally they have to provide top executives with accurate information about the company's image and how well it is perceived by shareowners. IR personnel play important boundary-spanning roles, assessing the stability of financial markets and their impact on the business's financial performance. They must be relatively permeable with regard to significant sectors of the market and industry, and they must have easy access to top decision makers to provide key input into the company's long-term strategies and growth goals. IR underscores the importance of activities designed to sustain reputable relationships with stockholders as well as the need to communicate these activities reliably and creatively to shape an image of a successful and credible organization. The larger and more important role of IR is to restore the confidence of financial markets and potential investors in the ability of the corporation to communicate honest information about its performance in a transparent and accountable way. Corporate managers and boards of directors are also required by government regulators and the Securities and Exchange Commission (SEC) to provide financial information about the companies they run to the public.

With regard to financing, most businesses rely heavily on the public, which, in turn, expects to be informed of the company's financial affairs. Keeping the public informed is an important management responsibility. Communication of financial information should be accurate, clear, and consistent. It should evolve into a system of accountability that enables investors to be more confident in the organization, thus enhancing corporate credibility and reputation. Companies with stained reputations are less likely to attract investors than companies with solid, reliable reputations. Reputation has more to do with direct experience than projected images, so constituents are more likely to trust and uphold a company's reputation. DeLapp (1996) discusses the key elements for a successful (proactive) reputation management program. First, know where you stand in the community and identify your current reputation. Next, develop a clear, consistent message that reinforces the projected reputation, and remember that reputation management is everyone's job. Furthermore, be visible on the big issues, and remember that you are only as good as your weakest link. Finally, enact a contingency or crisis-management plan so that if a crisis does occur, your company's reputation is less likely to be tarnished.

The recent corporate transgressions involving Enron, WorldCom, Adelphia, Quest, Global Crossing, Arthur Andersen, and others demonstrate the need for greater accountability of companies in following accounting principles and in communicating financial results. The latest conflict of interest between the convergence of government-insured commercial banks and the investment banks also shook up financial systems, forcing companies and IR departments in many of them to enact codes of ethics and develop communication activities aimed at rebuilding corporate character and restoring investor confidence. The Corporate Justice System established at Fannie Mae to investigate and adjudicate wrongdoers is one example of such a development.

The movie *Wall Street* depicts the story of capitalism at its best—or the best of the worst, if you will. In the movie, the nemesis, Gordon Gekko (played to perfection by actor Michael Douglas), triumphantly declares that "greed is good!" I wonder, to what extent, if any, is greed good? As a realist, one is hard pressed to agree with Gordon Gekko; however, as an ethical individual, one is bound to challenge it. In their book *The Ethical Challenge*, Tichy and McGill (2003) claim that one of the strengths of the free market system is that it emphasizes doing business ethically, a statement that is quite antagonistic in light of the recent corporate scandals and executive frauds that littered the corporate playing field. Let's look at some examples.

Enron: The Corporate Tactics

Warren Buffet (2002) once trumpeted, "You only find out who is swimming naked when the tide goes out" (Insurance Operations in 2001, ¶ 9). For Enron, the tide shifted in October 2001. Prior to that, Enron was widely heralded as the "the world's most successful energy company in that it was making an elegant leap to the absolute pinnacle—the biggest company in the *world*" (Flanagan, 2003, p. 53) and was easily the seventh largest corporation in America. How could such a Goliath fall so rapidly and without any ominous harbinger? One wonders if there was a corresponding David (in keeping with the "David and Goliath" story) that caused the arrogant giant to collapse. In fact, upon closer examination, it is clear that the cause of Enron's failure was simply its utter disregard for ethical standards.

In 1998, power officials in California stated that by 2000, there would be an acute energy shortage. A combination of inclement weather, relentless power consumption, a lack of new power plants, a botched deregulation scheme, and regulated consumer prices accelerated the onset of the energy shortage (Flanagan, 2003). Enron executives were not complaining, though; in fact, they had much to rejoice about. For one thing, California law imposed a ceiling of $250 per megawatt hour on power sold by in-state plants. However, if out-of-state plants supplied the energy, the ceiling was raised. And the price of power per megawatt hour in neighboring states was five times the rate in California. So Enron quite cleverly, though immorally, bought power in California and sold it to out-of-state buyers for a lucrative price. Another similar trading tactic employed by Enron, dubbed *ricochet* or *megawatt washing*, was to buy power in California at $250 per megawatt hour and ship it out of state to a friendly trader, who would then pass it back for resale in California at five times the original price and comfortably increase Enron's profit (Flanagan, 2003, p. 84). What about other stakeholders, primarily the residents of California? Enron's manipulation tactics looted Californians and created much anguish and fear. Summarizing the didactic in Confucius' *Analects* (Book 15), Donaldson (1996) advises people not to do to others what they do not want done to themselves. Enron clearly violated this notion. I doubt that any of the Enron employees would have approved of the company's dubious trading tactics if they had been California residents employed by another energy company. In fact, the "ethics of care" toward Californians was absent in Enron's actions. The issue of Enron's accounting fraud has been inordinately publicized and excessively analyzed; therefore the story will not be recounted here. However, the next section provides the details of how Arthur Andersen applied fraudulent measures to cover its unethical practices at Enron.

Arthur Andersen: Turning the Blind Eye

Accountants have long been in the limelight, perceived as someone "you could trust . . . to be honest and not make any mistakes" (Flanagan, 2003, p. 120). Indeed, most of us have trusted them with our tax returns and continue to do so. By 1978, Arthur Andersen was the largest professional services firm in the world, bringing in more than $500 million a year in revenue. It was also Enron's accounting firm and was paid about $1 million weekly. So when Enron blew up in October 2001, Andersen went into a panic (Flanagan, 2003). Stupidly and rather unethically, Andersen surmised that destroying the evidence—its auditors' stamp on Enron's financial statements—would make the firm nonculpable. In his book, Flanagan recounts that the blame for destroying the documents was placed on one low-level individual, David B. Duncan, who was Andersen's lead man on the Enron account. It is baffling to the masses that, to date, no top executive claimed responsibility for shredding the Enron papers. Thus, ironically, Duncan appears almost as a hero, insofar as ethics of responsibility is concerned; it disgusts many people to think that high-paid corporate executives would hide behind Fifth Amendment protection and the advice of their equally high-paid lawyers. It is hard to believe that a single low-level employee would have so much at stake in Andersen's downfall that he would act illegally, immorally, and independently on such a sensitive issue. It is a pity that despite upholding his moral belief, though late-coming, by admitting accountability, Duncan's name forever will be etched in the annals of corporate scandal as ignominious. For its actions, or lack thereof, Andersen was ultimately charged with obstruction of justice; however, the superordinate accusation against the firm should be one of immoral actions and lack of ethical judgment. For one thing, in helping

Enron on its misguided path, from the outset Andersen ignored the repercussions of its actions on one of its key stakeholder groups: the firm's partners. Most accounting firms are based on partnerships rather than being publicly owned. So those partners who retired years ahead of all these misdealings lost all their savings in Andersen. Where, then, was Andersen's ethics of care?

Botes (2000) differentiates between the ethics of justice and the ethics of care. The ethics of justice is a perspective by which ethical decisions are made on the basis of universal principles and rules, and in an impartial and verifiable manner with a view to ensuring the fair and equitable treatment of all people. The ethics of care, on the other hand, is a perspective in which the involvement of, harmonious relations with, and the needs of others play an important part in making ethical decisions in a given situation.

One important lesson we learn is that the Justice Department exemplified the ethics of justice. Knowing that the destruction of Andersen was not in the best interest of any of the stakeholders (e.g., the firm's partners, employees, creditors, the general public), the Justice Department strived to reach a deal that would save the firm from going to trial (Flanagan, 2003); clearly, all involved parties knew that a trial would find Andersen guilty. It was not until customers started to flee the firm that the negotiations started to deteriorate. Once the dust settled, the government got busy enacting new laws. The end result of all this was that the government established a new oversight board called the Public Company Accounting Oversight Board, which was given sweeping powers to set accounting industry standards for ethics and conflicts of interest.

Tyco: Stealing the Vanity

The story of Tyco is the pinnacle of corporate greed. One name that still emanates from the fall of Tyco is Dennis L. Kozlowski, the company's former CEO. With 250,000 employees in 80 countries, Tyco was heavily involved in aggressive takeovers of smaller, troubled companies and pruning the operating costs of the acquired companies by firing excess employees and top executives (Flanagan, 2003). Without regard to the human cost, Tyco believed in achieving a quick return to healthy, financial conditions. Little wonder that, with all its acquisitions, the company was growing by upwards of 30% a year. For example, when Tyco acquired ADT, the large security company, Kozlowski cut 1,000 out of 8,000 jobs, about 12.5% of ADT's workforce. As was the case with Andersen, Tyco completely and flagrantly ignored the ethics of care when it came to the employees. Financially it sounds injudicious, but to Tyco it made perfect sense because those costs did not appear until long after an acquisition was made. As a result, Tyco acquisitions looked highly lucrative in the short term.

At the apex of his years as Tyco's CEO, Kozlowski appeared as benevolent as a folklore king. As a member of the board of regents of his alma mater, Seton Hall University, he donated $5 million for a scholarship fund. Interestingly, at a ceremony thanking Kozlowski for his generous donation, the framed picture awarded to him fell, and the glass shattered to pieces. If one believes in fate, this could have been an omen of what was to follow. It was proven later that the donation came from the pockets of Tyco shareholders, not from Kozlowski. Sure enough, Tyco could have given Kozlowski some levity on granting generous gifts as part of maintaining the company's good corporate citizenship, but where were Kozlowski's ethics of truthfulness and full disclosure? In fact, he was completely comfortable with, and proud of, having Seton Hall go so far as to name a building after him. Sadly, even the university seems comfortable violating the ethics of justice by keeping the building name "Kozlowski Hall" (Flanagan, 2003).

Kozlowski was equally liberal in using company funds to pay for his personal expenses. He used Tyco's money to pay $13.2 million for two paintings by Renoir and Monet and $17 million for a duplex on Fifth Avenue in New York City. Furthermore, he tried to evade city sales taxes totaling about $1.1 million on those paintings. And what is even more outrageous is that he indulged in embezzlement and tax evasion when his compensation for a 3-year period totaled $332 million.

One outrageous accusation was that Kozlowski had diverted $242 million from an employee loan program to buy yachts, fine art, and luxury homes (Flanagan, 2003). Again, the ethics of care was nonexistent, but what more can one expect of an ignoble and unethical man? In 2002, the new Tyco CEO, Edward Breen, seized most of Kozlowski's physical assets, including the $17-million Fifth Avenue apartment. Sweet revenge, at last. Or one might just as well conclude that the ethics of justice had finally been served.

WorldCom: The Giant Falls

At the time of its full disclosure, WorldCom's was the biggest bankruptcy in American corporate history. That is a powerful statement that will lead many students and analysts to question the *why* and *how*, and it will make the unfortunate shareholders sigh in agony, begging questions of "if only." Where were WorldCom's moral values and ethical principles while it was atrophying? In this section, I focus on the causes of WorldCom's debacle from an ethical perspective. Before discussing the downfall, it is important to understand where WorldCom stood on a financial front. With assets of over $100 billion, it was once the second largest telecommunications company in America. Moreover, it was once the fifth most widely held stock in America, with tens of millions of mutual fund investors holding its stock. What started in 1985 as

Long Distance Discount Service, founded by four friends (Bill Fields, David Shingle, Murray Waldron, and Bernard J. Ebbers), turned into a telecom behemoth with a stock price that soared to $63.50 in 1999. The telecom industry and its investors were of the opinion that if they built the networks, the traffic and profits would come. In fact, in 2000 alone, telecoms spent billions on new equipment. Telecom was the next big thing that everyone was banking on, some for early retirement and some for earnings in the six- to nine-figure range. During this time, WorldCom was aggressively expanding by acquiring other companies, such as Advanced Telecommunications, Resurgens Communication Group, Metromedia-ITT, MFS Communications, and MCI (valued at $37.4 billion), to name a few. With all these acquisitions, WorldCom in effect became the nation's first fully integrated local and long-distance phone company since the breakup of Ma Bell (Flanagan, 2003).

Beginning in 2000, the demand for more telecom capacity began to slack off into single digits. The prevalent belief that the telecom industry's growth rate for the decade would be 20% was unrealistic. As cash flow decreased, so did the earnings; debt started piling up. As a result, stock prices started tumbling. Yet, by industry standards, WorldCom seemed to be defying gravity and was still strong. However, that would soon change. On March 11, 2002, the SEC's inquiry of WorldCom's accounting found numerous breaches. For one thing, WorldCom was counting its expenses as income. In addition, there were improper transfers of more than $3 billion in 2001, plus $797 million during the first quarter of 2002. This meant that WorldCom actually was losing money in 2001 and in the first quarter of 2002. After more revelations of accounting transgressions, it became apparent that WorldCom had misstated over $7 billion total. Although this fraud had been going on since 1999, Arthur Andersen, WorldCom's former auditor, had found nothing amiss (Flanagan, 2003). However, WorldCom was equally culpable. In *Business Week*, Ebbers proclaimed, "Our goal is not to capture market share or be global. Our goal is to be the No. 1 stock on Wall Street" (Barrett, 1997, ¶ 10). He supposedly viewed the investors and stockholders as the number one stakeholders, but in cooking the books, Ebbers cheated the very stakeholders he valued so much. Ebbers and WorldCom severely lacked even the basic ethical philosophy of the ethics of care in relation to the stockholders' well-being as well as the ethics of full and complete disclosure. The result of all this was that WorldCom's stock price dropped to pennies a share.

As with the executives at Andersen, it is sad to note that Ebbers was not mature enough to take responsibility for his actions, or rather his inactions, to uphold the ethical practices of the business. To the end, Ebbers professed that "no one will find me to have knowingly committed fraud" (Flanagan, 2003, p. 153). Whether he knew about WorldCom's accounting fraud is secondary in the larger context of responsibility and accountability. The more important issue is that it was Ebbers's responsibility to ensure legitimate accounting disclosure, and in the event of failure, as was the case, he should have held himself accountable for it. There are reports that Ebbers gave money to local charities, churches, a museum, and his alma mater, Mississippi College. But such charitable giving does not change the fact that by compromising his ethical standards at WorldCom, he jeopardized his reputation and, more important, tarnished the image and financial situation of the nation's second-largest telecom company.

Organizations around the world often struggle with various ethical issues and standards. For example, WorldCom maintained a positive image with regard to local charities but failed miserably in doing justice to its shareholders. Perhaps there is a need for guidelines that will prompt such corporations to stay on an ethical path. The globalization of today's business world has virtually dissolved national boundaries, leading to a new form of transnational organizations that operate like huge networks. One of the key factors in managing such an organization is to understand the diverse cultures that surround its many components. It is necessary not only to understand the cultural differences but also to comprehend local cultures' moral and ethical principles. The dichotomy between principle values in Western and non-Western traditions poses a bigger challenge to managers today than in the past. In Japan, for example, it is customary to exchange gifts, and it can be amusing for an American manager to get used to the idea of presenting gifts because the Western school of thought holds that accepting a gift can be like accepting a bribe. In Donaldson's (1996) terms, this reflects a lack of understanding of the cultural relativist's creed: When in Rome, do as the Romans do. Indonesians who are lax on accepting bribery are no better or worse than officials in Denmark who refuse to offer or accept bribes. On the other hand, some practices are clear violations of the ethical code. The Union Carbide case in India is a prime example.

Union Carbide

On December 3, 1984, operations went awry at a Union Carbide pesticide plant in Bhopal, India. Rapidly, a sequence of safety procedures and devices failed. Fugitive lethal vapors crossed the plant boundaries, killing 4,037 people and seriously injuring 60,000 more. In terms of human life lost, this was the worst sudden industrial accident ever. By underestimating the level of management involvement needed at the Bhopal plant to compensate for the country's poor infrastructure and regulatory capabilities, Union Carbide created a situation ripe for mismanagement and failure of safety systems. Rather than being socially responsive (do the best you can), Union Carbide was barely fulfilling its social obligation (meeting the legal requirement). In a networked transnational world, where criticisms of failure are swift, it is important for organizations to be on guard and to see that social obligation is fulfilled. One should refute the claim that divides accountability for this disaster into other spectrums—the Indian subsidiary, the Indian government, Bhopal officials, and others. For one thing, what is meant by "others"? Does it mean the innocent employees on duty or the operator, R. Khan, who violated instructions in the MIC processing manual? These breaches would never have happened if Union Carbide had had sufficient management operating in Bhopal in the first place. What is even more despicable is the company's disregard for the fundamental ethical principle of the protection of life (Loewenberg & Dolgoff, 1996). It was Union Carbide's decision to invest, for lack of a better term, in an impoverished nation and, being a behemoth global conglomerate, it was the company's duty to confirm that security devices functioned properly and in agreement with its American plants. One could only imagine the repercussions if this case had transpired in America. What is important here is not to absolve Indian officials but merely to point out Union Carbide's utter disregard for duty and responsibility.

However, Union Carbide did display empathy, and it upheld its social obligation in the aftermath of the gas leak. As soon as news of the Bhopal disaster reached the company's officials in America, they sent emergency medical supplies, respirators, oxygen (Union Carbide products), and an American doctor with extensive knowledge of methyl isocyanine, the chemical in the leaked vapor. I do not want to speculate about whether this reaction was intended as a face-saving activity or in fact as a fulfillment of the company's ethical responsibility. What is important is that Union Carbide sent help to its Indian subsidiary. The company's nearly 100,000 employees

displayed compassion by observing a moment of silence for the victims, canceling their Christmas party and setting up an emergency relief fund, thus upholding the ethics of care.

In such a complex world, it can be confusing to act ethically at all times. Exercising creativity by thinking out of the box helps. For instance, Coca-Cola has unfailingly refused requests for bribes from Egyptian officials but has managed to gain political support and public trust by sponsoring a project to plant fruit trees. Another example is Levi's solution to the problem of underpaid child workers in Bangladesh. Employment of children younger than 14 years old is allowed in Bangladesh, but it is a violation of Levi Strauss's corporate principles. Abolishing child employment in its Bangladeshi plant, however, would have had unfortunate implications: The children would not have had money to go to school, and more notably, it would have severely impacted the survival of the families who depend on the children's wages. So, after some deliberation, an agreement was reached. The suppliers in Bangladesh agreed to pay the children's regular wages, and Levi Strauss offered to pay for the children's tuition, books, and uniforms. Thus, by being more socially responsive, respecting the cultural relativist creed, and exercising moral creativity in ethical dilemmas, one can succeed in creating an ethical workplace. Today's complex transnational business models have further complicated ethical boundaries. To avoid Union Carbide's predicament, transnational organizations need to transcend cultural boundaries and be socially responsive companies rather than companies that merely fulfill the social obligation.

Financial Communication: The Sarbanes-Oxley Act of 2002

Companies like Enron and WorldCom found ways to manipulate accounting treatment of transactions, such as off-balance sheet activities. And auditors compromised their independence in trying to balance the pressures between their ethical values and audit fees, as well as other potential value-added services. There have been significant mandatory changes to the operation of public companies in light of such behavior. President Bush signed into law the Sarbanes-Oxley Act of 2002, which is designed to protect investors and restore public confidence in corporate accounting (Leone, 2003). The act addresses such issues as establishing the Public Company Accounting Oversight Board, auditor independence, corporate responsibility, enhanced financial disclosures, corporate and criminal fraud accountability, and penalties. The importance of corporate ethical standards is mandated by section 406, which states that publicly traded companies (i.e., issuers) must

> disclose whether or not, and if not, the reason therefor, such issuer has adopted a code of ethics for senior financial officers, applicable to its principal financial officer and comptroller or principal accounting officer, or persons performing similar functions.

Under the Sarbanes-Oxley Act, the SEC requires companies to file an internal control report with their annual report outlining management responsibilities for establishing and maintaining adequate internal controls as well as its conclusions about the effectiveness of those controls. The company's auditor must attest to management evaluation. The New York Stock Exchange, meanwhile, proposed new corporate governance standards that, if the SEC approves them, would require companies traded on that exchange to adopt corporate governance guidelines and a code of business conduct and ethics for all employees. Accountants can help employers or clients navigate these new rules and create a code of ethics that complies with all of the requirements. Once SEC rules are finalized, Section 404 of the act will require publicly traded companies to file in their annual reports an *internal control report* that outlines what steps management has taken to establish and maintain

adequate internal controls and financial reporting procedures, as well as management's conclusions about the effectiveness of those controls and procedures, a report CPAs and corporate finance departments likely will have a hand in drafting. The report must include a copy of the auditor's attestation to, and reporting on, management's evaluation of these controls and procedures. Sarbanes-Oxley defines a code of ethics in broad terms, so if companies already comply they do not need to develop a new code of ethics.

What's different now that Sarbanes-Oxley is on the books? The new law puts more emphasis on financial reporting (particularly on its accuracy), which could translate into more responsibility for accountants. Also, Section 301 mandates that companies put in place a mechanism for employees to raise concerns, confidentially and anonymously, about financial reporting matters. The SEC's proposed rules for implementing Section 406 say that a company's code of ethics should identify the person or persons to whom employees should deliver these anonymous reports. Establishing a process for rank-and-file employees to confidentially report code violations is a critical component of any ethics program. Most companies that have already established such procedures assign a case number to each complaint or tip an employee makes so he or she can track its progress. In addition, the person to whom employees report alleged violations is generally someone outside the ordinary chain of corporate command (e.g., an ethics or compliance officer, an ombudsman) who nonetheless has access to the company's top executives and its board of directors.

The WorldCom case amply illustrates the perils of having employees report complaints to a top executive with routine corporate responsibilities. Internal auditors who uncovered the company's accounting fraud reported it to the company's then CFO, Scott Sullivan. The federal government now alleges that Sullivan instigated the fraud and attempted to block the internal investigation. WorldCom did not finally acknowledge, make public, and address the fraud until its vice president of internal audit, Cynthia Cooper, took damaging evidence to the company's audit committee (Pulliam & Solomon, 2002).

The challenge companies face—whether they create an entirely new code of ethics or reassess and upgrade an existing one to comply with Sarbanes-Oxley—is to draft a document that is not just decoration on the company bulletin board, but instead helps employees live up to the ethical standards demanded by investors, legislators, and regulators. According to Myers (2003), the correct approach is to bring together a multidisciplinary team from all parts of the organization (e.g., finance, sales, human resources, operations, marketing, executive) to draft a code, communicate its importance to employees, and then involve them in seminars to help understand how the code applies to them and their colleagues. One way to make a code of ethics come alive for employees is for corporate communication staff to plan training sessions that engage employees in discussions about real-life ethical dilemmas they might expect to handle on the job. Such training should also include debates and discussions of such questions as "Now that you know the company is in trouble and your boss is aware of this, what do you do?" Enron had a rigorous code of ethics, for example, yet fell victim to unethical behavior in part because its board of directors twice voted to suspend the code to allow the company's former CFO, Andrew Fastow, to launch business activities that created, for him, a conflict of interest. Ethics professionals warn against viewing educational programs as a once-and-done procedure. Ethics training is perishable. To deal with problems continuously means to avoid short memory lapses. Companies should schedule regular refresher courses for all employees.

Implementation Challenges

Implementing the Sarbanes-Oxley Act is an expensive, time-consuming, yet necessary piece of legislative action. In 2004, Financial Executives International surveyed 321 public companies, who said that "on average they expected to expend 12,000 hours of internal work, 3,000 hours of external work, spend an additional $590,000 in auditor's fees (an average increase of 38 percent), and an additional $700,000 in software and IT consulting, for a total of $1.9 million in first-year compliance costs" (United Press International, 2004, ¶ 4). Not only are the upfront costs of the act significantly high, but there are stiff penalties that apply if a company is not up to speed in time. For a serious violation of the act, a company can be fined millions of dollars. The deadline to file compliant financial reports for companies with market caps greater than $75 million is November 15; for companies with market caps less than $75 million, the deadline is April 15 of the tax year. One of the major personnel issues resulting from the act is that accountants in publicly traded companies must now dedicate their time to compliance, and thus spend less time on efficiently running a business. In addition, the managers of these accountants must spend time reviewing the compliance financial data, which may impede their ability to effectively govern a team. A number of observers agree that a financial director's time is best spent directing, not checking figures and signing documents to attest to financial validity. Another issue raised by the act is that companies are adding more financial experts to their boards in order to protect themselves from the new laws, but this may not be a good business decision; the consequence of such an action can detract from the strategic planning and development of the organization. In short, just because a company is compliant with Sarbanes-Oxley does not necessarily mean it is being led by a quality management team.

There are different perspectives on the Sarbanes-Oxley Act. One perspective is that implementation should be seen as more than compliance; it should be seen as a way to enhance financial credibility and increase business performance. Section 302 of the act requires executive certification, and Section 404 requires disclosure requirements in the annual report regarding the adequacy of internal controls. For executives to feel comfortable in certifying that they have a strong internal control structure that mitigates the risk of deficiencies in their processes, business operations need to be streamlined. It is important to recognize that operating departments, not just finance, need to comply with the requirement to establish internal controls. Good governance extends beyond the finance and accounting departments; operating managers and staff need to understand the importance of internal controls, particularly the consequences of improper recording and reporting of financial and operational events. A regular training and reinforcement program will promote enterprise-wide awareness, but will only be effective if it is built upon solid policies, procedures, and systems. Strengthening current processes and systems can assure management of the quality of certifications for years to come, because activities around certifications are recurrent and far-reaching. Sarbanes-Oxley has changed the regulatory environment for public companies; they need to invest time and resources in complying with these changes. Rather than fighting the increased demands, companies should use the act as a means to improve their business processes and view it as a path toward competitive advantages that produce tangible results.

Another perspective regarding the act deals with the burdens it imposes. Executives are worried that shareholders are going to be harmed by the amount of time that companies will need to invest in complying with the act versus applying, which will take away from efforts toward making profits and gaining market share. Also, it is feared that private companies will not be so quick to go public due to the added work involved in compliance (Valley, 2003). A major area of concern is Sarbanes-Oxley's requirement for executives' certification. Executives are in a position of high risk because the burden of the companies' ethics and accounting policies rests heavily on them. One way that they are gaining comfort regarding certification is to require all managers to certify their data or to require an "upstream certification of data" (Leone, 2003, ¶ 6). Doing so gives the managers a sense of ownership and ethical obligation. Even with the upstream certifications, though, the executives are still ultimately responsible. As a result, they expect higher compensation due to the increased risk and responsibility.

Enforcement

In an attempt to instill ethical values into their management and employees, public companies must now adopt a code of ethics, or if not, they must explain why. A number of companies have been widely recognized for the scope and quality of their ethics programs. Xerox makes ethics training a requirement for every employee, all the way up to the CEO. The Texas Instruments employee ethics handbook dates to 1961, and the company has received three ethics awards for its leadership in the field. Texas Instruments also provides employees with a business-card-sized pamphlet that serves as a quick test for workers faced with an ethical dilemma:

1. Is the action legal?

2. Does it comply with our values?

3. If you do it, will you feel bad?

4. How will it look in the newspaper?

5. If you know it's wrong, don't do it.

6. If you're not sure, ask.

7. Keep asking until you get an answer.

Forcing ethical conduct on a company will not necessarily make it an ethical company. Companies can respond to the Sarbanes-Oxley Act in two ways. They can complain about the costs and view the act as harming their market share because management efforts are being focused on complying with regulations instead of on making a profit. Or companies can view the fall of companies such as Enron and WorldCom as a learning experience and accept the change. They can use the implementation as an attempt to gain market share by strengthening their operations, placing more control on their processes, and becoming more efficient. Furthermore, the act should be used to enhance the company's business structure as opposed to being seen as something that will cause a loss in market share. The business and regulatory environment has changed dramatically. If a company already has streamlined processes and internal controls that mitigate the risk of deficiencies in processes, then there is little effect in terms of efforts to implement the act. If the company needs to work on establishing control points in the business processes, doing so will help it identify areas of improvement, which could in turn increase company productivity.

Executives signing a representation letter for their company are also expected to be accountable for every reporting unit within the company. It only takes one department to have an unethical manager. One way to ensure that department heads are trustworthy is through upstream certification. Requiring managers to sign the representation letter will make them more hesitant to do something wrong, knowing that they are attesting to the fact that they are unaware of any deficiencies or fraud. For the quarterly and annual SEC filings, managers have to sign a representation letter, which is provided to the CFO. Doing so gives the CFO additional comfort in the underlying data that are submitted in the SEC filings. Managers can meet with legal counsel to discuss what each representation in the letter means and who in the organization can attest to it, thus giving the managers ownership of and responsibility for the data.

Sarbanes-Oxley was necessary to enforce corporate ethical behavior and help restore public confidence in the accounting industry. There needed to be something to remind accounting firms of their independence; they always struggle between the time it takes to perform an audit procedure and what they earn on the engagement or the budget. Due to time constraints, accounting staff might not be taught how to audit, and/or they do not fully understand the company's processes, so they might "power tick" or merely document that the test work was performed,

when it really was not. Also, staff and management are trained to identify areas that could bring value-added services to the firm, which interferes with the auditor's independence because its staff might overlook an unethical accounting treatment if it will bring additional services for a lot more money than the audit ever would. Enforcement of Sarbanes-Oxley will help bring the accounting industry back to its roots by reminding it what its function is supposed to be. However, as Thomas Bell, president and CEO of Cousins Properties, stated regarding Sarbanes-Oxley's influence of ethical conduct in the corporate environment, "it's not going to create different ethical behavior because ethical behavior comes from here . . . [holding his hand against his chest]. Ethical behavior doesn't come from somebody forcing you to be ethical" (Valley, 2003, ¶ 8).

Summary

Chapter 10 covers the lower right side of the CVFCC (marketing management covered the upper right side). The primary objective of financial communication is to promote the value, credibility, and reputation of the organization in order to achieve a favorable market image about its financial strength. Institutional investors and analysts receive a company's communications regularly, which helps them evaluate the company's earning potential and its intentions to materialize its potential and attain short- and long-term goals. This communication activity often involves producing and distributing financial reports and analyses regularly through annual meetings and quarterly distribution of mandatory reports, answering shareowners' questions and concerns, addressing long-term strategic issues with major institutional investors, and sending information to securities analysts and other Wall Street parties. Recent executive frauds and corporate scandals have prompted important reforms regarding how companies fulfill such responsibilities and engage in ethical behavior.

Review Questions

1. Examine the long-term relationship between financial communication and organizational reputation. Do you think that self-regulation is sufficient in establishing accepted management responses to stockholders' concerns?

2. Trace the steps taken by one or two companies to implement the Sarbanes-Oxley Act, and draw some conclusions about the relative success of such implementation. What barriers did they need to overcome?

3. The case of Arthur Andersen, which was Enron's auditor and consultant, raises important questions about who is watching the watchers. Discuss.

CASE STUDY

Illinois Power and *60 Minutes:* Communicating About the Communications

During the late 1970s there was something of a standing joke throughout the business world that a visit from the crew of *60 Minutes* was destined to ruin your day, if not your career. And the nuclear power industry seemed particularly vulnerable to such scrutiny after Three Mile Island and the release of a presidential commission report on hazards. The following case examines how one power company in the Midwest handled its treatment by the press—specifically its coverage by one of the fifth estate's most important and ferocious watchdogs, *60 Minutes*.

Background

In the 1970s, the residents of the central Illinois communities of Clinton and Decatur had mixed opinions about building a local nuclear power plant. Unemployment was high, and Illinois Power Company provided local officials hope for an upturn in the economy. A new reservoir was built, the fishing was excellent, and, at the height of the construction, the company and its contractors employed over 3,500 workers.

At the time of the *60 Minutes* visit, national media outlets had brought the issue of nuclear power into a world spotlight. On the local scene, reporters frequently covered the Illinois Power plant's detractors. Stories of rate increases and construction overruns were frequent media items.

In late September 1979, *60 Minutes*, producer Paul Loewenwarter wrote a short note to Illinois Power asking if the company would participate in interviews about the high cost of building nuclear generating facilities.

Corporate executives met to determine Illinois Power's (IP) "attitude" toward the dubious distinction of such coverage, and exactly how to handle it. IP officials believed *60 Minutes* was intent on covering the story. Refusing to participate could leave negative impressions in the minds of 24 million viewers. What had interested *60 Minutes* producers was a briefing they had received from critics of the construction. Thus a refusal of coverage implied "guilt" by insinuation, and left no means to expose the company's position or to enable rebuttal. Interdepartmental memos cited the "less than unanimous" agreement among executives to cooperate, supported by the belief that CBS had demonstrated an "anti-nuclear" and "antibusiness" bias in the past. Nonetheless, IP officials decided to cooperate, and more than that, the company would make every effort to provide access and information for the story.

Illinois Power specified only one condition. The company would videotape everything shot by *60 Minutes* crews. For every minute of film shot, there would be corresponding videotape shot by IP in-house media staff. In return for IP's cooperation, producer Loewenwarter assured them that there would be "fair and balanced" coverage of the issues involved.

The research and information gathering phase of the story took place during September 1979. Harry Reasoner conducted a 90-minute interview with W. C. Gerstner, executive vice-president of Illinois Power, on October 9. The next day Reasoner filmed interviews with employees at the plant construction site. Then a number of phone calls between CBS staff and IP representatives finalized the story. The 14-minute segment aired on the November 25, 1979, *60 Minutes*.

Reasoner introduced the segment by stating:

> The American Nuclear Power program is in trouble. And not only because of Three Mile Island and the presidential commission's report on hazards. It's in trouble because of the cost of building the plants has gone crazy. A China syndrome of cost.

> Take Illinois Power, for example. It wants its customers to help pay for a nuclear power plant whose costs have gone up three times since the original estimates. If the customers don't pony up, the company's financial rating, their ability to sell bonds and meet their customers' energy needs is in trouble. We went to Clinton, Illinois. . . .

The story went on to describe proposed rate increases in order to cover costs estimated at $30 million per month. Interviews with former employees critical of the project provided examples of expenditures without incentives for cost controls. One former employee stated, "It's like Watergate. They've got themselves committed, they went into it and all of a sudden they've got a bear by the tail and they don't know how to let go." Comparisons with other nuclear projects were discussed, delays were cited, and the segment concluded with Reasoner stating:

> Illinois Power was proud that it met one critical milestone in its schedule, albeit a revised, updated two-and-a-half-year schedule. It installed its nuclear reactor vessel right on the new timetable and called out the media to witness it one balmy day in October. But the work to come is far more complicated, the kind that has caused mistakes and delays at most other plants, forcing them to fall behind schedule.

> Illinois Power insists that won't happen here. But if the charts are right, it will happen here. And costs will rise again. The thing is, someone has to pay for all that. That someone, of course, will be, one way or another, sooner or later, the customers of Illinois Power.

> But what Illinois Power and its critics have learned about nuclear power, if they have, is important to us all because all energy is going to cost a lot more, so much more that anything extra from lessons not learned is simply something we can't afford. From the standpoint of the utility company or its customers or a nation, there is no percentage in solving energy crises by going broke.

Illinois Power was appalled by the broadcast and received an immediate barrage of calls from employees, customers, and the press. According to one document on the aftereffects of the coverage, the response in the stock market was shocking. "By 10 AM on the Monday following the broadcast 10,000 shares had been traded and the price (was) beginning to slip. By the end of the day three times as many shares had been traded as ever before in a single day and the price had fallen something over a dollar. Our employee morale was suffering badly and the hate letters began to arrive from ex-stockholders and the public" (H. Deakins, A Summary of a CBS Visit to Illinois Power Company, p. 3).

The Company Response

The broadcast occurred three days prior to a decision on Illinois Power's rate case before the Illinois Commerce Commission. The case before the commission was a request for money, part of which would be used to help the nuclear facility. A negative decision would seriously damage company plans.

(Continued)

(Continued)

By 10:00 a.m. on the Monday following the broadcast, IP decided to make a rebuttal videotape. It was produced by IP's own in-house media staff, under the direction of the public affairs department. The objective of the tape and the accompanying print efforts was to "defuse" the impact of the broadcast and to "get the facts" to employees, press, the financial community, IP stockholders, and the general public.

Company officials viewed the CBS broadcast several times to decide which positions were, from their perspective, most erroneous and damaging. It was determined that the IP response should be relatively brief (45 minutes) and designed to correct as many of the "major inaccuracies" as possible. The response would compare the *60 Minutes* broadcast with the in-house video shot at the same time. The in-house video would feature a staff narrator to tie together segments and reinforce particular counterarguments. Completed one week after the original broadcast, the production also contained sworn testimony and exhibits from the ongoing rate case.

The program, entitled *"60 Minutes/Our Reply,"* was narrated by Howard Rowe. Rowe began by asking:

> What happens when a major TV network comes to town to do a news feature on the power company? Plenty! And not much of it's very pleasant, as we learned when Illinois Power became the target . . . on *60 Minutes*.

> On November 25th, the CBS new program *60 Minutes* broadcast a feature on the construction costs of the Clinton nuclear power plant. The program was the result of interviews conducted by CBS early in October. They came to Clinton, and to Decatur, at the urging of one of the opponents to Illinois Power's rate case.

> In line with our policy of providing all news media with the facts about our operations, the company agreed to cooperate fully with the producer, Paul Loewenwarter. He assured us, in turn, that CBS was going to produce a balanced, factual presentation of the economics of building nuclear power plants. We told him that we were going to film anything that the *60 Minutes* crew chose to film on Illinois Power property. This turned out to be a good idea.

> What we're going to show you is the complete presentation as it appeared on *60 Minutes*. But what we're also going to do is to stop from time to time and expand on those areas that *60 Minutes* edited out, presented incorrectly, or chose to ignore.

The video went on to refute, point for point, facts and conclusions presented by *60 Minutes*.

Public and private release of the IP tape began immediately. Distribution included video set-ups at locations where customers paid bills, presentations by field representatives to service and civic organizations, employee showings during work times, complimentary copies to securities analysts, and distribution to local media editors and publishers. Requests for the tape from utility groups and major corporations exceeded IP's expectations.

A copy of the rebuttal tape and an open letter to IP stockholders was sent to Robert Chandler, CBS vice-president and director of Public Affairs Broadcasts. In the letter to stockholders, the chairperson and president of IP, Wendall Kelley, quoted an official of Standard and Poor's Corporation as saying in commerce commission testimony that Illinois Power's management of the power plant construction project was doing "a good job." Kelley's letter stated further that the *60 Minutes* telecast was "yet another example of sensationalism in journalism at the expense of the facts of the matter." He then provided five specific counterarguments to the broadcast.

1. Harry Reasoner stated that Illinois Power scheduled only two weeks to complete the full-system tests that on similar projects take an average of 14 months to make. He concluded by saying that we planned to accomplish in two weeks what no other nuclear builder had ever accomplished in that time period. In the complete interview with Mr. Gerstner, Mr. Reasoner was told that the chart he was looking at was not a construction schedule; it was a milestone chart. Its purpose is to let the Nuclear Regulatory Commission know the approximate time during which the test is to be made. The particular test itself requires only three days to complete. In addition, the same chart Mr. Reasoner

was using on camera shows the testing of some seventeen sub-systems which precede the full-system test, are scheduled individually over a 25-month period prior to the full-system test. The fact is that our schedule is reasonable and attainable.

2. Mr. Reasoner stated that against other plans of similar design, Clinton cost overruns are well ahead of the pack.

   Mr. Gerstner showed Mr. Reasoner, on camera, a list of all seven one-unit boiling water reactor nuclear plants being built in the United States. On this list, Clinton had the lowest cost increase.

3. Mr. Reasoner made the flat statement that Clinton was the Company's first nuclear project and the first for our contractor, Baldwin Associates.

   During [the] *60 Minutes* visit to the Company, it was explained to them that Baldwin Associates was a consortium of four major construction companies: Power Systems, Inc, Fruin-Colnon, McCartin & McAuliffe, and Kelso-Burnett. It was pointed out to *60 Minutes* two of these companies, prior to starting Clinton, had worked on 14 nuclear projects. It would be difficult, you would think, to refer to all of that as "no nuclear experience," but that's what *60 Minutes* did.

4. The major points of the *60 Minutes* program were based on the comments of three former employees of either the Company or its contractor. Two of these men were fired for cause and the third resigned because he was not satisfied with a seven per cent pay increase. All were associated with the Clinton project for short times only.

   The most vocal of these critics also appeared as an "expert" witness in opposition to our recent rate case before the Illinois Commerce Commission. After he was cross-examined in regard to his testimony, the hearing examiner ruled: "The witness has not demonstrated that he is qualified by educational experience or work experience concerning the subject matter of his testimony and should not be permitted to testify as an expert and provide opinions or arrive at all of the conclusions which are contained in his testimony." *60 Minutes* knew of this ruling, yet chose to present him on camera to recite those same opinions and conclusions.

5. Lastly, it was stated on *60 Minutes* that even the usual neutral staff of the Commerce Commission joined in asking that the rate increase be denied. This was not true. Just three days after the *60 Minutes* telecast, the Commission, at the recommendation of its staff, granted us the major portion of the rate increase we had requested, including additional revenues to cover part of the cost of capital we have already raised and spent on the Clinton plant. (Letter from Wendell J. Kelley, chairperson and president, to the stockholders of Illinois Power Company, December 14, 1979)

Chandler, responding on behalf of CBS in correspondence to Kelley dated January 21, 1980, stated simply that neither the tape nor the letter to stockholders "persuades us that our story was unfair." His letter went on to state that *60 Minutes* had found two inaccuracies in their story that would be corrected on Sunday, January 27. Specifically, Chandler stated:

1. We stated that the 14% rate increase was attributable to the cost of the Clinton construction. We were in error; despite the Commission's assertion that "unquestionably, the driving force for the requested electric rate increase is the Company's need to generate revenue to support the construction of Clinton Unit #1," we should have said that only part of the increase was requested to pay for Clinton and the balance for general revenue purposes.

2. We also stated that the "usually neutral staff at the Commerce Commission joined in asking that the rate increase be denied." That is in error; we should have said that the staff recommended that that the cost of Clinton construction not be included in the electric rate base. In short, it recommended that the part of the increase attributable to the construction be denied. (Letter from Chandler to Kelley, January 21, 1980)

(Continued)

(Continued)

Chandler's letter addressed the issues raised in Kelley's letter to stockholders and in the videotape. His point-by-point analysis concluded:

> In sum, it should be clear that far from being "used" by your opponents in the rate case, we went to considerable lengths to get at the facts, which were and perhaps remain in dispute. In this letter I have cited at length from the Commission order because the commission itself had access to all arguments and data, and was highly critical of the Clinton project, in terms of overruns, schedules, and the credibility of your own claims. We did time our broadcast just prior to the decision and said so, because that decision was to address questions in which the entire country has a stake.

> There remains one final area of concern. I note that you take pains to point out to users of your videotape that the *60 Minutes* material contained in the tape is copyrighted by CBS and you proscribe limits on its use. While I appreciate your own concern and efforts to avoid the abuse of our rights by others, I am nonetheless obliged to point out that your own use and distribution of the material constitute in themselves an infringement on our copyright.

Illinois Power, in response to the CBS letter, performed an extended analysis of the letter asserting that CBS's admission of inaccuracy on "two rather insignificant points was entirely unsatisfactory." The 15-page document went on to identify what IP believed were nearly 20 specific examples of unfairness, inaccuracies, invalid and nonrepresentative comparisons, and misleading though technically correct comments. The analysis document contained a number of accusatory remarks concerning responsible journalism, calculated use and omission of selected information, and questionable ethics. The document concludes with a discussion of how difficult it was for IP to "accept the *60 Minutes* presentation . . . as balanced and unbiased journalism." Furthermore, IP consulted its attorneys, who advised that redistribution of the CBS broadcast within the IP tape constituted "fair use" as part of "comment and criticism," and not an attempt to profit by its use.

Harold Deakins, IP public affairs manager, attempted to correspond personally with Harry Reasoner of *60 Minutes* concerning the company's treatment at the hands of the program. Reasoner responded that the correspondence from CBS executive Chandler to IP chairperson Kelley accurately described his own position. Although Reasoner "personally" regretted the way IP officials felt about the coverage, he also stated, "I think we were fair." And "treatment of Illinois power as a strong example was proper and reasonable." Reasoner maintained the network position, citing cost overruns in the nuclear business as "horrendous and endemic" (Letter from Reasoner to Deakins, February 28, 1980).

Case Questions

1. What are the organizational communication issues in this case? Describe the responsibilities of both Illinois Power and *60 Minutes* to communicate with the general public.

2. Describe the various communication constituencies of Illinois Power. Specifically, consider stockholders, the general public, regulatory agencies, and the media.

3. Describe the various communication constituencies of a program such as *60 Minutes*. Specifically, consider the agenda-setting and persuasive roles of the *60 Minutes* story with regard to the general public and Illinois Power's stockholders and regulatory agencies.

4. How can communication theory help us understand what happened at Illinois Power? Consider persuasion theory, media effects research, the public relations literature, and general systems theory.

5. What would you have done if you were in top management at Illinois Power? At *60 Minutes*? Discuss the value and ethical implications of your choices.

SOURCE: From Walker, Kim B., "*60 Minutes:* Communicating about the Communications," in *Understanding Organizational Communication* by Pamela Shockley-Zalabak. Allyn & Bacon/Longman (1994). Reprinted with permission.

11

Organizational and Management Communication

Internal communication as a field of study has coalesced around two broad perspectives: a coordinative functional rule perspective and the theory of bureaucratic control, which essentially view organizations as mechanistic systems; and a humanistic perspective that views organizations as interactive systems evolving around the sociopsychological needs of organizational members. The rule approach was positioned by management and organization theory as an efficiency-driven, control-oriented ideology with a strong emphasis on the centralization of decision making and clear roles and responsibilities. Communication is viewed as the transfer of symbolic information. The function of human communication is the regulation of consensus in order to coordinate human behavior, and the structure of human communication comprises the code and network rules involved in regulating consensus (Cushman, King, & Smith, 1988). Communication is improved by following explicit rules that constrain the content and sequence of the messages transmitted. Rules are prescriptive social conventions or normative guidelines that regulate social interaction and help highly interdependent players in social settings coordinate actions and mutually adjust their behaviors by relying on consensus concerning how to solve mutual problems (Moemeka & Kovacic, 1995). Max Weber epitomized this approach by postulating that bureaucracies are organized according to rational principles. The strict hierarchy and unchallenged authority are aimed at achieving compliance and facilitating administrative change. Leaders in these organizations are viewed as naysayers, monitors, and evaluators, trading disciplined behavior and good performance for rewards. Ultimately the goal of such an organization is to promote the stability, accountability, and legitimacy of organizational actions.

During the late 1960s, under the pretense of social and economic change, managers increasingly confronted problems that bureaucratic systems seemed ill suited to handle. It was in this context that a discourse on organizational culture and employee commitment began to attract the attention of management consultants and organizational researchers alike. The common view was that an altered approach was needed to help managers create adaptive, more effective systems. Surprisingly, however, the rationalistic approach continued to dominate the thinking and practice of organizational leaders, and much of the success of modern organizations during the 1970s was credited to their ability to inscribe the lessons of experience in codified rule structures. The Neo-Weberian movement portrayed modern, complex organizations as rule-driven systems. Rules increase efficiency by reducing uncertainty and by connecting individual action to collective outcomes. Compliance is achieved through employees' self-policing and assimilation, and through clear and unambiguous communication. Message fidelity, the degree to which a message received is the same as the message sent, is the standard by which communication effectiveness is evaluated. There is no place for ambiguity, contradiction, or paradox within the bureaucratic organization because they would confuse the well-ordered structure.

Rule Theory: Rationalistic Approach to Communication

The rule theory is based on three metaphysical models or assumptions of behavior: motion-action, information-processing coordination, and creative-standardized usage (Moemeka & Kovacic, 1995). In the motion-action model, rational actors define problems, choose alternative means for accomplishing stated goals, critique their performance, self-monitor progress, and respond to existing or emerging practical or normative forces. The information-processing coordination model assumes that adaptive players in social interactions abide by a regulated consensus needed to achieve desired outcomes cooperatively. Organizational members build consensus about the meaning of information available to them; in some way, they shape or regulate their perception of what is possible and, by regulating the set of possibilities, move more efficiently toward a decision. The creative-standardized usage model replaces emerging communication processes that generate rules in

creative, ad hoc situations with more verified rules that offer greater uniformity and predictability. When standardized usage is employed, it signals a willingness by the transacting parties to participate in communication relationships. Further, it points to the existence of tacit (unwritten or unspoken) understanding about the appropriate ways to interact and achieve mutual expectations. It also sends a clear message that distributive solutions (e.g., compromise) are preferred to nonsettlements as soon as the creative-standardized usage of the code has been accepted by both parties, that the parties have shared responsibility to achieve these solutions, and that any deviation from the rules would subsequently trigger sanctions. Such situations are typically verifiable through measurement and are reinforced through socialization processes by which the rules involved in regulating consensus about the task at hand are internally monitored and corrected by those involved in the coordination task. Cushman (1987) summarizes:

> Thus, a pattern of behavior becomes empirically verifiable as rule governed when a mutual expectation regarding what is appropriate behavior in a given situation can serve as a standard to judge and evaluate (so that one has the right to expect certain conduct) and not merely an expectation. While habits are descriptive of human behavior, rules are evaluative of such behaviors and thus monitored by those employing the rule. (p. 227)

Three dimensions of functional communicative rules exist: (a) rule homogeneity, or distribution of the rule structure in a given population; (b) rule conventionality, or the level of agreement on the standardized usage; and (c) rule stability, or the time period in which the rule is sustained. Higher scores on all three dimensions indicate greater acceptance of the rule, in effect constraining the options available for parties engaged in communication transactions about standardized solutions. The rule theory thus is a reductionism theory in that it restricts human actions in coordination situations to those that conform to existing, normative rules.

The Humanistic Approach

Communication in the humanistic approach is viewed as the key mechanism through which structure is created. Communication not only allows the parts of the organization to run smoothly but also is the force that creates, maintains, and sustains the organization. The role of the leader in this view is also altered from that of a monitor who keeps track of what's going on to one of an evangelist who articulates the vision. Message fidelity is no longer the only standard for evaluating the effectiveness and appropriateness of communication. As a result, the possibility exists for appropriate and effective communication to be ambiguous, contradictory, and paradoxical. The philosophy behind the humanistic approach is that, free from the burden of being overcontrolled, with more autonomy and discretion over the outcomes of work, employees will synergize their efforts and perform with excellence. Participative management and pushing decision making down to lower levels appear to have helped many companies become innovative and flexible, transform cultures, use cross-functional teams, do well in environments of change, and even deal with crisis situations. Apollo 13 (see discussion in chapter 2) is an excellent example of how teams function within a professional bureaucracy that adapted the humanistic approach in running its huge projects. What is so interesting is that the traditionally hierarchical (and even militaristic) structure of NASA had to break into teams of practice in order to solve life-and-death problems (Tompkins, 2005).

A key factor for successful, effective management communication is instilling corporate culture values and beliefs in employees and mobilizing support for the vision. The most productive organizations are ones in which individuals clearly understand the vision of the organization and their contributions to that vision. Culture provides employees with a sense of identity and commitment to a set of values and beliefs, which in turn create an atmosphere that encourages and seeks consistent alignment between employees' needs and organizational goals. People want to have a clear sense of where they fit into the organization and what impact their work has on the organization as a whole. Strong organizational culture is associated with high organizational performance and high employee satisfaction. Members who accept core values have greater commitment and loyalty. A strong culture gives everyone in the organization a clear and focused vision. When communication is clear and ideas are understood, relationships, participation, and satisfaction increase. Open and free-flowing communication encourages and produces an environment where members can co-create meanings and realities and seek clarity when understandings are muddled. When management communication aligns with the organization's vision and when organizational leaders assume the role of communication champions, thereby building trust and gaining commitment to that vision, organizational members develop a shared reality and accountability toward the attainment of corporate communication goals.

Rationalistic and Humanistic Communication Roles: A Competing Values Perspective

Whereas the rationalistic approach appears to be consistent with the lower part of the Competing Values Framework (CVF) because of its predominant emphasis on transactional communication, performance, and control, the humanistic approach aligns more with the top half of the model, focusing on relational communication, people, and change. These differences reflect biases in managers' views toward people, actions, and situations. The CVF highlights the contradictory nature inherent in organizational environments and the complexity of choices that managers face when responding to competing tensions. These responses include a variety of managerial roles differentiated by situational contingencies. The CVF displays the repertoire of managerial roles by aligning pairs of roles with specific organizational environments. These roles are complementary, but those in the opposite quadrant are seen as competing or contradictory (see Figure 11.1). For example, the innovator and broker roles rely on creativity and communication skills to bring about change and acquire the resources necessary for change management. In the opposite quadrant, the monitor and coordinator roles are more relevant for system maintenance and integration, and they require project management and supervision skills. And whereas the director and producer roles are geared toward goal achievement, the facilitator and mentor roles are aimed at generating a motivated workforce driven by commitment and involvement. The key to successful managerial communication is recognizing the contradictory pressures on managers. Successful managers know how to navigate across roles to balance the demands from the different environments on the organization (Pounder, 1999). Effective managers are also perceived, more often than those perceived as less effective, as displaying the eight CVF roles. Gender differences do not change this conclusion: Men and women are regarded as equally competent (or incompetent) managers when assessed objectively by their bosses, peers, or staff in terms of how well they display the CVF roles (Vilkinas, 2000). High-performing managers display behavioral complexity that allows them to master contradictory

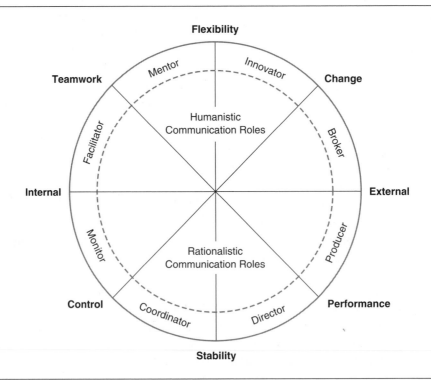

Figure 11.1   Competing Values Framework: Dimensions and Roles

SOURCE: Adapted from Quinn, R. E. (1988). *Beyond Rational Management*. San Francisco: Jossey-Bass. Reprinted with permission of John Wiley & Sons, Inc.

behaviors while maintaining some measure of integrity and credibility (Denison et al., 1995; Quinn, 1988).

The framework allows managers to identify their relative strengths and weaknesses through self-assessment or by measuring their perceptions about how well they perform the roles against the perceptions of others and, if necessary, taking steps to improve their deficiencies. Figure 11.2 is an example of self-analysis conducted by first-line supervisors in a service organization and direct evaluation by middle managers and top executives. Balancing the role behaviors across the CVF quadrants is important for effective communication. Studies show that when managers overemphasize one set of values (or play certain roles extensively without considering the other roles), they drift toward

the negative zone; consequently, the organization might become dysfunctional. In *Beyond Rational Management*, Quinn (1988) suggests that acquiring behavioral complexity could help managers avoid the consequences of the negative zone. Behavioral complexity involves (a) a conclusive command of the repertoire of leadership roles and (b) the ability to vary the emphasis on each role depending on the situation.

First-line supervisors appear to have a somewhat inflated view of their profile, but the middle managers' assessment was quite different. Their ratings of the first-line supervisors were lower (3 as opposed to 4) on all roles, especially the mentor role. The top executives saw the first-line supervisors as focusing on four distinct roles equally distributed across the CVF (innovator, producer, coordinator, and facilitator), with

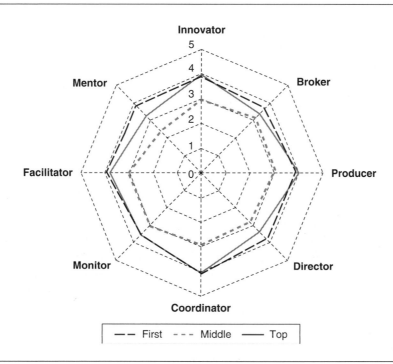

Figure 11.2   Assessment of First-Line Supervisors by All Levels

somewhat less emphasis on the remaining roles. An area of agreement was that first-line supervisors were relatively low in the mentor role. The only apparent change from the self-analysis was that first-line supervisors did not feel they should de-emphasize the role of mentor. Both middle managers and top executives also felt that the first-line supervisors should play the broker role less, which was a significant difference from the self-assessment. Top executives also pointed out the need for first-line supervisors to focus on the director role, which is a transactional role focusing on customers' needs.*

Facilitating Vertical Communication

The CVF can be also used to strengthen the vertical linkage within the chain of command by clarifying the roles and the expectations that managers have vis-à-vis the other levels (Belasen, 1998). DiPadova and Faerman (1993) observed that by "examining the transition from one managerial level to the next, managers can better understand how their expected behaviors differ across levels. . . . [T]hey can see how the roles [are enabled] in different ways in the different [administrative] contexts" (p. 162). An important advantage of using the CVF, then, lies in the creation and maintenance of effective management communication. Problems involving information underload or overload, distortions, and negative filtering can be anticipated and overcome. Clarifying managerial roles and expectations can help minimize role ambiguity and offset the costs associated with dysfunctional role conflicts. Likewise, interpersonal conflicts involving turf issues, status, and power can be avoided in favor of developing a constructive

dialogue and encouraging positive learning. As DiPadova and Faerman conclude,

> often the levels are experienced as so discrete and stratified that members see themselves as separate constituencies in the same organization, rather than as members of the same team. The common language offered by the CVF ameliorates the separateness because it is essentially an organizational language that identifies performance criteria which are common across the hierarchy. (p. 168)

How similar or different is the perceived importance of the eight CVF roles performed by managers across levels? To answer this question, Tables 11.1–11.4 report the results of a study involving managers in a large financial institution. One central finding is that there are many striking similarities regarding the importance of the roles played by managers at different levels. Overall, the evidence suggests that managers at each level were able to identify with all eight CVF roles.

The results suggest that first-line supervisors can be classified as *committed intensive*. These managers place greater emphasis on the innovator, broker, and producer roles than on all other roles. These managers serve as the primary point of contact for providing financial products and services to business clients within the assigned market area. Committed intensives are characterized by the high intensity that they bring to their work. They are almost obsessive about personal productivity for themselves and others, to the point that they may have difficulty understanding, and perhaps tolerating, individuals who are not willing to work as hard as they do (Quinn, 1988).

The middle managers in the sample can be described as *conceptual producers* who work well

---

*SOURCE: Reprinted by permission from *Leading the Learning Organization: Communication and Competencies for Managing Change* by Alan T. Belasen, the State University of New York Press. Copyright © 2000 State University of New York. All rights reserved.

Table 11.1   Similarities and Differences in Motivating Employees and Setting Goals

Level	Producer	Director
All managerial levels	• Maintains a high level of energy, motivation, and effort • Motivates others	• Makes important work decisions • Sets goals • Sets objectives for accomplishing goals • Defines roles and expectations for employees
First level	• Focuses on results and accomplishments • Gets others to excel in their work • Uses time- and stress-management strategies to handle delays and interruptions	• Assigns priorities among multiple goals
Middle level	• Creates high-performance expectations in others • Focuses on results and accomplishments • In motivating employees, considers their individual differences	• Garners support for goals from managers at lower levels
Top level	• Creates high-performance expectations in others • In motivating employees, considers their individual differences • Gets others to excel in their work	• Establishes context for decision making at lower levels

with developing and selling new ideas. This is consistent with the fact that these managers have a higher level of formal education than do first-line supervisors. These individuals perceive themselves as being conceptually skilled, production-focused, effective managers even though they pay little attention to details. This perception is supported by evidence that the managers in our sample emphasized the high importance of the innovator, broker, producer, facilitator, and director roles at their level. The coordinator, mentor, and monitor roles were assessed to be of less importance, as indicated by lower mean scores relative to the overall profile mean for middle managers.

Top executives appear to emphasize the external and human interaction CVF roles. Thus, they appear to be characterized as *open adaptive*. These executives scored high on the importance of the innovator, broker, producer, director, facilitator, and mentor roles relative to their management level's overall profile mean. It was evident that top executives placed less emphasis on the coordinator and monitor roles, which is consistent with empirical research suggesting that these managers spend more time dealing with the institutional environment and the well-being of the organization as a whole and are less concerned with internal processes at the micro level.

Information Communication Technology

Moon (2002) argues that information communication technology (ICT) enables many

Table 11.2 Similarities and Differences in Controlling Work and Tracking Details

Level	Coordinator	Monitor
All managerial levels	• Ensures that work is going according to schedule • Reallocates resources to accommodate the needs of work units • Coordinates tasks and people	• Disseminates information regarding policies and procedures • Relies on reports from others • Ensures flow of information among necessary personnel and units • Sets up and maintains necessary communication channels
First level	• Anticipates workflow problems	• Oversees compliance with procedures • Plans workload adjustments, as needed
Middle level	• Anticipates workflow problems • Schedules workflow of tasks and projects	• Interprets financial and statistical reports
Top level	• Determines subordinates' assignments based on individual skills and abilities • Coordinates units as well as individual employees	• Carefully reviews the work of others

Table 11.3 Similarities and Differences in Mentoring and Facilitating Interactions

Level	Mentor	Facilitator
All managerial levels	• Gives credit to subordinates for their work and ideas • Maintains an open, approachable, and understanding attitude toward subordinates • Takes a personal interest in employees	• Works to enhance employee participation • Creates a cohesive work climate in the organization • Creates a sense of belonging to the organization
First level	• Helps employees work toward and prepare for promotion • Does on-the-job training	• Fosters a sense of teamwork among employees • Facilitates and leads meetings
Middle level	• Does on-the-job training • Creates opportunities for first-line supervisors to challenge themselves	• Fosters a sense of teamwork among employees • Involves subordinates in discussions about work matters
Top level	• Advises lower level managers on how to handle difficult employee situations • Creates opportunities for lower level managers to challenge themselves	• Involves subordinates in discussions about work matters • Facilitates and leads meetings

Table 11.4   Similarities and Differences in Managing Change and Persuasion

Level	Innovator	Broker
All managerial levels	• Supports changes imposed on the organization • Nurtures contacts with external people even when disagreeing with the changes	• Builds coalitions and networks among peers • Represents the unit to clients and customers
First level	• Turns problems into opportunities • Encourages creativity among employees • Helps employees deal with ambiguity and delay • Helps subordinates see the positive aspects of changes	• Interacts with people outside the organization • Presents ideas to managers at higher levels
Middle level	• Turns problems into opportunities • Helps employees deal with ambiguity and delay • Assesses the potential impact of proposed changes • Comes up with ideas for improving the organization	• Represents the unit to others in the organization
Top level	• Assesses the potential impact of proposed changes • Encourages creativity among employees • Personally helps individual employees adjust to changes in the organization • Exerts lateral and upward influence in the organization • Helps subordinates see the positive aspects of changes	• Represents the unit to others in the organization

applications for managerial and corporate communication. Moon suggests that secure intranets and databases, which are already in place and being developed in public-sector organizations, are efficient managerial tools that collect, store, organize, and manage a large volume of data and are part of the strategy for improving internal managerial efficiency. However, Meijer (2001) highlights a conflict between individual autonomy and organizational control. The use of ICT often shifts control over the creation and management of information from centralized locations to individual operators. With the rise of personal computer usage, it is easy not to register

and file e-mails, and, paradoxically, individuals can place themselves outside the control of the organization and accountability. Whereas direct and open communication allows for using metaphors and sharing stories, electronic communication can be impersonal and is often misunderstood. Telling stories allows communicators to connect with people emotionally and intellectually; the stories inspire people to take action, connect with the message, and create a shared purpose and meaning. Does this mean that corporate communicators should minimize the use of electronic media? Not necessarily. But they should certainly consider the circumstances of the communication situation and, when important, hold crucial conversations more informally and directly. Face-to-face communication is more conducive to overcoming perceptual biases and increasing mutual understanding and acceptance.

The Role of Informal Networks in Management Communication

The fundamental idea underpinning effective communication in an organization involves understanding the dynamic of the relations among its internal and external contacts. Certain skills and competencies are essential for a corporate communicator to possess in order to function well in both arenas. In exploring this issue, it is necessary to focus attention on the relevance of *informal networks* as an organizational phenomenon that contributes to organizational productivity (Cross & Prusak, 2002). Such networks are often misunderstood or neglected by top executives because these systems are not part of the explicitly identifiable structure that managers oversee. Rather, top executives tend to

perceive them as a speed bump in the road to efficiency and productivity. However, upon a closer look at these different *webs of communication*, it is possible to expose and understand the potential contribution of the corporate communicators who enable these systems to exist and the interpersonal linkages that they produce. Once top executives are educated about this functionality, the different communication roles can be showcased as tools to transform ineffective informal networks into productive ones that support the goals of upper management. Figure 11.3 illustrates the relationship between communication factors, goals, and networks. The cyclical relationship among the factors suggests the ongoing process in which communication activities and organizational goals mutually interact; they represent a cause-and-effect relationship. They appear in a means-ends chain of objectives.

An overview of such communication factors and systems can be obtained by conducting a social network analysis that positions the different relationships into the foreground to identify areas for possible realignment or reprioritization (see also chapter 13). This analysis helps management understand whether or not priority

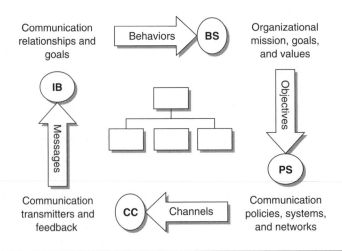

Figure 11.3   Network Map: Communication Influencers

areas are being served by current communication channels and exposes the potential for adjustments along the lines of the company's strategic objectives (Cross & Prusak, 2002).

Throughout these charted systems, the role of corporate communicators is represented in multiple, overlapping activities, which deliver different communication functions. First is the role of *central connectors* (CC), facilitators of communication for most organizational members in a network who disseminate essential information resources or provide knowledge on particular inquiries. These connectors are rarely elected to be officially in charge of a division or department, but through their ability to direct employees to the right people elsewhere inside or outside of the organization, they are frequently sought out for assistance. Sometimes these professionals are overutilized to the point that they become bottlenecks in the system and create the need to have management step in and reallocate responsibilities or initiate rotation among different positions (Cross & Prusak, 2002). Second is the role of *boundary spanners* (BS), who inform and relate parts of the network to other cross-functional areas internally and externally. Much of their time is spent as roving ambassadors who make connections with people outside the informal network. Therefore, their critical function is to facilitate communication among different areas of functionality and specialization, which puts organizational members within a few degrees of separation. Third is the role of *information brokers* (IB), who facilitate coherent communication across the subunits of the network and filter out unnecessary or irrelevant information to support the flow of effective communication. Essentially, what they do for the network, as a whole, is connect many of the more indirect associations into a working conglomerate, thus complementing the work of the more prevalent central connectors. Fourth is the role of *peripheral specialists* (PS), whose position as outliers in the organization's network allows them to serve as experts in particular areas. Being on the outskirts of the organization allows them to stay on top of the most current information relevant to their area or focus. This role requires that they not be engulfed in meetings and internal panels. Although upper management's tendency to bring them closer into the inside flap of the organization is common, doing so decreases their ability to be most effective (Cross & Prusak, 2002).

Aligning Communication With Structures

The traditional approach to corporate management views the organization as a collection of functional units that are linked vertically. Middle managers and first-line supervisors play key roles in vertical organizations because they help translate goals and evaluate how work is performed. Communication across administrative levels is formal and follows the chain of command, with managers assuming full responsibility over the work units. Managers are responsible for developing performance targets, auditing, evaluating, and rewarding personal and collective performance, and employees are expected to be loyal and implement the goals and directives. Communication flows downward and upward, mimicking the structure of authority and mirroring formal superior-subordinate relationships. One of the key points suggested by Larkin and Larkin (1994) is that first-line supervisors and middle managers provide the key communication link between the company's management and the workforce. Because managers and supervisors are positioned between the first-line workers and top executives, they form a natural conduit for information—up, down, and across the company. Yet despite managers' and supervisors' unique position within the company, most organizations fail to recognize the tremendous influence they exert on first-line employees and to empower them, not only as taskmasters but also as important opinion leaders and communication agents (Belasen, 2000).

Significant gaps exist between employees from different departments with no channels facilitating interaction and communication across organizational lines. The lower the level, the larger the communication gap between departmental employees. These gaps are further expanded by corporate growth. Problems can result when two departments need to communicate at the lower level. Typically, resolving an issue that occurs at a lower level requires communication with a higher authority where a channel exists. After the problem is resolved, the decision is then passed back down to the level where the problem originated. This phenomenon is referred to as *silo-ing*. Communication travels vertically through administrative layers, as well as up and down the various functional groups. Vertical organizations also tend to focus on organizational charts that show the authority lines and reporting relationships across levels (see Figure 11.4).

Horizontal Management

The wave of downsizing and restructuring during the 1990s gave rise to a new management communication model: horizontal management. Organizations have shrunk and flattened, replacing traditional authority lines with contemporary communication lines. In the process, many middle management and supervisory positions have been eliminated, allowing companies to become more efficient and productive (Skagen, 1992). Surviving middle managers must cooperate and work with each other to establish business and work processes to ease workflow and facilitate the flow of information across organizational lines (Belasen, 2000). The principal benefit of horizontal management is that, through the different functions, it facilitates smooth transition of intermediate products and services to the customer. Empowering employees, improving communication, and eliminating

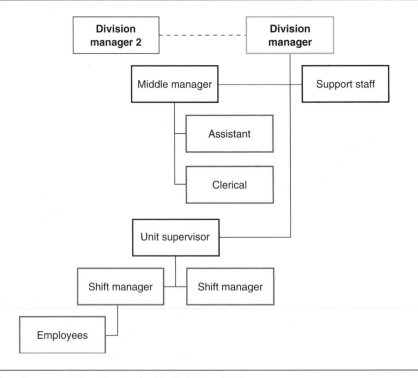

Figure 11.4   Communication Flow in the Vertical Organization

unnecessary work achieve this transition. Instead of the multilayer reporting structure, the pure form of horizontal management consists of core competencies. Payoff for such cooperation goes beyond efficiency, improved work culture, and satisfied customers; formulated correctly, it can become a strategic advantage for the company. Imagine the impact of a well-designed program to effectively minimize customer disputes. Thorough investigation of the causes of customer disputes may uncover hidden problems in the production, delivery, or invoicing process. Early identification of problems in the upstream process is a feedback tool that helps control these problems and facilitates the continuous flow of strategic information among departments. The company can therefore fully exploit the potential of the horizontal structure. When implemented properly, the horizontal organizational structure promises the dividend of a lean and responsive organization with better coordinated efforts in the production process, more responsive decision cycles, and savings from a flatter and more effective organizational structure. This structure,

as depicted in Figure 11.5, consists of a group of senior managers responsible for strategic decisions and policies and groups of empowered employees working together in different process teams.

Horizontal structures eliminate the need to devote resources to vertical communication lines and complex systems of coordination. In a horizontal organization, the internal machine uses fewer resources, and information is processed at the local level by multifunctional teams. Team members are typically empowered personnel from the respective functions working within the process. The process team, permitting the company to operate with flexibility and responsiveness in a continuously changing business environment, can resolve local problems quickly. Increased interaction between employees from different departments fosters close working relationships and better communication, and those employees can obtain a better understanding of each other's responsibilities, thus reducing costly conflicts that result from misunderstanding and disagreement among different departments.

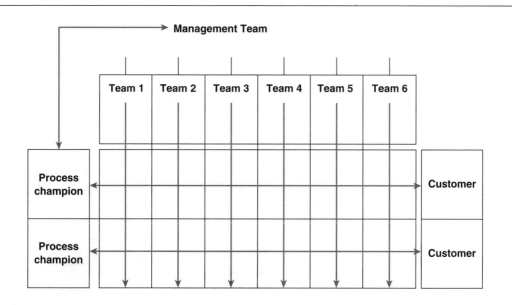

Figure 11.5   Horizontal Lines in a Team-Based Organization

Unlike traditional organizational structures that separate goals and work by functional lines, horizontal structures integrate people and units into self-contained groups with built-in coordination (Belasen, 1997). In other words, individuals with different skills are co-located and perform jobs that are driven by external goals or customer expectations. Because teams operate close to the front lines of the organization (upstream systems) and often communicate directly with customers, they need to be familiar with corporate communication goals and messages. Performing diverse organizational tasks and often faced with the need to handle boundary-spanning activities, team members must be familiar with core communication activities and products and act in accordance with corporate communication goals. A shift from vertical to horizontal structures also requires team members and managers to change their worldviews, social norms, and work practices to reflect the new roles and responsibilities.

Leadership is vital for the success of nonbureaucratic, team-based organizations. Vertical organizations can run virtually without leaders because centralization and high formalization are effective substitutes for leadership. Tall, hierarchically structured organizations run through middle managers, whose primary role is to manage functions, integrate units' efforts, and monitor their performance. Horizontal organizations, on the other hand, provide former supervisors and managers with new managerial opportunities to become coaches, consultants, and sponsors. This situation, however, also creates a vacuum that requires teams to co-opt traditional leadership roles. The shift to team-based structures is not an elimination of supervisory tasks but instead is a structured transfer of many of those tasks to the team (Belasen, 2000). In these organizations, the role of corporate communication directors becomes increasingly important. They need to help the different teams go through the socialization process and assimilate the new norms of behavior and shared understanding. Team members also perform important boundary-spanning activities and represent the organization to external audiences. Maintaining the identity of the organization across such highly decentralized work structures and ensuring that the corporate image is managed consistently is a challenging corporate communication task. This is precisely why a centrally located, strategically focused corporate communication function is needed to help organize the delivery of communication products and activities across decentralized organizational lines.

Aligning Communication Processes in Loosely Coupled Structures

Power and Rienstra (1999) researched the development of a corporate communication model for loosely coupled businesses in local governments. Their sample agency consisted of 18 businesses spread over 50 locations. They argue that communication is the "glue" for developing a workable model for loosely coupled systems. They claim that the success of change in such organizations depends on close attention to communication issues, especially during implementation. In addition, they highlight the need to develop the skills of the *educated communicator* to implement a change plan and be able to survey, facilitate, encourage, and persuade people. Generic plans and centralized communication processes are not successful for loosely coupled organizations; instead, they need to develop a culture and ethos for upward and horizontal communication, as well as offer training for staff in communication and people skills. To do so, clear aims and objectives for a communication plan must be established, and in order to build a common vision, they must be based on the organization's mission and goals and be conveyed at the grassroots level.

For one public-sector agency, a planning conference with representatives (communication advocates) from every business was proposed. For this agency, Power and Rienstra (1999) recommended a central, strategically managed communication function, but one with devolved local operational communication management and flexibility. This means that each unit was able to determine its information requirements, develop participative consultative processes and cross-functional teams, and use staff exchange procedures across business units. Along with local activities, various management communication initiatives were suggested (e.g., a news magazine delivered to the employee's home address to encourage corporate identity, a structured training program on the change process, development of links with management to hear information in face-to-face situations, informal opinion leaders and local managers to deliver important messages and validate information at workplace sites). Employee involvement and participation of staff in two-way communication are crucial to achieving organizational goals and bridging the gap between management and employees. To create such an open communication system, there must be recognition at the top that staff members have a voice and a commitment to follow up on plans and ideas. Therefore, the middle manager's role as facilitator and coach, clarifying and disseminating information, is especially important in order to ensure that employees have access to sources of information.

Managerial Ethics and Social Responsibility

In March 2002, President Bush unveiled his "Ten-Point Plan to Improve Corporate Responsibility and Protect America's Shareholders." The plan was based on three core principles: information accuracy and accessibility, management accountability, and auditor independence. However, imposed governance alone will not be enough; corporations need to do more. They must reform from the inside out in order to raise the bar of moral and ethical behavior. Social and behavioral mechanisms have to be put in place, and each company must determine how best to implement

them. These mechanisms must be employed from the top down, and all employees need to buy in. First and foremost, companies need to not only keep their employees actively engaged in organizational activities and decisions but also keep them committed. Second, companies need to practice results-based leadership that requires employees to have a sense of personal accountability. Third, companies need to establish a code of ethics that all employees, including management, must follow. This code of ethics should be integrated into the company's mission statement and permeate daily decision making. Employees should be trained with examples of ethical conduct, and ethical policies and procedures should be enforced. A whistle-blowers' hotline should be established to encourage the uncovering of fraud. An ethics officer or ombudsman should be put on the payroll to oversee and enforce all ethics policies and discipline all offenders. As a final defense, independent audits should be conducted to review all company books. Moreover, companies should emphasize that no one is above the ethical code.

According to Clarkson (1995), the term *social responsibility* has no clear meaning. However, *performance* and *nonperformance* are more easily measured. Clarkson suggests using a scale with the nominal values *reactive*, *defensive*, *accommodative*, and *proactive* to evaluate social performance. The scale is useful for characterizing management strategy and a posture toward different stakeholder groups. It is simple to use as long as organizational data are available; these data show what an organization has done and is currently doing regarding specific social issues. The key strategies in this area range from doing less to doing more than is required by law. Requirements come from a vast array of sources, including government, special interest groups, political action committees, social activists, press, and investors. Some requirements are determined by legislation, whereas others can stem from what a corporation does and promises to its stakeholders. Figure 11.6 is a CVFCC diagram that depicts these behaviors and corporate orientations in a way that signifies the relationships between diverse stakeholders and patterns of organizational responses. These relationships are further explored in the chapters on stakeholder power, bases of influence, and crisis communication.

Reactive and defensive behaviors are associated with when a company complies with laws and regulations or is satisfied "playing by the rules." These behaviors are often advocated by the principal-agent theory, which supports the notion that a manager's moral obligation is to the owner(s) and that using a firm's resources for social good is more like a liability or tax. Managers are not in the business to decide how much to tax and how tax is spent. Taxation should be left to the democratic process and, therefore, businesses that pursue social good subvert capitalism. Companies are in the business of running an efficient and effective business and providing valued goods and services to customers and profitable returns to owners. Reactive and defensive behaviors are therefore

reductionist in that companies minimize their involvement in social causes or their liability in particular cases by either denying responsibility or partially admitting responsibility but fighting it to shield their core business and retain credibility. The Firestone-Ford denial of responsibility for the SUV rollover and car accidents in early 2000 stands out as a case in point.

In May 2000, after rollovers caused serious injuries and claimed the lives of many motorists, the National Highway Traffic Safety Administration issued a probe into the failures of certain tires made by Bridgestone/Firestone that were used on Ford pickup trucks and SUVs, mostly Explorers. In August 2000, Bridgestone announced the recall of 6.5 million ATX, ATX II, and Wilderness tires produced by its Firestone unit in North America and offered to replace them. Ford and Firestone found fault with each other, severing the century-old relationship between the two companies. Firestone believed it had isolated the problem and that the flaw was related to the design of the Explorer itself. Ford, on the other

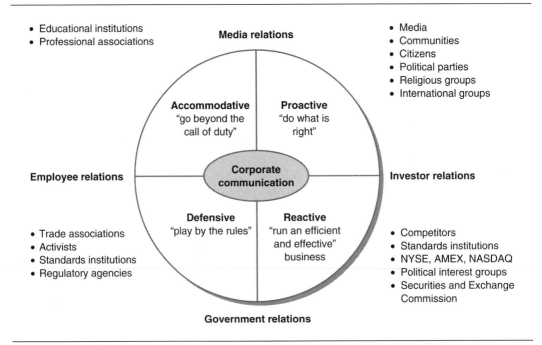

Figure 11.6   Patterns of Corporate Social Responsibility

hand, ferociously defended the design of its Explorer, demanding a wider recall of Firestone tires. In June 2001, executives from the two companies faced off in Congress, trading blame and using conflicting data to defend their positions. Shortly afterward, Ford decided unilaterally to replace 13 million Firestone tires that Bridgestone described as "world class." With both companies in deep denial, Ford and Firestone suffered significant blows to their image and reputation. In the several years that followed, it ended up costing the two companies billions of dollars in lost earnings, legal expenses, and settlements.

In contrast with reactive and defensive behaviors, accommodative and proactive behaviors fall under nonmaximizing value approaches that "go beyond the call of duty." We live in a complicated world that requires managers to think holistically about complex organizational and social issues. Companies use proactive behaviors in anticipation of social issues by voluntarily contributing to the overall wealth of society. Companies take a positive or exemplary stand by initiating social programs and by doing what is right to meet societal expectations beyond legal obligations. On June 26, 2006, U.S. investor Warren Buffett announced that he would give $31 billion of his Berkshire Hathaway stocks to the Bill and Melinda Gates Foundation to help support global health and disease research. In 2005 the Gates Foundation reportedly made grant awards of $1.36 billion, and it plans to spend at least $1.5 billion yearly on global health issues. Buffet's contribution will give the foundation at least $1.5 billion of additional resources for the first year (Akukwe, 2006).

Corporate social responsibility (CSR) requires not only ethical leaders but also effective strategy, strong corporate culture, and individual involvement. It requires corporate governance (board of directors), public disclosure (regulations), third-party verification (auditors), and stakeholder engagement (shareholders, customers, interest groups, citizens). Experts agree that the triangle of fraud requires need, opportunity, and rationalization. Without opportunity (which occurs because of poor internal and external controls, weak regulations, and lack of positive corporate culture), *fraud* and *dishonesty* will no longer be used to epitomize corporate society. An ethical corporate culture has an infrastructure that minimizes the possibility for ethical transgressions on the part of any of its members because that infrastructure promotes organizational integrity. An ethical corporate culture provides incentives for all employees to act both productively and ethically. An ethical corporate culture celebrates diversity, honors individual differences, and tries to find ways to harmonize individual self-interests with the interests of the company and of the greater good of the outside community. Individuals within such a culture are rewarded for behaviors that go above and beyond ethical duty.

The CEO and the Board of Directors

Socially responsible companies reevaluate their values and standards so that their decisions and actions are not just ethical but have the dual effect of maximizing shareholder interests and minimizing the social costs of their actions. For CSR to be effective, someone needs to he held accountable. In major corporations, this person is normally the CEO working closely with an effective board of directors (BOD). Some analysts consider *measure and disclosure* to be at the heart of managerial accountability, whether on financial statements or regarding social issues. Information provided by a business is used by investors, consumers, regulators, community groups, and other key stakeholders in their decision making; thus, it is important for such information to be credible. A lack of credible information has been at the forefront of the corporate accounting scandals involving major corporations such as Enron, WorldCom, and Global Crossing. Criticism of recent accounting scandals has fixated on the need for more independent BODs in corporations. Critics believe that having an independent board prevents unethical behavior by top executives, an idea that is underscored by the fact that the New York Stock Exchange (NYSE) and the National Association of Securities Dealers Automated Quotations (NASDAQ) recently issued principles of governance reform. These principles focus on the BOD independence and require that all boards have a majority of directors without ties to the company, a full separation between the role of chairman and the role of CEO, and regular meetings without the CEO.

Structural Regulations

Given that evidence suggests many BODs for large U.S. companies are already independent, it is ironic that regulators see these structural regulations as being crucial to ending the current corporate crisis. Enron, for example, had an independent board. Its members did not own equity in the company; thus, according to regulators' terms, they were considered independent. However, there was still strong evidence of conflict of interest. For example, it was noted that Enron made contributions to the political campaign of Senator Phil Gramm, husband of Wendy Gramm, audit committee chairman for Enron. Similarly, audit committee member Lord Wakeham had a consulting contract with Enron. The point is that defining *independence* only in terms of equity interest in a company and chairmanship is not sufficient; other factors can pose a conflict of interest. Additionally, independence is only one factor or principle of good governance. Other issues, such as conflict of interest (e.g., a board member receiving remuneration for services from the company), director quality and experience, and active BOD involvement in decision making, are much more critical. The most important characteristic of the BOD is not independence but the ability to influence

strategic decision making through knowledge of industry and experience. Any policy that restricts the pool of available director candidates makes it more difficult for firms to assemble boards with an optimal configuration of strategic experience. Some analysts believe that directors with a stake in the company are likely to be more involved and concerned about the long-term impact of policies on that company. Others argue that directors who are also owners (i.e., have equity positions in the company) are more likely to act fraudulently or unethically. The debate about the structure of governance and the appropriateness of authority and communication lines between the BOD and the CEO is still unsettled.

Policies and Standards

NYSE and NASDAQ policies impair a company's efforts to appoint directors who hold equity in it. The recent wave of scandals is not due to lack of independence by BODs but to fraudulent accounting practices and policies, as well as weak systems of internal and external controls. And the absence of social mechanisms such as a code of ethics, corporate culture, and, even more important, an ethical leader only serves to exacerbate the problems. CEOs set the ethical direction for the organization and are responsible for creating a corporate culture (based on principles of veracity, honesty, and integrity) within their organization; they must also communicate these principles to all employees, from top executives to line staff. Additionally, an ethical organization should have a medium through which employees can confidentially express their concerns and have them addressed effectively. The outcome for Enron might have been different if such a medium had been available to Sherron Watkins.

Standard accounting practices and policies, as well as potent systems of internal control (facilitated through the BOD) and external control (independent auditors and regulators), help maintain the credibility of a firm's information. In addition to structural reforms of the BOD, however, there must be structural reform of accounting practices, company-auditor relationships, and the role of regulators in ensuring that the wave of scandals, which has become an epitaph of major corporations, is brought to an end. Questionable accounting practices such as off-balance-sheet activities and mistreatment of intangible assets (goodwill), expenditures, revenue, and cost estimates have been identified as methods used by some organizations to defraud investors. Decades of financial deregulation, weak securities law, and general gray areas in laws and rules have exacerbated this problem. One example is Global Crossing, a recently bankrupt telecom company that was audited by Andersen, which treated future revenue as current revenue. Its system of accounting considered future contracts as current revenue even before they were realized (a contravention of the Generally Accepted Accounting Principles [GAAP] concept of prudence or conservatism). The company also amortized current expenses that were not capital expenditure, as opposed to matching these expenses against current revenue streams (a contravention of the GAAP concept of accrual or matching). The interesting issue here is that the internal audit committee failed to recognize this activity, and so did its "independent" auditor, Andersen. This failure has raised questions about the relevance or effectiveness of independent nonexecutive directors and provided empirical evidence that structural reform of corporate governance must go beyond a call for an independent BOD and must encompass systems of controls and accounting practices.

Reforms

There is a need for reform of the accounting rules set by the GAAP, the Financial Accounting Standards Board (FASB; the designated private-sector organization in the United States that establishes financial accounting and reporting standards), and the International Accounting Standards Board (IASB; which sets accounting standards) as well as reform of the approach to rule setting. Accountants should not be given the task of interpreting rough or general accounting principles; doing so lends itself to inconsistencies, ambiguities, and fraud. Rather, regulatory bodies should define precisely how to deal with each situation. Similarly, auditors should be independent and should not also be consultants. Keeping such functions separate prevents conflict of interest. The BOD, through its independent audit committee, has a role to play here also. The directors need to ensure that they are prudent, active, and diligent in overseeing the company's polices and actions and take proactive steps in recommending corrective actions when necessary. Direct involvement of an accountable BOD is especially necessary in ambiguous situations associated with the interpretation of rules and principles and the implementation of policies.

The Ethical CEO

The ethical CEO serves as an envoy or a liaison between the BOD and other corporate management. He or she not only communicates the mission, goals, and values of the company but also "walks the talk." True leaders are those who lead by doing; they believe that "talk is cheap" and "actions speak louder than words." The CEO is committed to corporate culture that values open dialogue with all stakeholders within and outside the company. He or she encourages open dissent from other senior management and company employees (e.g., whistle-blowers) by providing the appropriate channels for communication. The CEO encourages corporate communicators to engage with the outside community and with the media. He or she considers the possibility of new kinds of leadership within the company. For example, the CEO may consider hiring an ethics officer, a privacy officer, and/or an environmental officer. The CEO and the BOD may decide to increase ethical awareness within the company by introducing training and education requirements for all managers and employees. The CEO is committed to disclosing comprehensive and reader-friendly financial information to board members, company employees, investors, and other relevant stakeholders in a timely and organized fashion. In short, the CEO must be a moral manager who takes responsibility for the financial and social direction of the company.

Communication Between the CEO and Board Members

Hart and Quinn (1993) used the CVF to identify four important roles that CEOs play within four distinct domains: taskmaster (market), vision setter (future), analyzer (operating system), and motivator (organization). Effective CEOs spend time focusing on broad visions for the future and evaluating performance plans. Called "high performance leaders" (Belasen, 2000, p. 383), they pay attention to relational issues while also addressing tasks and action plans. Playing these four roles simultaneously helps increase the reputation of the CEO and boosts the business and financial performance of the firm.

The margin of error for a CEO is narrow because he or she must measure up to high standards of excellence in a relatively short period of time. The average amount of time that new CEOs are given to prove their effectiveness and win the BOD's confidence is about a year and a half, after which there is a full expectation for winning over Wall Street, increasing market cap, and turning the business around (Gaines-Ross, 2003). Meeting these expectations and developing a strategic vision for the organization require candid and frequent communication with board members, who expect the CEO to demonstrate a high capacity for

learning and to be creative and open-minded but also decisive and inspiring. Effective CEOs communicate the company's goals clearly, interact well with board members, and hold themselves and board members accountable for the consequences of strategic decisions.

Keeping the communication lines open, providing timely feedback, and developing relationships of trust with board members are particularly important when the CEO is a strong, high-performance leader and when the BOD includes nonexecutives. Nonexecutives are outside directors who often provide contrasting views or competing alternatives to business strategy. Inside directors with a good mix of strategic experience and depth of industry knowledge seem to favor CEO duality (i.e., the CEO is also the chairman of the board) because it promotes a unified and strong leadership (Pearce & Zahra, 1991). The recent scandals and executive frauds, however, have led many to question the validity of such a structure, calling for full separation of decision management systems from decision control systems. CEO duality tends to prevent outside directors from challenging the CEO's authority; separating the two systems promotes greater transparency and accountability as well as an improved public image. In some cases it also leads to better business performance (Rechner & Dalton, 1991).

Building an Effective Board of Directors

The separation of decision management (initiation and implementation of business strategy) and decision control (ratification and monitoring of strategic goals and outcomes) should help improve ethical leadership and performance credibility. This separation means that the highest level decision-management agent (the CEO) should not control the highest level decision control structure (the BOD). Effective separation of these two realms requires that the chairman of the board and the CEO be two different individuals. If done correctly, firms that switch to a dual-leadership structure should begin to experience improved performance (Fama & Jensen, 1983). Firms with such a structure consistently outperform (i.e., are more profitable and more cost efficient than) firms with a unitary leadership structure (Pi & Timme, 1993; Rechner & Dalton, 1991). Principal-Agency Theory, which was mentioned earlier in this chapter, views the relationship between the BOD and the CEO instrumentally. That is, the CEO's moral obligation is to the stockholders, as represented by the directors. Signs of mistrust between board members and the CEO could be harmful to the organization's public image and credibility. Board members can challenge the CEO by developing back channels to managers and collecting information that challenges the CEO's views. This type of rift can occur if the CEO fails to provide sufficient and timely information to board members or if board members pursue different interests or have different agendas (Sonnenfeld, 2002). Losing authoritative sources of power as a result of greater structural board independence from management, however, may prompt some CEOs to co-opt board members using persuasion, ingratiation, and assimilation tactics.

Building an effective BOD and creating a climate of trust and mutual respect are certainly goals that every CEO should work toward. An effective BOD projects a strong organizational image and strong internal identity. A climate of trust and candor helps support the corporate communication staff's goal of creating consistent and unambiguous messages that diverse stakeholder bases can understand and embrace. The CEO can take steps to proactively promote a culture of open dissent while pushing board members to question their own roles and

assumptions. At the same time, board members can develop mechanisms and outlets to collect external information, network outside the company to form a better understanding of the competitive challenges that exist in the business environment, and develop alternative scenarios to assess the strategic direction of the business. Ensuring board members' personal accountability and evaluating the their performance beyond their past accomplishments should help improve the quality of executive decision processes and ultimately increase the confidence and integrity in the BOD/CEO relationship (Sonnenfeld, 2002).

Summary

Chapter 11 covers the left side (upper and lower) of the CVFCC. One of the main points that the literature makes about management communication is the need to encourage internal corporate identity through various management communication initiatives. When management communication aligns with the organization's vision and organizational leaders assume the role of communication champion, building trust and gaining members' commitment, organizational members develop shared reality and accountability toward the attainment of corporate communication goals. Unlike vertical authority lines, horizontal structures eliminate the need to devote resources to formal systems of coordination. The internal machine of a flatter organization uses fewer resources, relying heavily on communication lines and networks as effective substitutes for hierarchy. This chapter also delves into ethics and social responsibility. Managerial accountability systems are necessary and important to improve trust within and around the organization as well as to create better communication relationships between board members and top executives.

Review Questions

1. Describe typical barriers (e.g., misfits between decision-making structures, communication flow, organizational strategies) to effective management communication and the means (e.g., structural, cultural) to overcome these barriers.

2. Evaluate the differences between communication systems in vertical and horizontal structures.

3. What is the role of networks of communication?

4. Describe the communication dynamics between a CEO and board members in CEO duality and nonduality roles.

5. How can trust in and around organizations can be improved?

6. Do you think that horizontal structures change the roles and responsibilities of corporate communication internally? Externally?

7. What are the theoretical and practical predicaments related to using defensive or reactive strategies in issue management? What are the limitations of such strategies?

CASE STUDY

The Paradoxical Twins—Acme and Omega Electronics

Part I

In 1983, a Cleveland manufacturer bought out Technological Products of Erie, Pennsylvania. The Cleveland firm had no interest in the electronics division of Technological Products and subsequently sold to different investors two plants that manufactured circuit boards. One of the plants, located in nearby Waterford, was renamed Acme Electronics; the other plant, within the city limits of Erie, was renamed Omega Electronics, Inc.

Acme retained its original management and upgraded its general manager to president. Omega hired a new president, who had been a director of a large electronic research laboratory and upgraded several of the existing personnel within the plant. Acme and Omega often competed for the same contracts. As subcontractors, both firms benefited from the electronics boom of the early 1970s, and both looked forward to future growth and expansion. Acme had annual sales of $10 million and employed 550 people. Omega had annual sales of $8 million and employed 480 people. Acme regularly achieved greater net profits, much to the chagrin of Omega's management.

Inside Acme

The president of Acme, John Tyler, was confident that had the demand not been so great, Acme's competitor would not have survived. "In fact," he said, "we have been able to beat Omega regularly for the most profitable contracts, thereby increasing our profit." Tyler credited his firm's greater effectiveness to his managers' abilities to run a "tight ship." He explained that he had retained the basic structure developed by Technological Products because it was more efficient for the high-volume manufacturer of printed circuits and their subsequent assembly. Acme had detailed organization charts and job descriptions. Tyler believed that everyone should have clear responsibilities and narrowly defined jobs, which would lead to efficient performance and high company profits. People were generally satisfied with their work at Acme; however, some of the managers voiced the desire to have a little more latitude in their jobs.

Inside Omega

Omega's president, Jim Rawls, did not believe in organization charts. He felt that his organization had departments similar to Acme's, but he thought that Omega's plant was small enough that things such as organization charts just put artificial barriers between specialists who should be working together. Written memos were not allowed, since as Rawls expressed it, "The plant is small enough that if people want to communicate they can just drop by and talk things over."

The head of the mechanical engineering department said, "Jim spends too much of his time and mine making sure everyone understands what we're doing and listening to suggestions." Rawls was concerned with employee satisfaction and wanted everyone to feel part of the organization. The top management team reflected Rawls's attitudes. They also believed employees should be familiar with activities throughout the organization so that cooperation between the departments would be increased. A newer member of the industrial engineering department said, "When I first got here, I wasn't sure what I was supposed to do. One day I worked with some mechanical engineers and the next day I helped the shipping department design some packing cartons. The first months on the job were hectic, but at least I got a feel for what makes Omega tick."

Part II

In 1986, integrated circuits began to cut deeply into the demand for printed circuit boards. The integrated circuits (ICs), or "chips," were the first steps into microminiaturization in the electronics industry. Because the manufacturing process for ICs was a closely guarded secret, both Acme and Omega realized the potential threat to their futures, and both began to seek new customers aggressively.

In July 1986, a major photocopy manufacturer was looking for a subcontractor to assemble the memory unit for its new experimental copier. The projected contract for the job was estimated to be $5 to $7 million in annual sales.

Both Acme and Omega were geographically close to this manufacturer and both submitted highly competitive bids for the production of 100 prototypes. Acme's bid was slightly lower than Omega's; however, both firms were asked to produce 100 units. The photocopy manufacturer told both firms that speed was critical because its president had boasted to other manufactures that the firm would have the finished copier available by Christmas. This boast, much to the designer's dismay, required pressure on all subcontractors to begin prototype production before final design of the copier was complete. This meant that Acme and Omega would have at most two weeks to complete the prototypes, or delay the final copier production.

Part III

Inside Acme

As soon as John Tyler was given the blueprints (Monday, July 11, 1986), he sent a memo to the purchasing department asking it to move forward on the purchase of all necessary materials. At the same time, he sent the blueprints to the drafting department and asked that it prepare manufacturing prints. The industrial engineering department was told to begin methods design work for use by the production department supervisors. Tyler also sent a memo to all department heads and executives indicating the critical time constraints of this job and how he expected that all employees would perform as efficiently as they had in the past.

The departments had little contact with one another for several days, and each seemed to work at its own speed. Each department also encountered problems. Purchasing could not acquire all the parts on time. Industrial engineering had trouble arranging an efficient assembly sequence. Mechanical engineering did not take the deadline seriously and parceled its work to vendors so the engineers could work on other jobs scheduled previously. Tyler made it a point to stay in touch with the photocopy manufacturer to let it know things were progressing and to learn of any new developments. He traditionally worked to keep important clients happy. Tyler telephoned someone at the photocopy company at least twice a week and got to know the head designer quite well.

On July 15, Tyler learned that mechanical engineering was way behind in its development work, and he "hit the roof." To make matters worse, purchasing did not obtain all the parts, so the industrial

(Continued)

(Continued)

engineers decided to assemble the product without one part, which would be inserted at the last minute. On Thursday, July 21, the final units were being assembled, although the process was delayed several times. On Friday, July 22, the last units were finished while Tyler paced the plant. Late that afternoon, Tyler received a phone call from the head designer of the photocopy manufacturer, who told Tyler that he had received a call on Wednesday from Jim Rawls of Omega. He explained that Rawls' workers had found an error in the design of the connector cable and taken corrective action on their prototypes. He told Tyler that he checked out the design error and that Omega was right. Tyler, a bit overwhelmed by this information, told the designer that he had all the memory units ready for shipment and that as soon as they received the missing component, on Monday or Tuesday, they would be able to deliver the final units. The designer explained that the design error would be rectified in a new blueprint he was sending over by messenger, and that he would hold Acme to the Tuesday delivery date.

When the blueprint arrived, Tyler called in the production supervisor to assess the damage. The alterations in the design would call for total disassembly and the unsoldering of several connections. Tyler told the supervisor to put extra people on the alterations first thing Monday morning and to try to finish the job by Tuesday. Late Tuesday afternoon the alterations were finished and the missing components were delivered. Wednesday morning, the production supervisor discovered that the units would have to be torn apart again to install the missing component. When John Tyler was told this, he again "hit the roof." He called industrial engineering and asked if it could help out. The production supervisor and methods engineer couldn't agree on how to install the component. John Tyler settled the argument by ordering that all units be taken apart again and the missing component installed. He told shipping to prepare cartons for delivery on Friday afternoon.

On Friday, July 29, fifty prototypes were shipped from Acme without final inspection. John Tyler was concerned about his firm's reputation, so he waived the final inspection after he personally tested one unit and found it operational. On Tuesday, August 2, Acme shipped the last fifty units.

Inside Omega

On Friday, July 8, Jim Rawls called a meeting that included department heads to tell them about the potential contract they were to receive. He told them that as soon as he received the blueprints, work could begin. On Monday, July 11, the prints arrived, and again the department heads met to discuss the project. At the end of the meeting, drafting had agreed to prepare manufacturing prints while industrial engineering and production would begin methods design.

Two problems that were similar to those at Acme arose within Omega. Certain ordered parts could not be delivered on time, and the assembly sequence was difficult to engineer. The departments proposed ideas to help one another, however, and department heads and key employees had daily meetings to discuss progress. The head of electrical engineering knew of a Japanese source for the components that could not be purchased from normal suppliers. Most problems were solved by Saturday, July 16.

On Monday, July 18, a methods engineer and production supervisor formulated the assembly plans, and production was set to begin on Tuesday morning. On Monday afternoon, people from mechanical engineering, electrical engineering, production, and industrial engineering got together to produce a prototype just to ensure that there would be no snags in production. While they were building the unit, they discovered an error in the cable connector design. All the engineers agreed, after checking and rechecking the blueprints, that the cable was erroneously designed. People from mechanical engineering and electrical engineering spent Monday night redesigning the cable, and on Tuesday morning the drafting department finalized the changes in the manufacturing prints. On Tuesday morning, Rawls was a bit apprehensive about the design changes and decided to get formal approval. Rawls received word on Wednesday from the head designer at the photocopier firm that they could proceed with the design changes as discussed on the phone. On Friday, July 22, the final units were inspected by quality control and were then shipped.

Part IV

Ten of Acme's final memory units were defective, while all of Omega's passed the photocopier firm's tests. The photocopier firm was disappointed with Acme's delivery delay, and incurred further delays in repairing the defective Acme units. However, rather than give the entire contract to one firm, the final contract was split between Acme and Omega with two directives added: (1) maintain zero defects and (2) reduce final cost. In 1987, through extensive cost-cutting efforts, Acme reduced its unit cost by 20% and was ultimately awarded the total contract.

Case Questions

1. Using the five hallmarks of high-reliability organizations described in chapter 2 (preoccupation with failure, reluctance to simplify interpretations, sensitivity to operations, commitment to resilience, and deference to expertise), determine which organization was more effective, and why, in responding to the pressures to develop the prototype on time and with high quality.

2. Use the CVF model (Figure 11.1 and Tables 11.1–11.4) to describe the communication roles played by the two presidents. Then use Table 8.1 (message orientations) to examine the types of communication used by each president. According to the CVFCC, Omega's communication climate fits more with that of relational communication, and Acme's is more compatible with promotional communication. What factors and behaviors account for this observation?

3. How can Acme's success be explained?

SOURCE: From Veiga, John F., "The Paradoxical Twins: Acme and Omega Electronics." In John F. Veiga and John N. Yanouzas, *The Dynamics of Organization Theory*, St. Paul: West Pub., 1984. Reprinted with permission.

PART E

Analysis and Control

12

Stakeholder Analysis

Whereas the market view of the corporate world focuses on the customer and the financial view centers on maximizing the value for the corporate shareholder, the extended stakeholder model breaks out of these conventions by including all persons, groups, or organizations with the ability to place claims against organizational goals, span of attention, resources, or outputs. Orts and Strudler (2002) believe that expansive views of stakeholders are often so broad that they are meaningless, and so complex that they are useless. As we examine stakeholders, we see various groups being highlighted by stakeholder theorists. For example, Freeman's (1984) listing of stakeholders includes such diverse constituencies as owners of various kinds, supplier firms, customer segments, employee segments, various members of the financial community, several levels of government, consumer advocacy groups and other activist groups, political groups, unions, and competitors. Hill and Jones (1992) list managers, stockholders, employees, customers, suppliers, and creditors. Clarkson (1995) lists the company itself, employees, shareholders, customers, and suppliers as primary stakeholders, with the media and various special interest groups classified as secondary stakeholders. Donaldson and Preston (1995) list investors, political groups, customers, employees, trade associations, suppliers, and governments. Others include entities such as community and the general public (Hill & Jones, 1992), public stakeholders (Clarkson, 1995), and the natural environment (Orts & Strudler, 2002).

A stakeholder approach encourages corporate executives to include external and internal groups and individuals, or stakeholders who value the goals and interests of the organization, in managerial decision-making processes. This approach also addresses what managers should do to shape their relationship with stakeholders (Berman, Wicks, Kotha, & Jones, 1999). According to Ledingham and Bruning (1998) a *relationship* is a "state which exists between an organization and its key publics in which the actions of either entity impact the economic, social, political and/or cultural well-being of the other entity" (p. 62). It is common to look at stakeholder theory as a wheel, with the corporation at the center and all of its stakeholders as the spokes (Frooman, 1999; Page, 2002). As time goes on, the wheel gets more spokes as more and more stakeholders views are considered to be valuable. The corporate communication professional is encouraged to think strategically about key stakeholders' concerns, map out their values and power bases, and make decisions to support and strengthen the alignment of organizational strategies with the most influential stakeholders. One way to focus the analysis on key stakeholders is to use a CVFCC map that highlights the importance of primary stakeholders such as customers, investors, regulators, and employees in addition to secondary stakeholders (see Figure 12.1).

According to Phillips (2004), a corporation is bound by moral obligations to its stakeholders. The main challenge is to recognize what stakeholders want. Complicating the issue, however, is the fact that different parts of an organization tend to deal with different stakeholders. For example, the HR department communicates with employees to find out what they want, whereas PR staff communicate with the community to find out what it wants. Corporate communicators should therefore take on more of the responsibility in finding out what stakeholders want

instead of relying solely on individual departments to do so. Better communication also helps prevent conflict before it has a chance to percolate. For example, if an employee is unhappy with the organization in any way, whether it is policy or activity related, it is best for management to be aware of this before it has a chance to escalate.

Communicating With Stakeholders: A CVFCC Approach

The CVFCC provides guidelines for communicating with various stakeholders, some with overlapping roles, using different message orientations (as shown in Table 12.1). The CVFCC quadrants form a framework that illustrates some of the potential conflicts or competing values that decision makers or corporate communicators may

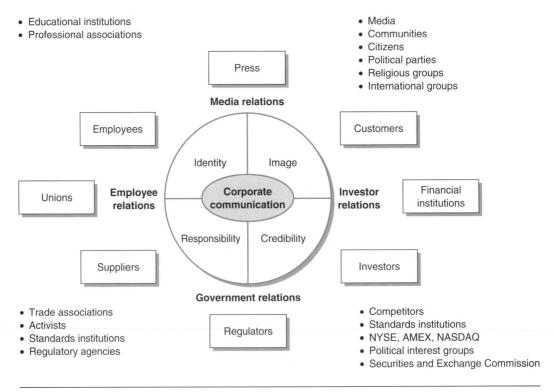

- Educational institutions
- Professional associations

- Media
- Communities
- Citizens
- Political parties
- Religious groups
- International groups

- Trade associations
- Activists
- Standards institutions
- Regulatory agencies

- Competitors
- Standards institutions
- NYSE, AMEX, NASDAQ
- Political interest groups
- Securities and Exchange Commission

Figure 12.1   Mapping Organizational Stakeholders: A Competing Values Framework for Corporate Communication Perspective

encounter in addressing a diverse set of stakeholders with different goals, interests, and values. For example, addressing stockholders requires insightful communication with a great deal of energy and enthusiasm, a strong belief in the company's future and growth potential, and a general sense of direction that is rooted in the vision. Top executives, corporate communication directors, and IR executives use storytelling and symbols, which are powerful media, to present an idea in a rich, colorful way that connects with the audience on impact. Addressing regulators requires a different tone and different language— a communication strategy that presents facts and figures both credibly and reliably. A company's representatives draw on the company's success stories to highlight the legality and ethical implementation of codes and standards imposed by regulators, but they also use messages that are confirming and validating. The communication is reactive and responsive, controlled and evaluative, accurate and well structured. At times it is also introspective; words and expressions are used to illustrate that the company's determination to follow up on promises and take the necessary steps to comply with external requirements.

Frooman (1999) suggests three questions about stakeholders that must be answered before a response strategy can be developed. First, who are they? This question refers to the stakeholders' attributes. Second, what do stakeholders want? Third, how are the stakeholders going to try to get what they want? This last question is not typically addressed in stakeholder literature; corporations should take this question into consideration when developing communication strategies to manage their stakeholders or when it is important to balance claims of multiple stakeholders.

The case of Walgreens and its conflict with stakeholders (Plowman et al., 1995) demonstrates the need for organizations to balance relationships with many stakeholder groups. The three major areas of conflict for Walgreens were the cost of drugs, consumers' freedom to choose their drug provider, and mail-order drugs. The retailer attempted to accommodate the needs of many stakeholder groups; it chose to use a collaborative (two-way symmetrical) negotiation strategy on the cost of drugs and customer freedom issues, but an avoidance technique on mail-order drugs. The two-way model seeks feedback from stakeholders toward the goal of mutual understanding. In the case of the first two (i.e., cost of drugs and consumer choice), some common ground existed between the different stakeholder groups: Most supported controlling the price of drugs and giving patients the ability to choose a drug provider. In contrast, the stakeholders had greatly differing agendas on mail-order drugs, so Walgreens found that the best strategy was to avoid the issue until government regulations were further addressed. Plowman et al. use the two-way symmetrical model of communication and negotiation strategies to explain the results of conflict resolution in the different areas of Walgreens's pharmaceutical business. This model promotes a win-win strategy in resolving conflict (see also chapter 4). However, the authors suggest that using the two-way symmetrical model alone may not resolve the conflict to all parties' satisfaction and suggest navigating between the two-way asymmetrical (win-lose) and the two-way symmetrical (win-win) models.

Firm-Stakeholder Relationships

Using resource dependence theory, Frooman (1999) developed a classification of four types of firm-stakeholder relationships: firm power, high interdependence, low interdependence, and stakeholder power. A resource is anything an actor finds to be valuable, and dependence is a state which one actor must rely on another actor's actions to get a particular outcome. The actor that is being relied upon is the one that has the power. Because organizations are not self-sufficient or self-contained, they must rely on the environment to support them. Therefore, through exchange or trade relationships, stakeholders have the power to demand certain things from the organization in return for

Table 12.1 Matching Message Orientations to Organizational Stakeholders

	Customers, press, venture capitalists		
Union members, professional associations, employee affiliations	**Relational** **Purpose:** establish integrity, rapport, trust, confidence, and commitment **Medium and tone:** conversational, familiar words; inclusive pronouns; personal examples; honesty; commitment **Focus:** receiver-centered **Example:** informal chats; cafeteria talks; reflective listening; personal, supportive, communicative, reinforcing feedback	**Transformational** **Purpose:** challenge receivers to accept mind-stretching vision **Medium and tone:** visionary, charismatic, vivid, colorful metaphors and symbols; oral delivery; enthusiastic, emphatic, unorthodox written communication **Focus:** idea-centered, futuristic, rhetorical **Example:** CEO speech, written strategic plan, smart talk, communicating vision	***Stockowners, financial analysts, market regulators, competitors***
	Hierarchical **Purpose:** provide clear directions to receivers **Medium and tone:** neutral, precise words; controlled, sequential, standard constructions; factual accuracy; structural rigor; logical progression; realistic presentation; conventional documents; concrete examples; lists; tables; audit reports **Focus:** channel-centered **Example:** policy statements, procedural specifications, rules, standards, written documents, computer printouts, unaddressed letters, memos, directives	**Promotional** **Purpose:** promote an idea, sell a product or service, persuade receivers, establish credibility **Medium and tone:** decisive, engaging, original, supported by credible evidence, prepositional, assertive, declarative, vivid examples, sense of urgency **Focus:** argument-centered **Example:** sales presentations, recommendations to senior managers, press releases, directives, quarterly results, financial reports	
	Regulators, suppliers, standards institutions		

SOURCE: Based on Rogers, P. S., & Hildebrandt, H. W. (1993). "Competing values instruments for analyzing written and spoken management messages," in *Human Resource Management Journal, 32*(1), 121-142; Alan T. Belasen (2000). *Leading the Learning Organization: Communication and Competencies for Managing Change*, p. 61, SUNY Press. Reprinted with permission.

supporting it. The firm's relative dependence gives external stakeholders leverage over it. Frooman (1999) goes on to discuss two types of influence strategies: withholding and usage. Stakeholders use a withholding strategy when they want the firm to change a particular behavior. For example, a stakeholder might discontinue or threaten to discontinue providing the firm with a resource it depends on. Examples of withholding strategies include consumers engaging in a boycott, employees going on strike, and suppliers no longer providing a product due to unpaid bills. Stakeholders employ a usage strategy to put conditions on supplying a resource. This type of strategy is usually used when the stakeholder is still partially dependent on the firm, such as when a stakeholder is a supplier. With a withholding strategy, the firm usually absorbs the costs of making a change to its behavior, but with a usage strategy the cost is usually divided between both parties.

Frooman (1999) also discusses two strategy influence pathways: direct and indirect. A stakeholder uses a direct strategy when it can manipulate the resource without any outside help. The stakeholder uses an indirect strategy when it lacks power, in other words, when the firm is not dependent on the stakeholder. In this case, the stakeholder needs the help of another stakeholder as an ally, someone that the firm is dependent on. Direct and indirect withholding and usage strategies are used by stakeholders to get a firm to change its behavior. How do stakeholders get what they want? Frooman's discussion of the conflict between StarKist Tuna and the Earth Island Institute (EII) in the 1980s provides one answer.

StarKist

The conflict arose because StarKist was purchasing a good portion of its tuna from a foreign tuna fishing industry, which used an effective and efficient netting method called *purse-seining* to catch the tuna. The problem was that, in catching the tuna, it was also trapping more than 100,000 dolphins a year, which is precisely why the United States had banned this tuna-catching method. Domestic fleets were no longer allowed to use purse-seining, so StarKist turned to the foreign fishing industry.

In 1988 EII attempted to stop StarKist from employing the foreign fishing industry that used this method. The first thing EII did was to turn to tuna consumers. It wanted consumers to boycott StarKist tuna, and to persuade them to do so, EII made an 11-minute video that contained many disturbing and gruesome scenes. The video showed half-drowned dolphins mangled in fishing nets and dolphins being thrown overboard as shark bait. In the spring of 1988, the video was aired in its entirety or in parts on all of the major networks. EII then mass-produced the video and began distributing it to schools all around the country. Over the next 2 years the environmental media began reporting on the story, and the general media slowly followed suit. By the spring of 1990, about 60% of the public was aware of the issue and the request for a boycott. By April 1990, StarKist announced that it would stop purchasing tuna caught by the purse-seining method. StarKist also insisted that members of the Inter-American Tropical Tuna Commission would monitor the foreign fishing fleets.

Some of the main stakeholders involved in this case were the consumers, the foreign fishing industry, EII, the media, investors, the Inter-American Tropical Tuna Commission, and StarKist employees. Figure 12.2 depicts these stakeholders. Notice the resemblance between the StarKist stakeholders in Figure 12.2 and the CVFCC stakeholders in Figure 12.1. The foreign fishing industry supplied StarKist with a less costly product because of the efficient and cost-effective method it used to catch fish. StarKist was one of the leading tuna companies at the time. StarKist relied on the foreign fishing industry, and the foreign fishing industry relied on StarKist. That industry knew that if a boycott were to occur, it would lose a large chunk of its sales. Because these two entities relied on each other, StarKist was able to use a direct usage strategy to avoid having to absorb all of the cost involved in the behavior change.

StarKist never threatened to stop purchasing tuna from the foreign fishing industry; instead it put conditions on their relationship. A different fishing method was instituted, and observers from the Inter-American Tropical

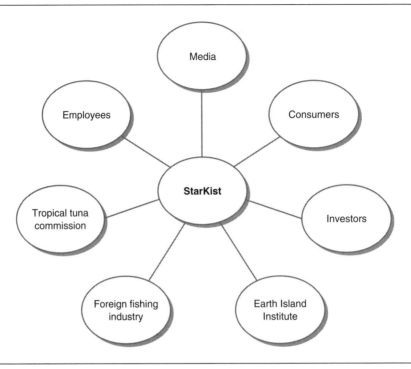

Figure 12.2 Stakeholders in StarKist's Environment

Tuna Commission would now be allowed on the ships. StarKist was able to split the cost with the industry fairly evenly (Frooman, 1999). The new required fishing method would cost the foreign fishing industry more money, as would having the commission's observers onboard, but the industry raised the cost of tuna only slightly. StarKist also had to absorb some of the costs, but did so without raising the price of canned tuna.

EII and StarKist had a low-interdependence relationship. EII was not a stakeholder until the purse-seining issue arose, but it became a stakeholder when it wanted StarKist to change its method of fishing. Indirectly, members of EII may have been stakeholders if they were consumers of StarKist tuna, but that alone would have been insignificant in making a difference. EII had to use an indirect strategy to affect StarKist's behavior. It chose to get the support of StarKist consumers, thus using them as its ally. To get their attention, EII

developed the aforementioned video. But it could not do this alone; it needed the support of the media to air the video. Through media exposure, consumers became informed about the issue and had the power to apply a withholding strategy to effect the behavior change that EII wanted. EII encouraged StarKist consumers to boycott the product, which would have a devastating effect on both StarKist and the foreign fishing industry. Without consumers purchasing the tuna, StarKist sales would plummet; moreover, it would not make any profit. The boycott would then affect the employees and the company's investors, not to mention its management.

StarKist employees could have been affected in more than one way, and they could have played the roles of multiple stakeholders. A StarKist employee might also be a StarKist consumer, a member of EII, and/or an investor in the company. A conflict arising from one of these roles could very negatively affect the employees of the organization. The effects could continue even beyond the solution that is reached. For instance, the employees could lose trust in the organization, and it may be difficult, if not impossible, to regain their trust and get them to believe in the organization's values again. This scenario is an example of how a negative image can affect the way employees identify with an organization (Corley et al., 2001). It shows how what happens externally can affect internal stakeholders.

Such a conflict could also affect employees by causing them to lose their jobs. For example, if StarKist had not given in to EII and had continued buying tuna that was caught using the purse-seining method, a full-scale boycott could have resulted. The boycott could have caused great economic loss for the company, resulting in the company going bankrupt and employees being laid off.

Investors would also have been affected by such a boycott because StarKist would have lost money by not making sales. Or investors could have pulled their support from the company even before a boycott could occur. The video that EII produced gave StarKist a very negative image and reputation. Investors could have seen continued association with such a company as a losing investment because a company's reputation and image greatly affect its success. Media relations could also have been affected by this conflict. The media communicated the issue to the public in support of EII and the consumers. If StarKist had not made changes, it might not have been able to maintain a good relationship with the media. The reporters might not have trusted the company if it had had a negative image and reputation, which would have led to negative media attention and the company's inability to have its story "spun" in a favorable light.

The consumers in this case had a large source of bargaining power. It was up to them to decide whether to put pressure on StarKist, and they were the stakeholder group with the most power to influence the company's behavior. Purchasing power and low switching costs allowed them to use a withholding strategy. The consumers were not dependent on StarKist; they could easily have started buying tuna from other companies. The consumers were able to threaten StarKist with a boycott if the company did not switch fishing methods. StarKist chose to protect its firm and change its behavior. And by insisting on having observers on the foreign fishing fleets, the company went above and beyond what was requested in order to further protect its image and reputation and to show stakeholders that it was willing to change.

Principles of Stakeholder Management

The concept of *stakeholder* was at the center of a 6-year project conducted by the Sloan Foundation. This project outlined the principles of stakeholder management, which are commonly referred to as the Clarkson Principles (Donaldson, 2002).

Principle 1—Managers should acknowledge and actively monitor the concerns of all legitimate stakeholders and should take their interests appropriately into account in decision making and operations. Managers must be aware of the diverse stakeholders in the corporate environment and the role that each stakeholder plays in and around the organization. Managers should listen to what each stakeholder wants; this does not mean that each request must be granted, but it does mean that each request must be evaluated and seriously considered.

Principle 2—Managers should listen to and openly communicate with stakeholders about their respective concerns and contributions, and about the risks that they assume because of their involvement with the corporation. Both internal and external communications are critical for successful stakeholder management. Effective communication involves not only sending messages but also receiving them; it involves discourse between managers and stakeholders. Managers should try to understand the multiple perspectives of the stakeholders.

Principle 3—Managers should adopt processes and modes of behavior that are sensitive to the concerns and capabilities of each stakeholder group. Because there is such a variety of stakeholder groups, managers must decide how to present information to each one. Each group of stakeholders varies in size, complexity, level of involvement, and primary interests. Methods of delivering information to stakeholders include shareholder meetings, collective bargaining agreements, advertising, public relations, press releases, personal contact, and, when dealing with entities such as government agencies, official proceedings. It is up to managers to decide which delivery method will be most effective in accomplishing the organization's goals and objectives.

Principle 4—Managers should recognize the interdependence of efforts and rewards among stakeholders and attempt to achieve a fair distribution of the benefits and burdens of corporate activity among them, taking into account their respective risks and vulnerabilities. Managers should distribute benefits and burdens (or externalities) that result from corporate activity fairly among the stakeholders. Each stakeholder is vulnerable on a different level.

Principle 5—Managers should work cooperatively with other entities, both public and private, to insure that risks and harms arising from corporate activities are minimized and, when they cannot be avoided, appropriately compensated for. Corporations and their managers sometimes need to rely on other organizations, so managers should be proactive in establishing contacts with relevant entities. Organizations should develop coalitions in order to reduce harmful impacts and compensate affected parties.

Principle 6—Managers should avoid altogether activities that might jeopardize inalienable human rights (e.g., the right to life) or give rise to risks, which if clearly understood, would

be patently unacceptable to relevant stakeholders. Corporate operations and managerial decisions often result in risky or unexpected outcomes. It is important for managers to communicate these risks to stakeholders that could be affected. An arrangement is considered satisfactory when stakeholders knowingly agree to accept a certain combination of risks and rewards. Sometimes an activity involves consequences for which no compensation would be sufficient. And sometimes an activity involves risks that are not fully understood or appreciated by critical stakeholders. When this occurs, managers may have to abandon the activity altogether or simply restructure it to eliminate the possibility of unacceptable consequences.

Principle 7—Managers should acknowledge the potential conflicts between (a) their own role as corporate stakeholders and (b) their legal and moral responsibilities to stakeholders, and they should address such conflicts through open communication, appropriate reporting and incentive systems, and, when necessary, third-party review. The fact that managers are also stakeholders in an organization is often overlooked. They have access to a great deal of privileged information that other stakeholders do not have access to, which creates asymmetrical relationships that often lead to tension. One way that managers can help reduce such tension is by subjecting themselves to periodic performance evaluation; another is by maintaining trusting relationships with diverse stakeholders based on mutual respect and credibility.

Communicating Messages to Stakeholders

Table 12.2 is a summary of the methodology developed by Lewis, Hamel, and Richardson (2001). It describes six models of stakeholder communication change, and although they are aimed at guiding nonprofit organizations, their significance for other organizations is also valuable.

Table 12.2 Models of Stakeholder Communication Change

Model	Description	Example	Costs
Equal Dissemination	This model focuses on distributing information to stakeholders of all sorts early and equally by means of meetings, postings on electronic lists, banners, and newsletters.	"We're talking about nearly every day, using almost every mode possible. We made a conscious effort to communicate until we were blue in the face—we didn't want the agencies to say we didn't know this change was coming."	There are tangible costs, and people offer unwanted advice and/or raise objections.
Equal Participation	Same as above; however, this model involves two-way communication—both disseminating information and soliciting input.	"If you are going to have change, you need to have consensus. If you spring it on them, you'll get problems."	This is an extremely tedious and political process. It is risky to solicit opinions before change and can be frustrating as well.
Quid Pro Quo	Something of value is exchanged for the communicative access granted by implementers. Implementers give more communicative attention to stakeholders who have something they need or desire (e.g., money, expertise, resources).	"There's a pecking order with our communication. Whoever pays the most dues gets listened to the most. Just like in any business, your biggest vendor or supplier will have the most clout."	Implementers run the risk of angering those who feel left out of the process.
Need to Know	Alternative to above. Implementers keep quiet about planned change except to those who really have to know or who explicitly express a desire for the information.	"Because we've had so many management changes in that one program, we were going to be monitored by the state. The CEO told us not to tell the board because he didn't want them to try and micromanage or get involved."	There is selective communication involving preferential treatment; it can be manipulative.
Marketing	This model focuses on constructing messages specific to individuals or to stakeholder groups—knowing who your stakeholders are and what motivates them.	"All stakeholders take a different communication strategy. You couldn't throw one message out and have it work for all the people you work with. They're too diverse and come from too many different places."	Customized messages make it difficult or impossible to carry out. Minor changes are very time-consuming.
Reactionary	This model is only apparent in a few cases. Implementers' communication has the flavor of crisis management—trying to survive a change, usually one that was forced on the organization or came up in response to an unexpected situation.	"Change happened so frequently that the grant agency would not accept a grant application from us because they didn't know what would come of the changes. We had to ride the wave of negativity until things calmed down and then we could communicate to everyone."	This is the least-planned approach. Implementers rarely have time to consider other approaches.

SOURCE: Based on Lewis, L. K., Hamel, S. A., & Richardson, B. K. Communicating change to nonprofit stakeholders, in *Management Communication Quarterly, 15*(1), 5–41. Copyright © 2001, by Sage Publications, Inc.

Factors that influence the selection of a model (or strategy) include structural and environmental variables (e.g., high specialization, functional differentiation, numbers of managers and communication channels), culture, and management style (Lewis et al., 2001). For example, the Equal Participation Model would be used if abundant communication channels are available, there is no urgency to implement change, and the organization perceives commitment to change as unproblematic. The Quid Pro Quo Model would be used if an urgent timetable exists, there is limited supply of resources and communication channels, and the organization needs to gain the commitment of key stakeholders. This model would probably be a common choice for nonprofit organizations due to their financial and political situations, but it may exclude non-resource-holding stakeholders from the communication process. Lewis et al. suggest that hybrid versions of these models are plausible (see Table 12.3), depending on corporate communication perceptions of two task dimensions: (a) the perceived need for communicative efficiency and (b) the perceived need for consensus building.

Steps in Stakeholder Analysis

The first step in a typical stakeholder analysis is for the corporate communication planning team to identify key internal, external, and interface stakeholders by mapping out the task environment of the focal organization. A typical task environment might include regulators, competitors, customers, investors, suppliers, unions, and even media and special interest groups (see Figure 12.1). Key stakeholders can be further classified as primary and secondary. Primary stakeholders (e.g., regulators, customers, investors, employees, affected communities) have a legitimate interest in the company's goals as well as an immediate, continuous, and powerful impact on executive decision- and policymaking processes. Secondary stakeholders (e.g., communities at

large) are less intimidating and typically use indirect sources of power to influence the organization.

The second step requires corporate communicators and analysts to rank the stakeholders by highlighting their relative bases of power. All stakeholders matter to a corporation in varying degrees. How does a corporate communication office determine which stakeholder matters more than another? Stakeholder salience is the degree to which managers give priority to competing stakeholder claims based on three attributes: power, legitimacy, and urgency (Mitchell, Agle, & Wood, 1997). These attributes are bound by cultural norms and behaviors and are often moderated by the values of the CEO (Agle, Mitchell, & Sonnenfeld, 1999). *Power* refers to the stakeholders' ability to structure the context of executive decisions. *Legitimacy* is the extent to which stakeholders' relationships or claims with the firm are rightful. *Urgency* is the degree to which the stakeholders' claims call for immediate attention. When a stakeholder has all three attributes, the manager must give that stakeholder high priority (Mitchel et al., 1997; Page, 2002). Often the legitimacy of a claim does not matter as much if the stakeholders have the power to make good on what they threaten to do. Power and legitimacy are core attributes of stakeholder salience; based on social cognition theory, managers are more likely to consider the power and legitimacy of a stakeholder group if they have prior experience with that group (Agle et al., 1999). Top executives and corporate communicators alike must consider all of the stakeholders' divergent interests through strategic decision making, and they should do so in a manner consistent with the claims of other stakeholder groups (Hill & Jones, 1992).

The third step in stakeholder analysis involves the evaluation of how well the organization performs against stakeholders' perceptions or criteria of effectiveness. This step is essential in gathering feedback about stakeholders' general satisfaction level and whether the organization tries to meet their expectations. A simple

Table 12.3   Factors Influencing the Choice of Communication Change System

		Need for Consensus Building	
		Low	High
Need for Communicative Efficiency	High	**Need to know model**—The change sparks little controversy and requires little in the way of commitment from stakeholders, and implementers themselves control the resources necessary for installation of the change. However, implementers are faced with a low budget for communication about the change, and/or a scarcity of available channels for communication, as well as possible time pressures. This model is efficient in targeting key individuals for communication and provides needed opportunities for interaction only with those whose opinions are pertinent to the change and/or who are specifically interested in the change.	**Quid pro quo and Marketing models**—Implementers are likely to concentrate efforts on those who "hold the most cards." Gaining consensus from the few stakeholders with something to offer comes to be viewed as more beneficial than attempting to communicate with everyone on a limited budget and limited time. A marketing approach might also be used for a few key stakeholders who receive a substantial portion of the communication
	Low	**Equal dissemination model**—Implementers consider communication channels to be abundant and affordable, have no overwhelming urgency to implement, and perceive that commitment to the change and cooperation will be unproblematic. This model provides the maximum information for the maximum number of stakeholders and forestalls any potential negativism through equal treatment and early notification. It also avoids creating unnecessary commotion about the change by encouraging interaction about it.	**Equal participation and Marketing models**—Nonprofit implementers who perceive that their organization has time, resources, and available communication channels are likely to use equal participation. Change may be controversial and intense; implementers will probably view participation in the process as necessary to gaining commitment to change. A marketing approach might also be used when the organization is small and most interaction occurs face to face.

SOURCE: Based on Lewis, L. K., Hamel, S. A., & Richardson, B. K. Communicating change to nonprofit stakeholders, in *Management Communication Quarterly, 15*(1), 5-41. Copyright © 2001, by Sage Publications, Inc.

methodology developed by Blair and Fottler (1990) for health care systems appears to work well. A modified version is described below.

1. Determine whether each stakeholder is internal, external, or interface and whether each is a "key" or not. To determine whether a stakeholder is a key, look at Figure 12.3 and select the stakeholders that rank high on influence and importance.

2. A map similar to the one depicted in Figure 12.4 can be used to place external, interface,

Stakeholder	Status	Key	
		Yes	No
1.			
2.			
3.			
4.			
(etc.)			

Figure 12.3   Classifying Stakeholders

and internal stakeholders around the CVFCC box. This activity should yield a network of the players identified in Figure 12.3. Any likely coalitions (i.e., networks) among these stakeholders should be indicated with a heavy line. External stakeholders function outside the boundaries of the organization in expectation that policies, decisions, or actions address their concerns or provide them with certain benefits; internal

stakeholders are members of the organization; and interface stakeholders operate both within and outside the organization with proximity to important networks of communication or decision authority centers.

3. Corporate communicators can identify the most relevant stakeholders to the organization. Doing so helps in assessing the relative power of the key stakeholders identified in the previous steps. With input from departmental managers, corporate communicators then assess the overall power of each stakeholder and whether it is increasing or decreasing (see Figure 12.5).

4. Figure 12.6 can be used to rate the stakeholders' sources of power. Typical sources include financial control, political support, expertise, and information (see also Figure 12.9).

5. Using Figure 12.7 as a guide, key stakeholders and their core values and interests can be listed and then audited by corporate communication staff. Recognizing these values and

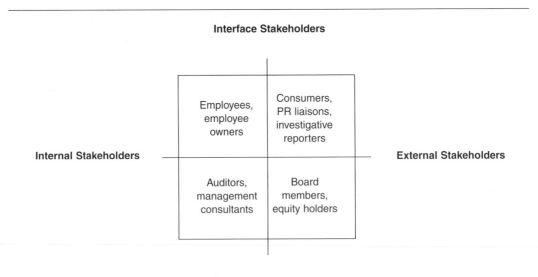

Figure 12.4   Using the Competing Values Framework for Corporate Communication to Organize Data About Stakeholders

Key Stakeholder	Overall Power Level	Significance
	(L) ——— (H)	(+) ——— (–)
1.		
2.		
3.		
(etc.)		

Figure 12.5   Rating Stakeholders' Power

Key Stakeholder	Sources of Power
1.	1.
	2.
	3.
2.	1.
	2.
	3.
3.	1.
	2.
	3.
(etc.)	

Figure 12.6   Rating Stakeholders' Sources of Power

Key Stakeholder	Core Values and Interests
1.	1.
	2.
	3.
2.	1.
	2.
	3.
3.	1.
	2.
	3.
(etc.)	

Figure 12.7   Identifying Core Values and Interests

interests is essential for determining which issues are likely to be important for different stakeholder management strategies.

6. Figure 12.8 can be used to identify strategic issues that face the organization. Each key stakeholder is then assessed in terms of how important each issue is in relation to the stakeholder (Blair & Fottler, 1990).

Sources of Power

Several important sources of social power are typically recognized in the literature: legal power that relies heavily on administrative power and centralized authority; reward power that establishes the dependence of others by virtue of controlling essential (e.g., financial) resources and having discretion over the allocation of such resources; referent power that achieves compliance because of admiration, a desire for approval, or identification processes (e.g., when consumers identify with the core values of socially responsible organizations); and expert power that creates dependence of others due to knowledge advantages and other core competencies. These power sources are used by actors (e.g., stakeholders, social systems) to influence or shape policies, create favorable economic conditions, gain relative advantage over others, or affect the public image or credibility of some actors. Power relationships are asymmetrical (i.e., one is powerful, the other powerless) and therefore fluid because vulnerable actors try to offset the equation of power and change the dynamics of dependence. They extract themselves from relationships, seek alternative sources, or develop resources that powerful actors need to obtain, thus changing the equilibrium from dependence to interdependence, or from control relationships to exchange or trade relationships. Of course, if they benefit from the current relationship, powerful actors tend to resist attempts by more vulnerable actors to withdraw or change the power relationship.

Key Stakeholders	Strategic Issues		
	1.	2.	3.
	CI, SVI, or NI?		
1.			
2.			
3.			
(etc.)			

Figure 12.8   Identifying Strategic Issues

NOTE: CI indicates critically important to stakeholder; SI, somewhat important to stakeholder; NI, not at all important to stakeholder.

Thus the conditions for conflict arise as both parties try to frustrate each other's efforts. The message here is that it is virtually impossible for social actors to fully insulate themselves from influences or interactions with others. Social systems are interdependent by definition; they are connected through a supply value chain. The organization depends on input markets (called *upstream systems*) for resources and on output markets (*downstream systems*) for distribution of its value-added goods or services.

A diagram of sources of power from the perspective of the CVFCC appears in Figure 12.9. Notice how the model distinguishes between two sources of power: organizational and managerial. Organizational sources of power relate to administrative discretion, as with the option to allocate or withhold resources. Managerial sources of power relate more to personal biases, preferences, or interests. As discussed earlier, the CVFCC/ Stakeholder/Power model provides structure for communicating and interacting with diverse stakeholders. For example, it would justify Walgreens's choice of a collaborative negotiation strategy in dealing with the cost of drugs and customer freedom because such issues seem to be located in the lower right quadrant (but closer to the resources dimension) along with customer

and vendor stakeholders. The other strategy used by Walgreens—avoidance—was also related to the regulating agencies dimension. In the StarKist case, EII applied pressure through the upper right quadrant with threats of using sources of power from the lower right quadrant.

The prioritizing matrix (Table 12.4) is a good tool that enables corporate communicators to rate stakeholders and assign quantitative value, if necessary, to those in need of most attention. Ranking the stakeholders by the extent of their importance and influence can help decision makers weigh in on their interests and respond to their concerns. Estimating or making a value judgment about the criteria that stakeholders use to assess the organization's performance is an integral aspect of this method.

Assessing Stakeholders' Perceptions Using the CVFCC

The CVFCC can also be used as an ongoing assessment tool to identify the gap between how well corporate communication executives balance the set of contradictory pressures coming from different directions and to organize communication responses both proactively and

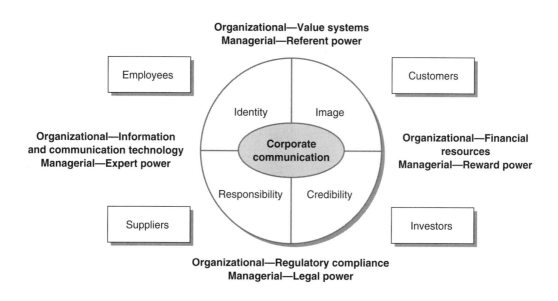

Figure 12.9   Competing Values Framework for Corporate Communication: Sources of Stakeholders' Power

strategically to deal with these pressures. The CFVCC model has two important parts: (a) the communication performance profile in which the relative importance of certain elements of corporate communication can be identified along the lines of current and desired profiles and (b) the measurement model in which the gap between the two profiles, as illustrated in Figure 12.10 can be translated into an action plan leading to revisions in corporate communication strategies and activities. Thus, the CVFCC can serve as a barometer that registers the perceptual biases of corporate executives and the variation in communication emphases. The framework allows executives to review the current status of corporate communication activities in a single communication report and make choices about resource allocation and the trajectory of communication activities and products, as well as measure the distance between reality and perceptions and take steps to close the gap.

The CVFCC is also useful in auditing stakeholders' views about the overall effectiveness of corporate communication, identifying communication strengths and weaknesses, and realigning communication strategies with external environments. A typical assessment can be conducted at several levels, including the actual corporate identity (how the organization presents itself to various stakeholders) and the communicated identity (the identity as projected to stakeholders via different cues, which represent lenses that the organization would like its stakeholders to use in order to perceive it favorably). It is possible for one organization to have multiple corporate identities, or images, depending on the views of its multiple stakeholders. This reality underscores the essential link between image and strategic management, or the importance of integrating different communication systems into a strategic perspective.

Summary

Chapter 12 is an important milestone in this book. It draws on the CVFCC and other methodologies to help map out the most important

Table 12.4   Prioritizing Stakeholders

| | | Importance of Stakeholder | | | |
		Unknown	Little/no importance	Some importance	Significant importance
Influence of Stakeholder	Unknown				
	Little/no influence				
	Some influence				
	Significant influence				

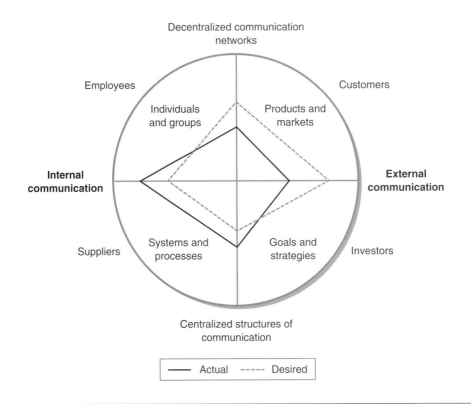

Figure 12.10   Competing Values Framework for Corporate Communication: Actual and Desired Profiles

stakeholders, their values and bases of power, and strategies that corporate communication staff can use to strategically address the concerns of influential stakeholders. The chapter presents important concepts, process guidelines, and case applications to illustrate the significance of stakeholder analysis and its value to the field of corporate communication, both in theory and in practice.

Review Questions

1. Discuss the strategic importance of stakeholder analysis for corporate communication.

2. Discuss the value of the CVFCC as a tool for identifying key stakeholders.

3. Identify an organization with which you are familiar (e.g., workplace, university, hospital). Use Figure 12.1 to map out the primary and secondary stakeholders of this organization. Then use Figure 12.9 to briefly describe the sources of power of these stakeholders. What are the lessons that you can draw from this exercise?

CASE STUDY

Granite City: Doing More With Less

It was not the typical morning after a general election in the office of Roger Peytons, the city manager. The results of the November election in Granite City had been expected to bring new council members and possibly a new mayor but no one expected an entirely new council and the tax limitation amendments. As Roger Peytons reviewed the results in the morning paper he knew that his administration was going to be called on to do more with less and to do it quickly.

Granite City, with a population of 450,000, has experienced rapid growth during most of the last decade. Only in the last three years has an industry-wide slump in electronics manufacturing slowed employment and growth opportunities. During the past ten years Granite City has been a haven for developers: The city council has frequently overridden city planner recommendations for modest development in favor of more aggressive plans. Although general property taxes are low, several special property improvement districts have defaulted on bonds, which [has] substantially raised taxes in some portions of the city. Granite City is the lowest-cost utilities market in the nation among cities of comparable size with a utility monopoly run by city government. Roger Peytons was surprised that the citizens of Granite City did not have a more favorable picture of their city government.

The tax limitation amendments were Roger Peytons' real challenge at the meeting of his senior staff. Amendment 3 provided no new taxes without voter approval. He could live with that and even saw some advantage to the amendment because it provided for extensive public debate concerning needed projects and improvements. Amendment 4 was the disaster for the city budget. It mandated a tax rollback over a two-year period. The impact in the coming fiscal year would be over $12 million from an annual operating budget of $112 million. The new council had run on a platform supporting the amendments and would certainly want rapid action from the city manager's office.

As Peytons began his meeting with senior staff he sensed the despair and concern around the table. His public relations director had four calls from media asking for his response to the elections and his plan to bring city spending and programs [into] compliance. Peytons described the challenges he saw ahead— reductions in services and programs that would affect the public; elimination of jobs to reduce overhead; and communication with members of a new council, most of whom had strong convictions about the types of services and programs the city should provide. Senior staff members were given two weeks to prepare budget reduction proposals for all departments except uniformed services, namely police and fire. Peytons decided to postpone a news conference until he had an opportunity to meet privately with the mayor and council.

(Continued)

(Continued)

Peytons' first meeting with the mayor and council convinced him that he had a difficult job ahead. He had to persuade the council of the need for balanced cuts across the budget rather than the elimination of specific programs, which might meet with the disapproval of particular council members. Peytons was relieved when the mayor seemed to side with his plan. At the end of the meeting the council moved to accept for consideration a budget reduction plan from the city manager's office before asking the staff support to devise a council-directed plan.

At the next meeting of his senior staff, Peytons listened to the proposals for budget reduction in 12 program areas, with heavy emphasis on reductions in street improvements and repair and the development of parks and recreational facilities. The program reductions would, over a two-year period, eliminate approximately 400 jobs. Senior staff seemed unwilling to go to the public for hearings on the proposed changes, much less take the proposal to the council. Peytons directed public hearings to be set for two weeks from the day of the meeting. Moreover, he asked the human resources director to work with him to notify all city employees of the types of program proposals that would soon appear in the local press. Peytons also set up a meeting with the mayor to review the proposals.

The human resources director recommended that all department heads have brief information meetings with their employees. No firm decisions would be reached for several months, so the goals of meetings were to inform employees of the magnitude of the budget program and to communicate the commitment of management to minimize the number of jobs subject to layoffs. The human resources director told Peytons he hoped to achieve at least one-third of the reduction through normal attrition. He did suggest that some employees would have to be moved laterally to fill positions where job needs required replacements.

The mayor approved the initial proposals and the establishment of public hearings to gather reactions to the reduction plans. He advised Peytons to wait until after the public hearings to take proposals to the council at large. Press coverage would keep the council generally informed and they, of course, could attend all hearings. Peytons was somewhat uncomfortable making public plans that the remainder of the council had not reviewed. He chose to take the mayor's advice because he knew the mayor was politically astute in such matters.

The public hearings were frustrating. The 12 areas of program reduction affected citizens in all sectors of the city and met the overall budget reduction goals. Citizens who had led the fight for the tax rollback called the proposals punitive and designed to exaggerate the impact of Amendment 4. They contended a significant reduction in payroll would minimize reductions in programs. Various public constituencies supported all 12 of the proposed programs or projects.

Council members attending the public hearings became concerned about the complexity of the overall problem. In addition to members of the public who wanted specific programs and projects, council members had received letters and telephone calls from over 300 city employees voicing concerns about their jobs and the overall perception of the quality of city services.

Media stories on the city's budget problems were daily front-page news. Two companies considering Granite City for plant locations expressed concern to the chamber of commerce economic development committee; they felt the political climate was less favorable than it was at the time they had put Granite City on their short selection lists.

The city manager's office had increasing inquiries from employees about their futures with the city, and morale in general seemed low. Roger Peytons decided he needed to establish a comprehensive communication plan for the internal organization and, to a lesser extent, to deal with public inquiries. He called his staff together and suggested they design a communication program to address council issues, employee concerns, public inquiries, and the media in general. Although his staff members were concerned about their capability to do so, they agreed that many of their current problems may have resulted from the lack of a comprehensive information plan prior to the election.

Case Questions

1. Use Figures 12.1 and 12.9 to diagram the key stakeholders in this case and assess their sources of power.

2. Discuss the gap between stakeholders' desires in the environment of Granite City and the pattern of organizational responses, including typical channels and message orientations.

3. What, if anything, should Roger Peytons and his staff do to prevent the problems they are facing?

4. Should the city manager have separate communication plans for employees, the council, the public, and the media?

5. What is needed in each of the plans? Based on the information in Table 12.1, what communication channels and message orientations would you use? How would you monitor the effectiveness of Roger Peytons (clue: use Figure 12.10)? How should he proceed?

SOURCE: From Pamela Shockley-Zalabak, *Understanding Organizational Communication: Cases, Commentaries, and Conversations*. Published by Allyn & Bacon, Boston, MA. Copyright © 1994 by Pearson Education. Reprinted by permission of the publisher.

13

Communication Audits Within Organizations

Effective communication audits can alert managers to gaps or blind spots that might exist between observed and expected communication performance. Audits provide feedback about strengths and weaknesses of organizational culture as well as managerial roles and styles; they also help develop measures to deal with glitches and other communication breakdowns. As such, a communication audit is an excellent diagnostic and intervention tool to reduce communication anxiety and increase the effectiveness and efficiency of communication flow within and outside the organization. Typical communication audits (see Figure 13.1) include policies, procedures, and rules (systems of control); communication roles and message orientations (systems of interaction); transmitters of communication, media, and channels (systems of delivery); and culture, goals, and decision-making communication (systems of performance).

Functionalism

Most communication audits follow a functionalist perspective based on identification, measurement, and evaluation of observed communication behaviors and activities. The functional perspective views communication as an information conduit or *pipeline*. The goal is to send messages through the pipeline as efficiently and accurately as possible to improve productivity. Any elements that hinder or reduce the efficiency and effectiveness of communication transactions or communication relationships become potential targets for assessment and intervention, the goal of which is to restore smoothness and accuracy on both ends of the communication process: senders and receivers. Through diagnosis and measurement, the typical communication audit helps highlight "energy leaks," "white spaces," or "blind spots" that are both the cause and outcome of communication failures.

Communication audits that follow the functionalist approach touch on many aspects of organizational activities, including the boundaries of the organization and its interface with the environment. Environmental scanning and stakeholder analysis, for example, are different means to assess key players in the external environment and their potential impact on the organization's activities. On the other hand, network

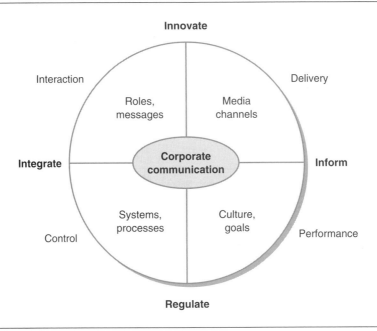

Figure 13.1   Typical Communication Audits

analysis or interaction analysis relies on socio-metric methods aimed at tracing communication patterns and processes across formal and informal systems to determine communication interdependencies and key access points to the system. Systematic audits usually cover six important steps: planning to establish the purpose of the audit; assessing top executives' attitudes toward communication and perceptions of specific communication strengths and weaknesses; collecting and analyzing written communication material; conducting focus groups, interviewing, and collecting firsthand data; designing and running a survey instrument to get the broadest possible coverage; and tabulating and communicating the results. Content analysis, which looks at messages according to specific criteria and vocabulary usage, is often utilized to gain perspective about the fit between the objectives of the message and its form or substance.

Interpretivism

Whereas functionalists use quantitative methods and direct assessments (e.g., attitude surveys) to evaluate the "distance" between actual communication performance (the baseline) and desired performance (benchmarks) and suggest measures to close that gap, interpretivists look at communication as part of the fabric of organizational life. Interpretivists are more interested in uncovering underlying values, beliefs, and latent dynamics and tensions that may result in conflicts and failures through listening to employees' daily discourse (Jones, 2002). Instead of using surveys and measurements to identify potential causes for information underload (e.g., when upward communication is lacking) or overload (e.g., when vertical communication lines are saturated, thus creating bottlenecks) or determining the extent to which employees are satisfied with the flow of information, interpretivist auditors listen to employees' accounts to develop an understanding of how they feel about what is happening around them. Interpretivists then try to identify emerging themes and meaningful behaviors that are part of the daily makeup of the organization. One method used by interpretivist auditors to help form their understanding about social discourse is textual analysis; any printed material or field notes that document exchanges of communication can be used for such an analysis. A second method is ethnomethodology; organizational communication is understood through dramas, metaphors, and symbols, with members playing different roles. Most data are collected through observations, member responses to oral or written questions, and transcriptions of organizational stories and texts (Meyer, 2002). Content analysis is then used to identify emerging themes, key events, or symbols that represent reflections of the unconscious routines that guide members' discourse and behavior without being clearly noticed. Unlike functionalist auditors, who compile the data using statistical methods and charts and present their findings in bulleted conclusions and suggestions for improvement, interpretivists write reports that look more like the organizational life history of key events.

The study conducted by Morgan et al. (2004) is a good example of typical interpretivist research. It was conducted via surveys but focused mainly on the storytelling parts of the surveys. The two open-ended items ("share a personal, specific experience that further explains your response to, or simply relates to, any one of the 28 statements" from a close-ended portion of the questionnaire; "reflect on your history as an AGRON employee, and describe the role, if any, the company has played in your life") illustrate the sort of data that are solicited by the interpretivist investigator. By reading all the personal accounts several times, the researchers can categorize emerging themes and differentiate one source of employee identification from another. The merit of this method

is that employees do not need to choose from any one source, but rather all sources identified come from employees' personal experiences. These sources are authentic and can engender further conceptualizations from employees if communicated back to them.

Both functionalism and interpretivism have their own merits; each is more suitable than the other in particular situations. If what is being measured is clear and specific, a functionalist model with designed questions is more efficient. But if the problems are unclear or exist deep within the daily discourse of organizational life, the interpretivist method might be more useful. And sometimes it is most productive to use both methods in a complementary way; in doing so, established themes can be measured and new themes can be detected, enabling researchers to arrive at a much fuller assessment of observed and underlying organizational discourse.

Uncertainty Reduction

Communication audits can be best understood from an uncertainty reduction perspective. Organizational members, particularly during transition, have both predictive and explanatory needs about the future (Hargie, Tourish, & Wilson, 2002). They need to know what is going to happen and how changes in communication policies, activities, and directives might affect their status and work conditions. As uncertainty increases, they seek more information to help answer questions and relieve stress and role ambiguity. When communication lines are not used properly or when managers withhold information, employees perceive this as a threat. Consequently, they look for alternative means of communication such as cliques and grapevines to satisfy their need for information. Communication audits help uncover this need through a gap analysis that looks at the perceived and actual flow of communication. When linked with organizational effectiveness criteria such as those in the CVF (see the section on Cultural Types later in this chapter), a communication audit becomes a powerful tool to measure the alignment of communication practices and media appropriateness against the strategies and goals of the organization. Moving from assessment to intervention, a communication audit helps improve management practices, creates a better organizational climate, and leads to higher level of employee satisfaction.

The Process of a Communication Audit

According to Hunn and Meisel (1991), the audit process generally consists of surveying the organization's employees, observing its operations, and analyzing formal and informal reports or messages used to communicate information internally and externally. The first step in a communication audit is to conduct top management interviews. These interviews are important in understanding management's attitudes and beliefs about communication within the organization, and they are used to highlight problems in management communication practices and styles. Among the items collected could be orientation packets, policy and procedural manuals, organization publication materials, and memos. In addition, analysis of organizational messages provides insight into the strengths and weaknesses of the organization's current communication practices, thus adding data to support the findings. The next step in the communication audit is to conduct employee interviews, which should be done via focus groups representing different functional areas of the organization. For example, one group could be employees who have direct contact with the customers, and another group could be employees who package the goods sold by the company. The next step in the communication audit is to prepare and administer the questionnaires, which should be based on the communication areas identified during the planning meeting

and the management and employee interviews. In order to analyze the data, and to aid in compiling a report for the organization, the data must be put in some form that allows the researchers to run tests and develop statistics. If the goal of the audit is to assess the organization's external communication practices, the methodology also usually includes some form of stakeholder analysis.

Benefits

Communication audits have many benefits for the organizations that sponsor them. They highlight not only deficiencies in organizational communication that cause major breakdowns and limit an organization's effectiveness but also ways to improve. Communication audits typically illustrate the differences between the organization's intended goals and objectives and the actual performance of its managers. Differences often lie in the definitions of work objectives and performance expectations as well as in how people interact, exchange information, or support the organization's values and goals. When there are discrepancies between the organization's goals and objectives and how the employees perform their specified duties, the organization may not run as efficiently and effectively as it could. The communication audit is useful in highlighting those discrepancies and facilitating change. Another benefit of the audit is that many organizations justify certain budget expenses based on the identification of communication effectiveness. For example, if a communication audit yields positive feedback for company-wide publications, the organization may be more apt to continue to fund the publications in the future.

At the personal level, the results of communication audits often promote an increase in productivity and improved interpersonal communication, decision-making, and problem-solving practices. There is a substantial agreement among experts that internal communication audits help managers increase confidence in their communication abilities and skills and gain greater proficiency in dealing with employees, customers, and executives (Robson & Tourish, 2005). Managers who use the CVFCC communication audit tools reportedly develop better understanding across managerial and functional lines and work together as a management team. They are able to develop a shared understanding of the core leadership competencies required to support organizational capabilities and business growth strategies. Content analysis is another communication audit tool that can improve business and interpersonal communication because it sensitizes managers to the appropriateness of message composition and message form or substance. Crafting and articulating a message has long been recognized as a skill that helps support communication relationships (Barge, 1994; Conger, 1996). Managers can learn to identify characteristics and orientations that tend to dominate their messages, and, more important, they can learn about which characteristics are lacking in their messages.

Sometimes, the goal of the communication audit is simply to better understand the different functions of communication or to offer basic feedback about the current state of communication practices in the organization. When best communication practices are used to reflect the desire to remedy deficiencies or to remove communication barriers to optimize organizational performance, the communication audit methods are also diagnostic. These diagnostic methods, such as those described in the next sections, allow corporate executives to measure existing communication practices against future needs and goals and to take proactive steps to improve communication performance.

Identifying Communication Activities Across Managerial Levels

Although all managers require a blend of conceptual, technical, and HR skills to perform their jobs effectively, top executives are expected to have greater conceptual skills than those of middle managers or first-line supervisors. This higher expectation is due to the fact that the depth of top managers' responsibilities is much greater and requires significant mental, analytical, and diagnostic abilities to acquire and interpret information from multiple sources to make complex decisions that affect the whole organization. Technical skills, including job skills and functional expertise, are more important for first-line supervisors. Middle managers, who function as communication links between upper and lower management, must have strong HR skills; their proximity to the top may also require strong conceptual skills. These skills, however, must be balanced against the functional skills that are essential to middle management decision making at the unit or division level. These important skill variations support the various managers' distinct responsibilities.

It is important for managers at all levels, however, to ensure that the eight universal leadership roles described in chapter 11 are manifested in their behaviors. For example, managers at all levels perform the monitor role. First-line supervisors use short-range scheduling, expense budgets, operations management, and measurement tools to oversee the activities of subordinates and meet performance targets specified by upper management. Top executives are engaged more in reading and evaluating financial statements and reports, and they are concerned with strategic planning and control systems to meet performance and profit targets at the organization level. Middle managers, on the other hand, are involved more in functional deployment and intermediate planning, and they frequently use output control systems to monitor the activities at lower levels. Thus, although managers at all levels perform the role of monitor, each level has different nuances and objectives. The scope of activities is also different. Top executives focus more on broader issues and concerns as well as shape and control business and financial performance and respond to stakeholders' concerns. Middle managers pay more attention to internal processes, functional interfaces, and how first-line supervisors handle the details of subordinates' performance. As managers move up the chain of command and as they become removed from specific information about customers, performance, and so on, they typically rely more on interpretation of the details rather than keeping track of the details themselves. These differences are crucial for the proper functioning of the organization because they provide the foundation for effective organizational integration. The three management levels appear as part of a means-ends chain of objectives: Accomplishing the goals of lower levels serves as a means to achieve the goals of higher levels.

The Importance of Contextual Factors

Belasen (2000) reports on the results of communication audits conducted in four different organizations: telecommunications, bank, power lab, and dining services. One common thread that emerged from the audits was the importance of the effects of contextual factors on the predominant roles and message orientations used by managers at all levels. The managers in the sample from the bank placed greater emphasis on the external roles, particularly those of broker, innovator, and producer. Whereas the bank's emphasis on external roles stemmed from marketing outreach and client relationships, the makeup of the power lab, which comprised primarily specialists, naturally demanded more emphasis on the facilitator role. In both the bank and the power lab, virtually all levels of management viewed the coordinator role as less important, but for different reasons. In the bank, it was because of a greater emphasis on boundary-spanning, brokering, and linking activities outside the organization; in the power lab, it was due to the nature of specialists whose activities are coordinated primarily via mutual adjustments and lateral relations. The managers in the dining

service organization, however, perceived the coordinator role as important primarily because of quality control and an emphasis on workflow operations. Another interesting finding was that, in the bank, the innovator and broker roles were perceived as important by all managers regardless of their hierarchical location. This perception may have been a result of the sales-driven culture and the bank managers' high degree of understanding about the importance of creative thinking, effective presentation of ideas, and other primary characteristics of effective innovators and brokers.

Although managers at all levels perform the four fundamental functions of planning, organizing, leading, and controlling, their managerial responsibilities tend to vary. This variation typically occurs along the lines of time horizon (e.g., long-term planning versus short term operational goals), span of attention toward different domains (e.g., market positioning, internal processes, management of professional intellect, organizational productivity), and range or scope of activities (e.g., micro versus macro issues, external versus internal focus). Top executives' time horizon and span of attention, for example, are strategic; they focus on the competitive advantages of the firm and its overall strength and positioning within the market. Managers at lower levels, on the other hand, pay more attention to individuals and groups working together to accomplish the unit's goals. In the telecommunications organization, for example, the profile of the first-line supervisors tilted toward the upper-left quadrant of the CVFCC (i.e., interactions, teamwork), whereas that of top executives tilted toward the upper-right quadrant of the CVFCC (i.e., change, delivery). These results pinpoint that top executives favor external communication roles, especially in a highly competitive market; first-line supervisors value internal roles, particularly those associated with mentoring employees and facilitating group interactions; and middle managers fall right in the middle, illustrating the importance for them to maintain a balance between the internal and external system requirements.

Assessment of Managerial Communication Roles and Skills

To gain insights into a person's managerial strengths and weaknesses, it is helpful to gather information from people who work together in different capacities and different working relationships. In assessing a manager's abilities, these individuals articulate their perceptions of the behaviors manifested in the roles played by the manager. These individuals' assessments are essential for balancing or validating the way managers perceive themselves. The smaller the gap between self-perception and the perception of others, the greater the strength in particular areas; the larger the gap, the greater the weakness. By rank ordering any discrepancies in perception from least to most important, managers determine the priority they place on each role and skill in terms of job needs or future professional development. Self-improvement efforts tend to focus on the following questions:

- Was anything in the assessments surprising?
- What "rang true"?
- How do you account for the discrepancies between your personal profiles and those provided by others?
- What value was gained from these assessments?

By comparing the results of self-assessment against the assessment by others, a manager can take steps to deal with higher expectations (e.g., by increasing personal involvement) or lower expectations (e.g., by decreasing an overemphasis on monitoring behavior), thus reducing tension and the potential for conflict in interpersonal relations. The same communication audit and gap analysis can be used to identify blind spots across

managerial levels. For example, although middle managers who participated in a communication audit of a service organization believed that their attention was equally distributed across the CVF communication roles, top executives (their bosses) and first-line supervisors (their subordinates) perceived the middle managers' role behaviors quite differently; they felt that the middle managers did not pay enough attention to the producer role. Furthermore, they seemed to signal an overall dissatisfaction with the scope of the middle managers' role performance (see Figure 13.2). Note how first-line supervisors felt that the middle managers should increase their mentor and facilitator responsibilities, a need that relies on more communication and feedback between the two levels. Interestingly, the same middle managers wanted to see a decrease in the mentor and facilitator activities displayed by first-line supervisors (see also Figure 11.2).

Notice how the assessments by others contain and even go beyond the scope of the middle managers' self-assessment. Of course, these profiles present only one side of the story; a true gap analysis should also involve a comparison between the actual (i.e., current) and desired (i.e., preferred or idealized) profiles. Such a comparison gives evaluators, communication analysts, and communication directors a sense of what needs to be improved (target of audit) and how important the improvement is (outcome of audit). Figure 13.3 presents the idealized profiles for the middle managers. Remember that the middle managers provide their self-perceptions of how they would like to see themselves performing these communication roles. Of course, the self-perceptions do not always align with the perceptions of others. For example, middle managers agree that the scope of their attention should include all the roles, but it is evident that the first-line supervisors and top executives think differently. In fact, top executives ended up pushing the desired profile further toward the right. Is this reasonable? You be the judge.

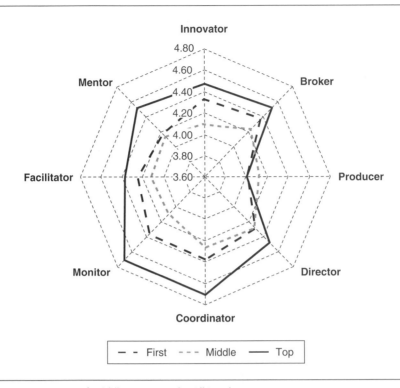

Figure 13.2   Assessment of Middle Managers by All Levels

Diagnosing Organizational Culture

Chapter 8 introduced the concept of *culture* and the importance of aligning employees' attitudes and commitments with corporate values and overall direction. Cameron and Quinn (1999) define organizational culture as "the taken-for-granted values, underlying assumptions, expectations, collective memories, and definitions present in an organization" (p. 14). Organizational culture represents a set of commonly shared values, beliefs, and ways of thinking that provide members with a sense of organizational identity. It is this sense of identity that provides unwritten, and often unspoken, guidelines for how social systems develop and how things are done in an organization. An organization's culture is initially formed as a result of collective memories, past experiences, and influence by strong leadership, past and present. Over time, assumptions about how to operate become so implicitly embedded in the underlying structure of interactions that they are difficult, if not impossible, to articulate. Organizational culture goes largely undetected because it is not tangible, but rather it is found in the prevailing ideology of organizational members. These members are often unaware of the culture until it is challenged or the organization is faced with a new culture, which underscores the importance of understanding organizational culture especially during transitions so that members know where they stand in relation to their environment.

Successful organizations must continually and appropriately respond to environmental changes. Because of the dramatic changes taking

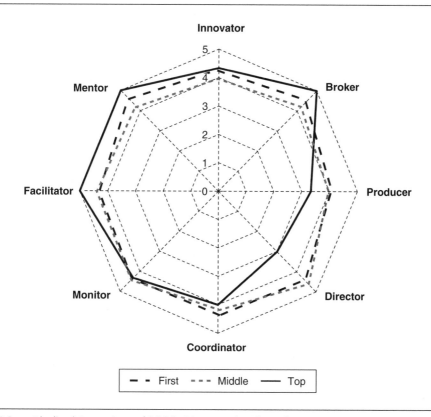

Figure 13.3   Idealized Perceptions of Middle Managers by All Levels

place in today's marketplace, such as the rate of technological change associated with the shift to an information-age economy, organizations no longer have a choice—they must determine how to change in order to increase their effectiveness. Weick and Sutcliffe (2001) propose that managers create an atmosphere that encourages individuals to monitor, challenge, and discuss each other's ideas in order to be receptive to new ways of doing things. When organizational members are willing to consider multiple perspectives and try innovative ideas, they add complexity to the organization, which allows it to more effectively meet the challenges posed by a complex environment. Effective organizations are those that are able and willing to change in response to their environment. Change efforts such as total quality management, downsizing, and reengineering initiatives have been used and

implemented by many organizations to increase and enhance effectiveness, and yet the desired change was not achieved. The success of these changes was limited because they focused on program changes while leaving the culture the same (Belasen, 2000). New strategies, tools, and/or techniques can be implemented, but unless the values, beliefs, and ways of thinking and doing things (i.e., the culture) change, organizational effectiveness will most likely be less than optimal. Organizational culture has a powerful effect on the long-term business and financial performance of organizations.

Although other frameworks for measuring organizational culture have been proposed, Cameron and Quinn (1999) advocate their model, claiming that it offers several advantages. Specifically, it captures the practical key dimensions of culture that research has shown to foster organizational success, it can be completed in a relatively short period of time, the steps required actively involve all organization members in the process, it measures dimensions of organizational culture on both quantitative and qualitative (i.e., stories and symbols) levels, and the framework that the model is built on is supported by extensive empirical research with valid scholarly foundations. The cultural gap analysis allows researchers to diagnose what critical theory scholars refer to as the *deep structure* of the organization: the unexamined beliefs and values that serve as the basis for organizational action. This structure is what the CVF instrument was designed to identify and diagnose.

Cameron and Quinn (1999) provide a methodology to help managers and other change agents make sense of their organizational culture. The methodology, which includes a theoretical framework and validated instruments, allows for the systematic diagnosis of an organization's predominant current and preferred cultures. The authors explain that such a diagnosis is a necessary precursor to implementing effective change efforts. They assert that their methodology is useful because it helps managers and their organizations adapt to the demands of their environment and enhance organizational performance. Specifically, Cameron and Quinn's methodology allows for a comprehensive culture audit that maps out the cultural profile of a target organization along the lines of four culture types: clan, adhocracy, market, and hierarchy.

Cultural Types

The hierarchy culture is characterized by a formalized and structured workplace. Rules and procedures govern organization members' actions. Leaders are good coordinators and organizers who help maintain a smooth-running organization. Value is placed on stability, predictability, and efficiency. The market culture is characterized by a focus on performance and results. Leaders are hard-driving producers and competitors. Value is placed on competitive actions and meeting goals and targets. The clan culture is a manifestation of common understandings, mutual support, and social interactions. Success is defined in terms of the internal climate and concern for organizational members. Finally, the adhocracy culture is characterized by a dynamic, entrepreneurial, and creative workplace. Organizational members are risk takers. Leadership is predominantly visionary, innovative, and risk oriented. Value is placed on being on the leading edge of new knowledge, products, and/or services and being ready for change and meeting challenges. As discussed in chapter 8, these cultural types are consistent with Deal and Kennedy's (1982) typology, which is based on the dimensions of risk tolerance and feedback and rewards. The work-hard, play-hard culture goes with the clan culture; the tough-guy, macho culture aligns with the adhocracy culture; the process culture fits with the hierarchy culture; and the bet-the-company culture matches the market culture (see Figure 8.2).

The characteristics used to classify cultural types include six criteria:

1. Dominant organizational characteristics, which identify whether an organization is (a) personal, like a family, (b) entrepreneurial and risk taking, (c) competitive and achievement oriented, and/or (d) controlled and structured

2. Leadership style, which can be described as (a) mentoring, facilitating, or nurturing; (b) entrepreneurial, innovative, or risk taking; (c) no-nonsense, aggressive, results oriented, and/or (d) coordinating, organizing, and efficiency oriented

3. Management of employees, which emphasizes (a) teamwork, consensus, and participation; (b) individual risk taking, innovation, freedom, and uniqueness;

(c) competitiveness and achievement; and/or (d) security, conformity, and predictability

4. Organizational glue, which consists of (a) loyalty and mutual trust, (b) commitment to innovation and development, (c) emphasis on achievement and goal accomplishment, and/or (d) formal rules and policies

5. Strategic emphasis on (a) human development, high trust, and openness; (b) acquisition of resources and creating new challenges; (c) competitive actions and winning; and/or (d) permanence and stability

6. Criteria for success, which is defined as (a) developing human resources, teamwork, and concern for people; (b) having the newest and most unique products and services; (c) winning in the marketplace and outpacing the competition; and/or (d) being dependable, efficient, and low cost

Cultural Audit in a Health Care Organization

The Health Care Organization (HCO) is comprised of several decentralized facilities and a centralized office or headquarters. The facilities are regionally dispersed and together employ approximately 1,000 staff members, the majority of which are direct caregivers (front-line employees). The facilities provide 24-hour nursing care and supervision to adults who are chronically ill or in need of intensive rehabilitative care. The mission of the HCO is to provide the motivation and support to allow residents/patients to attain the highest possible level of physical and mental well-being, whether the goal is to return home or to make the facility their home. Each facility is under the direction of both a licensed nursing home administrator and a director of nursing. The staff of the home

office provides support and oversight to all facilities in areas such as nursing, rehabilitation, administrative, operational, and support services. All employees are well informed of the aging, medical, and nursing needs of their patients/residents and are committed to exceptional customer service. A cultural audit of the HCO was conducted to identify differences in the preferred profiles between the centralized office and the field units. Figures 13.4 and 13.5 depict the preferred profiles.

Although the HCO is highly regulated, it makes efforts to encourage open and honest communication in all directions, which explains the presence of a competing tension between the clan and hierarchy cultures. This tension, however, is typical in highly regulated environments in which the demands for compliance, accountability, and control are high. It should be noted that competing tensions do not necessarily signal a sign of strength or weakness for the organization; effective organizations are able to behave in flexible and sometimes contradictory ways. The analysis of the profiles suggests that, on average, the HCO desires a culture that emphasizes the clan and hierarchy cultures and de-emphasizes the adhocracy and market cultures. Organizations with a strong hierarchy culture are highly formalized and structured workplaces where procedures govern what people do. Success is defined in terms of dependable delivery, smooth scheduling, and low cost. The desire to increase the clan and hierarchy cultures is likely the result of placing importance on people (professionals treating patients) and process (adhering to rules and regulations). Although adhocracy characteristics (change, development) and market characteristics (achievement, competition) are present in the HCO profiles, they are less important than the more predominant characteristics of the clan and hierarchy. As discussed above, these findings underscore the significance of contextual factors in the internal and external organizational environments.

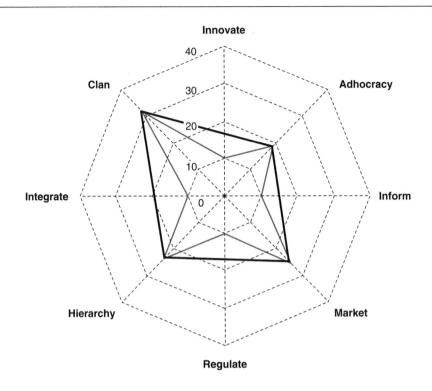

Figure 13.4   Competing Values Framework for Corporate Communication Preferred Profile of Field Units

Summary

Diagnosing communication characteristics such as roles, values and culture, and message orientations (including those discussed in chapters 8 and 12) help sensitize managers to the appropriateness of message composition and the relevant mode of delivery for effective communication performance. Corporate communication professionals at all levels can use the CVFCC diagnostically to initiate organization-wide self-improvement programs. Aligning organizational culture with managerial roles and message orientations helps sustain organizational identity and subsequently enhances the public image of the organization, its credibility, and its reputation. The strength of the linkage between organizational identity and external image is vital for the functioning and effectiveness of corporate communication and performance. Communication audits help discover missing links, highlight energy leaks, and spot gray areas that require attention. By using audits to obtain desired communication profiles, corporate communication executives can demonstrate to key stakeholders that ongoing improvements in corporate communication activities, both internally and externally, are important corporate communication goals.

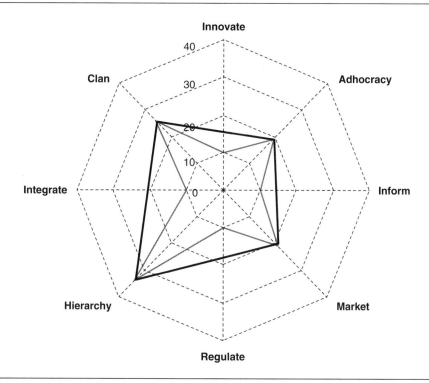

Figure 13.5   Competing Values Framework for Corporate Communication Preferred Profile of Centralized Office

Review Questions

1. What is the purpose of a communication audit?

2. Discuss how the CVFCC can be used as a method to facilitate understanding across managerial levels in different types of organizations.

3. What is the value of a communication audit from the perspective of organizational legitimacy and the need to manage organizational image and reputation?

4. Collaborate with team members to conduct Internet research on the topic of organizational communication AND training OR consulting, and write a 4- to 6-page report summarizing your main findings: What are the topics, concepts, tools, or models of communication described or used by the consultants? Who are their clients? What are the intervention methods or improvement programs that they support? What kind of expertise or credentials do they have? If you were a top executive in an empowered organization, would you use this consulting service to improve your organizational communication practices?

CASE STUDY

Planning the Project

A large insurance company recently completed a communication audit. The audit was conducted by its in-house personnel and covered all levels of the hierarchy. The results were compiled into a 54-page study entitled "Communication Practices," and sent to managers throughout the organization. Many communication problems are highlighted in the study. One is the apparent failure of the company's open-door policy. Over 80 percent of the employees feel that their boss discourages them from coming by to discuss problems or get advice. A second is the perception that each hierarchical group has its own behavior and that the behavior of the level above it is quite lacking. For example, when it comes to willingness to communicate change in advance, give praise and encouragement, and follow through on promises, the data in Tables 13.1, 13.2 and 13.3 show perceptual gaps. A third is the failure of management to understand how to effectively use the informal organization in getting things done.

On an overall basis, the report concludes that management at all levels of the structure needs communication training. In fact, notes the audit, most managers are surprised that management has not provided such training in the past. After reading the report and holding a meeting with the top management staff, the president has decided to call in a training and consulting group to provide management [with] the assistance it needs. A number of consulting groups would like to bid on the job, and the president has decided to make the final choice on the basis of the proposal that is submitted. Each is to examine the data in Tables 13.1–13.3 and spell out the type of training it will offer. The firm with the best proposal will get the job.

Table 13.1   How Often Does Your Boss Communicate Change in Advance? (How Often Do You?)

Personnel	Often	Usually	Sometimes	Seldom	Never
Vice presidents	5(45)	15(45)	20(10)	30	30
General managers	4(52)	13(43)	19(5)	36	28
Foremen[/women]	3(57)	10(41)	18(2)	39	30
Supervisors	2(63)	9(37)	16	41	32
Workers	1	7	15	45	32

Table 13.2   How Often Does Your Boss Give Praise and Encouragement to You? (How Often Do You?)

Personnel	Often	Usually	Sometimes	Seldom	Never
Vice presidents	25(60)	35(35)	30(5)	10	—
General managers	20(70)	45(30)	25	10	—
Foremen[/women]	15(78)	30(22)	20	15	20
Supervisors	14(87)	21(13)	33	23	9
Workers	1	6	22	35	36

Table 13.3   How Often Does Your Boss Follow Through on Promises? (How Often Do You?)

Personnel	Often	Usually	Sometimes	Seldom	Never
Vice presidents	32(60)	28(38)	20(2)	15	5
General managers	26(67)	24(30)	15(3)	20	15
Foremen[/women]	21(75)	22(24)	27(1)	23	7
Supervisors	10(95)	18(5)	30	28	14
Workers	5	15	34	30	16

Case Questions

1. Assume you are the member of your consulting firm who has been charged with this assignment. Develop eyeball CVFCC cultural profiles (current and preferred) for this firm.

2. What behavioral objectives would you set for your improvement program? What type of training would you recommend? Describe the specific approaches you would take.

3. How would you go about conducting a posttraining evaluation that includes a comprehensive audit of managerial roles, message orientations, and culture? Be complete in your write-up.

SOURCE: Gibson, J. W., & Hodgetts, R. M., *Organizational Communication: A Managerial Perspective*, copyright © 1991, pp. 469-470. Reprinted by permission of Pearson Education, Inc., Upper Saddle River, New Jersey.

PART F

Crisis Communication and Patterns of Corporate Response

14

Crisis Communication and Message Strategies

crisis is an "event that brings, or has the potential for bringing, an organization into disrepute and imperils its future profitability, growth, and possibly, its very survival" (Lerbinger, 1997, p. 4). This definition, however, should also include reference to the media as a way to communicate instant messages to the public. Another definition emphasizes the verbal, visual, and/or written interaction between the organization and its external audiences prior to, during, and after the negative occurrence (Williams & Olaniran, 2002). A crisis usually causes an interruption in what is going on and poses certain risks to an organization, potentially affecting reputation, image, brand equity, credibility, publicity, financial viability, legitimacy, and/or community standing (Smudde, 2001). Because an organizational crisis can potentially escalate in intensity, fall under close government or media scrutiny, jeopardize the current positive public image of an organization, or interfere with normal business operations, an organization could be placed at serious risk for survival (Stephens, Malone, & Bailey, 2005).

According to Melillo (2003), it is important for an organization to always respond to a crisis in some way. The organization can use various strategies to deliver messages that explain the situation; its choice of message strategy affects both how people perceive the crisis and the image of the organization experiencing the crisis (Stephens et al., 2005). However, according to Leonard (2001), the three most important things an employer can do in a crisis are communicate, communicate, and communicate. Research has shown that communication and openness are central to organizational reputation at times of crises (Borda & Mackey-Kallis, 2004). Most experts also agree that one of the roles of a leader is to create and sustain the organization's credibility and trust among organizational stakeholders (Lockwood, 2005).

Following a fire at Deloitte's office in Madrid, the company issued the following crisis communication media statement, which provides a useful example of how to structure such a statement.

Fire at Deloitte Office Tower in Madrid:
Deloitte Spain Maintains Activity

Madrid, February 14, 2005—The recent building fire in Madrid has destroyed the local Deloitte office. In response, Deloitte Spain would like to communicate the following:

- Deloitte greatly appreciates the work of the fire, police and emergency departments for ensuring the safety of all its professionals and building residents. There have been no casualties reported as a result of this fire. Currently, our Madrid office is working to recover its IT and information systems. We have activated contingency plans, which include the help and support of Deloitte Touche Tohmatsu, our global office.

- Except for the local phone lines and other communication sources in Madrid, all other Deloitte offices in Spain have not been affected. Communications from our Madrid office are being redirected to other firm locations, as part of the contingency plans.

- Most Deloitte professionals in Madrid will resume work on Monday. Client service operations will not be impacted by this event. All 19 Deloitte offices outside Madrid will continue with their normal operations.

- Deloitte has started researching several options for the new location of its Madrid office. The Firm expects to resolve this situation in a few days.

- Deloitte thanks the unconditional support and collaboration from its clients, suppliers and professionals, which is helping the Firm to normalize its activity.

Deloitte will make further official communications through www.deloitte.com or its online Spanish pressroom, accessible via http://deloitte.acceso.com

SOURCE: "Fire at Deloitte Office Tower in Madrid: Deloitte Spain maintains activity," 2/22/05. Used with permission of Continuity Central.

The leader's role is not only to restore trust in the organization's ability to resume performance but also to sustain the organization's brand image and overall value in the marketplace (Schoenberg, 2005). Top executives should therefore bring to their posts a combination of strategic thinking, broad communication skills, honesty, integrity, and the ability to accept responsibility for failure. Take the response of Southwest management to the crisis involving one of the airline's flights as an example.

Southwest Airlines

On December 8, 2005, Southwest flight 1248 ended in tragedy when, trying to land in the midst of a Chicago snowstorm, it veered off the runway, breaking down barriers before finally careening into a crowded intersection. The plane collided with at least two cars; a 6-year-old boy in one car did not survive the accident. Southwest's PR team had to not only save face for the company (in terms of both internal and external image) but also handle matters in an ethically responsible fashion, particularly in dealing with the 11 people who were injured in the accident as well as their families. Within hours of the crash, Southwest posted a press release on its Web site, officially confirming the incident and communicating that it was already cooperating with the National Transportation Safety Board and the Federal Aviation Administration to identify the cause of the accident. The names of the passengers and motorists involved were not released, and would not be until Southwest employees had finished contacting the families of those affected. Ethically, this was the right course of action, because releasing the names of those involved via mass media could have sent entire families into turmoil as they frantically tried to find out what had become of their loved ones.

A few hours after issuing the first press release, Southwest released a second one, again proactively providing more information on the event (even though it was approaching 1:30 a.m. EST), rather than waiting until the start of most business hours. Doing so allowed the company to further facilitate the news by expanding upon (or updating) previous statements, proving to the public that it was not trying to hide or cover up the incident, but rather was trying to disseminate information to the public as timely as possible. By being expeditious with its press releases, Southwest had a fair amount of control over what news and facts were out in the open and avoided the potentially catastrophic problem of public opinion reaching the point of rampant speculation. Beginning with the second press release, the company made sure to include contact numbers so that members of the media could reach Southwest's media/PR department and the public could call if they had any questions about the incident. Openness and accessibility are key in maintaining a positive relationship with the media, and in the case of this crisis, Southwest proved that it had no intention of being anything but cooperative.

Communication Failures

Stanton (2002) presents 10 communication mistakes that an organization should avoid when responding to crisis situations. First, do not rush to judgment. It is essential to understand the facts of the situation before engaging in communication; do not speculate or make a judgment in the absence of complete information. It is much more difficult to retract statements than to make them right the first time. Second, do not overreact. It is easy to fall into the trap of treating every difficulty as a crisis, but it is important for an organization to determine how to differentiate between a crisis and an emergency. During an emergency, an organization typically continues to function essentially as normal. On the other hand, a crisis gains public attention, prevents management from conducting business as usual, and requires a specialized level of intervention and response. Third, do not fail to act. Many organizations still believe that if they ignore a crisis it will go away, which is rarely, if ever, the case. The primary objective in a crisis is for an organization to restore its trusting relationship with its constituencies. Fourth, do not bend the facts. Communication during a crisis does not need to be a blunt admission of wrongdoing, but neither should it be an invented exoneration if the facts do not support that position. The truth is usually the best place to start.

Fifth, do not show a lack of concern, empathy, or sympathy. The organization's concern for stakeholders, profitability, and return on investment should not take precedence over expressions of concern when people's lives are affected. The organization can remain personable and human by having someone speak to people and express emotion appropriately and sincerely. Showing concern and empathy for those affected, providing for the victims and their families, and indicating that the first priority is to address their needs strengthen any statements that the organization makes about how it is handling the situation. Sixth, do not assign blame. Instead, an organization should discuss how it plans to address the situation, cooperate with investigating authorities, and work with its internal and external resources to develop fair and equitable compensation strategies. Doing so demonstrates that at an early stage the organization is focused on the issue and working to address it.

Seventh, do not remain insular. Most organizations have teams of talented people who are well equipped to address crises; however, these people have the corporate perspective foremost in their minds. Seeking an external perspective avoids the mistake of relying only on an inward focus. The organizations best prepared to manage crises are those that have identified, in advance, outside experts in a variety of key areas who can advise management and potentially serve as credible third parties. Eighth, do not show an absence of teamwork. A frequent tendency is for one communicator, or "sacrificial lamb" (Stanton, 2002, p. 22), to handle all aspects of the response by working nights and weekends, burning the candle at both ends. A core team approach, however, drawing on the best talents of individuals from several departments and disciplines, ensures effective communication as well as a highly productive, collaborative process of crisis management. Ninth, do not restrict information internally. Failing to think about internal communication means failing to realize that employees are an organization's front-line communicators, and often its consumers. Employees should be used as ambassadors to test messages and gather opinions and insights. Tenth, do not fail to plan. It is impossible to plan for every crisis scenario, but organizations should make plans regarding how they will make decisions in a crisis. This plan should include determining who will be involved in the decision-making process as well as specific roles and responsibilities (Stanton, 2002).

In addition to the 10 communication mistakes, it is important for an organization to consciously avoid Gustin and Sheehy's (2003) seven sins of crisis communication: unpreparedness, absence, ignorance, silence, distance, untruthfulness, and naiveté. Unpreparedness involves not having a crisis communication plan that clearly defines who will speak to the media, government officials, and other crucial audiences. When an organization is not available to the media and not willing to share the latest information, it is viewed as absent, which can be damaging to its image. Ignorance involves not understanding the priorities or information needs of families, the media, and the general public. At this point credibility and trust are at stake, and an organization needs to disclose important information or declare its accountability. Following a crisis, an organization should be open to the public. If it remains silent or avoids tough questions, it may lose control of the flow of information. Distance can involve pulling back too soon by putting distance between the organization and the issue. Untruthfulness involves not responding to inquiries quickly or effectively, which only harms the organization in the end. When an organization is naïve, it does not deal with the situation realistically and opens itself up to media and public criticism.

Failure at Dow Corning

In 1991, Dow Corning, the world's largest manufacturer of silicone-gel breast implants and the leading supplier of medical devices to the U.S. breast-surgery industry, was hit by one of the worst crises in the company's history. The company came under growing criticism for failing to disclose information about the health hazards caused by the breast implants it manufactured and for reckless endangerment of the lives of thousands of women who received these implants nationwide. In December 1991, a federal district court jury in San Francisco awarded $8.6 million to a woman who claimed she was suffering from an autoimmune disease resulting from her breast implants. The jury also found that Dow Corning acted with fraud, malice, and oppression, because of its failure to disclose information about the implant hazards. Company executives reacted to the ruling with outrage and blamed the finding on sensationalist media reports.

During a crisis, the public is often more offended by an organization's lack of honesty than by the crisis itself. Dow Corning's lack of honesty continued to work against it as reports of hidden information and cover-ups continued to leak to the press. Public outrage increasingly focused less on the growing evidence of health risks posed by the breast implants and more on the perception that Dow Corning had known of the potential hazards for many years. One of the company's most blatant violations was its PR team's failure to release vital information regarding the implants. Soon after the 1991 court settlement, and despite the company's efforts to prevent their publication, hundreds of pages of internal Dow Corning documents used in the case were released. The documents highlighted several pieces of pertinent information. First, some employees had known as early as 1971 that the manufacturer lacked sufficient scientific data to guarantee the implants' health safety. Second, Dow Corning had paid millions of dollars in out-of-court settlements to keep claims about health risks secret. And finally, warnings of the need for more thorough testing by the company's scientists had been repeatedly ignored. Additionally, the company failed to show concern after numerous implant-induced health complications were revealed, refrained from any public action, and misled rather than worked with regulators, physicians, and federal watchdog groups. When all of this information was released, it caused substantial damage to Dow Corning.

Even the company's proactive measures turned out to be destructive. In mid-1991, it set up a toll-free hotline to address breast-implant questions and concerns. However, the FDA shut down this line in early 1992 because the information that Dow Corning was providing to callers was either false or used in a confusing or misleading way. In 1992, the company's newly appointed CEO supervised the public release of sensitive Dow Corning documents dealing with the safety of devices, as well as a proposal to pay for the removal of implants for low-income women. These actions, although well intended, came too late to rescue the corporation's declining public image. By assuring women and their doctors for years that breast implants were safe, the company failed to show concern for thousands of women with serious health problems resulting from the implants. Essentially, Dow Corning had placed its corporate interest before public responsibility.

The PR effort at Dow Corning failed on all accounts. The company neglected to take a proactive stance immediately following the first public outcry regarding health risks. It failed to release factual data as soon as it became available or to appoint a credible spokesperson. It failed to demonstrate sympathy for victims of implant-related health problems, cooperate with key public figures, or publicly correct its behavior. It reduced its credibility by covering up mistakes with out-of-court claim settlements. And it met media inquiries with defensive allegations and consistently committed actions deemed unsympathetic by the thousands of women adversely affected by this crisis (Borda & Mackey-Kallis, 2004).

Failure at the University of Maryland

On June 19, 1986, the University of Maryland was faced with a crisis after the sudden and unexpected death of basketball player Len Bias. Bias collapsed in his dormitory room at 6:30 a.m., after celebrating through the night with several of his teammates. The unconscious Bias was transported by paramedics to a local hospital, where he was pronounced dead at 8:50 a.m. There were no signs of foul play or obvious reasons for Bias's death, but within 8 hours, a Washington, D.C., television station reported that Bias had died from cocaine intoxication.

The crisis escalated over the next few days and lasted several months. Bias's use of cocaine resulted in charges that the University of Maryland was a haven for drug use. Reporters gathering information for detailed stories about Bias's career also discovered that the athletic department at the University of Maryland appeared to exploit its student-athletes. For example, Bias was more than 18 months from graduation, although he was in his fourth year at the university. During the spring 1986 semester, he failed two classes and withdrew from three others. Five of the other fourteen players on the men's basketball team also failed out of school the previous semester, but were later reinstated.

The chancellor of the University of Maryland and his senior administration decided that the director of public information, Roz Hiebert, would handle all requests for information regarding Bias. They believed that funneling information through one person would prevent inaccurate reporting. On June 24, five days after Bias died, the chancellor sent a confidential four-paragraph memo to vice chancellors, the provost, deans, directors, and department chairs, instructing all faculty and staff to refer any media inquiries to Hiebert. However, the magnitude of the story quickly overwhelmed Hiebert. The volume of calls generated by the crisis, combined with her staff's inability to respond to requests for information, prevented Hiebert from handling the enormous number of requests for information as quickly as they needed to be. Using a single spokesperson did not work because it was a big story covered by a number of different news organizations. Hiebert had other responsibilities besides performing damage control regarding Bias's death, so it was not practical for her to be available 24 hours a day to accept and fulfill interview requests. As a result, the media often made requests for interviews but would not hear back from Hiebert for several hours or sometimes until the next day. Because this

news story often had new developments daily, the media and the public found this delay to be unacceptable. In addition, it was a mistake not to give the University of Maryland PR staff the authority to release information. When Bias died, no one from the PR department was at the hospital. When the case went to the grand jury, no one from the PR department was outside the courthouse. Therefore, there was no way for the media to present the University of Maryland's point of view. Instead of having someone from the PR staff available to monitor the case, speak about it publicly whenever necessary, and know the media members covering the story, the media were forced to go back to Hiebert each time a question came up. The media felt there should have been someone present each day to monitor them (Marra, 2004).

Although it is undoubtedly impossible to determine whether or not the crises experienced by Dow Corning and the University of Maryland could have been avoided, it is possible to ascertain whether or not they could have been handled more efficiently and effectively. According to Duke and Masland (2002), a good crisis plan should fulfill four requirements. First, it should establish that the interests of the people concerned will be the first priority. Second, it should make clear that the organization will be as open about what happened as the facts and conditions permit. Third, it should give priority to resolving the emergency and protecting the people affected. And fourth, it should emphasize that the organization will be fair to all, including critics or opponents who may have instigated the problem. In addition, Hoffman (2001) states that there are four Ps to effective crisis communication: prevent, plan, prepare, and practice. To prevent a crisis, management teams should sit down together in regular or special staff meetings to brainstorm what in their organization could go wrong and develop into a crisis. During the planning phase, a written crisis communication plan should be developed that details the first actions to be taken in a crisis. Preparing for crisis includes providing a good deal of thought to deciding which aspects of the crisis and the organization should be emphasized. Finally, practice involves role-playing the organization's response to a stimulated crisis once every 6 months in order to increase retention and effectiveness.

Success for NASA

On February 1, 2003, the space shuttle Columbia broke apart on re-entry into the earth's atmosphere after a 16-day journey through space, killing all seven astronauts on board, including the first Israeli astronaut, and sending debris across Texas and Louisiana. At first it was unclear what caused Columbia's demise so close to home, but with the world bracing for a U.S. war with Iraq and terrorism fears heightened, NASA had to respond quickly, openly, and honestly (Grunwald, 2003). In the early days of the response, it was clear that NASA's chief spokespeople were more focused on the personal loss of their friends and colleagues and the human tragedy being experienced by family, friends, and the nation. This gave the organization credibility; no one could doubt the sincerity or pain experienced by these professionals. NASA also had an independent agency lead the investigation, which reassured the public through the media that the job would be done right, thus removing concern about credibility and conflict of interest. NASA spokespeople spoke openly, honestly, and forthrightly about emerging information; in doing so, they avoided putting the media in the position of having to turn elsewhere to find anyone who appears to have something worthwhile to say, regardless of how positive or negative it is. In fact, NASA was almost omnipresent from the beginning and throughout the crisis. It also utilized the Internet as a vital medium for delivering public information. A crisis site, updated frequently, was linked to the agency's home page; it was a solid source of information for the public and the media, on everything from space shuttle debris to the investigation progress.

NASA was successful in managing its reputation in this instance because it seemed clear that it was not focused on either reputation management or legal management. NASA representatives wanted to share their feelings about the event and whatever information was available to them that might help the public understand what happened and why. The media always looks for someone or something to blame, but NASA did not allow the blame to be laid at its feet (Baron, 2003). During the Columbia disaster, NASA avoided the seven sins of crisis communication management (Gustin & Sheehy, 2003) discussed earlier. It was prepared to communicate, was not absent from the scene, seemed to understand its priorities, was open to the public, stayed in the public eye, was truthful, and dealt with the situation realistically.

NASA management was prepared for communication because of its crisis plans, which included clear lines of authority for speaking to media and government officials, as well as other critical audiences. This preparedness was evident in not only the frequent updates that the agency began to broadcast within an hour of initial reports of a problem but also the speed with which the first press conference was convened. NASA administrators were present and available to the media within hours; shuttle manager Ron Dittemore was a consistent and steady voice, sharing the latest available information. NASA set its priorities intelligently by recognizing the information needs of the astronauts' families, the media, and the general public. The administration appeared to provide full disclosure of critical information early on, which served it well as time passed. Even when it came to admitting errors in judgment, NASA did so apparently realizing that credibility and trust were at stake. The management team recognized the importance of declaring its accountability, something that is seldom found in a crisis but is critical in establishing credibility. NASA was open to the public in the days, weeks, and months following the accident. It held press conferences twice a day, and press staff were readily available. The agency did not appear to avoid tough questions, which is a strong characteristic because questions met with no response only get tougher when the public demands answers. NASA stayed in the public eye and did not pull back too soon before the public and the media were ready to return to a more normal cycle of news on the topic. As time goes on, pressure on a management team can build to the point at which it tries to put some distance between itself and the issue. NASA's management team avoided doing this. There may have been problems with the internal flow of information related to the safety of the Columbia mission, but there was no sign that NASA had been untruthful. It responded to inquiries quickly and effectively and, when necessary, acknowledged and clarified information and put it into context. NASA dealt with the situation realistically by understanding that almost any action by a company or organization can prompt an inquiry and become a pathway to media coverage and criticism (Gustin & Sheehy, 2003).

Success for Texas Eastern Transmission Corporation

On March 23, 1994, a Texas Eastern Transmission Corporation pipeline erupted in Edison, New Jersey. Natural gas exited the pipeline and entered a 1,000-unit apartment complex. The flames from the fire caused by the eruption could be seen 20 miles away in New York City. This event was especially dramatic because the pipeline erupted in a residential area. Hundreds of people lost prized possessions and nearly their lives during the

fire. This was a crisis in which lawsuits and punitive damages were a threat. Public opinion initially turned against Texas Eastern Transmission because of the assumption that it had cut costs and thereby allowed its facilities to deteriorate to an unsafe level. Once they became aware of the explosion and fire, senior executives, including management, operations, and public affairs, went to the scene to express concern for the personal injuries and property damage and to seek to set things right in order to regain control. The objectives of this team and the crisis response effort were to (a) take care of human needs, (b) cooperate with investigators to determine the cause of the incident, and (c) return the pipeline to safe operation as soon as possible. Company executives responded to the human needs within their limits by supplying financial support to people whose property had been harmed by the fire. The company cooperated with federal, state, and local officials to determine the cause of the accident. And instead of trying to single-handedly assume responsibility for getting the pipeline up and running again, company executives yielded to the government officials who needed to assume their role in doing so. This enacted partnership gained approval for the restoration of pipeline service, which occurred 21 days after the explosion (Heath, 2004).

Success can be defined in many ways. The success stories of NASA and Texas Eastern Transmission Corporation prove the value of crisis communication planning in gaining a desired outcome. Both organizations were able to overcome crisis while maintaining their reputations in the eyes of their consumers, stakeholders, and the media.

Verizon: Effective Corporate Communication

September 11, 2001, was the most significant crisis that Verizon has ever had to face. The attack on the World Trade Center knocked out 300,000 voice access lines and 4.5 million data circuits, and made 10 cellular towers inactive. The damage left 14,000 businesses and 20,000 residential customers without service. Verizon's corporate communication executives responded quickly and proactively by keeping the public informed about the damage and how the company was going to resolve the problem. They had a press center that operated 24 hours a day, 7 days a week. The company set a goal of restoring the necessary systems so that the NYSE would be up and running by the following Monday, and it accomplished this goal, thanks to a great deal of hard work from many employees who worked through the whole weekend.

Verizon's CEO, Ivan Seidenberg, worked closely with the communications team to reach out to his employees and keep them informed. Seidenberg went to personally inspect the damage that was done to the Verizon building. He was there for his employees and customers in the middle of everything that was happening. This kind of responsiveness is what people want in the middle of a crisis; they want to hear directly from the leader of their organization (Argenti, 2002). As a result, the company received a great deal of positive news coverage. Verizon received both national and international attention, including an entire section dedicated to the company in the book *After*, written by Steven Brill (2003), and a BBC documentary about what the company accomplished during 9/11. Verizon came out of this crisis stronger than before. The crisis enhanced its reputation and increased its recognition as a socially responsible company.

Protecting the Image

The purpose of communication during a crisis is to influence the public's perception of the organization and to maintain a positive image or restore a damaged image among stakeholders. Organizations in crisis seek to protect their image by modifying public perception of responsibility for the crisis or to manage impressions of the organization itself. Communication objectives during a crisis may also include informing, convincing, or motivating certain stakeholders to action. A key objective of message strategies at such a time is damage control—preventing negative relationships with external parties. A secondary objective is for the organization to use the opportunity to tell the public about its mission, values, and operations (Stephens et al., 2005). It may be the CEO who sends the message of personal involvement, honesty, and compassion to the public (O'Rourke, 2004). Compare, for example, the methods used by Union Carbide's (Bhopal, India) executives and Johnson & Johnson's (Tylenol) executives in responding to their respective crises depicted (see Table 14.1). Although it is impossible to plan for all possibilities, a crisis plan with a well-rehearsed crisis communications team can prevent a crisis from turning into a catastrophe. Ideally, crisis preparation takes place well in advance of an eruptive situation. It is nearly impossible to handle a full-blown crisis while, at the same time, preparing a crisis management plan. Stanton (2002) defines a crisis communication plan as "a method for planning and thinking about situations in day-to-day operations, business and company communities, and preparing company people to understand and respond to the special demands of crisis conditions" (p. 19). Developing a crisis communication plan before you encounter an emergency can help an organization turn around a disaster (Marsh & Robbins, 2004).

According to Stephens et al. (2005), crises are generally composed of five dimensions: (a) they are highly visible, (b) they require immediate attention, (c) they contain an element of surprise, (d) they have a need for action, and (e) they are outside the organization's complete control. Crises may be considered a function of external and environmental

Table 14.1   Anatomy of Corporate Responses

Union Carbide	Johnson & Johnson
• Failed to identify as a crisis the public perception that the company was a negligent, uncaring killer	• Identified as a crisis the public perception that Tylenol was unsafe and Johnson & Johnson was not in control
• Did not plan before reacting: CEO immediately went to India to inspect damage	• Planned before reacting: CEO picked one executive to head crisis team
• All executives involved	• Rest of company involved only on a strict need-to-know basis
• Set no goals	• Set goals to – stop the killings – find reasons for the killings – provide assistance to the victims – restore Tylenol's credibility
• Action (CEO) – damage control, stonewalling – distanced himself – misrepresented safety conditions – did not inform spokespeople – adopted bunker mentality	• Action – gave complete information – worked with authorities – pulled Tylenol from shelves (first year cost: $150 million) – used strong marketing program – reissued Tylenol with tamper-proof packaging
• Chronic problems continued • Public confidence was low • Costly litigation followed • No formal crisis plan resulted	• Crisis resolved • Public confidence was high • Sales regained strength • Well-documented crisis management plan resulted

SOURCE: From Bateman, T. S. & Snell, S. A., "Management: Building Competitive Advantage," in *Management* 4/e. Copyright © 1999, The McGraw-Hill Companies, p. 100. Reprinted with permission.

threats or internal and organizational weaknesses. In addition, most crises seem to share the following characteristics: a surprise, a trigger, a threat, an uncontrollable event, and a quick response. Surprise relates to timing as well as the event itself. A trigger is an unexpected event, action, or incident that alters the public's view of the organization. A threat can involve human lives, property, and/or the environment. An uncontrolled event results in turbulent circumstances, placing the situation out of management's control for a period of time. A quick response involves responding immediately to employees, stakeholders, customers, and the media to protect the organization and

regain control. Nearly all crises unfold in similar stages. The first stage consists of early warning signals of a threatening disaster, which can be faced or ignored. The next stage involves preparation and prevention, and includes such aspects as developing crisis teams and conducting training and exercises. The third stage is damage containment, the goal of which is to limit the effects of the crisis, to prevent it from contaminating other parts of the organization or environment not immediately affected. The final two stages are recovery and evaluation, which typically involve re-establishing organizational routines and creating feedback systems and procedures to deal with future crises

(Stephens et al., 2005). The benefits of recreating the public image and retaining long-term credibility by far exceed the cost of facing the brutal facts and confronting the crisis head on. The industry playing field is littered with examples of unanticipated consequences by companies shielding or defending themselves rather than following the rules of disclosure, transparency, and accountability. The American Home Products and the Dalkon Shield, and Johns Manville and asbestos, serve as reminders of companies that were forced into Chapter 11 bankruptcy when medical science eventually proved their misdeeds.

Organizing the Exchange of Information

One way to organize the exchange with internal and external audiences during a major crisis is to follow the simple rules of disclosure, transparency, and accountability. The CVFCC is a good start (see Figure 14.1). Corporate communication staff can implement a well-synchronized response system that includes sharing information with the public (INFORM), using internal communication to mobilize employees to tackle deficiencies (REFORM), developing rules and codes of ethics to guide future actions (CONFORM), and moving on to meet new goals and expectations (PERFORM).

Organizations have various rights and obligations to interact with the public and their communities (Troester, 1991), especially during times of crisis. An organization might need to provide the public/community with instructions on how to respond to the situation. For example, people might need to evacuate the area, as in the aftermath of the September 11 terrorist attacks or Hurricane Katrina. Or an organization might need to provide coping information to the public. For example, both United Airlines and American Airlines used the Web to convey messages to the public (and employees) about how to cope with the September 11 terrorist attacks (Greer & Moreland, 2003). When a crisis occurs, communication is one of the most effective tools in limiting the damage to an organization, its image, and its identity and averting decline. Wrigley, Salmon, and Park (2003) found that 70% of the companies in their sample had crisis management plans in place. Yet only 12% had specific plans dealing with bioterrorism, which

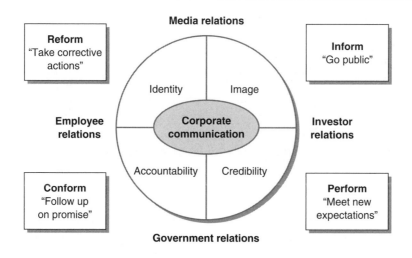

Figure 14.1 Organizing Corporate Responses: A Competing Values Framework for Corporate Communication Road Map

was always a risk but an even higher one following 9/11. And 90% of these same companies stated that if this crisis was to occur it would have resulted in "severe consequences" for their corporation. This study highlights the unwillingness of many organizations to prepare for this type of external factor/disaster. But most organizations would agree that crisis planning is imperative. Therefore, the possibility that many organizations wait for a crisis to occur and then learn from it through trial-and-error methods is a real and often true limitation of organizations and their crisis management plans. According to Hearit (1994), "most corporations wait until a public relations problem reaches a 'crisis' status before they respond; they publicly address the problem only when it becomes clear, for example, that their actions have hurt people, have cut into profits, or have damaged their carefully crafted images" (p. 114).

Restoring the Image

Benoit's (1997) theory of image restoration discourse based on *message options* is another approach to understanding crisis occurrence and patterns of organizational response. This theory offers five broad categories of strategies to repair a corporation's image (see Figure 14.2). The first strategy is denial. Denial comes in the form of simply refuting a claim made by another party; during a price war between Pepsi and Coke, Coke denied Pepsi's accusation that Coke had charged increased prices for some customers. A second form of denial is placing the blame on others; after the Exxon Valdez oil spill, Exxon's chairman blamed state officials and the U.S. Coast Guard for delaying the authorization to begin the cleanup efforts, implying that if Exxon was not at fault for the delay, its image should not be tarnished (Benoit, 1997). The second strategy is evasion of responsibility. After charges of auto repair fraud claimed that Sears employees persuaded customers that their vehicles needed additional (and often unnecessary) work in expectation of higher bonuses from the company, the Sears chairman

characterized the auto repair mistakes as inadvertent, rather than intentional. The third and fourth strategies are reducing the perception of offensiveness and taking corrective action (followed by a formal announcement of future prevention). Following a blackout in 1993, the AT&T chairman presented plans to conduct a thorough examination of the company's practices from the ground up and to spend billions of dollars to make these practices even more reliable. Thus, he promised not only to correct the current problem but also to prevent future problems (Benoit, 1997).

The fifth strategy is mortification, or pleading for forgiveness. In March 2005, after a fraud ring stole the personal and financial information of more than 100,000 consumers from computer databases maintained by ChoicePoint, the company's chairman and CEO testified before the House Energy and Commerce Committee's Subcommittee on Commerce, Trade, and Consumer Protection by offering an apology and asking for forgiveness:

> But regretfully, I know that I am not here today to talk only about the good things ChoicePoint has done. I know I am here because your committee and your constituents are concerned about the harm that may have been done to approximately 145,000 Americans, whose information may have fallen into the hands of criminals who accessed ChoicePoint systems. Let me begin by offering an apology on behalf of our company, as well as my own personal apology, to those consumers whose information may have been accessed by the criminals whose fraudulent activity ChoicePoint failed to prevent. Beyond our apology, I want to assure the public and the members of this committee that we have moved aggressively to safeguard the information in our possession from future criminal theft. We have also moved promptly to provide assistance to every affected individual to help him or her avoid financial harm. We also welcome participating in the efforts of this Committee and other policy-makers seeking to provide an appropriate regulation of our industry. (*Protecting Consumer's Data*, 2005, p. 2)

The example of ChoicePoint illustrates the importance of discourse and cultural readiness

Substrategies

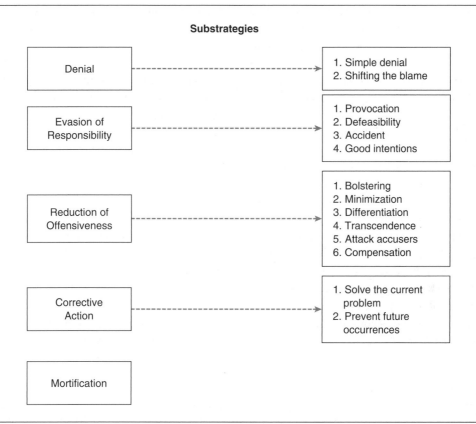

Figure 14.2   Benoit's (1997) Image Restoration Strategies

SOURCE: Based on "Image Repair Discourse and Crisis Communication," by W. L. Benoit, 1997, *Public Relations Review*, *23*, pp. 177-186.

to deal with crises and reduce risk. We have already studied the convergence of external factors and an organization's responsibility to its public during a crisis. However, the organization is also obligated to communicate messages internally. Hearit and Courtright (2003) address this idea through a social constructionist approach to crisis management: Much of what is required during crisis management occurs through the utilization of communication as the crisis unfolds. They argue that crises are, above all, communicative creations; as such, their successful management and resolution are fundamentally perceptual. Discourse is the main way in which organizations and stakeholders communicate during a crisis. Basically, as a crisis develops, the discourse is created to resolve the crisis by

changing how stakeholders perceive the crisis in order to favor the organization. Therefore, in applying this idea internally to organizations, it is important to begin developing a culture with readiness and sensitivity to handle predictable surprises (Hearit & Courtright, 2003).

Stages of Crisis

Duke and Masland (2002) present four basic stages of crisis communication: crisis preparedness, initial response, maintenance of ongoing corrective actions and reactions during the course of the crisis, and evaluation and follow-up. Crisis preparedness involves having a comprehensive crisis plan that has been updated in the past year. Initial response involves a crisis team that convenes immediately, gathers facts, issues a preliminary news release, and communicates with key people. Maintenance of ongoing corrective actions and reactions involves keeping in close touch with members of the crisis response team. During this stage, information continues to be gathered and media inquiries responded to. Evaluation and follow-up are done in the aftermath of a crisis, but should still reflect concern and response. These stages can also be viewed in terms of precrisis, crisis, and postcrisis periods.

The precrisis period includes preparation, planning, and testing phases. During the preparation phase time should be spent on creating a crisis management team, gaining management support for a crisis plan, identifying corporate vulnerabilities, and training employees. The purpose of the crisis management team is to maintain up-to-date information about every aspect of the organization so that it is prepared in the event of a crisis. According to Borda and Mackey-Kallis (2004), the crisis management team should be composed of people who are creative, knowledgeable about the business, powerful, and able to bring a variety of unique perspectives to bear on solving the problem. Once the team is in place, gaining management support for a crisis plan should become its primary goal. It is important for management to understand and approve the need for a crisis plan. To identify corporate vulnerabilities, the team should talk to top executives, technical personnel, and even outside sources to discover potential risks. The risks should be assessed, researched, and monitored to prevent them from actually occurring. It is important to give employees all the training they need and to establish positive employee relations before a crisis strikes. Employees are the foundation of any organization, and they are the people who will present corporate identity and messages during times of crisis. To complete precrisis preparations the team should finalize as much of the communication effort as possible before a

crisis happens. This can include preparing media packets, setting up an information hotline, and gathering employees' home contact information (Borda & Mackey-Kallis, 2004).

In the planning phase, the organization should create a message action plan, define target audiences, establish techniques needed to communicate the message, and assign responsibility. A message action plan "combines all elements of a public relations or communications plan into a single, easily read document that helps assure a company's key message will be conveyed in a coherent, disciplined, and organized fashion in times of crisis. It allows for quick understanding of what must be accomplished including when, how, and by whom" (Borda & Mackey-Kallis, 2004, p. 123). The message action plan should define target audiences, including employees, politicians, the media, and stock market analysts. Potential messages and the order of importance should be decided to prevent wasting time during a crisis. Once the target audiences are defined, all techniques that will be used to communicate the organization's message should be determined, such as press releases, media packets, audio and video communications, and paid media advertising. In assigning responsibility, the organization should clarify who is accountable for each task in order to meet deadlines and to prevent missed opportunities.

During the testing phase, the organization should simulate a crisis situation to test the crisis communication plan. This simulation should take the form of drills that are repeated over time to help the organization cover as many hypothetical crises as possible. Testing is essential because it allows the crisis plan to be re-evaluated and refined.

The crisis period includes phases of gathering, packaging, and delivering information. The information-gathering phase involves performing background research. Short- and long-term problems and effects should be defined immediately to minimize potential damage later on. Opinion polls are good tools to identify these problems and to focus on what the public is thinking and feeling. The crisis management team must understand the background of the situation as well as the scope and dimensions of the organization's position before meaningful recommendations can be made. After the initial crisis alert is received, a list of possible actions based on an understanding of the problems and team members' experiences should be developed.

The information-packaging phase involves a crucial part of managing a crisis: appointing one spokesperson to reach the media first with a unified message. Public perception is an important factor if a corporation is going to cope successfully with crises. Communicating explicitly and reliably reassures the public that the organization is taking appropriate measures rather than falling back on a bunker mentality. When disclosing information to the media, the organization should do so honestly, accurately, and fully. If it does not, the media will most likely uncover it anyway, which will prolong the crisis. According to Borda and Mackey-Kallis (2004), 95% of people are more offended by a company's lack of honesty than by the crisis itself. Once a crisis occurs, it is imperative that the organization present a human face and show concern immediately to the people involved (e.g., victims' families, survivors).

During the information-delivery phase, the crisis response message should be presented quickly, and the spokesperson should be assertive with the media. Providing information as quickly as possible is crucial. According to Borda and Mackey-Kallis (2004), letting the story dribble out only prolongs the agony and results in new and potentially damaging headlines with each dose of new information. The organization's spokesperson should provide human-interest stories to the media to help portray a sensitive, understanding, and people-oriented organization.

The postcrisis situation includes phases of evaluation, congratulation, and continuing to control the situation. After the immediate crisis passes, the organization should conduct an evaluation to recommend improvements and highlight vulnerabilities. Borda and Mackey-Kallis

(2004) suggest that it is helpful to prepare a detailed summary of how the plan operated, mistakes that were made along the way, and aspects that could have been better anticipated. After a crisis, morale in the organization may be low and its employees may be distraught. It is important not only to thank everyone involved in managing the crisis, but also to lift employees' spirits. Although the crisis may have ended, the media coverage may not have. The organization's crisis team should be prepared to respond to any inquiries and counteract negative publicity. With all of these phases in place, an organization is more likely to handle a crisis in the manner it chooses. Each section of the crisis communication model should be seen as equally important because they work together to provide an organization with its desired outcome.

The Importance of Culture in Managing Crises

The social constructionist approach places high importance on the need to develop a culture that recognizes the existence of crises. Just how do we do this? Wise (2003) offers an examination of crisis response by a hospital that was faced with an anthrax case. Following protocol, the hospital treated the anthrax patient with the antibiotics recommended by the Centers for Disease Control and Prevention and reported the case to the appropriate authorities. The FBI demanded that hospital officials refrain from making any public announcements regarding this occurrence. Top executives grappled with this request because their organizational culture was being challenged. The culture in this hospital had always been one of frequent communication. The hospital's president stated that he felt it was wrong to go against the culture of openness and transparency even during this crisis situation. Therefore, the top executives went against the FBI request and not only spoke with the 200 hospital employees but also released a statement during a press conference to their external stakeholders and posted this news release on the hospital's Web site along with information regarding anthrax. This culture was more powerful than both the standard crisis management thinking and even the FBI. In fact, Wise's findings state that the established culture at the hospital was the most important factor in the successful handling of the case. Furthermore, Wise states that the "core value that influenced the organization [the hospital] during crisis was open communication with its employees and other publics. It was this value that guided Charmel and Powanda [the top executives] as they made their decisions, not pages from a crisis plan book" (p. 470). This case shows that it is possible to recreate positive communicative actions throughout a crisis and that a strong organizational culture can prepare an organization for a crisis positively so that its chance of overcoming the crisis increases. Having strong precrisis relationships with internal and external stakeholders and having crisis management teams and clear media policies are key success factors in managing crises.

Summary

Chapter 14 shifts the emphasis from managing daily corporate communication tasks and routines to handling crises and communicating uncertainty. A crisis usually causes an interruption in business as usual and poses certain risks to an organization, potentially affecting reputation, image, brand equity, credibility, publicity, financial viability, legitimacy, and community standing. Because an organizational crisis can potentially escalate in intensity, fall under close government or media scrutiny, jeopardize the current positive public image of an organization, or interfere with normal business operations, an organization could be at serious risk for survival.

Review Questions

1. What is the role of corporate communication in diffusing the negative effects of organizational crises?

2. Discuss the dynamics associated with crisis management from the perspective of the primary functions of corporate communication.

3. Use examples to illustrate how organizations have dealt with crises in their corporate environments. What kind of methods did they use to reduce or avert the negative effects of crises?

CASE STUDY

Tylenol Tampering Scare

In 1982, Johnson & Johnson experienced a major crisis when it was discovered that numerous bottles of its Extra-Strength Tylenol capsules had been laced with cyanide. By the end of the crisis, seven people had died. How Johnson & Johnson dealt with this situation set a new precedent for crisis management. The company was lauded for its quick decisions and sincere concern for its consumers. Despite initial losses, Johnson & Johnson regained and exceeded its previous market share within months of the incident.

Reacting to the News

When Johnson & Johnson was faced with the initial situation, it had to make some tough decisions that would severely impact the future of the company. Rather than think in financial terms, however, CEO James Burke immediately turned to the company's Credo. Written by Robert Johnson in 1943, the document defines the focus of the company as its customers. With this as its inspiration, Tylenol used the media to promptly begin alerting people of the potential dangers of the product. It dispatched scientists to determine the source of the tampering.

Setting a New Standard

Johnson & Johnson then made a decision that would set a new standard for crises involving product tampering. The company ordered a massive recall of more than 31 million bottles at a cost of more than $100 million. It also temporarily ceased all production of capsules and replaced them with more tamper-resistant caplets. This type of drastic response had never been attempted, which prompted much criticism. However, Johnson & Johnson stood firm behind its decision—and for good reason. The company was able to "use the crisis to demonstrate to [its] customers [its] commitment to customer safety and to the quality of the Tylenol product." In addition, the company's willingness to be open with the public and communicate with the media helped the company maintain a high level of credibility and customer trust throughout the incident. Burke also maintained a high profile and repeatedly assured the public of the company's commitment to its customers' safety.

Regaining Lost Ground

Directly following the incident, Johnson & Johnson's stock fell seven points, and it dropped from having 35 percent of the nonprescription pain-reliever market to having only eight percent of the market. However, these tough times would not last. The company aired commercials within days to regain the public's trust, and a month after the recall, the company embarked on an aggressive campaign to rebuild the Tylenol brand. In November, it promised to have the product back on the shelves in a new triple-tamper-resistant package—the first of its kind—by the end of the year. It offered incentives, such as a free replacement of caplets for the capsules and special coupons, to try to maintain its customer base. The company's attempts were successful, and by the following spring, Johnson & Johnson had regained its previous market share. When another poisoning involving a New York woman occurred four years later, Johnson & Johnson once again had to take action. "Because the company had been through it before—the tampering, the tragedy, the scrutiny of news organizations—its executives knew how to handle it." Despite the fact this case was soon identified as an isolated incident, Johnson & Johnson decided to permanently discontinue capsule products—once again demonstrating its commitment to putting safety first.

Case Questions

1. Examine Johnson & Johnson's quick responses to the incident using corporate advertising and its willingness to be open with the public and communicate with the media. Use Figure 14.1 to help support your conclusion.

2. Was Johnson & Johnson successful in restoring its reputation through effective marketing communication? Use Internet resources to trace the company's strategic moves to deal with the incident.

SOURCE: From *Johnson & Johnson's Tylenol Scare*, by J. Hogue, 2001, University of Florida. Retrieved March 22, 2007, from http://iml.jou.ufl.edu/projects/Spring01/Hogue/tylenol.html. Reprinted with permission.

15

Conclusion

Corporate Communication: The Maestro

Corporate communication is like the conductor or the maestro, and the decentralized communication operatives are like the musicians in a symphony orchestra. The musicians (corporate communication functions) display specialized knowledge and use different tools with unique sound bites, and the conductor (centralized corporate communication) creates harmony by synchronizing the various parts for more coherent and meaningful sound effects (corporate messages). Much as the relationship between the conductor and the musicians affects the quality of the orchestra performance and its public image, corporate communication, too, is responsible for linking the primary functions into a coherent whole. Viewing internal and external communication as connected functions shifts the focus of corporate communication to answering questions about how an organization can communicate consistently with its many audiences in a way that represents a coherent sense of self. As chapter 3 highlighted, that sense of self is needed to maintain credibility and reputation inside and outside the organization through strong organizational identity and a positive external image.

A delicate balance must always exist between the musicians (extraordinary, complex, and highly specialized individuals) and the group as a whole. Like effective conductors who present interpretive vision and direction to the orchestra musicians (Hunt, Stelluto, & Hooijberg, 2004), corporate communication, too, must ensure that the different voices emanating from media relations, investor relations, government relations, and employee relations are in sync with the overall corporate message. In doing so, conductors must play all the CVF roles (discussed in chapter 11) well: monitor, coordinator, facilitator, and mentor to maintain the integrity of the orchestra and the director, and producer, broker, and innovator to achieve high ratings with external audiences and maintain performance credibility. Similarly, corporate communication must maintain the *value congruence* of the sociotechnical system and at the same time help attain the company's *value proposition*. Corporate communication works to increase the harmony among the functional areas to maximize the fit between corporate strategy, organizational identity, and external image; sustain the effort to institutionalize the corporation through branding and legitimization; and facilitate the coordination of communication activities for optimal implementation of policies and decision making (Van Riel, 1995).

Effective conductors are the masters of their domain. They have strategic awareness of institutional requirements and stakeholders' expectations, and they have the operating experience needed to transform independent musicians into an interdependent cohesive group. Similarly, strategic corporate communication transforms the network of connected functions into a structure of interconnected and well-synchronized communication responsibilities and activities. As discussed in chapter 4, strategic corporate communication issues include an orientation of communication toward an organization's priorities as well as the external environment. Those internal and external priorities include responsibility to investors, media relations, a strong organizational culture, and relationships with government and regulatory agencies—the areas covered by the CVFCC.

Strategic Corporate Communication

Strategy serves as the basis for organizing, implementing, and evaluating communication activities within and outside the organization. As discussed in chapter 4, effective communication strategy links the mission and goals of the organization with its markets ("What business will we be in?"); clarifies the means to achieve the stated objectives ("How will we get there?"); identifies the organization's unique characteristics (e.g., corporate identity, reliability of service, reputation) and core competencies that help differentiate it from its competitors ("How will we win over customers?"); and identifies a sequence of activities, timing, or staging (e.g., pursuit of early wins, building credibility) to achieve growth ("What are our moves and how will we obtain our returns?"). Strategies are altered based on changes in the environment, competitors' responses, and new choices and initiatives made by top executives (Hambrick & Fredrickson, 2001). Creating appropriate messages and choosing the right communication channels to deliver

those messages can help companies align their goals with the interests of key stakeholders. Organizations must adapt quickly to changes in the environment. As Jack Welch once said, "Change before the environment changes." Organizations do so by developing strategic flexibility, which draws on the capabilities used to respond to various demands and opportunities that exist in dynamic and uncertain competitive environments (Hitt, Ireland, & Hoskisson, 2003).

Corporate communication integrates the different communication functions, roles, and activities on which a company can base its strategic actions. It is therefore internally and externally focused. Crafting the strategy that shapes the organization's image and identity is probably the most important responsibility of corporate communication staff. Whereas image helps the organization differentiate itself from others, identity enables the organization to integrate itself from within. Corporate communication is valued for its strategic input into decision making and the overall corporate strategy, not just for its operational excellence in managing communication resources and programs already deployed within the organization.

Corporate communication leverages the organization's communication resources, capabilities, and core competencies to accomplish its goals in the competitive environment (see Figure 15.1). *Sustained* competitive advantage occurs when a firm implements a value-creating strategy that competitors find difficult to imitate. Corporate communication can help top executives and policy makers form an accurate picture about the company's strategic intent for the public and *attain* the support the company's needs for its action. As discussed in chapter 9, a good advertising campaign, for example, helps a corporation achieve sustainable competitive advantage by propagating the company's vision, purpose, and scope of operations to its various stakeholders, particularly capital market stakeholders (i.e., shareowners, customers, regulators). At the same time, corporate communication helps maintain the systems of communication needed to support managerial competencies. Such competencies include the systems of control as well as the processes and structures essential for organizational operations—the organizational and technological resources needed to create and communicate a strategic vision. Helping to mobilize support for the strategic vision requires intangible resources such as human capital or knowledge, skills, trust, commitment, and managerial communication. As discussed in chapter 8, to be competitive a company must retain its best employees—the internal stakeholders—through effective employee relations, strong identity programs, and a view of human capital as a strategic organizational asset. Other intangible resources include innovation and ideas (e.g., capacity to learn) and reputational resources such as brand name, perceptions of service quality, and, as covered in chapters 9–11, overall organizational attractiveness (e.g., organizational integrity, social accountability).

The dominant culture and the creation of meaningful and collaborative communication relationships lie at the heart of the strategy of managing human capital. Organizational culture represents a set of values, beliefs, and ways of thinking that are commonly shared and that provide members with a sense of organizational identity. It is this sense of identity that communicates unwritten, and often unspoken, guidelines for how social systems develop and how things are done in an organization. As described in chapter 13, an organization's culture is initially formed as a result of collective memories, past experiences, and influence by strong leadership, past and present. The dominant culture must also be in line with the strategic intent and strategic vision of the organization. Whereas strategic intent is a manifestation of how the organization leverages its core competencies to attain its goals, the strategic vision includes its dreams and the communication strategies and messages to formulate future directions.

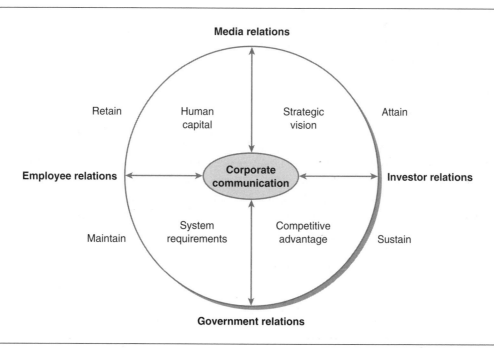

Figure 15.1   Strategic Corporate Communication: A Competing Values Framework for Corporate Communication Perspective

The Theory and Practice of Corporate Communication

The overall value of the CVFCC is that it provides a fuller view of corporate communication in which a dynamic interplay of complementary and often competing orientations takes place. The framework supports the notion of communication functions (i.e., investor relations, government relations, employee relations, media relations) and communication systems (i.e., information, regulation, integration, innovation) that are both independent and interdependent. These functions and systems must be balanced and managed strategically. The CVFCC offers an integrated view in which the relative value of each perspective is not mitigated by the value of the other perspectives. It affords an excellent opportunity to describe these perspectives while at the same time weighing the tradeoffs among the perspectives to enrich the analysis. The framework is particularly useful in helping communication researchers and practitioners form a better understanding of the scope and range of communication activities that affect the organization both internally and externally. As shown in chapter 12, the CVFCC promotes the development of communication responses that consider the objectives and consequences of employing different messages when addressing different audiences.

A helpful summary of the value of this book comes from one of its reviewers: Existing textbooks on corporate communication simply do not integrate diverse corporate communication practices into a coherent theoretical framework. This book is more than a collection of tips and best practices. It is more than a how-to guide for corporate communicators. The challenge in writing this book was to first introduce and then have students and practitioners become engaged with a theoretical approach to corporate communication—in other words, to learn a vocabulary that would help them understand the practices with which they are engaged. The book broadens their understanding of corporate communication beyond "what they do at work" in order to see how what they do fits into a much bigger and intellectually stimulating frame. Corporate communication is a serious subject that is amenable to intellectual study and analysis.

Corporate communication professionals have a responsibility not only to the clients and stakeholders they serve, but also for the meanings that permeate organizational culture, which, in turn, create the basis of values, attitudes, beliefs, and members' relationships with one another. We need to understand corporate communication theoretically—how it works, what its place is, and what impacts it will have. Any attempt to describe it in terms of tips and best practices without the insight of theory might compromise the integrity of this important (and serious) topic. The CVFCC helps pull together theoretical insights and practical applications, which distinguishes this book from any other book on the subject. This book's value to students is that it enables them to think about corporate communication in a sophisticated and critical way. Not only will they learn how to do their jobs well, they will also understand why.

As Elliot Luber stated in his Foreword to this book—here is a gift to those who study or use communication on a daily basis. May the four forces be with you!

Integrative Case Study: The Acquisition of Abbott Hospital

The Setting

In late July 1990, the *Auston Transcript* reported that Sister Mary Theresa, on behalf of Mt. Mercy Hospital, had received notification of acceptance of her offer to purchase Abbott Hospital, a 108-bed nonsectarian short-term acute general care facility located in the growing northwest portion of Auston, Oklahoma. Mt. Mercy Hospital—headed by Sister Mary Theresa and run by the Sisters of the Sacred Heart—is a 372-bed short-term acute general care facility and is Auston's dominant medical force. News of the impeding acquisition of Abbott by Mt. Mercy fueled a controversy that threatened to split much of the Auston medical community. One prominent doctor accused Sister Mary Theresa of attempting to have the Holy Roman Empire control the northwest portion of town.

Auston is a city of 200,000 people located 70 miles from Oklahoma City in Oklahoma's wheat and oil production belt. The latest census lists Auston as the fastest growing city in the state. The city's labor force has a high percentage of skilled white-collar and professional employees. Auston is also the home of Adams University, which has a student body of 20,000 and a new medical school scheduled to open in late 1993. The general economy is stable, primarily due to federal facilities. A national postal training center, Anderson Air Force Base, and the Center for Solar Design inject a half-billion dollars annually into the local economy. Major electronics firms form the base of private sector employment.

The eight civilian and military hospitals in Auston have a combined bed capacity of 1,500. There are approximately 338 physicians, surgeons, dentists, and dental surgeons operating from these hospitals. The chamber of commerce and the medical community predict that this level of care will not be adequate to service Auston's population expansion at its present growth rate.

Sister Mary Theresa, Chief Administrator of Mt. Mercy Hospital

At the center of the Abbott–Mt. Mercy controversy is Sister Mary Theresa, chief administrator of Mt. Mercy Hospital. A member of the order of the Sacred Heart nuns, she is the eldest of six children in a devoutly religious Catholic family. She entered the convent at age 17 and initially trained as a teacher. After teaching for six years, she entered nurse's training and obtained both her B.S. in nursing and a graduate degree in hospital administration. She became the administrator of Mt. Mercy Hospital 16 years ago.

During her tenure as administrator of Mt. Mercy, Sister Mary Theresa has become a controversial figure in Auston. Her supporters describer her as a strong-willed, articulate, well-organized woman who deserves credit for developing Mt. Mercy into a regional force in both medical care and basic research. Her enemies in the lay and medical communities contend that she is a cold, calculating opportunist who works only for the interests and gains of Mt. Mercy Hospital, the Sisters of the Sacred Heart, and the Catholic Church. Sister Mary Theresa describes herself as a hard worker with little patience for incompetence. Both supporters and detractors agree she is persuasive, intelligent, unafraid of confrontation, and a tough competitor.

Sister Mary Theresa has spent much of the past 16 years building a solid core of well-trained, capable physicians who admit primarily to Mt. Mercy Hospital. The restrictions for full staff privileges at Mt. Mercy are stringent in comparison with other hospitals in Auston. Many doctors who have practiced elsewhere in the county feel these rules are too strict and object to spending five years on courtesy staff privileges before they may become full staff members. As a result, some choose not to admit to Mt. Mercy.

Mt. Mercy and Abbott Hospitals

Mt. Mercy Hospital was opened by the Sisters of the Sacred Heart 22 years ago. The 372-bed facility is run as a not-for-profit hospital, as are the other six institutions located throughout the country and operated by the Sisters of the Sacred Heart based in Orange, New Jersey. Sister Mary Theresa credits the not-for-profit concept with generating the revenues to finance the expansion and development of Mt. Mercy.

(Continued)

(Continued)

In 1985, Mt. Mercy Hospital retained Kenner, Kenner, and Olson of Detroit to assist the hospital board of directors in the development of a long-range plan. This long-range plan was to address itself to the projected shortage of hospital beds in Auston. Whereas much of the plan called for the renovation of the existing facility located in the center of Auston, it also provided for the acquisition of property for construction of a satellite hospital in the northwest sector of the city.

Subsequent to the completion of Mt. Mercy's long-range plan and prior to any property acquisition by Mt. Mercy, Abbott Hospital was constructed and opened. Abbott Hospital was owned by MEDICO, a professional hospital management firm located in Los Angeles and operated as a not-for-profit corporation with no sectarian affiliations. Abbott is located in northwest Auston, which is in the heart of the city's growth pattern. In 1990, of the 30 new doctors in Auston, 27 located their offices near the Abbott facility.

During Abbott's first year of operation in 1988, MEDICO lost over $2 million. Late in the year, MEDICO management fired the administrative staff at Abbott and offered Dr. John Coletti the position of chief administrator. Dr. Coletti had been with MEDICO while completing his doctorate in hospital administration. His reputation in the company was based on his experience in several difficult administrative situations. MEDICO management viewed Coletti as a strong, decisive, and self-confident administrator.

Coletti spent much of his first months at Abbott staffing departments with people he characterized as strong leaders. Coletti revised the wage and benefits program for employees in order to stabilize what had become an excessive turnover rate. Coletti liked Abbott and the city of Auston. He was extremely pleased when, within 14 months, Abbott was operating at break-even. MEDICO management consequently viewed him as one of their successful administrators.

The Acquisition Period

Early in 1990, Sister Mary Theresa, Sister Mary Joseph, director of nursing at Mt. Mercy, and Dr. John Cassler, Mt. Mercy medical chief of staff, began reviewing the long-range plan for Mt. Mercy. Both Sister Mary Joseph and Dr. Cassler are strong supporters of Sister Mary Theresa. The three mutually agreed that a contact with MEDICO with intent to purchase Abbott might be timely after MEDICO's initial financial losses. Sister Mary Theresa felt the acquisition of Abbott was the best way to pursue the satellite hospital concept outlined in Mt. Mercy's long-range plan. Sister Mary Theresa contacted only select members of the board of directors of Mt. Mercy regarding her decision to approach MEDICO.

Sister Mary Theresa was frustrated when MEDICO management refused to answer her telephone calls. Dr. Cassler and Sister Mary Joseph received no responses either. MEDICO seemingly would not communicate directly with anyone at Mt. Mercy. Sister Theresa, once again with only informal approval of selected board members, hired McGill Associates of Chicago to act as an intermediary for discussing the purchase of Abbott with MEDICO.

In late May 1990, a McGill representative notified Sister Mary Theresa that MEDICO would entertain an offer somewhere in the vicinity of $20 million. Sister Mary Theresa and Sister Mary Joseph met with financial advisors to the Sisters of the Sacred Heart and determined that an offer of $18 million was in order. It was the verbal acceptance of the offer by MEDICO that made headlines in the *Auston Transcript* in July 1990.

Sister Mary Theresa called a board of directors meeting immediately after the *Auston Transcript* article announced the tentative agreement between Mt. Mercy and MEDICO. At the meeting she obtained unanimous approval to proceed with the necessary steps to finalize the purchase. And although some members of the Mt. Mercy board felt she was again operating autocratically, they could not fault the results of her efforts.

In order to finalize the Abbott purchase, Sister Mary Theresa began the formal application process for a certificate of public necessity. Oklahoma state law requires that transfer of ownership of an acute care facility be preceded by obtaining a State Certificate of Public Necessity for Construction or Modification of Acute care facilities. The procedure to obtain state consent for transfer of ownership involves formal documentation of projected benefits to the community and clients within the service area of the facility. Part of this documentation includes public testimony from hearings held in the local community and at the state level. Timing of the hearings was important to Sister Mary Theresa because the purchase agreement between Mt. Mercy and MEDICO called for an additional $96,000 per month for the months of January, February, and March 1991 if closing and transfer of ownership did not occur prior to December 31, 1990.

The Public Response

The certificate of public necessity had to be presented to the Project Review Board of the Auston Council of Governments, the Northeastern Oklahoma Health Systems Agency, and the State of Oklahoma Health Services Agency. Mt. Mercy personnel were expected to present and defend their position with regard to the Abbott purchase. Any interested parties from the community or health service field were invited to present information relevant to the proposed transfer of ownership.

On September 19, 1990, at a meeting of the Northeastern Oklahoma Health Systems Agency, the certificate of public necessity was presented to the public and affected agencies. Sister Mary Theresa had developed a purchase rationale centered on the efficiencies of cost and service from a multi-hospital concept.

Sister Mary Theresa began her formal statement to the group by indicating the significance of changing from a single autonomous institution to a multi-hospital system. The multi-hospital system was defined as a combination of distinct operating institutions under the single ownership and operation of one management unit. Sister Mary Theresa proposed that a multi-hospital system would achieve economies that could possibly contain or even reduce cost of patient care. She proposed that economies of scale are possible through central management and judicious consolidation of services, equipment, and personnel. She further argued that the smaller institution (Abbott) could improve care by its linkage to the larger comprehensive institution with its greater technology and scope of resources and services. And the shifting population of Auston would be better served by the branch hospital concept; Sister Mary Theresa contended that competition among local hospitals had not benefited patients. The multi-hospital system would still be locally operated while effecting cost containments that could not be achieved by the duplication of services necessary for single unit care facilities. Her final argument centered on the advantages of a combined medical staff and administrative services. Sister Mary Theresa submitted in writing a detailed plan of proposed economies that would substantiate Mt. Mercy claims of debt service capability through combined operating revenues of Mt. Mercy and Abbott.

Sister Mary Theresa's written statement confirmed publicly the purchase price of $18 million. An initial $2 million was available from the operating reserves of Mt. Mercy Hospital. The hospital's operating budget would assume associated expenses for acquisition estimated at $300,000. The Monroe Foundation of St. Louis had made a $2 million donation to be applied directly to the purchase price. The balance of $14 million was to be obtained through the issuance of tax-exempt bonds.

Sister Mary Theresa estimated consolidation savings during the first year of acquisition at $373,000. These savings would result from the elimination of the Abbott management contract with MEDICO, the utilization of Mt. Mercy data-processing capabilities, and the combination of maintenance contracts with Mt. Mercy's existing suppliers. Additional revenue economies were projected to exist in laboratory services, purchasing, nursing administration, admitting, and electrocardiography.

Staff of the health systems agency did not take issue with Sister Mary Theresa's rationale of the multi-hospital concept. Instead their line of questioning centered around determination of a purchase price. They were concerned about the lack of formal assessment of the value of Abbott Hospital. Sister Mary Joseph responded that assessors qualified to evaluate the worth of a hospital were extremely rare, and in any case, MEDICO and Mt. Mercy had mutually agreed on the price. At this point, the staff recommended approval, and Sister Mary Theresa's plans had cleared their first public test.

On October 1, 1990, a meeting of the Auston County Medical Society featured extensive discussion of the proposed acquisition of Abbott by Mt. Mercy. Many local doctors went on record opposing the purchase. Among the most vocal was Dr. Martin Leeham, a powerful member of the "old guard" of the medical society. Dr. Leeham, noted for having a hot temper and being very outspoken, is considered a fine doctor and surgeon by his colleagues. He was one of the first doctors in Auston to perform legalized abortions. During the past 16 years he has not exercised his admitting privileges at Mt. Mercy Hospital, even for cases not expected to run afoul of the Catholic Code of Ethics.

Six years ago Dr. Leeham organized a group of doctors and businesspersons in the community to approach the city council with a certificate of public necessity to build a 200-bed hospital in the northwest section of Auston. The hospital was to be doctor-owned and administered with no religious affiliation.

(Continued)

(Continued)

Sister Mary Theresa and her board were very vocal in their opposition to such a plan and attended all public hearings to voice their objections. The plan for the doctor-owned hospital was defeated and left Dr. Leeham with a bitter attitude toward Sister Mary Theresa.

The morning following the county medical society meeting, the *Auston Transcript* carried excerpts of Dr. Leeham's remarks charging Mt. Mercy and Sister Mary Theresa with an attempt by the Holy Roman Empire to take over the northwest section of town. Upon reading the account, Sister Mary Theresa is credited with smiling and saying, "Oh, good, then I'll be the Holy Roman Empress."

The second public hearing for approval of the certificate of public necessity was scheduled for October 10, 1990, with the project review board of the Auston Council of Governments. Publicity from the county medical society meeting had aroused broad community interests. The Catholic Code of Ethics and the subject of legalized abortions and sterilizations received widespread press coverage.

Legalized abortions and sterilizations constituted 25 percent of the surgical revenues at Abbott. The Catholic Code of ethics prohibits abortions or sterilizations in hospitals under Catholic ownership and operation. Opponents of the acquisition claimed that many of the new doctors locating their offices near Abbott intended to utilize the surgical facility at Abbott for abortions and sterilizations.

Sister Mary Theresa expected the project review board meeting to be emotional with strong opposition to approval of the certificate. During the meeting she refused to answer any questions relating to a description of the Catholic Code of Ethics. She stated the code would be operational at Abbott and consistently confined her comments to advantages from the multi-hospital concept and cost economies. The public opposition from the lay and medical community was not well organized and failed to mount any significant counterarguments. The project review board voted to approve the certificate of public necessity, thus clearing the way for a final hearing to be held in Oklahoma City with the State Department of Health Facilities Advisory Council of the Oklahoma Health Systems Agency.

The final public hearing was scheduled for December 5, 1990, just days short of the purchase penalty deadline. Sister Mary Theresa felt pressure to obtain immediate approval from the Oklahoma Health Systems Agency in order to avoid activating the price escalation clause. A delay through the holidays could cost Mt. Mercy $96,000 on January 1, 1991.

Sister Mary Theresa, Dr. John Cassler, Sister Mary Joseph, and Dwight Morris, attorney for Mt. Mercy, attended the meeting. Mt. Mercy representatives expected the state staff of the health facilities advisory council to be well prepared this time. Sister Mary Theresa repeated her basic remarks about the multi-hospital concept. The health facilities advisory council staff immediately challenged the validity of her projected economies and raised the issue of closing emergency room services at Abbott. Sister Mary Theresa countered with a flat refusal to consider closing emergency room services without a thorough needs analysis. She supported her figures by asking council staff to specifically indicate areas of possible error in her projections. The council attorney, Jim Redden, launched into a lengthy statement about the power and influence of Mt. Mercy. He questioned community willingness to allow further expansion of that influence. He cited newspaper publicity following the county medical society meeting. The representatives from Mt. Mercy were somewhat alarmed at what they considered Redden's lack of objectivity. During a noon recess in the hearings, Sister Mary Theresa and her advisors gathered to consider their approach during the afternoon session.

Case Questions

1. Describe the organizational change issues in this case.

2. Use stakeholder analysis (see Figure 12.1) to map out the key players in the environment of Mt. Mercy. Then discuss the impact of the acquisition of Abbott from the perspectives of the medical community, the management at Abbott, the public, and Mt. Mercy's leadership.

3. Identify a variety of sources of potential conflict as leaders of Mt. Mercy acquire Abbott. Describe the differing values, interests, and influences in the medical community and at Mt. Mercy.

Determine how past events have contributed to the present situation. Use Table 8.1 (entations) to compare and contrast the types of communication used by Sister Mary address the concerns of the different stakeholders.

4. Use Figure 11.1 to trace the leadership roles played by Sister Mary Theresa in the various situa. How effective was she? Should members of her board support her actions without more informa- tion? Why or why not?

5. What are the value and ethical issues in this case?

[Handwritten notes:]
- 25% of rev from hospital from abortion + sterilization
- doctors set up shop near hospital to use hospitals for abortions
- Negative impact on community to the people! to people + doctors

---

CASE STUDY

Mt. Mercy Acquires Abbott

On December 6, 1990, a certificate of public necessity was granted by the state of Oklahoma to Mt. Mercy for the acquisition of Abbott Hospital in Auston, Oklahoma. Sister Mary Theresa had won her battle over the opponents of Mt. Mercy's expanding influence in the medical community.

Upon receipt of the certificate, Mt. Mercy retained Kidder, Kidder and Company to handle a private placement of tax-exempt bonds to finalize the $18 million purchase. Bonds were quickly placed, and com- bined with operating reserve and foundation monies, the acquisition was completed.

Sister Mary Theresa planned for Mt. Mercy to begin operating Abbott on February 15, 1991. She con- tacted Dr. John Coletti, Abbott administrator under MEDICO, and asked him to remain. Coletti agreed, feeling the progress he had made at Abbott would continue.

Early in January 1991, Sister Mary Theresa requested that the Mt. Mercy personnel department inter- view all Abbott staff members, who were asked to sign a letter of intent with regard to their continued services on the combined Mt. Mercy/Abbott staffs. Staff members were notified that signing the letter would insure them of continued employment for a three-month probationary period, at the end of which permanent placement would be discussed. Staffs of both hospitals were to be informed they could be transferred between hospitals at administrative discretion. No seniority and accrued benefits from Abbott would transfer to Mt. Mercy/Abbott staff status. John Coletti was not consulted or notified of these actions by the Mt. Mercy personnel department. He complained directly to Sister Mary Theresa and expressed concern that these actions would seriously undermine morale.

Sister Mary Theresa nevertheless directed the personnel department to continue with the interviews. Sister Mary Joseph was instructed by Sister Mary Theresa to advise all Abbott department heads that they were to report directly to their counterparts at Mt. Mercy. Abbott department heads thus became assis- tant department heads. John Coletti was furious and threatened to resign his position immediately unless this policy was altered. Sister Mary Theresa held to her basic reorganization plan, and Coletti resigned on February 1, 1991. Five departments' heads from Abbott also resigned.

The First Six Months

Amidst turbulent conditions, Abbott Hospital became an operating satellite of Mt. Mercy Hospital on February 16, 1991. The Catholic Code of Ethics became the governing code [at] Abbott on the same day.

Within two weeks of the Mt. Mercy takeover, six doctors had resigned from the staff of Mt. Mercy at Abbott. They had transferred their staff privileges to Memorial, a local hospital permitting legalized abor- tions and sterilizations in its surgical facilities.

(Continued)

(Continued)

Sister Mary Theresa addressed herself to the task of replacing John Coletti. She was disturbed by reports that the management of Memorial had offered Coletti a position, and that he would join their staff on March 1. In late February 1991, Sister Mary Theresa hired Adam Sampson to become assistant administrator for Mt. Mercy at Abbott.

Adam Sampson is from a family of physicians. After an unsuccessful semester at medical school, Sampson returned to hospital administration and has met both success and failure during his career. At his last position, the hospital's financial problems were dramatically turned around. Sampson has taken the credit for the progress, although reliable sources consider the hospital staff to be the major change factor. Sampson considers himself an idea man who will work to avoid confrontation if possible. Observers generally describe him as a nice person who takes orders well. Adam Sampson assumed his duties at Mt. Mercy at Abbott on March 1, 1991. Sister Mary Theresa asked him for monthly reports summarizing the general operating and financial status of the new satellite.

During the same month, Sister Mary Theresa formed a Mt. Mercy at Abbott Operational Review Committee composed of Sister Mary Joseph, Dr. John Cassler, and Adam Sampson. The committee was to meet monthly to review all phases of the Abbott operation. Sister Mary Theresa had set a goal for Abbott to break even within 13 months. She intended to make whatever adjustments necessary to facilitate the goal.

The Early Results

During April, May, and June 1991, revenues for Abbott ran 15 to 20 percent below projected levels. Revenues from surgery and associated patient care days were the hardest hit, with a decline of 62 percent. The pediatrics occupancy rate was an unacceptably low 21 percent. Mt. Mercy staff doctors were not admitting patients to Abbott at a greater rate than before the purchase. Administrative costs were up 6 to 8 percent, within the anticipated range for the change to Mt. Mercy procedures.

In June 1991, a somewhat frustrated Adam Sampson indicated he was not getting cooperation from the Abbott staff. Sampson asked Sister Mary Theresa and the other committee members to consider transfer of Mt. Mercy personnel to Abbott to give him a staff that might be more responsive to his needs for operating information. Furthermore, he was finding it difficult to fill the administrative vacancies that had followed the Coletti resignation.

Sister Mary Theresa and Sister Mary Joseph both agreed that Sampson was premature in requesting additional changes at Abbott. Sister Mary Theresa assured Sampson the staff discontent caused by the initial takeover would take some time to dissipate.

Sister Mary Theresa expressed concern about Abbott revenues to Dr. Cassler. She reminded him that cost economies from consolidation were meaningless if she could not keep her operating revenues at a level to service the acquisition debt.

The July Operational Review Committee Meeting

When the committee met in July, Abbott revenues were running 18 percent below projections. Surgery revenues had improved slightly but still registered a 58-percent decline. The pediatrics occupancy rate remained a dismal 21 percent. Administrative cost increases had leveled off at 6 percent. Sampson's specific analysis of doctor admissions confirmed Mt. Mercy staff doctors were not increasing their utilization of Abbott facilities. A somewhat surprising picture surfaced with emergency room revenues running ahead of projections for break-even.

Dr. Cassler confirmed John Coletti's appointment as director of planning for Memorial Hospital. He further reported Dr. Leeham's latest efforts to persuade several new doctors to move their practices to Memorial. Committee members were aware that Memorial had applied for a certificate of public necessity to add 26 additional beds. Sister Mary Theresa felt it prudent to support the application.

Sampson indicated he was impressed with the competency of the Abbott staff but did not feel he was getting helpful input to facilitate correcting the bleak revenue picture. Sister Mary Theresa and the committee agreed on corrective action. The committee discussed how to approach the various facets of the problem.

Sister Mary Theresa was opposed to transferring personnel between the two facilities. She proposed immediate reinstatement of accrued benefits from Abbott tenure to all Abbott staff members remaining on the combined staffs. Sister Mary Joseph strongly concurred, emphasizing the linkage between overall staff morale and the high quality of staff-patient relations for which Mt. Mercy and Abbott had been known. Sampson seemed hesitant about their proposal but did not challenge it. Dr. Cassler proposed initiation of formal conversations with a number of his colleagues to determine what types of services might attract both new doctors and increased admissions to Abbott from doctors currently exercising staff privileges at Mt. Mercy. All committee members agreed a public response to Dr. Leeham was inappropriate.

Sister Mary Theresa asked Sister Mary Joseph to compile a detailed analysis of the Mt. Mercy pediatrics ward. Sister Mary Theresa instructed the Operational Review Committee to look for possible consolidation of services, which would revise the operating structure of Mt. Mercy in order to strongly encourage Mt. Mercy staff doctors to utilize Abbott for all pediatrics and related cases. The beds vacated by pediatrics at Mt. Mercy could accommodate a planned surgical ward expansion. Sister Mary Theresa was curious about the emergency room revenue reports from Abbott. She asked the committee to consider what implications this might have for other services.

Case Questions

1. Evaluate the effectiveness of the first six months of Mt. Mercy's operation of Abbott. Specifically consider the communication events leading to John Coletti's resignation. Develop a rationale for Sister Mary Theresa's approach to Abbott's personnel status at the time of the merger with the Mt. Mercy staff.

2. What are the major change issues in this case? Use Figure 8.2 (types of organizational culture) and Table 8.1 (message orientations) to describe communication problems in merging two separate organizations.

3. How would you describe Sister Mary Theresa's leadership style during the merger period? Develop a rationale for her decision to ignore John Coletti's advice. Evaluate his decision to leave Abbott.

4. What changes would you recommend to the approach that management took at Abbott? What, if any, should remain the same?

5. Use Figure 15.1 (strategic corporate communication) to describe the major strategic issues in this case.

CASE STUDY

The End of the First Six Months

By the end of July 1991, accrued benefits had been reinstated for the original Abbott staff members. Sister Mary Theresa and Sister Mary Joseph had begun plans to relocate all pediatrics services from Mt. Mercy to Abbott. An *Auston Transcript* article outlining plans for the consolidation portrayed a favorable community reaction. Several staff doctors had expressed mild displeasure to Dr. Cassler but did not seem to be contemplating any serious opposition. Cassler also reported success in forming a group of staff doctors to study service needs that could be accommodated specifically at Abbott. No decision was made concerning emergency room service.

(Continued)

(Continued)

Sister Mary Theresa, without committee or board knowledge, began seeking additional foundation monies for debt service in the event revenues were not sufficient within 13 months to meet the debt service schedule. As she looked ahead, Sister Mary Theresa saw many difficulties but was exhilarated by the challenges of making a multi-hospital concept work.

Case Questions

1. Use the communication audit model described in chapter 13 to develop a comprehensive plan to help Sister Mary Theresa and Sister Mary Joseph improve internal and external communication.

2. Would Sister Mary Theresa and Sister Mary Joseph benefit from reading *The Theory and Practice of Corporate Communication*? If so, how?

SOURCE: From Pamela Shockley-Zalabak, *Understanding Organizational Communication: Cases, Commentaries, and Conversations.* Published by Allyn & Bacon, Boston, MA. Copyright © 1994 by Pearson Education. Reprinted by permission of the publisher.

CASE STUDY

Integrative Case Study: BelBeck Production

The case of BelBeck illustrates communication issues from several perspectives. As the executive vice president for corporate communication, Amy Bell's task is to find a way to improve communication among the three divisions, each of which has several operating units. The president, Ossie Becker, just handed her a report from a turnaround strategist with a consultancy group, Ariel Think Inc., which specializes in designing effective corporate communication strategies with proven methodologies in stakeholder analysis and relationship management. The group also specializes in change management and has successful experience working with corporate clients to transform business strategies into action. The consultant, Moti Brown, conducted an internal communication audit and recommended a set of action plans for improving the flow of communication both internally and externally. Becker was particularly concerned with the conclusion of that report: "Steps must be taken immediately to reconfigure the systems of communication both internally and externally. . . . BelBeck's financial results, performance credibility, and customer retention are on the line. . . . In a TV/radio/film industry with cutthroat competition, any inaction would result in a loss of business." The report analyzed BelBeck's capabilities and resources and compared them against its long-term goals and strategies, with a primary focus on four systems of communication within BelBeck:

Innovative—The three divisions and the units within them have little or no interaction and therefore lack the synergistic effects that typically breed innovative ideas and insights. Customers receive services and products that are typically good but lack the cutting edge that other companies offer.

Integrative—Operating units are highly specialized, with professionals developing different lingo, sagas, and norms of behavior reflecting different goals, areas of expertise, and interpersonal communication. Although the work units are quite cohesive, the communication between them is poor.

Regulative—Coordination across functional lines at BelBeck takes too much effort and time, and there are a great deal of redundant communication and unnecessary messages. Most work is performed sequentially by different functions in the organization (e.g., from marketing and accounts receivable to editing and producing) using rules and standard operating procedures that are not always enforced. Managers, account executives, and professionals often develop competing interpretations of work outcomes with tension and conflict over who broke the rules and who is accountable for the mishap.

Informative—Boundary-spanning activities at BelBeck are less than optimal. Most information about new trends, client expectations, and developments in the industry reaches top executives late, and most decisions are made in crisis mode. BelBeck lags behind competitors in responding to changes in the marketplace and therefore misses opportunities to grow and sustain the business.

Becker is furious. He just received a phone call from John Green, a venture capitalist who actively worked with him on strategies that could potentially improve the bottom line. In fact, it was Green who suggested retaining the services of Ariel Think Inc. In previous correspondence, Green made it clear that his partners provided financing to help BelBeck grow to a critical mass to attract public financing through a stock offering. He was concerned by BelBeck's underperformance and was worried that his private partners (i.e., the private and public pension funds that provided the funds) will be pushing for a merger or acquisition with another company by providing liquidity and exit for the company's founders, including Becker and Bell. Green wants to meet with Becker immediately. Becker still remembers Green's last message to him: "Either fix this company or face the brutal facts head on." He gave the report prepared by Brown to Bell and asked her to call the management team for an urgent meeting. He then left for his meeting with Green.

Bell is pondering her options. Several years ago she was hired away from a Canadian company that she headed to lead the expansion efforts at BelBeck. Becker offered her equity-based incentives that included a substantial stake in the company. Through strong advertising, marketing, promotion, and PR campaigns, she turned BelBeck into one of the leading production companies in California. Within 2 years after she assumed her position, revenues hit $160 million, up 25% from the previous year, and the company posted a net gain of $6 million. She decided to call Susan Gold, BelBeck's customer relations director, and Brenda Diamond, the HR director, both close allies, to review the options. After reviewing the situation, they agreed that BelBeck would benefit from considering the following measures:

1. A more tightly integrated customer relationship system

2. Better integration across functional lines

3. Improved downward and upward flow of communication

4. More opportunities for lateral communication

5. Better tracking and monitoring information systems

6. Greater accountability for work processes and outcomes

7. Better management of the company's key stakeholders

Gold and Diamond also pointed out that Brown and others at Ariel Think Inc. talked informally about a full-scale reconfiguration of the company's structure and communication systems. Gold noticed a chart in the report that flipped BelBeck's structure sideways, replacing functions with processes. A comment below the chart stated that creating self-contained units "with all of the skills necessary to respond to clients' needs" should help resolve BelBeck's structural and communication deficiencies. "Looks invigorating," Gold whispered over the phone, "but I don't know if the other managers will buy into the idea." Later, as Bell was heading into the meeting with the management team, she recalled Becker's last message to her before leaving for his meeting with Green: "The only way to get out of the hole is to stop digging."

BelBeck's three divisions are headed by three vice presidents. The vice president for account management, Abby Wright, has several layers of account supervisors, each with a cluster of account executives. The vice president for media and production, Jeremy Elliott, is responsible for operating units that include television studio, radio, television field, film and nonlinear editing, writing, directing, producing, advertising, and broadcasting. Each of these units is led by a manager with added staff that include technical support, clerical, and documentation. The vice president for marketing and advertising, Daniel Stevens, is responsible for marketing, production, promotion, and advertising.

(Continued)

(Continued)

Four more departments, each with a designated director, report directly to Bell: employee relations, investor relations, public relations, legal and external affairs. These departments handle most of BelBeck's external communication, including dealing with reporters, financial analysts, vendors and agents, trade associations, union representatives, and investors. Bell also has a small unit of corporate communication staff headed by a corporate communication manager, Amanda Sharp, and a strategic planning manager, Anat Singer. A liaison position staffed by Molly Black helps connect corporate communication with the four directors that report to Bell. The entire organization has approximately 660 employees, about two thirds of whom work in the media and production division.

Case Questions

1. What should Bell tell her management team?

2. Who are the key stakeholders in this case? What kind of power do they have?

3. How would you describe the culture at BelBeck? The company's pattern of communication?

4. What are the organizational issues confronting Bell?

5. Create a chart of BelBeck's organizational structure.

6. How would you reconfigure the structure of BelBeck? What are the benefits of such a configuration? Chart the new structure.

7. Develop a communication plan for monitoring the success of the reorganization.

8. Evaluate the success of the communication plan from the perspective of employees, managers, founders, customers, and equity holders.

References

Agle, B. R., Mitchell, R. K., & Sonnenfeld, J. A. (1999). Who matters to CEOs? An investigation of stakeholder attributes and salience, corporate performance, and CEO values. *Academy of Management Journal, 42,* 507-525.

Akchin, D. (2001). Nonprofit marketing: Just how far has it come? *Nonprofit World, 19*(1), 33-35.

Akukwe, C. (2006). *Bill and Melinda Gates and Warren Buffet: Reshaping global health.* Retrieved March 22, 2007, from http://www.worldpress.org/Americas/2408.cfm

Alessandri, S. (2001). Modeling corporate identity: A concept explication and theoretical explanation. *Corporate Communications, 6*(4), 173-183.

Altria Group. (2007a). *Enhancing standards and regulatory frameworks.* Retrieved March 17, 2007, from http://www.altria.com/responsibility/4_5_3_standardsandregulatory.asp

Altria Group. (2007b). *Phillip Morris International.* Retrieved March 17, 2007, from http://www.altria.com/about_altria/01_00_02_PhilipMorrisIntl.asp

American National Red Cross. (2006). *Government relations.* Retrieved March 18, 2007, from http://www.redcross.org/aboutus/

American National Red Cross. (n.d.). *About us.* Retrieved March 17, 2007, from http://www.redcross.org/aboutus/

American Red Cross charity report. (2005). Retrieved March 17, 2007, from http://charityreports.give.org/Public/Report.aspx?CharityID=679

Argenti, P. A. (1994). *Corporate communication.* New York: McGraw-Hill.

Argenti, P. (2002, December). Crisis communication: Lessons from 9/11. *Harvard Business Review,* 103-109.

Arndorfer, J. B. (2005, August 1). McDonald's lovin' its new model, *TelevisionWeek, 24*(31), 17.

Baker, T. (2001a). Cutting through the e-maze: Marketing strategy (Part I). *Fund Raising Management, 32*(3), 28-31.

Baker, T. (2001b). Cutting through the e-maze: Marketing strategy (Part II). *Fund Raising Management, 32*(4), 32-36.

Baker, T. (2001c). Involvement strategy. *Fund Raising Management, 32*(7), 41-42, 46.

Balmer, J. M. T., & Gray, E. R. (2000). Corporate identity and corporate communications: Creating a competitive advantage. *Industrial and Commercial Training, 32*(7), 256-261.

Barge, K. (1994). *Leadership—Communication skills for organizations and groups.* New York: St. Martin's Press.

Barnett, P., & Malcolm, L. (1997). Beyond ideology: The emerging roles of New Zealand's crown health enterprises. *International Journal of Health Services, 27,* 89-108.

Baron, G. (2003). The blame game: Lessons learned from NASA. *Public Relations Tactics, 10*(5), 26.

Barrett, A. (1997, July 14). Making WorldCom live up to its name. *Business Week.* Retrieved March 27, 2007, from http://www.businessweek.com/1997/28/b353598.htm

Bateman, T. S., & Snell, S. A. (1999). *Management: Building competitive advantage.* Boston: Irwin/McGraw-Hill.

Baysinger, B. D., Kein, G. D., & Zeithaml, C. P. (1985). An empirical evaluation of the potential for including shareholders in corporate constituency programs. *Academy of Management Journal, 28,* 180-200.

Beder, S. (1998). *Marketing to children.* Retrieved February 12, 2007, from http://www.uow.edu.au/arts/sts/sbeder/children.html

Belasen, A. (1988). *The New York State Returnable Beverage Container Law: Economic effects, industry adaptation, and guidelines for improved public environmental policies.* Albany, NY: Nelson Rockefeller Institute of Government.

Belasen, A. (1997). An application of the competing values framework to self-managed teams. In

A. M. Rahim, R. T. Golembieski, & L. E. Pate (Eds.), *Current topics in management* (Vol. 2, pp. 79-111). Greenwich, CT: JAI Press.

Belasen, A. T. (1998). Paradoxes and leadership roles: Assessment, development and application. *Management Development Forum Journal, 1*(2), 65-86.

Belasen, A. T. (1999). Non-directive change: Leveraging the collective intelligence of organizational members. *Management Development Forum Journal, 2*(1), 5-20.

Belasen, A. T. (2000). *Leading the learning organization: Communication and competencies for managing change.* Albany: State University of New York Press.

Benoit W. L. (1997). Image repair discourse and crisis communication. *Public Relations Review, 23,* 177-186.

Berman, S. L., Wicks, A. C., Kotha, S., & Jones, T. M. (1999). Does stakeholder orientation matter? The relationship between stakeholder management models and firm financial performance. *Academy of Management Journal, 42,* 488-511.

Blair, J. D. & Fottler, M. D. (1990). *Challenges in health care management.* San Francisco: Jossey-Bass.

Boje, D. M. (1995). Stories of the storytelling organization: A postmodern analysis of Disney as "Tamara-Land." *Academy of Management Journal, 38,* 997-1035.

Borda, J. L., & Mackey-Kallis, S. (2004). A model for crisis management. In D. P. Millar & R. L. Heath (Eds.), *Responding to crisis: A rhetorical approach to crisis communication* (pp. 117-138). Mahwah, NJ: Lawrence Erlbaum.

Bormann, E., Cragan, J., & Shields, D. (1994). In defense of symbolic convergence theory: A look at the theory and its criticisms after two decades. *Communication Theory, 4,* 259-294.

Botes, A. (2000). A comparison between the ethics of justice and the ethics of care. *Journal of Advanced Nursing, 32,* 1071-1075.

Boudreaux, D. J. (1995). "Puffery" in advertising. *The Free Market, 13*(9).

Bowie, N. E. (1998, January). Companies are discovering the value of ethics. *USA Today Magazine.* pp. 22-24.

Boyd, J. (2003). A quest for cinergy: The war metaphor and the construction of identity. *Communication Studies, 54,* 249-316.

Brill, S. (2003). *After: How America confronted the September 12 era.* New York: Simon & Schuster.

Brown, L. F. (1995). Getting a grip on investor relations. *Directors & Boards, 19*(2), 44-47.

Bruning, S., & Ledingham, J. (2000). Perceptions of relationships and evaluations of satisfaction: An exploration of interaction. *Public Relations Review, 26,* 86-95.

Buffet, W. (2002, February 28). *Chairman's letter.* Retrieved March 19, 2007, from http://www.berkshirehathaway.com/2001ar/2001letter.html

Burrell G., & Morgan, G. (1979). *Sociological paradigms and organizational analysis: Elements of the sociology of corporate life.* Brookfield, VT: Ashgate.

Cameron, K. S., & Quinn, R. E. (1999). *Diagnosing and changing organizational culture.* New York: Addison-Wesley.

Caplan, J. (2005). Perks at work. *Time, 166*(11), 112-113.

Carson, E. D. (2002). Public expectations and non-profit sector realities: A growing divide with disastrous consequences. *Nonprofit & Voluntary Sector Quarterly, 31,* 429-436.

Caudron, S. (1997). Forget image. *Industry Weekly, 246*(3), 13-16.

Challenger, J. A. (2006, January). Perks are perking up again. *USA Today Magazine,* 19.

Cheney, G. (2002). *Values at work: Employee participation meets market pressure at Mondragon.* Ithaca, NY: ILR/Cornell University Press.

Cheney, G., & Christensen, L. T. (2001). Organizational identity: Linkages between internal and external communication. In F. M. Jablin & L. L. Putnam (Eds.), *The new handbook of organizational communication: Advances in theory, research, and methods* (pp. 231-269). Thousand Oaks, CA: Sage.

Chiles, A. M, & Zorn, T. E. (1995). Empowerment in organizations: Employees' perceptions of the influences of empowerment. *Journal of Applied Communication Research, 23*(1), 1-25.

Clampitt, P., DeKoch, R., & Cashman, T. (2000). A strategy for communicating about uncertainty. *Academy of Management Executive, 14*(4), 41-57.

Clampitt, P. G., Berk, L., & Williams, L. M. (2002, May-June). Leaders as strategic communicators. *Ivey Business Journal,* 51-55.

Clarke, G., & Murray, L. W. (2000). Investor relations: Perceptions of the annual statement. *Corporate Communications, 5*(3), 144-151.

Clarkson, M. (1995). A stakeholder framework for analyzing and evaluating corporate social performance. *Academy of Management Review, 20,* 92-117.

Coleman, R. (2004). Satisfied stakeholders. *CMA Management, 78*(1), 22-26.

Comrie, M. (1997). Media tactics in New Zealand's Crown Health Enterprises. *Public Relations Review, 23*, 161-176.

Conger, M. (1996). How a comprehensive IR program pays off. *Financial Executive, 20*(1), 30-35.

Constance, D. H., & Bonanno, A. (2000). Regulating the global fisheries: The World Wildlife Fund, Unilever, and the Marine Stewardship Council. *Agriculture and Human Values, 17*(2), 125-139.

Coombs, W. T. (1999). *Ongoing crisis communication.* Thousand Oaks, CA: Sage.

Corley, G. K., Cochran, P. L., & Comstock, T. G. (2001). Image and the impact of public affairs management on internal stakeholders. *Journal of Public Affairs, 1*, 53-67.

Cornelissen, J. (2004). *Corporate communication theory and practice.* London: Sage.

Crooke, R. E. (1996). How the cult of cost efficiency destroys credible communications. *Public Relations Quarterly, 41*(3), 8-13.

Cross, R., & Prusak, L. (2002, June). The people who make organizations go—or stop. *Harvard Business Review,* 105-112.

Cushman, D. P. (1987). The rules approach to communication theory: A philosophical and operational perspective. In L. D. Kincaid (Ed.), *Communication theory: Eastern and Western perspectives* (pp. 223-234). New York: Academic Press.

Cushman, D. P., King, S. S., & Smith, T. (1988). The rules perspective on organizational communication research. In G. M. Goldhaber & G. A. Barnett (Eds.), *Handbook of organizational communication* (pp. 55-94). Norwood, NJ: Ablex.

Deal, T. E., & Kennedy, A. A. (1982). *Corporate cultures: The rites and rituals of corporate life.* Reading, MA: Addison-Wesley.

Deetz, S., & Kersten, A. (1983). Critical models of interpretive research. In L. Putnam & M. E. Pacanowsky (Eds.), *Communication and organizations: An interpretive approach* (pp. 18-47). Beverly Hills, CA: Sage.

Deetz, S., & Mumby, D. K. (1990). Power, discourse, and the workplace: Reclaiming the critical tradition. In J. Anderson (Ed.), *Communication yearbook 13* (pp. 18-47). Newbury Park, CA: Sage.

DeLapp, T. (1996). Reputation management: Building and maintaining a positive public image and process. *Thrust for Educational Leadership, 25*(4), 10-13.

Denison, D. R., Hooijberg, R., & Quinn, R. E. (1995). Paradox and performance: Toward a theory of behavioral complexity in managerial leadership. *Organization Science, 6*, 524-540.

Dickie, R. B. (1984). Influence of public affairs offices on corporate planning and of corporations on government policy. *Strategic Management Journal, 5*, 15-34.

Dionisopoulos, G. N., & Crable, R. E. (1988). Definitional hegemony as a public relations strategy: The rhetoric of the nuclear power industry after Three Mile Island. *Central States Speech Journal, 39*(2), 134-145.

DiPadova, L. N., & Faerman, S. R. (1993). Using the competing values framework to facilitate managerial understanding across levels of organizational hierarchy. *Human Resource Management, 32*(1), 143-174.

Dolphin, R. R. (2003). Approaches to investor relations: Implementation in the British context. *Journal of Marketing Communication, 9*, 29-43.

Dolphin, R. R. (2004). The strategic role of investor relations. *Corporate Communications, 9*(1), 25-42.

Dominiak, M. (2006). Use creative tactics to retain staff. *Television Week, 25*, 112-113.

Donaldson, T. (1996, September-October). Values in tension: Ethics away from home. *Harvard Business Review, 74*, 48-62.

Donaldson, T. (2002). The stakeholder revolution and the Clarkson Principles. *Business Ethics Quarterly, 12*(2), 107-111.

Donaldson, T., & Preston, L. E. (1995). The stakeholder theory of the corporation: Concepts, evidence and implications, *Academy of Management Review, 20*, 65-91.

Duke, S., & Masland, L. (2002). Crisis communication by the book. *Public Relations Quarterly, 47*(3), 30-35.

Duncan, T. (2002). *IMC: Using advertising and promotion to build brands* (International Ed.). New York: McGraw-Hill.

Dye, R. A. (1998). On the frequency, quality, and informational role of mandatory financial reports. *Journal of Accounting Research, 36*, 149-160.

Eisner, M. A. (2004). Corporate environmentalism, regulatory reform, and industry self-regulation in the United States. *Governance: An International Journal of Policy, Administration, and Institutions, 17*(2), 145-167.

Ensman, R. G., Jr. (1993). Communication trends and the small shop (How non-profit organizations can cope with changing fund raising climate). *Fund Raising Management, 24*(9), 51-52.

Fairhurst, G. T., & Putnam, L. L. (2004). Organizations as discursive constructions. *Communication Theory, 14,* 5-26.

Fairhurst, G. T., & Sarr, R. A. (1997). *The art of framing: Seizing leadership moments in everyday conversations.* San Francisco: Jossey-Bass.

Fama, E. F., & Jensen, M. C. (1983). Separation of ownership and control. *Journal of Law & Economics, 26,* 301-325.

The federal charter of the American Red Cross. (n.d.). Retrieved March 17, 2007, from http://www.red cross.org/museum/history/charter.asp

FedEx. (1995–2007). *Our culture: People-service-profit.* Retrieved February 27, 2007, from http://www.fedex.com/br_english/about/careers/ourcul ture.html

Ferris, R. D., & Newman, R. M.. (1991). Building better financial communications: IR specialists cooperate with others in corporate structure. *Public Relations Journal, 47,* 18-23.

Flanagan, W. G. (2003). *Dirty rotten CEOs: How business leaders are fleecing America.* New York: Citadel Press.

Freeman, R. E. (1984). *Strategic management: A stakeholder approach.* Boston: Pitman.

Frooman, J. (1999). Stakeholder influence strategies. *Academy of Management Review, 24,* 191-201.

Frost, A. R., & Cooke, C. (1999). Brand vs. reputation. *Communication World, 16*(3), 22-25.

Gaines-Ross, L. (2003). *CEO capital: A guide to building CEO reputation and company success.* San Francisco: John Wiley.

Gallagher, K., & Weinberg, C. B. (1991). Coping with success: New challenges for nonprofit marketing. *Sloan Management Review, 33*(1) 27-42.

Gaywood, C. L. (Ed.). 1997. *The handbook of strategic public relations and integrated communications.* New York: McGraw-Hill.

Gerber, B. J., & Teske, P. (2000). Regulatory policymaking in the American states: A review of theories and evidence. *Political Research Quarterly, 53,* 849-886.

Gibbins, M., Richardson, A., & Waterhouse, J. (1990). The management of corporate financial disclosure: Opportunism, ritualism, policies, and processes. *Journal of Accounting Research, 28,* 121-143.

Gibson, D. C. (1997). A quantitative description of FBI public relations. *Public Relations Review, 23,* 11-30.

Gibson, J. W., & Hodgetts, R. M. (1991). *Organizational communication: A managerial perspective.* Upper Saddle River, NJ: Pearson Education.

Goodman, M. B. (1994). *Corporate communication: Theory and practice.* Albany: State University of New York Press.

Goodman, M. B. (1998). *Corporate communication for executives.* Albany: State University of New York Press.

Goodman, M. B. (2001). Current trends in corporate communications. *Corporate Communications, 6*(3), 117-123.

Gordon, C. D., & Kelly, K. S. (1999). Public relations expertise and organizational effectiveness: A study of U.S. hospitals. *Journal of Public Relations Research, 11,* 143-165.

Gore, A., Jr. (1994). The new job of the federal executive. *Public Administration Review, 54,* 317-321.

Gotsi, M., & Wilson, A. M. (2001a). Corporation reputation: Seeking a definition. *Corporate Communications, 6*(1), 24-30.

Gotsi, M., & Wilson, A. M. (2001b). Corporate reputation management: "Living the brand." *Management Decision, 39*(2), 99-104.

Great Places to Work Institute. (2007). *100 best companies to work for in America: 2006.* Retrieved March 19, 2007, from http://www.greatplaceto work.com/best/list-bestusa-2006.htm

Greer, C. F., & Moreland, K. D. (2003). United Airlines' and American Airlines' online crisis communication following the September 11 terrorist attacks. *Public Relations Review, 29,* 427-441.

Grunwald, M. (2003). Columbia is lost. *The Washington Post,* February 2, A01.

Gustin, C., & Sheehy, J. (2003). Avoiding the seven sins of crisis communication. *Electronic Perspectives, 28*(4), 5-6.

Gwin, J. M. (1990). Constituent analysis: A paradigm for marketing effectiveness in the not-for-profit organization. *European Journal of Marketing, 24*(7), 43-48.

Hambrick, D. C., & Fredrickson, J. W. (2001). Are you sure you have a strategy? *Academy of Management Executive, 15*(4), 48-59.

Hargie, O., Tourish, D., & Wilson, N. (2002). Communication audits and the effects of increased information: A follow up study. *Journal of Business Communication, 39,* 414-436.

Hart, S. L., & Quinn, R. E. (1993). Roles executives play: CEOs, behavioral complexity, and firm performance. *Human Relations, 46,* 543-574.

Hearit, K. M. (1994). Apologies and public relations crises at Chrysler, Toshiba, and Volvo. *Public Relations Review, 20*, 113-125.

Hearit, K. M., & Courtright, J. L. (2003). A social constructionist approach to crisis management: Allegations of sudden acceleration in the Audi 5000. *Communication Studies, 54*, 79-95.

Heath, R. L. (1997). *Strategic issues management: Organizations and public policy challenges.* Thousand Oaks, CA: Sage.

Heath, R. L. (2004). Telling a story: A narrative approach to communication during crisis. In D. P. Millar & R. L. Heath (Eds.), *Responding to crisis: A rhetorical approach to crisis communication* (pp. 167-188). Mahwah, NJ: Lawrence Erlbaum.

Heath, R. L., & Nelson, R. A. (1986). *Issue management: Corporate public policymaking and information society.* New Delhi: Sage.

Henley, T. K. (2001a). Integrated marketing communications for local nonprofit organizations: Communications tools and methods. *Journal of Nonprofit & Public Sector Marketing, 9*(1-2), 157-168.

Henley, T. K. (2001b). Integrated marketing communications for local nonprofit organizations: Developing an integrated marketing communications strategy. *Journal of Nonprofit & Public Sector Marketing, 9*(1-2), 141-155.

Hill, C. W., & Jones, T. M. (1992). Stakeholder agency theory. *Journal of Management Studies, 29*, 131-154.

Hitt, M. A., Ireland, R. D., & Hoskisson, R. E. (2003). *Strategic management* (5th ed.). Mason, OH: Thomson/South-Western.

Hoffman, J. C. (2001). Stakeholder focus: Effective crisis communication. *Chemical Market Reporter, 260*(12), 27-29.

Howard, C. (1995). "Building cathedrals"—Reflections on three decades in corporate PR and a peek at the future. *Public Relations Quarterly, 40*(2), 5-9.

Howard, T. (2001). Target ads hit right note by mixing music, color. *USA Today*, February 19. Retrieved March 27, 2007, from http://www.usatoday.com/money/advertising/adtrack/2001-02-19-target-adtrack.htm

Hunn, M., & Meisel, S. (1991). Internal communication: Auditing for quality. *Quality Progress, 24*(6), 56-60.

Hunt, J. G., Stelluto, G. E., & Hooijberg, R. (2004). Toward new-wave organization creativity: Beyond romance and analogy in the relationship between orchestra conductor leadership and musician creativity. *Leadership Quarterly, 15*(1), 145-162.

Hutton, J. G., Goodman, M. B., Alexander, J. B., & Genest, C. M. (2001). Reputation management: The new face of corporate public relations? *Public Relations Review, 27*, 247-261.

Ihator, A. (1999). Society and corporate public relations—Why the conflict? *Public Relations Quarterly, 44*(3), 33-40.

Jackson, P. (1997). Reputation management: Who needs an image? *Techniques: Making Education & Career Connections, 72*(6), 26-28.

Jernigan, D. H. (1997, July/August). Thirsting for markets: Corporate alcohol goes global. *Multinational Monitor*, 34-35.

Johnson, P. M. (1992). Closing the communication gap. *Training & Development, 46*(12), 19-21.

Johnson & Johnson. (1907–2007). *Our company.* Retrieved March 27, 2007, from http://www.jnj.com/our_company/our_credo/index.htm

Jones, D. (2002). The interpretive auditor, reframing the communication auditor. *Management Communication Quarterly, 15*, 472-479.

Judd, V. C. (2001). Toward a customer-orientation and a differentiated position in a nonprofit organization: Using the 5th p-people. *Journal of Nonprofit & Public Sector Marketing, 9*(1-2), 5-17.

Kaplan, T. (1998). *The Tylenol crisis: How effective public relations saved Johnson & Johnson.* The Pennsylvania State University. Retrieved February 13, 2007, from http://www.personal.psu.edu/users/w/x/wxk116/tylenol/crisis.html

Kearns, K. P. (1996). *Managing for accountability: Preserving the public trust in public and non-profit organizations.* San Francisco: Jossey-Bass.

Key, W. B. (1973). *Subliminal seduction: Ad media's manipulation of a not so innocent America.* Englewood Cliffs, NJ: Prentice-Hall.

Kjellerup, N. (n.d.). *The GE case files.* Retrieved March 8, 2007, from http://callcentres.com.au/gecase.htm

Kiriakidou, O., & Millward, L. (2000). Corporate identity: External reality or internal fit? *Corporate Communications, 5*(1), 49-58.

Kitchen, P. J., & De Pelsmacker, P. (2004). *Integrated marketing communications: A primer.* London: Routledge.

Kitto, J. A. (1998). The evolution of public issue management. *Public Relations Quarterly, 43*(4), 34-38.

Kurz, P. (2000). Intellectual capital management and value maximization. *Technology, Law, and Insurance, 5*, 27-32.

Lamb, L. F., & McKee, K. B. (2005) *Applied public relation: Cases in stakeholder management.* Mahwah, NJ: Lawrence Erlbaum.

Lang, M. H., & Lundholm, R. J. (1996). Corporate disclosure policy and analyst behavior. *Accounting Review, 71,* 467-492.

Larkin, T. J., & Larkin, S. (1994). *Communicating change: Winning employee support for new business goals.* New York: McGraw-Hill.

Laskin, A. V. (2006). Investor relations practices at Fortune 500 companies: An exploratory study. *Public Relations Review, 32,* 69-70.

Ledingham, J., & Bruning, S. (1998). Relationship management in public relations: Dimensions of an organization-public relationship. *Public Relations Review, 24,* 55-65.

Lee, M. (1998). Public relations is public administration. *New Bureaucrat, 27*(4), 49.

Leeper, R., & Leeper, K. (2001). Public relations as "practice": Applying the theory of Alasdair MacIntyre. *Public Relations Review, 27,* 461-473.

Leonard, B. (2001). A job well done. *HR Magazine, 46*(12), 34-38.

Leone, M (2003). *CFOs: Risk magnets.* Retrieved February 13, 2007, from http://www.cfo.com/article.cfm/3009142

Lerbinger, O. (1997). *The crisis manager: Facing risk and responsibility.* Mahwah, NJ: Lawrence Erlbaum.

Lewis, L. K., Hamel, S. A., & Richardson, B. K. (2001). Communicating change to nonprofit stakeholders. *Management Communication Quarterly, 15,* 5-41.

Loewenberg, F. M., & Dolgoff, R. (1996) *Ethical decisions for social work practice* (5th ed.). Itasca, IL: F. E. Peacock.

Lockwood, N. R. (2005, December). Crisis management in today's business environment: HR's strategic role. *SHRM Research Quarterly,* 2-10.

Lovstrom, S. (1998). *Deceptive on-line advertising to children.* Retrieved February 13, 2007, from http://iml.jou.ufl.edu/projects/Students/Lovstrom/steve.htm

MacArthur, K. (2006). McD's to shops: Make "lovin' it" more than tag. *Advertising Age, 77*(11), 8.

Markwick, N., & Fill, C. (1997). Towards a framework for managing corporate identity. *European Journal of Marketing, 31,* 396-409.

Marra, F. J. (2004). Excellent crisis communication: Beyond crisis plans. In D. P. Millar & R. L. Heath (Eds.), *Responding to crisis: A rhetorical approach to crisis communication* (pp. 311-326). Mahwah, NJ: Lawrence Erlbaum.

Marsh, C., & Robbins, L. (2004). Expect the unexpected. *Pit & Quarry, 96*(11), 10-12.

Maryland Association of Nonprofit Organizations. (2002). *Protecting the trust: Revisiting attitudes about public charities in Maryland.* Retrieved March 19, 2007, from http://www.marylandnonprofits.org/html/explore/documents/public_trust.pdf

McCord, L. B., & Richardson, J. E. (2000). Trust in the marketplace. In *Annual Editions: Business Ethics 02/03* (pp. 106-107). Guilford, CT: McGraw-Hill/ Dushkin.

McDonald's. (2003). *McDonald's unveils new global packaging system.* Retrieved March 8, 2007, from http://www.marketwire.com/mw/release_html_b1?release_id=61125

McDonald's. (2005–2006). *About McDonald's . . .* Retrieved March 27, 2007, from http://www.mcdonalds.com/corp/about.html

Meijer, A. (2001). Electronic records management and public accountability: Beyond an instrumental approach. *Information Society, 17,* 259-270.

Melillo, W. (2003). Crisis management. *Adweek, 44*(40), 26-27.

Meyer, J. (2002). Organizational communication assessment. *Management Communication Quarterly, 15,* 472-479.

Meznar, M. B., & Nigh, D. (1995). Buffer or bridge? Environmental and organizational determinants of public affairs activities in American firms. *Academy of Management Journal, 38,* 975-996.

Miller, R. (1988). Ethical challenges in corporate-shareholder and investor relations: Using the value exchange model to analyze and respond. *Journal of Business Ethics, 7,* 117-132.

Mitchell, R. K., Agle, B. R., & Wood, D. J. (1997). Toward a theory of stakeholder identification and salience: Defining the principle of who and what really counts. *Academy of Management Review, 22,* 853-886.

Moemeka, A., & Kovacic, B. (1995). The rules theory of interpersonal relationships by Cushman, Nicotera, and Associates. In D. P. Cushman & B. Kovacic (Eds.), *Watershed research traditions in human communication theory* (pp. 141-171). Albany: State University of New York Press.

Moon, M. J. (2002). The evolution of e-government among municipalities: Rhetoric or reality? *Public Administration Review, 62,* 424-433.

Morgan, J. M., Reynolds, C. M., Nelson, T. J., Johanningmeier, A. R., Griffin, M., & Andrade, P. (2004). Tales from the fields: Sources of employee identification in agribusiness. *Management Communication Quarterly, 17,* 360-395.

Moyer, L. (2005). The most charitable companies. *Forbes,* November 14. Retrieved March 30, 2007, from http://www.forbes.com/2005/11/11/charities-corporations-giving-cx_lm_1114charity_print.html

Myers, R. (2003). Ensuring ethical effectiveness: New rules mean virtually every company will need a code of ethics. *Journal of Accountancy, 195*(2), 28-33.

Nichols, D. R. (Ed.). (1989). *The handbook of investor relations.* Homewood, IL: Dow Jones-Irwin.

Oliver, S. (1997). *Corporate communication: Principles, techniques, and strategies.* London: Kogan Page.

On Target. (2004). *The Economist,* October 16, pp. 58-59.

O'Rourke, M. (2004). Protecting your reputation. *Risk Management, 51*(1), 14-18.

Orts, E. W., & Strudler, A. (2002). The ethical and environmental limits of stakeholder theory. *Business Ethics Quarterly, 12*(2), 215-233.

OSHA's mission. (n.d.). Retrieved March 27, 2007, from http://www.osha.gov/oshinfo/mission.html

Ospina, S., Diaz, W., & O'Sullivan, J. F. (2002). Negotiating accountability: Managerial lessons from identity-based nonprofit organizations. *Nonprofit & Voluntary Sector Quarterly, 31,* 5-31.

Page, C. G. (2002). The determination of organization stakeholder salience in public health. *Public Health Management Practice, 8*(5), 76-84.

Peterson, G. (Ed.). (2000). *Communicating in organizations: A case book* (2nd ed.). Boston: Allyn & Bacon.

Petrecca, L. (2002). A need to make sense of financial matters. *Advertising Age, 73*(39), 17.

Pfeffer, J., & Sutton, R. (1999, May-June). The smart-talk trap. *Harvard Business Review, 77,* 135-142.

Phillips, R. (2004, March/April). Some key questions about stakeholder theory. *Ivey Business Journal,* 1-4.

Pi, L., & Timme, S. G. (1993). Corporate control and bank efficiency. *Journal of Banking & Finance, 17,* 515-530.

Pearce, J., & Zahra, S. (1991). The relative power of CEOs and boards of directors: Associations with corporate performance. *Strategic Management Journal, 12,* 135-153.

Plowman, K. D., ReVelle, C., Meirovich, S., Pien, M., Stemple, R., Sheng, V., et al. (1995). Walgreens: A case study in health care issues and conflict resolution. *Journal of Public Relations Research, 7,* 231-258.

Post, J., Lawrence, A., & Weber, J. (1999). *Business and society: Corporate strategy, public policy, ethics* (9th ed.). Boston: Irwin/McGraw-Hill.

Pounder, J. S. (1999). Organizational effectiveness in higher education: Managerial implications of a Hong Kong study. *Educational Management & Administration, 27,* 389-400.

Power, M., & Rienstra, B. (1999). Internal communication in new corporate conglomerates: Developing a corporate communication model for loosely coupled businesses in local government. *International Journal of Public Sector Management, 12,* 501-515.

Prickett, R. (2002, September). Sweet clarity. *Financial Management,* 18-21.

Protecting consumer's data: Policy issues raised by ChoicePoint: Hearing before the Subcommittee on Commerce, Trade, and Consumer Protection, of the House Committee on Energy and Commerce, 109th Cong. (2005) (testimony of Derek Smith). Retrieved March 25, 2007, from http://energycommerce.house.gov/reparchives/108/Hearings/03152005hearing1455/Smith.pdf

Pulliam, S., & Solomon, D. (2002). Uncooking the books. *The Wall Street Journal,* October 30, p. A1.

Putnam, L. L. (1983). The interpretive perspective: An alternative to functionalism. In L. L. Putnam & M. E. Pacanowsky (Eds.), *Communication and organizations: An interpretive approach* (pp. 31-54). Beverly Hills, CA: Sage.

Quinn, R. E. (1988). *Beyond rational management.* San Francisco: Jossey-Bass.

Radtke, J. M. (1998). *Strategic communication for nonprofit organizations: Seven steps to creating a successful plan.* New York: John Wiley & Sons.

Rafter, M. V. (2005). Welcome to the club. *Workforce Management, 84*(4), 40-46. Retrieved February 26, 2007, from http://www.workforce.com/section/02/feature/24/00/24/index.html

Ragan's PR Intelligence Report. (2003). *McDonald's re-energizes brand.* Retrieved March 8, 2007, from http://www.igorinternational.com/press/printel-tag-line-brand-agency.php

Rao, H., & Sivakumar, K. (1999). Institutional sources of boundary-spanning structures: The establishment of investor relations departments in the

Fortune 500 industrials. *Organization Science, 10,* 27-42.

Rechner, P. L., & Dalton, D. R. (1991). CEO duality and organizational performance: A longitudinal analysis. *Strategic Management Journal, 12,* 155-160.

Renfro, W. L. (1987). Issue management: The evolving corporate role. *Futures, 5,* 545-554.

Reynolds, M. (1995). From PR to PA: A natural fit. *Communication World, 12*(1), 27-31.

Richardson, S. (2001). Discretionary disclosure: A note. *Abacus, 37,* 233-247.

Roberts, P. W., & Dowling, G. R. (2002). Corporate reputation and sustained superior financial performance. *Strategic Management Journal, 23,* 1077-1093

Robson, P., & Tourish, D. (2005). Managing internal communication: An organizational case study. *Corporate Communications, 10*(3), 213-222.

Rogers, P. S., & Hildebrandt, H. W. (1993). Competing values instruments for analyzing written and spoken management messages. *Human Resource Management Journal, 32*(1), 121-142.

Rose, C., & Thomsen, S. (2004). The impact of corporate reputation on performance: Some Danish evidence. *European Management Journal, 22,* 201-210.

Sabate, J., & Puente, E. (2003). Empirical analysis of the relationship between corporate reputation and financial performance: A survey of the literature. *Corporate Reputation Review, 6,* 161-177.

Samsung. (1995–2007). *Corporate identity: Samsung wordmark.* Retrieved March 8, 2007, from http://www.samsung.com/AboutSAMSUNG/SA MSUNGGROUP/CorporateIdentity/index.htm

Sapienza, H. J., & Korsgaard, A. M. (1996). Procedural justice in entrepreneur-investor relations. *The Academy of Management Journal, 39,* 544-574.

Schlosser, J. (2004). How Target does it. *Fortune, 150*(8), 100-112. Retrieved March 27, 2007, from http://money.cnn.com/magazines/fortune/for tune_archive/2004/10/18/8188073/index.htm

Schoenberg, A. (2005). Do crisis plans matter? A new perspective on leading during a crisis. *Public Relations Quarterly, 50,* 1, 2-7.

Schultz, D. E., & Kitchen, P. J. (2000). *Communicating globally: An integrated marketing approach.* London: Palgrave-Macmillan.

Scott, S., & Lane, V. (2000). A stakeholder approach to organizational identity. *Academy of Management Review, 25,* 43-63.

Seitel, F. (1994). The 10 commandments of corporate communications. *Vital Speeches of the Day, 60*(7), 202-204.

Shaffer, B. (1995). Firm-level responses to government regulation: Theoretical and research approaches. *Journal of Management, 21,* 495-514.

Shaffer, B., & Hillman, J. A. (2000). The development of business-government strategies by diversified firms. *Strategic Management Journal, 21,* 175-190.

Sharon, P. (1990). Communicating in the 1990s—Are we ready? The simple answer is no—We are not. *Communication World, 7*(6), 170-175.

Sharp Paine, L. (1994, March-April). Managing for organizational integrity. *Harvard Business Review, 72,* 106-117.

Shockley-Zalabak, P. (1994). *Understanding organizational communication: Cases, commentaries, and conversations.* New York: Longman.

Shockley-Zalabak, P. S. (2006). *Fundamentals of organizational communication: Knowledge, sensitivity, skills, values* (6th ed.). New York: Allyn & Bacon.

Singh, R., & Smyth, R. (2000). Australian public relations: Status at the turn of the 21st century. *Public Relations Review, 26,* 387-401.

Skagen, A. (1992). The incredible shrinking organization: What does it mean for middle managers? *Supervisory Management, 37,* 1-3.

Smith, E. B. (2004). Target sticks to its decision to ban Salvation Army kettles. *USA Today,* December 6, p. 5b.

Smith, L. (1996). Accountability in PR: Budgets and benchmarks. *Public Relations Quarterly, 41*(1), 15-19.

Smircich, L. (1983) Implications for management theory. In L. L. Putnam & M. E. Pacanowsky (Eds.), *Communication and organizations: An interpretive approach* (pp. 221-241). Beverly Hills, CA: Sage.

Smudde, P. (2001). Issue or crisis: A rose by any other name. *Public Relations Quarterly, 46*(4), 34-36.

Sonnenfeld, J. (2002, September). What makes great boards great? *Harvard Business Review,* 106-113.

Southwest Airlines Click 'n Save e-mail updates. (n.d.). Retrieved February 27, 2007, from http://www .southwest.com/email/mailhelp.html

Spencer, D. G. (1986). Employee voice and employee retention. *Academy of Management Journal, 29,* 488-502.

Stanton, P. V. (2002). Ten communications mistakes you can avoid when managing a crisis. *Public Relations Quarterly, 47*(2), 19-22.

Stephens, K. K., Malone, P. C., & Bailey, C. M. (2005). Communicating with stakeholders during crisis. *Journal of Business Communication, 42*, 390-419.

Stewart, T. (1998). America's most admired companies. *Fortune, 137*(4), 70-82.

Strenski, J. B. (1998.) Public relations in the new millennium. *Public Relations Quarterly, 43*(3), 25-25.

Stuart, H. (2002). Employee identification with the corporate identity: Issues and implications. *International Studies of Management and Organization, 32*(3), 28-44.

SWA in a nutshell. (n.d.). Retrieved February 27, 2007, from http://www.swamedia.com/swamedia/swa_nutshell.pdf

Target.com. (2006a). *Target and the Salvation Army announce partnership.* Retrieved February 22, 2007, from http://news.target.com/phoenix.zhtml?c=196187&p=irol-newsArticle&ID=805037&highlight=

Target.com. (2006b). *To our shareholders.* Retrieved February 22, 2007, from http://investors.target.com/ phoenix.zhtml?c=65828&p=irol-govHighlights

Target.com. (2007). *About Target: Philosophy and values.* Retrieved February 22, 2007, from http://sites.target.com/site/en/corporate/page.jsp?contentId=PRD03-001086

Taylor, D. W. (1990). A meso-level understanding of business-government relations. *International Journal of Public Sector Management, 3*, 54-60.

Taylor, J. R., & Van Every, E. J. (2000). *The emergent organization.* Mahwah, NJ: Lawrence Erlbaum.

Tichy, N. M., & McGill, A. R. (2003). *The ethical challenge.* New York: John Wiley and Sons.

Theaker, A. (2001). *The public relations handbook.* London: Routledge.

Tompkins, P. K. (1990). *Organizational communication imperatives: Lessons of the space program.* Los Angeles: Roxbury.

Tompkins, P. K. (2005). *Apollo, Challenger, Columbia: A study in organizational communication.* Los Angeles: Roxbury.

Trevino, L. K., Daft, R. L., & Lengel, R. H. (1990). Understanding managers' media choices: A symbolic interactionist perspective. In J. Fulk & C. W. Steinfield (Eds.), *Organizations and communication technology* (pp. 71-94). Newbury Park, CA: Sage.

Troester, R. (1991). The corporate spokesperson in external organizational communication. *Management Communication Quarterly, 4*, 528-540.

Turban, D. B., & Greening, D. W. (1997). Corporate social performance and organizational attractiveness to prospective employees. *Academy of Management Journal, 40*, 658-672.

United Press International. (2004). *Sarbanes-Oxley's compliance conundrum.* Retrieved March 27, 2007, from http://accounting.smartpros.com/x43534.xml

Vahouny, K. (2004). Opportunities for improvement. *Communication World, 21*(3), 32-37.

Valley, M. (2003, January 1). Sarbanes-Oxley is onerous. *National Real Estate Investor.* Retrieved February 15, 2007, from http://nreionline.com/commentary/firstword/real_estate_sarbanesoxley_onerous/

Van Riel, C. B. M. (1995). *Principles of corporate communication.* London: Prentice Hall.

Van Riel, C. B. M., & Balmer, J. (1997). Corporate identity: The concept, its measurement and management. *European Journal of Marketing, 31*, 340-351.

Veiga, J. F., & Yanouzas, J. N. (1984). *The dynamics of organization theory: Gaining a macro perspective.* St. Paul, MN: West.

Verchere, I. (1991). *The investor relations challenge: Reaching out to global markets.* London: Economist Intelligence Movement.

Vilkinas, T. (2000). The gender factor in management: How significant others perceive effectiveness. *Women in Management Review, 15*, 261-271.

Wagner, M. (1998). Nonprofits face hurdles. *InternetWeek, 732*, 79.

Wayne, G. F., & Connolly, G. N. (2002). How cigarette design can affect youth initiation into smoking: Camel cigarettes 1983-93. *Tobacco Control, 11*(Suppl. 1), 32-39. Retrieved March 19, 2007, from http://tc.bmj.com/cgi/content/full/11/suppl_1/i32

Wakefield, R. I., & Coleman, B. F. (2001). Communication in the unfettered marketplace: Ethical interrelationships of business, government, and stakeholders. *Journal of Mass Media Ethics, 16*(2/3), 213-233.

Weick, K. E. (1979). *The social psychology of organizing* (2nd ed.). New York: Norton.

Weick, K. E. (1983). Organization communication: Toward a research agenda. In L. L. Putnam & M. E. Pacanowsky (Eds.), *Communication and organizations: An interpretive approach.* (pp. 31-49). Newbury Park, CA: Sage.

Weick, K. E. (1990). The vulnerable system: An analysis of the Tenerife disaster. *Journal of Management, 16*, 571-593.

Weick, K. E., & Roberts, K. H. (1993). Collective mind in organizations: Heedful interrelating on flight decks. *Administrative Science Quarterly, 38,* 357-381.

Weick, K. E., & Sutcliffe, K. M. (2001). *Managing the unexpected: Assuring high performance in an age of complexity.* San Francisco: Jossey-Bass.

Williams, D. E., & Olaniran, B. A. (2002). Crisis communication in racial issues. *Journal of Applied Communication Research, 30,* 293-313.

Winston, C., Crandall, R. W., Niskanen, W. A., & Klevorick, A. (1994). Brookings papers on economic activity. *Microeconomics, 1994,* 1-49.

Wise, K. (2003). The Oxford incident: Organizational culture's role in an anthrax crisis. *Public Relations Review, 29,* 461-472.

Wright, D. K. (1995). The role of corporate public relations executives in the future of employee communications. *Public Relations Review, 21,* 181-198.

Wrigley, B. J., Salmon, C. T., & Park, H. S. (2003). Crisis management planning and the threat of bioterrorism. *Public Relations Review, 29,* 281-290.

Yamauchi, K. (2001). Corporate communication: A powerful tool for stating corporate missions. *Corporate Communications, 6*(3), 131-137.

Young, M., & Post, J. E. (1993). Managing to communicate, communicating to manage: How leading companies communicate with employees. *Organizational Dynamics, 22,* 31-43.

Index

Abbott Hospital
  acquisition of, 239–243
  operating under Mt. Mercy, 243–246
Accountability, negotiated, 53
Accounting
  policies and standards, 168–169
  reforms, 169
  structural regulations, 168
Acme, 172–175
Adhocracy culture, 106
Adobe Systems, 98
Adolph Coors Company, 65–72
Advertising, corporate, 33, 47
  to children, 130, 131
  ethics in, 130–132
  issue management and, 125–126
  logos in, 46–48, 59–60
  by nonprofit organizations, 127–128
  public relations and, 126–127
  reputation and, 59–60
  slogans in, 49–50, 59–60
  subliminal seduction in, 130
  See also Marketing communication
Advertising Age, 47
AFL-CIO, 65–66, 68–72
After, 225
Agilent Technologies, 53–54
Akchin, D., 127
Alexander, J. B., 58
Altria, 91–92
American Airlines, 45
American Express, 45
American Home Products, 226
American Red Cross, 48, 92–93, 128
Anticipation of the unexpected, 19–20
AOL Instant Messenger, xxvi
Apollo 13, 18–19, 153
Apple Computer, 98
Argenti, P. A., 6–7
Argonaut Group, 81–82
Ariel Think, Inc., 246–247
Arnold, Stephen, 134
Arousal, emotional, 17

Arthur Andersen, 88–89, 137–138, 139–140
Asbestos, 226
AT&T, 228
Attainment, enactive, 17
Audits, communication
  benefits of, 202–203
  cultural types and, 208–209
  diagnosing organizational culture, 206–208
  functionalism and, 199–200
  in Health Care Organizations, 209
  identifying communication activities across
    managerial levels, 203–204
  importance of contextual factors in, 204–205
  interpretivism and, 200–201
  process of, 202
  and reviewing corporate
    identity programs, 31
  uncertainty reduction in, 201–202
Auston Transcript, 239, 242, 245

Baker, T., 129
Balancing competing tensions in corporate
    communications, 22–24, 32–33, 155, 238
Barksdale, James, 98
Barriers, communication, 36
Barry, Jan, 119–120
Becker, Ossie, 246–248
Behavioral complexity and
    high-reliability organizations, 19–22
Belasen, Alan, 11, 104, 204, xxiv–xxv, xxvii
BelBeck Production, 246–248
Bell, Amy, 246–248
Bell, Thomas, 145
Benoit, W. L., 227
Berkshire Hathaway, 59, 167
Bernstein, Madeline, 119–120
Bet-the-company culture, 107
Bevins, Jane, 84
Beyond Rational Management, 155
Bias, Len, 221–222
Bill and Melinda Gates Foundation, 167
Bird Eye Walls, 96
Blair, J. D., 189

Blandings, Cary, 120
Blogging, xxv
Board of directors
    building an effective, 170–171
    communication between CEO and, 170
    structural regulations and
        independence, 167–168
Body Shop, The, 126
Boje, D. M., 104
Borda, J. L., 229–231
Botes, A., 138
Boudreaux, D. J., 131
Boundary spanners, 33, 93–94, 161, 164
Bowie, N. E., 83
Boycotts, 69, 185
Boyd, J., 31
Branding image and identity, 60–61
Breast Cancer Research Foundation, 48
Breen, Edward, 139
Bridgestone/Firestone, 166–167
Brill, Steven, 225
Brokers, information, 161
Bruning, S., 179
Buffering and bridging functions
    in government relations, 92–93
Buffet, Warren, 59, 136, 167
Burger King, 50
Bush, George W., 88, 89, 165
Business Week, 139

Cameron, K. S., 105, 107, 206, 207–208
Carruth, Nancy, 47
Case studies
    Abbott Hospital and
        Mt. Mercy Hospital, 239–246
    Acme and Omega Electronics, 172–175
    Adolph Coors Company, 65–72
    Agilent Technologies, 53–54
    Argonaut Group, 81–82
    BelBeck Production, 246–248
    Granite City, 195–197
    Hanover Software, 119–120
    Illinois Power, 146–150
    Microsoft anti-trust case, 98–99
    Ostern Corporation, 84
    Satellite Systems, 25–26
    Starbucks Coffee Company, 38–39
    Tylenol-tampering incident, 232–233
    Wal-Mart, 133–134
Cassler, John, 242, 244
CBS News, 65–66, 71–72
Central connectors, 161
Centralized communication
    structures, 22, 23 (figure)

CEOs. *See* Chief executive officers
Challenger disaster, 19, 21–22
Chandler, Robert, 148, 149–150
Change process, 17–18, 104
    communication, 186–188
    culture and, 107–109
    managerial level and, 159 (table)
Channel selection in the
    communication process, 36–37
Cheney, G., 62, 101
Chicago Tribune, 52
Chief executive officers, 167–168, 169–171
Children's advertising, 130, 131
ChoicePoint, 228
Christensen, L. T., 62, 101
Clan culture, 106
Clarkson, M., 165, 179
Clarkson Principles, 185–186
Coates, Michael, 62–63
Coca Cola, 141, 228
Coffee, John C., 90
Coletti, John, 240, 243
Columbia space shuttle, 222–225
Committed intensive supervisors, 156
Communication, corporate
    attempts to integrate the field of, 5–6
    change, 186–188
    as a community of practice, 4–5
    construct space of, 6–7, 12–15
    corporate identity and image in, 12
    effective, 235–236
    employee relations in, 33–34
    external, 52–53
    as a field of study, 3–4
    goals, 7–8, 22, 73–74, 101, 123, 135–136
    government relations in, 34–35
    holistic perspective of, 6–7
    integrated, 5–6, 22, 23 (figure), 29
    internal *versus* external, 5, 12
    investor relations in, 35
    loosely couple social systems in, 6–7
    as a matrix, 37–38
    media relations in, 33
    need for theoretically based
        organizing framework in, 8
    primary functions of, 32–33, 37–38
    process, 35–37, 164–165
    with stakeholders, 29–30, 35,
        180–181, 186–188
    strategic, 41–45, 51–52, 236–237
    systems, 22, 23 (figure)
    vertical, 156–157, 162
Community of practice,
    corporate communication as a, 4–5

Competing Values Framework for
    Corporate Communication
  balancing perspectives and systems
      in, 22–24, 32–33, 238
  communication audits and, 202–203,
      209, 210 (figure), 211 (figure)
  crisis communication in, 226–227
  development of, 11, xxiii–xxv
  dimensional qualities in, 11–12
  diverse stakeholders addressed by, 27–28
  employee relations in, 101–102
  functionalism in, 13–15, 199–200, 201
  government relations in, 85–86
  high-reliability organizations and, 19–22
  interpretivism in, 13, 15–16, 200–201
  investor relations in, 73–74
  marketing communication in, 123
  media relations in, 57–58
  message orientations in, 111–113
  radical structuralism and
      radical humanism in, 13, 14, 16
  rationalistic and humanistic
      communication roles in, 153–156
  stakeholders in, 180–181, 192–193
  strategic communication in, 236–237
Comrie, M., 43
Conceptual producers, 156–157
Confidence, stockholder, 76–77
Confrontational journalism,
    65–66, 71–72, 146–150
Connectors, central, 161
Consensus building, 189 (table)
Constituent policy field, 87
Construct space of corporate
    communication, 6–7, 12–15
Containment of the unexpected, 20–22
Context in the communication
    process, 36, 204–205
Conversation, strategic, 103–104
Cooke, C., 59
Coombs, W. T., 60
Cooper, Cynthia, 142
Coors, Adolph, 66
Coors, Adolph, III, 67
Coors, Adolph, Jr., 66, 68
Coors, Joseph, 65–66, 67
Coors, William, 65–66, 66–67
Corporate Communication:
    Theory and Practice, 3–4
Corporate Communications for Executives, 4
Corporate Reputation Review, 58
Corruption, corporate
  Arthur Andersen, 88–89, 137–138, 139–140
  Enron, 87–90, 136–137, 141, 167

  financial communication and, 135–136
  Tyco, 138–139
  Union Carbide, 140–141, 225, 226 (table)
  WorldCom, 87–90, 139–140, 141, 142, 167
  See also Social responsibility, corporate
Costco Wholesale Corporation, 111
Costello, Richard, 45
Council of Better Business Bureaus, 130
Courtright, J. L., 228
Cousins Properties, 145
Cox, James D., 89
Crable, R. E., 51
Credibility and integrity, 43–45
  in advertising, 131–132
  CEO and board of directors, 167–171
  corporate corruption and, 87–90
  public relations and, 61–62, 64
  social contract with employees and, 116–117
Crisis communication
  definition of crisis and, 217–218
  by Dow Corning, 220–221
  failures in, 219–222
  importance of culture in, 231
  by NASA, 222–224
  organizing exchange of
      information in, 226–227
  potential mistakes in, 219–220
  protecting corporate image, 225–226
  restoring corporate image through, 227–228
  by Southwest Airlines, 218–219
  stages of crisis and, 229–231
  successful, 218–219, 222–225
  by Texas Eastern Transmission Corporation, 224
  by University of Maryland, 221–222
  by Verizon, 224–225
Critical theories of human communication, 16
Crooke, R. E., 52
Crown Health Enterprises (New Zealand), 43
Culture, corporate
  audits, 209
  crisis communication and, 231
  diagnosing, 206–208
  humanistic approach to
      communication and, 153
  mapping, 107–109
  types of, 105–107, 125, 208–209
Curry, William N., 52
Curtis, Bill, 25–26
Cushman, D. P., 152
CVFCC. *See* Competing values framework
    for corporate communication

Daley, Bill, 90
Dalkon Shield, 226

Darrow, Clarence, xxi
Data collection, 201
Deakins, Harold, 150
Deal, T. E., 106, 208
Decentralized communication
   networks, 22, 23 (figure)
Deep structure of organizations, 208
DeLapp, T., 59, 136
Deloitte, 217, 218 (box)
De Pelsmacker, P., 124
Dialogue in employee relations, 103
Diamond of interactions, 115–116
Dionisopoulos, G. N., 51
DiPadova, L. N., 156
Discernment in employee relations, 103
Disclosure of financial information, 77–79
Discrimination, 69–70
Disneyland, 31
Distributive policy field, 87
Donaldson, T., 137, 140, 179
Dow Corning, 220–221
Drudge, Matt, xxv
Duke, S., 222, 229
Duncan, David B., 137
Duncan, T., 123–124
Dye, R. A., 77, 78, 79

Eastwood, Clint, 66
Ebbers, Bernard J., 139–140
Eberts, Shari, 47
Educated communicators, 164
EII, 183–185
Einstein, Albert, xxi–xxii
Eisenhower, Dwight, 66
Eisner, Michael, 104
E-mail, 114–115, 128, 130, 159
Emotional arousal, 17
Employee relations, 33–34
   avoiding the trap of knowing-doing, 109–110
   corporate identity and
      image and, 101, 102–103
   culture and, 105–107
   diamond model of interactions and, 115–116
   and employees as stakeholders, 184–185
   at FedEx, 117
   goals of, 101
   horizontal management and, 162–164
   message orientations and, 111–115
   motivating employees through, 104–105
   in nonprofit organizations, 129
   positive communication
      relationships and, 110–111
   providing solutions to challenges, 104

social contract with employees
   and, 116–117
strategic conversation and, 103–104
in the Training Organization, 107–109
vertical communication and, 162
See also Management
Enactive attainment, 17
Enron, 87–90, 136–137, 141, 144, 167
Ensman, R. G., Jr., 62, 127
Environmental Protection Agency, 85
Equal dissemination model of
   communication, 187 (table)
Equal participation model of
   communication, 187 (table)
ER. *See* Employee relations
Ethical Challenge, The, 136
Ethics, 116–117
   advertising, 130–132
   CEOs and, 169–170
   financial, 83
   managerial, 165–167
   Sarbanes-Oxley Act and, 88–89, 141–145
   See also Corruption, corporate
Ethnomethodology, 201
Evans, Donald L., 88
Evolution, xxi
Executives, top, 155–157
Expedia, 125
Experience, vicarious, 17
External communication, 52–53
   government regulations and, 94
   See also Marketing communication
Exxon, 228

Family Literacy Foundation, 48
Fannie Mae, 136
Fastow, Andrew, 143
Federal Aviation Administration, 218
Federal Bureau of Investigation, 52, 231
Federal Emergency Management Agency, 92
Federal Trade Commission, 130
FedEx, 117–118
Feedback loops, 36, 103–104, 107
Ferris, R. D., 76
Fields, Bill, 139
Fill, C., 12, 29, 30, 103
Financial analysts, 75–76
Financial ethics, 83
Financial information
   communication of, 5, 35
   corporate credibility and, 43–45
   investor relations departments and, 75
   public relations and, 63

reporting of, 77–79
    Sarbanes-Oxley Act and, 88–89, 141–145
Financial performance and
        corporate reputation, 80–82
Financial reporting, 77–79
Financial Times, 97
Flanagan, W. G., 137
Forbes, 48
Ford, Gerald, 66
Fortune, 59, 117, 125
Fottler, M. D., 189
Freeman, R. E., 179
Friedman, Thomas, xxvi
Front-line supervisors, 155–157, 203–205
Frooman, J., 181–183
Frost, A. R., 59
Functionalism, 13–15, 199–200, 201

Gallagher, K., 128, 129
Gates, Bill, 98–99, 167
General Electric, 45–47
General Motors, 14–15
Genest, C. M., 58
Gerstner, W. C., 147, 149
Gibbins, M., 77, 78–79
Gibson, D. C., 52
Girl Scouts of America, 92
Glauber, Robert R., 88
Global Crossing, 167
Goals of corporate communication,
        7–8, 22, 73–74, 101, 123, 135–136
    audits illustrating, 202–203
Gold, Susan, 247
Goldschmid, Harvey J., 90
Goodman, Michael, 3–4, 7
    on corporate advertising, 59
    on corporate image, 30
    on corporate reputation, 58
    on integrity and credibility of organizations, 44
    on logos, 46–47
    on media relations, 33
    on public relations, 61
Gordon, C. D., 52
Gorton's, 96
Gotsi, M., 43
Government relations, 34–35, 44–45
    at Altria, 91–92
    American Red Cross, 92–93
    boundary-spanning function, 93–94
    buffering and bridging
        functions, 92–93
    government regulations
        and, 85–87, 88–89, 141–145

importance of, 90–91
industry regulation and, 90–91, 91–92
and interdependence of
        government and business, 94–95
issue management through, 95–97
personnel, 87, 91, 92–93
policy fields, 87–90
supplier relations and, 97
GR. *See* Government relations
Granite City, 195–197
Graves, Michael, 47
Green, John, 247
Greenpeace, 96
Greenspan, Alan, xxiii, xxiv
Gustin, C., 220
Gwin, J. M., 128

Hamel, S. A., 186
Hanover Software, 119–120
Hart, S. L., 170
Hatch, Orrin, 99
Health Care Organizations, 209
Hearit, K. M., 228
Henley, T. K., 127, 128, 129, 130
Heritage Foundation, 67
Hewitt, Don, 71
Heye & Partner, 49
Hiebert, Roz, 222
Hierarchy culture, 105–106, 107
High-reliability organizations, 19–22
Hildebrandt, H. W., 111
Hill, C. W., 179
Hill and Knowlton Canada, 63
Hoffman, J. C., 222
Holistic perspective corporate
        communication, 6–7
Holmes Report, 28
Hood, George, 49
Hoover, J. Edgar, 52
Horizontal management, 162–164
Howard, C., 64
HROs. *See* High-reliability organizations
Hubbard, R. Glenn, 88, 89
Humanism, radical, 13, 14, 16
Humanistic approach to
        communication, 153–156
Hunn, M., 202
Hurricane Katrina, 48–49, 51, 227
Hutton, J. G., 58, 59

IBM, 28
ICT. *See* Information communication
        technology

Identity, corporate, 12
    auditing and reviewing, 31
    branding, 60–61
    CVFCC and, 28–29
    employee relations and, 101
    external communication of, 52–53
    General Electric's, 45–47
    government relations and, 34–35
    interaction with stakeholders and, 29–30
    link to corporate image, 27–28, 102–103
    McDonald's, 49–51
    program standards and, 31
    sustaining and managing
        programs for, 29–31
    Target Corporation's, 47–49
    transforming, 45–47
    visual, 30–31, 60
    See also Image, corporate
Ihator, A., 62
Image, corporate, 12, 22
    branding, 60–61
    crisis communication to protect, 225–226
    CVFCC and, 28–29
    employee relations and, 101
    enhanced through issue management, 60
    of General Electric, 45–47
    link to corporate identity, 27–28, 102–103
    restoration through crisis
        communication, 227–228
    strategic corporate communications
        and, 43–44
    See also Identity, corporate
IMC. *See* Integrated marketing communications
Informal networks in management
        communication, 160–161
Information brokers, 161
Information communication
        technology, 157–160
Innovation, corporate
        communication, 22, 23 (figure)
Insider trading, 63
Instant messaging, xxvi
Integrated marketing
        communications, 61, 123–125
Integration, corporate communication
    internal and external, 5–6, 22, 23 (figure), 29
    strategic, 42–43
Integrity. *See* Credibility and integrity
Intelligent Design, xxi
Interactions, diamond of, 115–116
Inter-American Tropical
        Tuna Commission, 184
Interdependence of government
        and business, 94–95

Internal *versus* external corporate
        communication, 5–6, 12, 22, 23 (figure)
    See also Marketing communication
*International Journal of
        Corporate Communication,* 3
Internet, the
    advertising on, 33, 128
    blogging on, xxv
    e-mail, 114–115, 128, 130, 159
    financial reporting and, 78
    marketing for nonprofit
        organizations, 129–130
    Microsoft and, 98–99
    varieties of communication on, 114, xxv–xxvi
Interpretivism, 13, 15–16, 20, 200–201
Investor relations, 35
    corporate reputation and, 79–80
    corporate social responsibility and, 80
    different stakeholders and, 74–75
    financial analysts and, 75–76
    financial ethics and, 83
    financial media and, 75
    financial performance,
        corporate reputation and, 80–82
    financial reporting and, 77–79
    goals, 73–74, 135–136
    public relations and, 63
    responsibilities, 73–74
    Sarbanes-Oxley Act and, 88–89, 141–145
    stockholders and, 74–75, 76–77
IR. *See* Investor relations
Issue management, 60, 95–97, 125–126

Jackson, P., 59, 80
John Birch Society, 67
Johns Manville, 226
Johnson, P. M., 104
Johnson, Robert, 232
Johnson & Johnson,
        62–63, 75, 225, 226 (table), 232–233
Jones, T. M., 179
Journalism, confrontational,
        65–66, 71–72, 146–150
Judd, V. C., 127, 129

Kelleher, Herb, 125
Kelley, Wendall, 148
Kelly, K. S., 52
Kennedy, A. A., 106, 208
Key, W. B., 130
Key Bank Web, 83
Khan, R., 140
King, Rollin, 125
Kiriakidou, O., 27

Kitchen, P. J., 123, 124
Kitto, J. A., 61
Klum, Heidi, 50
Kmart, 47
Knowing-doing trap, 109–110
Kohl's, 47
Kozlowski, Dennis L., 138–139
Kraft Foods, Inc., 91–92

Labaton, Stephen, 90
Labor unions, 65–66, 68–72
Landor, 45–46
Lang, M. H., 76
Larkin, T. J., 161
Ledingham, J., 179
Leeham, Martin, 241, 244
Leeper, K., 61
Legal departments and
        corporate communication, 5
Levi Strauss, 141
Lewis, L. K., 186
Light, Larry, 49
Listening in employee relations, 103
Litan, Robert E., 89
Lobbying and government relations, 93, 96
Loewenwarter, Paul, 146
Logos, corporate, 46–48, 59–60
Luber, Elliot, 238
Lundholm, R. J., 76

Mackey-Kallis, S., 229–231
Management
    accounting and reporting reforms and, 169
    aligning communication with
            structures, 161–162
    CEO and board of directors, 167–171
    communication functions, 7
    communication roles and skills
            assessment, 205
    communicators, 161
    competing values framework, xxiii–xxv
    culture, 105–107
    ethics, 165–167
    horizontal, 162–164
    humanistic approach to, 153–156
    identifying communication activities
            across levels of, 203–204
    informal communication networks
            and, 160–161
    issue, 60, 95–97, 125–126
    leadership style, 208–209
    levels, 155–157, 161, 203–205
    of loosely coupled structures, 164–165
    policies and standards, 168–169

positive communication
        relationships and, 110–111
    rationalistic and humanistic
            communication approaches, 152–156
    self-assessment, 155–156
    of stakeholders, 185–186
    string theory applied to, xxii
    trap of knowing-doing, 109–110
    vertical communication and, 156–157
    See also Employee relations
Mann Gulch disaster, 19–20
Maraynes, Allan, 65, 71–72
Marketagon, xxiii–xxiv
Market culture, 106, 107
Marketing communication
    e-channels for, 129–130
    to employees in nonprofit organizations, 129
    ethics in, 130–132
    goals of, 123
    integrated, 61, 123–125
    issue management through, 125–126
    by nonprofit organizations, 127–128, 128–130
    public relations and, 126–127
    Southwest Airlines', 124–125
    stakeholder analysis and, 128, 188–191
    sustainability and, 125, 236
    See also Advertising, corporate
Marketing model of
        communication, 187 (table)
Markwick, N., 12, 29, 30, 103
Martha Stewart Living Omnimedia, 63
Marx, Karl, xxii
Mary Theresa, Sister, 239–248
Masland, L., 222, 229
Matrix, corporate communication as a, 37–38
MC. *See* Marketing communication
McCarty, John, 65
McDonald's, 48, 49–51, 60
McEwen, Todd, 119, 120
McGill, A. R., 136
MCI, 139
Media relations, 33
    branding image and identity through, 60–61
    corporate spokespersons in, 63–64
    government organizations and, 51–52
    issue management and, 60
    Johnson & Johnson, 62–63
    public relations and, 61–62
    reputation and, 58–60
    specialists, 57–58
    stakeholders and, 184
    strategic corporate
            communications and, 43–44
Meijer, A., 159

Meisel, S., 202
Melillo, W., 217
Mentoring, 158 (table)
Message
    fidelity, 152
    options in crisis communication, 227–228
    orientations, 111–115, 182 (table), 203
Metaphors and corporate identity, 31
Metz, Tim, 75
Meznar, M. B., 92
Microsoft, 52, 98–99
Middle managers, 155–157, 203–205
Miller, R., 81
Millward, L., 27
Mitchell, Mike, 84
Mizrahi, Isaac, 47
Monopolies, 98–99, 133
Moon, M. J., 130, 157, 159
Moore, Michael, 14–15
Morgan, J. M., 201
Morris, Dwight, 242
Morse, Bob, 119, 120
Motivation of employees, 104–105
MR. *See* Media relations
Mt. Mercy Hospital
    Abbott Hospital under, 243–246
    acquires Abbott Hospital, 239–243
Myers, R., 142

NASA, 18–19, 21–22, 153, 222–224
National Association of Securities Dealers
    Automated Quotations, 168
National Grocers Association, 133
National Highway Traffic Safety
    Administration, 166
National Investor Relations Institute, 73
National Transportation Safety Board, 218
Need to know model of
    communication, 187 (table)
Negotiated accountability, 53
Netscape Communications, 98
Newman, Paul, 66
Newman, R. M., 76
New York Stock Exchange, 168
New York Times, xxv
Nigh, D., 92
Nike, 48
Nonprofit organizations
    advertising by, 127–128
    e-channels for, 129–130
    marketing communications in, 128–129
    marketing to employees in, 129
Nuclear Regulatory Commission, 51–52

Occupational Safety and
    Health Administration, 86–87
Oliver, S., 4, 5–6, 8
Olympic Games, 50
Omega Electronics, 172–175
Open adaptive executives, 157
Open communication and
    employee relations, 103
Opportunism, 79
Orbitz, 125
Organizations
    culture, 105–107, 125, 206–208
    deep structure of, 208
    high-reliability, 19–22
    integrity and credibility of, 43–45, 116–117
    interactions with stakeholders, 29–30, 35
    loosely coupled, 164–165
    nonprofit, 127–128, 128–130
    philosophy, 41, 47, 102–103, 105
    reactive and defensive behaviors by, 166–167
    reputations, 27, 43–44, 46–47
    stakeholders relationships, 181–183
    vertical, 162
Organizing, communication as
    Apollo 13 and, 18–19
    enactment and retention in, 17–18
Orientations, message,
    111–115, 182 (table), 203
Orts, E. W., 179
Ostern Corporation, 84
Overconfidence, 19–20

Park, H. S., 227
Parker, James F., 77
Paulson, Henry M., Jr., 88, 89
Pepsi, 228
Perceptions, stakeholder, 188–189, 192–193
Peripheral specialists, 161
Persuasion, verbal, 17
Peytons, Roger, 195–197
Philanthropy, corporate, 48, 50–51, 59
Philip Morris USA, 91–92
Phillips, R., 180
Philosophy, corporate,
    41, 47, 102–103, 105, 117–118
Physics, xxi–xxii
Policies and standards, 168–169
Policy fields in government relations, 87–90
Political contributions and
    government relations, 93
Positive communication
    relationships, 110–111
Post, J. E., 109

Power, M., 164
Power, stakeholder, 188, 190, 191–192
Preston, L. E., 179
Proactive planning and initiation of
    communications, 43–44, 96
    See also Crisis communication
Process
    communication, 35–37, 164–165
    communication audit, 202
    culture, 107
Productivity and communication
    audits, 202–203
Public relations, 43–44, 119–120
    confrontational journalism and, 65–66, 71–72
    corporate spokespersons in, 63–64
    credibility and, 61–62, 64
    investor relations and, 63
    media relations and, 61–62
    by nonprofit organizations, 127–128
    professionals, 61, 126
    public safety and, 62
    See also Image, corporate; Media relations
Puffery, 130, 131–132
Putnam, L. L., 16

Quality-control systems, 116
Quid Pro Quo model of
    communication, 187 (table)
Quinn, R. E., 11, 105,
    107, 155, 170, 206, 207–208

Radical humanism, 13, 14, 16
Radical structuralism, 13, 14, 16
Radtke, J. M., 128
Rationalistic approach to
    communication, 152–156
Rawls, Jim, 172–175
Reactionary model of
    communication, 187 (table)
Reactive and defensive behaviors
    by corporations, 166–167
Reagan, Ronald, 67
Reasoner, Harry, 148–149, 150
Redistributive policy field, 87
Reduction, uncertainty, 201–202
Redundancy, support of, 78–79
Regulations, government, 85–87
    Sarbanes-Oxley Act, 88–89, 141–145
    structural, 168
Regulatory policy field, 87
Reluctance to simplify interpretations, 20
Renfro, W. L., 60
Reporting, financial, 77–79

Reputation, corporate, 27, 43–44, 46–47
    financial performance and, 80–82
    investor relations and, 79–80
    management, 58–59
    media relations and, 58–60
    See also Crisis communication
Reputation Management, 58
Retreats, employee, 34
Richard, Shirley, 65–66, 70–71
Richardson, A., 77, 78
Richardson, B. K., 186
Rienstra, B., 164
RJR Nabisco, 131
Roberts, K. H., 20
Roger and Me, 14
Rogers, David, 133
Rogers, P. S., 111
Ronald McDonald House, 50
Rose, C., 80, 81
Rowe, Howard, 148
Rowley, Cynthia, 47
Rule theory, 152–153

Safety, public, 62
Salmon, C. T., 227
Salvation Army, 48–49
SAM's Club, 133
Samsung, 30–31
Sarbanes-Oxley Act, 88–89, 141–145
Satellite Systems, 25–26
Schlosser, J., 47
Schueler, Joseph, 66
Schultz, D. E., 123
Schultz, Howard, 38
Scopes, John T., xxi
Scott, Hal S., 88, 89
Sears, 48
Securities and Exchange
    Commission, 136, 142, 145
Seduction, subliminal, 130
Seidenberg, Ivan, 224–225
Self-efficacy, 16–17
Self-regulation, 94
Seminars, employee, 34
Sensitivity to operations, 20
Sharp Paine, L., 117
Sheehy, J., 220
Shingle, David, 139
Shockley-Zalabak, P., 57
Sickler, David, 69–70, 71
Silo-ing, 162
Singh, R., 126
Six Sigma certification, xxii

60 Minutes
    Adolph Coors Company and, 65–66, 71–72
    Illinois Power and, 146–150
Slogans, 49–50, 59–60
Smith, Adam, xxii
Smith, Frederick, 117
Smyth, R., 126
Social contract with employees, 116–117
Social responsibility, corporate
    corruption and, 140–142
    creative solutions for, 141
    image and, 44–45
    investor relations and, 80
    managerial ethics and, 165–167
Social systems, loosely coupled, 6–7
Sogo, 28–29
Southwest Airlines, 50, 77,
        78, 124–125, 218–219
Specialists, peripheral, 161
Spencer, D. G., 110
Spitzer, Elliot, 88
Spokespersons, corporate, 63–64
Staff units and corporate
        communication, 5, 33–34
Stages of crisis, 229–231
Stakeholders
    analysis and marketing
        communication, 128, 188–191
    communicating with,
        29–30, 35, 180–181, 186–188
    consensus building and, 189 (table)
    consumers as, 183–185
    corporate moral obligations to, 180
    employees as, 184–185
    ethics and, 117
    management principles, 185–186
    organizational reputations and, 43–44
    perceptions, 188–189, 192–193
    relationships, firm-, 181–183
    socially responsible organizations and, 44–45
    sources of power, 188, 190, 191–192
    StarKist, 183–185
    stockholders as, 74–75
    task environment and, 188
    two-way symmetrical model of
        strategic communication with, 43
    varieties of, 179
    See also Investor relations
Stanton, P. V., 219, 225
Starbucks Coffee Company, 38–39, 47, 53
StarKist, 183–185
Steel, Robert K., 88
Stephens, K. K., 225

Stewart, Martha, 63
Stockholders, 74–75
    confidence, 76–77
    financial reporting to, 78–79
Strategic conversation, 103–104
Strategic corporate communication
    defined, 41–42
    effective strategies in, 51–52, 236–237
    integrated approach to, 42–43
    proactive planning and, 43–44
    top management connected to, 43
    two-way symmetrical model of exchange
        with stakeholders in, 43
Strategic fit, 27
Strenski, J. B., 59
String theory, xxi–xxii
Structuralism, radical, 13, 14, 16
Strudler, A., 179
Study of corporate communication, 3–4
Subliminal seduction, 130
Sullivan, Scott, 142
Super Size Me, 50
Supplier relations, 97
Support of redundancy, 78–79
Sustainability and marketing
        communication, 125, 236
Sutcliffe, K. M., 19, 207
Symbolism, 16, 133–134
Systems, communication, 22, 23 (figure)
    informal, 160–161

TagClouds, xxvi
Taiwan, 126
Target Corporation, 47–49
Task environment, 188
Tatung Company, 126
Taylor, D. W., 87
Taylor, J. R., 13
Terrorist attacks of September 11, 2001,
        223, 224–225, 227
Texas Eastern Transmission
        Corporation, 224
Textbooks on corporate communication, 3–4
Thomas, Linda, 84
Thomsen, S., 80, 81
Thornton, John L., 88
Three Mile Island nuclear accident, 51–52
Tichy, N. M., 136
Tiger Woods Foundation, 48
Timberlake, Justin, 49
Tough-guy macho culture, 107
Training Organization, the, 107–109
Tyco, 138–139

Tylenol-tampering incident,
    62–63, 75, 225, 226 (table), 232–233
Tyler, John, 172–175

Ulrich, Bob, 48
Uncertainty reduction, 201–202
Unexpected, the
    containment of, 20–22
    expectation of, 19–20
Unilever, 96–97
Union Carbide, 140–141, 225, 226 (table)
University of Maryland, 221–222

Value Exchange Perception Process, 81
Van Every, E. J., 13
Van Riel, C. B. M., 3, 6
    definition of corporate communication, 7–8
Verbal persuasion, 17
Verchere, I., 73
Verizon, 28, 224–225
Vertical communication, 156–157, 162
Vicarious experience, 17
Visual identity, 30–31, 60

Waldron, Murray, 139
Walgreens, 181
Wallace, Mike, 65, 71
Wall Street, 136
Wall Street Journal, 75
Wal-Mart, 30, 47, 48, 133–134
Walt Disney Company, 104
Walton, Sam, 133
Warhol, Andy, 47
Waterhouse, J., 77
Weber, Max, 151

Webs of communication, 160
WebTV, 98
Weick, K. E.
    on ecological change, 17
    on error catching, 19
    on functionalism and interpretivism, 16
    on organizational culture, 207
    on the reluctance to simplify
        interpretations, 20
    on social systems, 6
    on variety and repetition, 18
Weinberg, C. B., 128, 129
Welch, Jack, 46, 236
Wendy's, 50
Wilson, A. M., 43
Wise, K., 231
Workforce Management, 111
Work-hard, play-hard culture, 106–107
WorldCom, 87–90,
    139–140, 141, 142, 144, 167
World Is Flat, The, xxvi
World Jam, 28
World Wide Fund for Nature, 96
Wright, D. K., 104
Wrigley, B. J., 227

Xerox, 144

Yamauchi, K., 41
Young, M., 109
Youngren, Brad, 84
YouTube, xxvi

Zaucha, Thomas, 133
Zuccarelli, Jennifer, 88

About the Author

Alan Belasen is professor of management at Empire State College, State University of New York, where he has held a leading role designing and implementing the MBA program, which he currently chairs. For more than 15 years Professor Belasen has taught organizational and leadership communication, communication audits, and corporate communication in the Department of Communication at the University at Albany. He has also taught management, ethics, and communication in the MBA program at Union Graduate College. Professor Belasen has provided communication audit consulting and management development and training to government, nonprofit, business, and academic institutions. His research focuses on the effects of change on managerial communication and leadership roles. Professor Belasen has also published *Leading the Learning Organization: Communication and Competencies for Managing Change* (2000, State University of New York Press).